THE PROCEEDINGS OF THE 3rd INTERNATIONAL HUMANITIES CONFERENCE

ALL & EVERYTHING 1998

Harry Bennett
Robert Bryce
Keith Buzzell
Robert Curran
Wim van Dullemen
Seymour Ginsburg
Stuart Goodnick
Jim Gomez
Richard Liebow
Forrest McIlwain
Adam Petts
Bert Sharp
Sophia Wellbeloved

Published by All & Everything Conferences
2010

Second Edition Published 2010
Published by All & Everything Conferences (on behalf of the Planning Committee)
© Copyright 2010 by Seymour B. Ginsburg and Ian C. MacFarlane

First Edition Privately Published 1998
Published by the Conveners of the International Humanities Conference: All and Everything 2001
© 2001 Seymour B. Ginsburg, Dr. H. J. Sharp, and Nicolas Tereshchenko, F.R.C.S. Eng.

The contents of this publication may not be reproduced or copied in whole or part in any book, magazine, periodical, pamphlet, circular, information storage or data retrieval system, or in any other form without the written permission of the Planning Committee.

Any profit from the sale of these Proceedings will be devoted to the funds for the organization of future Conferences of a similar nature.

Published by All & Everything Conferences

Website: www.aandeconference.org
Email: info@aandeconference.org

Second Edition Print

ISBN-10: 1-905578-16-4
ISBN-13: 978-1-905578-16-0

Also Published as
Second Edition eBook

ISBN-10: 1-905578-17-2
ISBN-13: 978-1-905578-17-7

Table of Contents

Foreword 5
Conference Invitation 6
Conference Program 10
Planning Committee 13
Advisory Board 14
Speakers 16
Sittings 19
Introduction and Opening of the Conference 21
The Transcaucasian Kurd 25
    The Transcaucasian Kurd - Questions & Answers 37
    Appendix - Summary of Astrological Themes 38
The Nature and Sources of Conviction 43
    The Nature and Sources of Conviction - Questions & Answers 55
Gurdjieff, Blavatsky and the Masters of Wisdom 58
    Appendix - Taking the Life Cure in Gurdjieff's School 87
    Gurdjieff, Blavatsky and the Masters of Wisdom - Questions & Answers ... 88
First Open Forum - Secrecy and the Work 91
The Kunderbuffer: The Kundalini Alchemy and Creation of the Soul 100
    Appendix - Quotes Related to Sacred Sexuality 113
    The Kunderbuffer - Questions & Answers 116
Time in the Cosmology of Mr. Gurdjieff 119
    Time in the Cosmology of Mr. Gurdjieff - Questions & Answers 140
Mysterious Coincidences: Gurdjieff, the Enneagram and Tradition 142
    Mysterious Coincidences - Questions & Answers 150
    Appendix - Mysterious Coincidences 162
Gurdjieff in Practice: The Liebovian Method 176
Second Open Forum - Gurdjieff, the Past, Present and Future Tense of the Work 180
Joy Without a Cause: Work on the Emotional Centre in Daily Life 192
The Evolution of Evolution 196
    Appendix - The Evolution of Evolution 218
    The Evolution of Evolution - Questions & Answers 224
Approaching the Neologisms of the First Series 229
    Approaching the Neologisms of the First Series - Questions & Answers 237
Tracking Oskiano In Beelzebub's Tales 243
    Addendum - Tracking Oskiano in Beelzebub's Tales 259
    Tracking Oskiano In Beelzebub's Tales - Questions & Answers 263
Beyond the Life-Death Antagonism: Prayer and Compassion in the Gurdjieff Hymns 265
Third Opern Forum - What is Authentic Form of the Work 272

The Organ Kundabuffer 286
    The Organ Kundabuffer - Questions & Answers 294
The Origins, Meaning and Purpose of the Movements 299
    The Origins, Meaning and Purpose of the Movements - Questions & Answers ...304
Fourth Open Forum - Where Do We Go From Here? 306
Appendix 1 - Gurdjieff by Carl Zigrosser 319
Appendix 2 - List of Attendees 325
Appendix 3 - Planning Committee for 1998-1999 326
Index 327

Foreword

The Planning Committee would like to take this opportunity of thanking all the Presenters for their help in producing these Proceedings. We have all done our best to produce a permanent record of what some of us believe to have been the third important and definite Conference under the title of "All and Everything".

It is hoped that this will lead to further creative interaction of those in the Work in the near future.

In the case of this Conference the individual Presenters have been responsible for providing a written paper covering the material they presented at the Conference and also for the transcription of the recording of their particular Question and Answer session. Bert Sharp has been largely responsible, however, for the checking and editing to produce the final master from which the Proceedings have been printed. Any topographical errors or other errors are therefore his responsibility and he apologizes for them. In addition to thanking all the contributors, Bert would in particular like to thank Frank Brzeski for his invaluable help and support in producing these Proceedings.

Conference Invitation

You are invited to...

THE 3RD INTERNATIONAL HUMANITIES CONFERENCE

ALL & EVERYTHING '98

WEDNESDAY EVENING MARCH 18TH TO SUNDAY MARCH 22ND, 1998
Royal Norfolk Hotel, The Esplanade Bognor Regis, West Sussex PO21 2LH/UK
Telephone: 01243 826222/Fax: 01243 8326325

The All & Everything Conference has now become established as one of the foremost independent forums on the work of G.I. Gurdjieff, attracting leading international scholars, artists, group leaders, students and speakers from around the world.

Originally conceived as a congenial meeting of the 'Companions of the Book', the conference has developed into a major forum for the presentation and discussion of recent writings, music and exercises associated with 'The Work'.

It is open, by invitation, to serious students of All & Everything and is not under the auspices or sponsorship of any Gurdjieff group or umbrella organization.

All & Everything 98 is designed to provide a vibrant forum for the discussion of all aspects of 'The Work' and will address the important question of where humanity stands today in the context of the teaching of Gurdjieff.

The conference seeks to keep the work of Gurdjieff contemporary, alive and relevant to global scientific, spiritual and sociological developments in the approach to the new millennium.

The aspiration of the Planning Committee is that the Conference should achieve a balance in the presentation of material relating to the practical stimulation and development of the three centres – moving, feeling and intellectual.

Individual presentations will be welcomed that have a specific relevance to the application of 'The Work' to any or several of the three centres.

Topics at previous A&E Conferences have included:

Analogues to the Esoteric Teaching of Gurdjieff
The Enneagramatic Structure of Beelzebub's Tales
Examples of the Law of Three and Seven in the Music of Gurdjieff/De Hartman
First and Second Conscious Shocks
Gurdjieff's Neuroanatomy of Man and Modern Science
The Heptaparaparshinokh as Defined by Mr. G. in Beelzebub's Tales
A Law Conformable Schematic for Awakening Higher Centers
A Reflection on the Obligolnian Strivings

Conference Invitation

ALL & EVERYTHING '98

REGISTRATION:

To register, please complete and return the coupon on the facing page with your registration fees as follows:

Registration Fee: £30($48) per person.

Optional advance purchase discount price of £22 (U.K. & Europe), £27/$43 (U.S. & other) payment including postage for your copy of a transcript of the 1998 proceedings.

ACCOMMODATION:

Delegates are asked to make their own hotel reservations directly with the Royal Norfolk Hotel. The group rate is £40 per person, per night, (up to 4 nights) inclusive of dinner, bed and breakfast, whether in a single or double bedded room.

For a 5-7 night stay the rate is £36. *Early booking is recommended to avoid disappointment.* Please specify that you are a delegate to the International Humanities Conference, All & Everything 98.

CALL FOR PAPERS FOR ALL & EVERYTHING '98 CONFERENCE

You are invited to propose a title and theme for any topic you wish to present, although inclusion cannot be guaranteed.

Suggested topics for consideration for A&E '98 include the following:

- *Parallels between the ideas of Gurdjieff and current scientific thinking*
- *Gurdjieff and the Diagram of Everything Living – its Relevance to Today!*
- *Gurdjieff and History*
- *Science, Evolution and the Three Brained Being*
- *Man as a Self-Developing Organism*
- *The Limitations of Logical Thinking*

I wish to make a presentation at the All and Everything 98 conference:

Title: _____

A draft or outline is enclosed or will be submitted subsequently. (If to be included, a final paper is required by 31 Jan 1998. It shall be the presenter's responsibility to prepare a transcript from the tape of questions and answers to the presentation by 30 April 1998.) In consideration of my talk and presentation being included in the proceedings of this conference, I do hereby consent to the publication worldwide of my talk and presentation and related textual material and questions, answers and discussion following, in all print and electronic media as part of the proceedings of this conference, and waive any remunerative rights therein. I grant authority for the above publication to Dr. H.J. Sharp on behalf of the conference planning committee. I understand that any profits from such publication will be used for producing future conferences. This consent does not limit my rights of presentation and publication of my submission at other conferences.

Please enclose a short biographical note listing your interests and/or publications.

Name *(please print)* _____

Signature: _____ Date: _____

Kindly clip and return this coupon, or a photocopy, with your registration information to: Dr. H.J. Sharp, 1 St. Winefrides Road, Littlehampton, West Sussex BN17 5NL, U.K.

All & Everything Conference 1998

ALL & EVERYTHING '98 CONFERENCE PLANNING COMMITTEE

The detailed planning and arrangements for the conference are the responsibility of the following Planning Committee, any of whom may be contacted for further details of the conference.

FRANK BRZESKI, 71 Tarrant Street, Arundel W.S., BN18 9DN, UK;
Tel: 01903-883829; Fax: 01903-884126; magcreat@dircon.co.uk

MARLENA BUZZELL, R3 Box 1123B, Upper Ridge Rd., Bridgeton, ME 04009, US;
Tel & Fax: 207-647-3521; email: kbuzzell@ime.net

SY GINSBURG, 532 Commodore Circle, Delray Beach, FL 33483, US;
Tel: 561-278-6116; Fax: 561-278-8979 email: SyGinsburg@compuserve.com

DIMITRI PERETZI, 13 Thermopylon Street, Haslandri 15233 Athens, GREECE;
Tel & Fax: 30+1+68.40.908; email: peretzi@hol.gr

H.J. SHARP, 1, St.Winefrides Rd., Littlehampton, W.S. BN17 5NL, UK;
Tel: 01903-715432; Fax C/O LEA 01903-726318; email: magcreat@dircon.co.uk

MICHAEL SMYTH, P.O. Box 1048, Mulino, OR 97042, US;
Tel: 503-829-7142; Fax: 503-829-7175; email: abintra@molalla.net

JEFF TAYLOR, 62, Ferris Mead, Warminster, Wilts, BA12 9PY, UK;
Tel: 01985-847781; Fax: 01985-213969; email: 101761.2467@compuserve.com

PROF PAUL BEEKMAN TAYLOR, 35, Cret de la Neige, Vessy, SWITZERLAND;
Tel: 41+22+784-2732; Fax: 41+22+320-0497; email: taylor@uni2a.unige.ch

NICOLAS TERESHCHENKO, 87 rue Vercingetorix, 75014 Paris, FRANCE;
Tel & Fax: 33+1+45.39.73.93

ALL & EVERYTHING '98 CONFERENCE ADVISORY PANEL

The Planning Committee is delighted to announce the formation of an Advisory Panel, constituted of distinguished individuals who have earned a significant reputation in Gurdjieff studies through academic, literary, musical and other sectors. The majority have a first hand practical experience of the All and Everything Conferences, having already attended the previous gatherings. A list of the members of this Advisory Panel is included overleaf.

REGISTRATION COUPON:

To: Dr. H.J. Sharp, 1 St. Winefrides Road, Littlehampton, West Sussex BN17 5NL, U.K.
Please register me (us) for: All & Everything '98
(Kindly clip and return this coupon, or a photocopy, with your registration information)

Name (s): _____ Telephone: _____

Street Address: _____

City/State/Region/Country: _____ Postal Code: _____

Fee(s) enclosed:
Registration fee: _____ person(s) @ £ 30 ($48)   £ ($) _____
Advance order: Proceedings @ £ 22 UK&EU; £ 27/$43 US & other   £ ($) _____
                                              Total remittance   £ ($) _____
Please make cheques payable in £ or $ to H.J. Sharp
Excellent train connections: approx. time: Gatwick-Bognor 1 hour; London-Bognor 2 hours
Please send an additional invitation to:

Name & Address: _____

Conference Invitation

ADVISORY PANEL

PROFESSOR MASASHI ASAI holds the chair of English Literature and Cultural Studies at Kyoto Tachibana Women's University and has made a significant contribution to studies of D.H. Lawrence (who visited the Prieure in February 1924.) As an undergraduate in Kyoto, he contacted a working group (which he now leads) instituted in Japan by Gurdjieffians from California. His unprecedented contribution to the dissemination of Gurdjieff's ideas in Japan include the translation of *Beelzebub's Tales to His Grandson*, *Life is Real Only Then: When `I Am`*, and *In Search of the Miraculous*. His translation of Moore's *Gurdjieff: The Anatomy of a Myth* will appear in 1998.

PROFESSOR HOLLY BAGGETT is an historian with a focussed interest in the gifted lesbian writers, editors, and artists drawn to Gurdjieff in Paris in the 1930s. Her study extends beyond `The Rope` (Elizabeth Gordon, Kathryn Hulme, Alice Rohrer, and Solita Solano.) Her doctorate (University of Delaware) was awarded for her thesis *Aloof from Natural Laws: Margaret C. Anderson and the `Little Review, 1914-1929*. Dr Baggett has now embarked on an in-depth study of Jane Heap, and is in wide consultation.

J. WALTER DRISCOLL is an independent scholar focussed on Gurdjieff studies since the 1960's. He met and corresponded with Wilhem Nyland and his groups in Warwick, New York and Seattle from 1970 until Mr Nyland's death in 1975. Following postgraduate training in librarianship in 1978, he embarked on his major work *Gurdjieff: an Annotated Bibliography* (Garland Publishing, 1985), in collaboration with The Gurdjieff Foundation of California. He is now engaged on a second edition (for which he solicits material) and is associate editor of the *Gurdjieff Homepage* at http://www.gurdjieff.org/#/. He assisted George Baker with *Gurdjieff in America: an overview,* (*American Alternative Religions*, 1995.)

WIM van DULLEMEN is a Dutch musician and musicologist who has placed his gifts at the service of the Work. Shortly after completing his studies under the composer W. Wijdeveld and becoming a professional concert pianist, he had a crucial meeting (in 1968) with J.G. Bennett. For 13 years he was the Class pianist for the eminent French Movements teacher Solange Claustres. He has propagated the Gurdjieff/de Hartmann musical *oeuvre* in `workshops`, articles, courses, lectures, and concerts - sometimes independently and sometimes in collaboration with Mme Claustres and the French pianist Alain Kremski.

Dr. MASSIMO INTROVIGNE is managing director of CESNUR, the Centre for Studies on New Religions in Torino, Italy. CESNUR's library hosts one of the most significant collections of Fourth Way books in Southern Europe. He teaches at Queen of The Apostles University in Rome and is the author of twenty books in the field of sociology of religion and contemporary esotericism. He has lectured often and sympathetically on Fourth Way-related subjects.

JAMES MOORE, who serves on the International Editorial Board of *Journal of Contemporary Religion*, has pursued practical Gurdjieffian studies for over 40 years. He first entered Dr Kenneth Walker's group in 1956 but his principal teacher was Madame Henriette Lannes. In 1980, having shared in every phase and facet of the Work in London, he was mandated to lead groups. His biographic study *Gurdjieff and Mansfield* (1980) challenges the *canard* of Gurdjieff's responsibility for Katherine Mansfield's death; his biography *Gurdjieff: the Anatomy of a Myth* (1992) is a standard work, widely translated. In 1994 he constituted in London the *Gurdjieff Studies Group*. (He co-ordinates the Advisory Panel.)

Dr ANDREW RAWLINSON has been Lecturer in Buddhism at the University of Lancaster, England, and visiting professor at the University of California at Berkeley and the University of California at Santa Barbara. Now retired from teaching and living in France, he remains an active researcher and writer with a long-standing interest in the Gurdjieffian field. His lengthy study *The Book of Enlightened Masters: Western Teachers in Eastern Traditions* (Open Court Publishing Company, 1997) contains a significant module on The Work.

Dr LEON SCHLAMM is Lecturer in Religious Studies at the University of Kent at Canterbury and co-convenor of the only British MA programme on The Study of Mysticism and Religious Experience. For his modules on Gurdjieff and Ouspensky - taught at both undergraduate and post-graduate levels - he draws on extensive reading and on his membership of The School of Economic Science (1970-1979.) He has sustained a lifetime's interest in the depth-psychology of religion as propounded by C.G. Jung (the early mentor of Gurdjieff's pupil Dr Maurice Nicoll.) Dr Schlamm's work in progress is a book entitled *C.G. Jung as mystic*.

PROFESSOR PAUL BEEKMAN TAYLOR (who for the past 30 years held the chair of Medieval English languages and literatures at the University of Geneva) grew up at the Prieure and was thus from earliest childhood immersed in a Gurdjieffian milieu. Later adopted by Jean Toomer, he lived in New York City and Doylestown Pennsylvania, and after the war sustained contact with Gurdjieff in New York and Paris. He has published five books and over a hundred articles. His work in press *Shadows of Heaven: Toomer and Gurdjieff* draws on his, and his mother's, experiences with both men.

KAREN-CLAIRE VOSS is Adjunct Professor of Religious Studies at San Jose State University where she taught for five years. She is Associate Editor of Modern Esoteric Spirituality edited by Jacob Needleman and Antoine Faivre, which contains a substantial chapter entitled `G. I. Gurdjieff and his School.` Presently living and working in Istanbul, Professor Voss is *inter alia* studying Gurdjieff's period there. She has a particular concern that academia's approach to Gurdjieff should not be dominated methodologically by the reductionist tendencies currently fashionable in certain scholarly circles.

Conference Program

THE 3RD INTERNATIONAL HUMANITIES CONFERENCE

ALL & EVERYTHING '98

Royal Norfolk Hotel
The Esplanade
Bognor Regis, West Sussex, PO21 2LH, UK
Telephone: 01243 826222 Fax: 01243 8326325

Wednesday 18th 1998
Thursday 19th 1998
Friday 20th 1998
Saturday 21st 1998
Sunday 22nd 1998

Planning Committee
*USA - Seymour B. Ginsburg, Marlena Buzzell,
Michael Smyth
EUROPE - Dimitri Peretzi, Nicholas Tereshchenko FRCS,
Prof. Paul Beekman Taylor
UK - Herbert J. Sharp, Frank M. Brzeski, Jeff Taylor*

Advisory Panel
*Professor Masashi Asai, Professor Holly Baggett,
J. Walter Driscoll, Wim van Dullemen,
Dr. Massimo Introvigne, James Moore,
Dr Andrew Rawlinson, Dr Leon Schlamm,
Professor Paul Beekman Taylor, Karen-Claire Voss.*

CONFERENCE PROGRAMME

CONFERENCE PROGRAMME

DAY 1 WEDNESDAY MARCH 18th

14.00-16.00 Meeting of Planning Committee *(To be joined by any members of the Advisory Panel present)*

20.30-22.00 Getting to know you session. Informal. Delegates to be welcomed by Marlena Buzzell on behalf of the Planning Committee. Any members of the Advisory Panel present will be introduced.

DAY 2 THURSDAY MARCH 19th

08.00-09.00 Sitting.

09.30-09.45 **INTRODUCTION.** Sy Ginsburg. *Greetings, messages, announcements, history of the genesis of the conference, copying, recording and ordering facilities*

Session 1 09.45-10.00 Introduction.
10.00-11.00 **The Trans-Caucasian Kurd.**
(45 min talk, 15 min Q&A) Sophia Wellbeloved.

11.00-11.15 Morning Coffee.

Session 2 11.15-11.30 Introduction.
11.30-12.30 **Sources of Conviction.**
(45 min talk, 15 min Q&A) Keith Buzzell.

12.30-14.30 Lunch Break.

Session 3 14.30-14.45 Introduction.
14.45-15.45 **Gurdjieff, Blavatsky and the Masters of Wisdom.**
(45 min talk, 15 min Q&A) Seymour B. Ginsburg.

15.45-16.15 Afternoon Tea.

Session 4 16.15-17.30 **What is a Messenger from Above?**
(75 min Open Forum) First Open Forum.
Prof. Paul Beekman Taylor to Chair.

17.30-20.00 Dinner.

Session 5 20.30-20.45 Introduction.
20.45-21.45 **The Kunderbuffer: The Kundalini, Alchemy and Creation of the Soul.**
(45 min talk, 15 min Q&A) Adam W. Petts.

DAY 3 FRIDAY MARCH 20th

08.00-09.00 **Sitting.** Robert Ennis: Tayu Meditation.

Session 6 09.30-09.45 Introduction.
09.45-10.45 **Time in the Cosmology of Mr. Gurdjieff.**
(45 min talk, 15 min Q&A) Forrest McIlwain

10.45-11.15 Morning Coffee.

Session 7 11.15-11.30 Introduction.
11.30-12.30 **Mysterious Coincidences – Gurdjieff, The Enneagram and Tradition.**
(45 min talk, 15 min Q&A) Jim Gomez.

12.30-14.30 Lunch Break.

Session 8 14.30-14.45 Introduction.
14.45-15.45 **Gurdjieff in Practice: The Liebovian Method.**
(45 min talk, 15 min Q&A) Richard Liebow and his Group.

15.45-16.15 Afternoon Tea.

Session 9 16.15-17.30 Second Open Forum.
Gurdjieff, the past, present and future tense of the work.
(75 min Open Forum) James Moore to Chair.

17.30-20.00 Dinner.

Session 10 20.00-20.15 Introduction.
20.15-21.15 **Joy without a Cause. Work on the Emotional Centre in Daily Life.**
(45 min talk, 15 min Q&A) Robert Bryce.

DAY 4 SATURDAY MARCH 21st

08.00-09.00 **Sitting.** Robert Ennis: Tayu Meditation.

Session 11 09.30-09.45 Introduction.
09.45-10.45 **The Evolution of Evolution.**
(45 min talk, 15 min Q&A) Bert Sharp

10.45-11.00 Morning Coffee.

Session 12 11.00-11.15 Introduction.
11.15-12.15 **Approaching the Neologisms of the First Series.**
(45 min talk, 15 min Q&A) Harry J. Bennett.

12.15-14.00 Lunch Break.

Session 13 14.00-14.15 Introduction.
14.15-15.15 **Tracking Oskiano in Beelzebub's Tales.**
(45 min talk, 15 min Q&A) Bob Curran.

15.15-15.30 Short Break.

Session 14 15.30-16.30 **Beyond the Life-Death Antagonism: Prayer and Compassion in the Gurdjieff Hymns.**
(45 min talk, 15 min Q&A) Wim Van Dullemen.

16.30-16.45 Afternoon Tea.

Session 15 16.45-18.00 Third Open Forum.
What is an Authentic Form of the Work.
(75 min Open Forum) Dr. Andrew Rawlinson to Chair

19.30 Conference Dinner.

Recital by Wim Van Dullemen.

DAY 5 SUNDAY MARCH 22nd

08.00-09.00 Sitting.

Session 16 09.30-09.45 Introduction.
09.45-10.45 **The Organ Kundabuffer.**
(45 min talk, 15 min Q&A) Stuart Goodnick (to be read by Martin Butler).

10.45-11.00 Morning Coffee.

Session 17 11.00-11.15 Introduction.
11.15-12.15 **The Origins, Meaning and Purpose of the Movements. Demonstration. Video.**
(45 min talk, 15 min Q&A) Wim Van Dullemen.

12.15-14.00 Lunch Break.

Session 18 14.00-15.15 Fourth Open Forum.
Where Do We Go from Here?
(75 min Open Forum) Prof. Paul Beekman Taylor to Chair

15.15 Closing of Conference.

All & Everything Conference 1998

SPEAKERS

PROF. PAUL BEEKMAN TAYLOR
Prof. Paul Beekman Taylor lived for some years with Jean Toomer in New York and Pennsylvania as a young boy, studied with Gurdjieff in Paris after World War 2, before turning to a teaching career in Medieval Germanic languages and literature, first in Iceland and for the past thirty years in Geneva, where he lives with his wife and two teenage children. Prof. Taylor retires from teaching this year and his book "Shadows of Heaven" will be published in May by Samuel Weiser.

HARRY J. BENNETT
Harry Bennett tells us simply that he is a carpenter living and working in Portland, Maine.

ROBERT BRYCE
Robert Bryce was born in Australia and was trained as a Shipwright, Chartered Engineer and Dispute Mediator. He now lives in the UK. He first came across Gurdjieff's thinking through reading Meetings with Remarkable Men at the age of 21. This led him to study the Work with a group in Sydney, Australia. This was led by Dr. Philip Groves.

DR. KEITH BUZZELL
Dr. Buzzell is a 1960 graduate of the Philadelphia College of Osteopathic Medicine. He is presently a member of the staff of Northern Cumberland Memorial Hospital in Bridgton and of clinical Medicine in Beddeford. Dr. Buzzell speaks from a broad perspective deriving from his life as a musician, musicologist, author, teacher, researcher, and physician. He is presently in Family practice in Fryeburg where he also serves as Medical Director of Hospice of Western Maine.

ROBERT CURRAN
Born in April 1943, Robert Curran participated in Lord Pentland's Work group in San Francisco from 1966 - 1987 and now continues the Work in Washington D.C.

WIM VAN DULLEMAN
Wim van Dulleman is a Dutch musician and musicologist who has placed his gifts at the service of the Work. He met John G. Bennett in 1968 and this was to have a decisive influence on his life. He became a member of the Gurdjieff Institute in France, and for 13 years he was the Class pianist for the eminent French Movements teacher, Solange Claustres. He was propagated the Gurdjieff/ de Hartmann musical oeuvre in workshops, articles, courses, lectures, and concerts - sometimes independently and sometimes in collaboration with Mme. Claustres, having organized seminars - open to all-for her in 1995 and 1996 in Amsterdam. His current C.D. is entitled "The Music of G. I. Gurdjieff" (Ars Floreat label, Amsterdam)

ROBERT DANIEL ENNIS
Robert Daniel Ennis has been teaching in the Fourth Way tradition since 1976. He has worked with E. J. Gold and Robert de Ropp, among others.
Mr. Ennis is the founder of Tayu Meditation Center, and the author of "The Way of Tayu," an introduction to Fourth Way spiritual practice. His work includes new approaches to Self-Observation and an external considering practice called Co-meditation.

SEYMOUR B. (SY) GINSBURG, J.D.
Sy Ginsburg was born in Chicago in 1934 and currently resides in Florida. He was introduced to the Gurdjieff work in 1978 by Sri Madhava Ashish, an eminent theosophical scholar and Hindu monk, who become his mentor over a 19 year period. Ginsburg was a member of the Gurdjieff Society of Florida and later a co-founder of the Gurdjieff Institute of Florida. Currently he is a Director of The Theosophical Society in Miami & South Florida and facilitator of the Gurdjieff Study Group at The Theosophical Society.

STUART GOODNICK
Stuart Goodnick holds degrees in Physics from the California Institute of Technology and the University of California at Santa Cruz. He is a member of the teaching staff at Tayu Centre, a Fourth Way school in Sebastopol, CA, where he lectures, writes and leads group work. He also works as the manager of the Power Products Engineering Group at Parker Compumotor, an electronics manufacturing firm.

JIM GOMEZ
Jim was born in San Francisco, California, in 1967. He moved to Portland, Oregon in 1968 and met Mrs. Staveley during that year, becoming involved in her Gurdjieff groups at Two Rivers Farm in Aurora. He became an increasingly active member of Mrs. Staveley's groups, living and working on the farm and studying the ideas of Gurdjieff rather intensively from 1986-1993.
In 1989 Jim met Dr. Keith Critchlow, F.R.C.A., noted authority on Sacred Geometry and architectural advisor to HRH The Prince of Wales. He renewed contact in 1991, after a period of intensive study of Sacred Geometry and Islamic Spiritual Pattern, and was invited to participate in The Prince of Wales's Institute of Architecture in London as a foundation student in 1993-4. He has graduated from the POWIA and The University of Greenwich BA (Hons) and is now working in an architectural practice in London.

RICHARD LIEBOW
Richard Liebow was born in 1928 in Iowa, USA. He spent one year in residence at the Prabhavananda Isherwood Ramamkrishna Hindu Organisation in 1952. His first glimpse of Gurdjieff/Ouspensky literature was in 1954. Then came a serious scrutiny of Gurdjieff/Ouspensky literature from 1966 to the present. He became a member of the Gurdjieff Foundation of San Francisco in 1967. Connection with Nyland Groups in San Francisco1988-1991. Organiser/sustainer of an independent Gurdjieff/Ouspensky study group in San Francisco - focused primarily on Ouspensky's Search. Producer of compacted versions of Beelzebub's Tales, Meetings with Remarkable Men, Ouspensky's Psychology, and Ouspensky's Search.

FORREST McILWAIN
Forrest McIlwain came across the Work in early 1972. He had begun a correspondence with Hugh B. Ripman, who was the leader of the Work Group in the Washington, D.C. area until his death in 1980. He continued to actively participate in the Washington Group until 1985. After Mr. Ripman's death, Mrs. Ripman replaced her husband. Whilst he was working with the Washington Group, Mrs. Ripman gave him the honour of leading the Beelzebub reading group. Mrs. Ripman observed on numerous occasions that he had a deep love for Beelzebub, and it is his continuing love which says why he wishes to present on this occasion a paper on "Time".

JAMES MOORE
Born in Cornwall in 1929, James Moore lives in London. After entering Dr. Kenneth Walker's group at age 26 he went on to study with Mme Henriette Lannes for 22 years until her retirement in 1979. Thereafter he studied under Maurice Desselle and M. Henry Tracol, enjoying the priviledge of regular contact with Mme Jeanne de Salzmann. In 1980 he was mandated to lead groups. He has participated in every phase of the Work, meeting many senior pupils of Gurdjieff, including Olga de Hartmann, Jane Heap, Jessmin Howarth, Rowland Kenney, Louise March, Rose Mary Nott, Jessie Orage and Lord Pentland.
As a writer, James Moore set himself the additional task of contributing to the propagation of Mr Gurdjieff's teaching. His interview with Peter Brook in The Guardian heralded the forthcoming film *Meetings with Remarkable Men*. In 1980, he published the biographic study *Gurdjieff and Mansfield*, challenging the canard of Gurdjieff's responsibility for Mansfield's death. January 1992 saw the publication of Moore's major work, the biography *Gurdjieff: the Anatomy of a Myth*.

ADAM W. PETTS
Adam Petts has had a motivation to seek a deeper meaning to his own existence for as long as he can remember. This led him into many different areas of practice and study. Seven years ago he came across a group in London known as The Gnostic Institute of Anthropology. This is part of an international organisation formed as the result of the teaching of Samuel Aun Weor. Born in 1917, in the light of his own experiences he began to teach, write books and give lectures and as a result a group formed around him. He wrote over 60 books dealing with many aspects of esoteric initiatic knowledge, fourth way psychology etc.,. He used the term Gnosis to indicate that his teachings were a fundamental blueprint of techniques for the self-perfection of the human being that can be found at the root of all world religions.

DR. ANDREW RAWLINSON
Dr. Andrew Rawlinson has been Lecturer in Buddhism at the University of Lancaster, England, and visiting professor at the University of California at Santa Barbara. Now retired from teaching and living in France, he remains an active researcher and writer with a long-standing interest in the Gurdjieffian field. His lengthy study "The Book of Enlightened Masters: Western Teachers in Eastern Traditions" (Open Court Publishing Company, 1997) contains a significant module on The Work.

DR. H. J. SHARP
Dr. Sharp took a first degree in Physiology, and an M.Sc., in Metallurgy by private study while working in industry. He later took a Ph.D., in Material Science. Subsequently he has become involved in the psychological transformation of himself and others, a much more difficult field of endeavour. In this he has been helped by many, including Ronald and Muriel Oldham and Lewis Creed, when he was able to visit the Dicker, John Castanios Flores, who led a large work group in Mexico and came to Littlehampton to end his days, and Nicolas Tereshchenko and Sy Ginsburg. There have been many others speaking through the written page and in other ways and perhaps most of all, in a very special way, his dear wife and daughter.

SOPHIA WELLBELOVED
Sophia Wellbeloved was a member of the Gurdjieff Society in London from 1962-1976. She is now doing a Doctoral Research at King's College, London into Beelzebub's Tales To His Grandson, in the Theology & Religious Studies Department.
She has given seminars on Beelzebub's Tales To His Grandson at King's College and at The School of Oriental and African Studies (SOAS), London University and has lectured on Gurdjieff at the Royal College of Art, London and at King's College and SOAS.

Planning Committee

USA

Seymour B. Ginsburg
Marlena Buzzell
Michael Smyth

EUROPE

Dimitri Peretzi
Nicholas Tereshchenko FRCS
Professor Paul Beekman Taylor

UK

Herbert J. Sharp
Frank M. Brzeski
Jeff Taylor

Advisory Board

Professor Masashi Asai holds the chair of English Literature and Cultural Studies at Kyoto Tachibana Women's University and has made a significant contribution to studies of D. H. Lawrence (who visited the Prieure in February 1924.) As an undergraduate in Kyoto, he contacted a working group (which he now leads) instituted in Japan by Gurdjieffians from California. His unprecedented contribution to the dissemination of Gurdjieff's ideas in Japan include the translation of *Beelzebub's Tales to His Grandson, Life is real only then, when "I am"*, and *In Search of the Miraculous*. His translation of Moore's *Gurdjieff: The Anatomy of a Myth* will appear in 1998.

Professor Holly Baggett is an historian with a focused interest in the gifted lesbian writers, editors, and artists drawn to Gurdjieff in Paris in the 1930s. Her study extends beyond 'The Rope' (Elizabeth Gordon, Kathryn Hulme, Alice Aohrer, and Solita Solano.) Her doctorate, University of Delaware) was awarded for her thesis "Aloof from Natural Laws: Margaret C. Anderson and the 'Little Review, 1914-1929." Or Baggett has now embarked on an in-depth study of Jane Heap, and is in wide consultation.

J. Walter Driscoll is an independent scholar focused on Gurdjieff studies since the 1960's. He met and corresponded with Wilhem Nyland and his groups in Warwick, New York and Seattle from 1970 until Mr. Nyland's death in 1975. Following postgraduate training in librarianship in 1978, he embarked on his major work *Gurdjieff: an Annotated Bibliography* (Garland Publishing, 1985), in collaboration with The Gurdjieff Foundation of California. He is now engaged on a second edition (for which he solicits material) and is associate editor of the Gurdjieff Homepage at www.gurdjieff.org. He assisted George Baker with *Gurdjieff in America: an overview*, (American Alternative Religions, 1995.)

Wim van Dullemen is a Dutch musician and musicologist who has placed his gifts at the service of the Work. Shortly after completing his studies under the composer W. Wijdeveld and becoming a professional concert pianist, he had a crucial meeting (in 1968) with J. G. Bennett. For 13 years he was the class pianist for the eminent French Movements teacher Solange Claustres. He has propagated the Gurdjieff/de Hartmann musical 'oeuvre' in 'workshops', articles, courses, lectures, and concerts - sometimes independently and sometimes in collaboration with Mme Claustres and the French pianist Alain Kremski.

Dr. Massimo Introvigne is managing director of CESNUR, the Centre for Studies on New Religions in Torino, Italy. CESNUR's library hosts one of the most significant collections of Fourth Way books in Southern Europe. He teaches at Queen of the Apostles University in Rome and is the author of twenty books in the field of sociology of religion and contemporary esotericism. He has lectured often and sympathetically on Fourth Way-related subjects.

Advisory Board

James Moore, who serves on the International Editorial Board of *Journal of Contemporary Religion*, has pursued practical Gurdjieffian studies for over 40 years. He first entered Dr. Kenneth Walker's group in 1956 but his principal teacher was Madame Henriette Lannes. In 1980, having shared in every phase and facet of the Work in London, he was mandated to lead groups. His biographic study *Gurdjieff and Mansfield* (1980) challenges the 'canard' of Gurdjieff's responsibility for Katherine Mansfield's death; his biography *Gurdjieff: the Anatomy of a Myth* (1992) is a standard work, widely translated. In 1994 he constituted in London the Gurdjieff Studies Group. (He co-ordinates the Advisory Panel.)

Dr Andrew Rawlinson has been Lecturer in Buddhism at the University of Lancaster, England, and visiting professor at the University of California at Berkeley and the University of California at Santa Barbara. Now retired from teaching and living in France, he remains an active researcher and writer with a long-standing interest in the Gurdjieffian field. His lengthy *study The Book of Enlightened Masters: Western Teachers in Eastern Traditions* (Open Court Publishing Company, 1997) contains a significant module on The Work.

Dr. Leon Schlamm is Lecturer in Religious Studies at the University of Kent at Canterbury and co-convener of the only *British* MA programme on The Study of Mysticism and Religious Experience. For his modules on Gurdjieff and Ouspensky - taught at both undergraduate and post-graduate levels - he draws on extensive reading and on his membership of the School of Economic Science (1970-1979.) He has sustained a lifetime's interest in the depth-psychology of religion as propounded by C.G. Jung (the early *mentor* of Gurdjieff's pupil Or Maurice Nicoll.) Dr. Schlamm's work in progress is a book entitled *C. G. Jung as Mystic*.

Professor Paul Beekman Taylor, who for the past 30 years held the chair of Medieval English languages and literatures at the University of Geneva) grew up at the Prieure and was thus from earliest childhood immersed in a Gurdjieffian milieu. Later adopted by Jean Toomer, he lived in New York City and Dutchtown, Pennsylvania, and after the war sustained contact with Gurdjieff in New York and Paris. He has published live books and over a hundred articles. His work at press, *Shadows of Heaven: Toomer and Gurdjieff*, draws on his and his mother's, experiences with both men.

Karen-Claire Voss is an Adjunct Professor of Religious Studies at San Jose State University where she taught for five years. She is Associate Editor of *Modern Esoteric Spirituality* edited by Jacob Needleman and Antoine Faivre, which contains a substantial chapter entitled "G. I. Gurdjieff and his School." Presently living and working in Istanbul, Professor Voss is 'inter alia' studying Gurdjieff's period there. She has a particular concern that academia's approach to Gurdjieff should not be dominated methodologically by the reductionist tendencies currently fashionable in certain scholarly circles.

Speakers

Prof. Paul Beekman Taylor lived for some years with Jean Toomer in New York and Pennsylvania as a young boy, studied with Gurdjieff in Paris after World War 2, before turning to a teaching career in Medieval Germanic languages and literature, first in Iceland and for the past thirty years in Geneva, where he lives with his wile and two teenage children. Prof. Taylor retires from teaching this year and his book *Shadows of Heaven* will be published in May by Samuel Weiser.

Harry J. Bennett tells us simply that he is a carpenter living and working in Portland, Maine.

Robert Bryce was born in Australia and was trained as a Shipwright, Chartered Engineer and Dispute Mediator. He now lives in the UK. He first came across Gurdjieff's thinking through reading *Meetings With Remarkable Men* at the age of 21. This led him to study the Work with a group in Sydney, Australia. This was led by Dr. Philip Groves.

Dr. Keith Buzzell is a 1960 graduate of the Philadelphia College of Osteopathic Medicine. He is presently a member of the staff of Northern Cumberland Memorial Hospital in Bridgton and of clinical Medicine in Beddelord. Dr. Buzzell speaks from a broad perspective deriving from his life as a musician, musicologist, author, teacher, researcher, and physician. He is presently in Family Practice in Fryeburg where he also serves as Medical Director of Hospice of Western Maine.

Robert Curran was born in April 1943. Robert participated in Lord Pentland's Work group in San Francisco from 1966 - 1987 and now continues the Work in Washington D.C.

Wim van Dullemen is a Dutch musician and musicologist who has placed his gifts at the service of the Work. He met John G. Bennett in 1968 and this was to have a decisive influence on his life. He became a member of the Gurdjieff Institute in France and for 13 years he was the Class pianist for the eminent French Movement teacher, Solange Claustres. He has propagated the Gurdjieff/de Hartmann musical oeuvre in workshops, articles, courses, lectures and concerts - sometimes independently and sometimes in collaboration with Mme. Claustres, having organized seminars - open to all - for her in 1995 and 1996 in Amsterdam. His current CD is entitled "The Music of G. I. Gurdjieff" (Ars Floreat label, Amsterdam)

Robert Daniel Ennis has been teaching in the Fourth Way tradition since 1976. He has worked with E. J. Gold and Robert de Ropp, among others. Mr. Ennis is the founder of Tayu Meditation Center and the author of *The Way of Tayu*, an introduction to Fourth Way spiritual practice. His work includes new approaches to Self-Observation and an external considering practice called Co-meditation.

Speakers

Seymour (Sy) B. Ginsburg, J. D., was born in Chicago in 1934 and currently resides in Florida. He was introduced to the Gurdjieff work in 1978 by Sri Madhava Ashish, an eminent theosophical scholar and Hindu monk, who become his mentor over a 19 year period. Ginsburg was a member of the Gurdjieff Society of Florida and later a co-founder of the Gurdjieff Institute of Florida. Currently he is a Director of The Theosophical Society in Miami & South Florida and facilitator of The Gurdjieff Study Group at The Theosophical Society.

Stuart Goodnick holds degrees in Physics from the California Institute of Technology and the University of California at Santa Cruz. He is a member of the teaching staff at Tayu Centre, a Fourth Way school in Sebastopol. CA, where he lectures, writes and leads group work. He also works as the manager of the Power Products Engineering Group at Parker Compumotor, an electronics manufacturing firm.

Jim Gomez was born in San Francisco, California, in 1967. He moved to Portland, Oregon in 1985 and met Mrs. Staveley during that year, becoming involved in her Gurdjieff groups at Two Rivers Farm in Aurora. He became an increasingly active member of Mrs. Staveley's groups. Living and working on the farm and studying the ideas of Gurdjieff rather intensively from 1986 - 1993. In 1989 Jim met Dr. Keith Critchlow, F.R.C.A., noted authority on Sacred Geometry and architectural advisor to HRH the Prince of Wales. He renewed contact in 1991, after a period of intensive study of Sacred Geometry and Islamic Sacred Pattern, and was invited to participate in The Prince of Wale's Institute of Architecture in London as a foundation student in 1993-4. He has graduated from the POWIA and The University of Greenwich BA (Hons) and is now working in an architectural practice in London.

Richard Liebow was born in 1928 in Iowa, USA. He spent one year in residence at the Prabhavananda Isherwood Ramamkrishna Hindu Organisation in 1952. His first glimpse of Gurdjieff/Ouspensky literature was in 1954. Then came a serious scrutiny of Gurdjieff/Ouspensky literature from 1966 to the present. He became a member of the Gurdjieff Foundation of San Francisco in 1967. Connection with Nyland Groups in San Francisco 1988-1991. Organiser/sustainer of an independent Gurdjieff/Ouspensky study group in San Francisco - focused primarily on Ouspensky's Search. Producer of compacted versions of *Beelzebub's Tales*, *Meetings With Remarkable Men*, Ouspensky's *Psychology*, and Ouspensky's *Search*.

Forrest McIlwain came across the Work in early 1972. He had begun a correspondence with Hugh B. Ripman, who was the leader of the Work Group in the Washington, D.C. area until his death in 1980. He continued to actively participate in the Washington Group until 1985. After Mr. Ripman's death, Mrs. Ripman replaced her husband. Whilst he was working with the Washington Group, Mrs. Ripman gave him the honour of leading the *Beelzebub* reading group. Mrs. Ripman observed on numerous occasions that he had a deep love for *Beelzebub*, and it is his continuing love which says why he wishes to present on this occasion a paper on 'Time'.

James Moore was born in Cornwall in 1929. He lives in London. Alter entering Dr. Kenneth Walker's group at age 26, he went on to study with Mme Henriette Lannes for 22 years until her retirement in 1979. Thereafter he studied under Maurice Desselle and M. Henry Tracol, enjoying the privilege of regular contact with Mme Jeanne de Salzmann. In 1980 he was mandated to lead groups. He has participated in every phase of the Work, meeting many senior pupils of Gurdjieff, including Olga de Hartmann, Jane Heap, Jessmin Howarth, Rowland Kenney, Louse March, Rose Mary Nott, Jessie Orage, and Lord Pentland. As a writer, James Moore set himself the additional task of contributing to the propagation of Mr. Gurdjieff's teaching. His interview with Peter Brook in The Guardian heralded the forthcoming film *Meetings With Remarkable Men*. In 1980, he published the biographic study *Gurdjieff and Mansfield*, challenging the canard of Gurdjieff's responsibility for Mansfield's death. January 1992 saw the publication of Moore's major work, the biography *Gurdjieff: the Anatomy of a Myth*.

Adam Petts has had a motivation to seek a deeper meaning to his own existence for as long as he can remember. This led him into many different areas of practice and study. Seven years ago he came across a group in London known as The Gnostic Institute of Anthropology. This is part of an international organisation formed as the result of the teaching of Samael Aun Weor. Born in 1917, in the light of his own experiences he began to teach, write books and give lectures and as a result a group formed around him. He wrote over 60 books dealing with many aspects of esoteric initiatic knowledge, fourth way psychology, etc. He used the term Gnosis to indicate that his teachings were a fundamental blueprint of techniques for the self-perfection of the human being that can be found at the root of all world religions.

Dr. Andrew Rawlinson has been Lecturer in Buddhism at the University of Lancaster, England, and visiting professor at the University of California at Santa Barbara. Now retired from teaching and living in France, he remains an active researcher and writer with a long-standing interest in the Gurdjieffian field. His lengthy study *The Book of Enlightened Masters: Western Teachers in Eastern Traditions* (Open Court Publishing Company, 1997) contains a significant module on The Work.

Dr. H. J. Sharp took a first degree in Physiology, and a M.Sc. in Metallurgy by private study while working in industry. He later took a Ph.D. in Material Science. Subsequently he has become involved in the psychological transformation of himself and others, a much more difficult field of endeavour. In this he has been helped by many, including Ronald and Muriel Oldham and Lewis Creed, when he was able to visit the Dicker, John Castanios Flores, who led a large work group in Mexico and came to Littlehampton to end his days, and Nicolas Tereshchenko and Sy Ginsburg. There have been many others speaking through the written page and in other ways and perhaps most of all, in a very special way, his dear wife and daughter.

Sophia Wellbeloved was a member of the Gurdjieff Society in London from 1962-1976. She is now doing a Doctoral Research at King's College, London into *Beelzebub's Tales to His Grandson*, in the Theology & Religious Studies Department. She has given seminars on *Beelzebub's Tales to His Grandson* at King's College and at The School of Oriental and African Studies (SOAS). London University and has lectured on Gurdjieff at the Royal College of Art, London and at King's College and SOAS.

Sittings

These took place beginning on Thursday morning 08:00 to 09:00
The sittings on Friday and Saturday morning were led by Robert Ennis using the Tayu Meditation method.

Robert Ennis has been teaching in the Fourth Way tradition since 1976. He has worked with E. J. Gold and Robert de Ropp, among others. Robert Ennis is the founder of the Tayu Meditation Centre, and the author of *The Way of Tayu*, an introduction to Fourth Way spiritual practice. His work includes new approaches to Self-Observation and an external considering practice called Co-meditation.

A brief synopsis of the Tayu meditation program follows:

Many people in the West do not understand why one would ever want to meditate. Some people have gotten the idea that it is a good way to reduce stress, and calm the mind. Of course this is true. But meditation can be much more than this. Meditation is the best way to confront our essential unhappiness, loneliness, and confusion in this strange but wonderful experience that is a human lifetime. It permits us to address the fundamental questions of life: "Who am I? What am I doing? Why am I doing it?" Meditation creates space in oneself in which real understanding can flourish. Only from such understanding can real change come about in one's life. With this understanding one can begin to act both consciously, and with conscience.

Tayu meditation is different from that with which most people in this culture are currently familiar. Most traditional forms of meditation which focus the awareness inwards, were developed to aid those growing up in Eastern cultures. In those cultures, the primary social emphasis for centuries has been upon humility and cooperation. These meditations were designed to balance the spiritual development of such people by strengthening their personal identities, by creating a kind of internal cave in which to engage in the process of learning to confront Self.

In Western culture, the primary social emphasis has been upon personal identity and achievement. One is taught from childhood to be independent, to complete for ones place in life, to be self-reliant. While these are certainly virtues, they can leave one feeling isolated, cut-off, and very lonely. The traditional forms of solo sitting meditation, when employed alone by a Westerner without proper guidance, may only heighten an already strongly developed sense of isolation and separateness.

Further, these meditations were generally expected to be performed either in the context of a monastic community, or by oneself in a solitary location. They are not well adapted to the Western model of householder and family living, and the demands of supporting oneself at a job, rather than by begging. Tayu meditation, in contrast, is designed to be effective under the normal conditions of life in Western culture. It does not demand that one adopt a special or restrictive lifestyle, or separate oneself from the world. Indeed, it is based upon the idea that one must learn how to make the world one's teacher.

Tayu meditation has several forms. The first, and most important, is called Self-observation. Self-observation is a form of continuous meditation, or meditation-in-action. It is intended to be used in the midst of daily life. That is how one will discover what one is like under the ordinary conditions of existence. Not in special surroundings or circumstances. Unfortunately, in the beginning the difficulty is to remember what one is trying to do. Ordinarily one becomes so wrapped up in, or identified with, one's everyday affairs that one has no attention left over to really observe anything.

But with a strong enough intention, and with persistent practice, eventually one will remember to observe oneself in this way at least part of the time during every day. And the more one remembers to do one's Self-observation, the easier and more rewarding it will become. One will begin to develop a picture of one's life upon which one can rely when the time comes to begin making changes. And some things will begin to change simply by one's having gotten a good look at them.

Self-observation is more difficult in the beginning than the common forms of meditation which involves sitting in a quiet room; because one does not have the advantage of being constantly reminded by one's circumstances that one is engaged in meditation. But done properly, it is ultimately more efficient, because one automatically learns how to apply the insights gained to one's ordinary life. There is no artificial separation between one's meditative practice and one's daily activities. It is also possible to engage in extensive meditation in this way without the necessity for extended retreats or stays in a monastery.

There is also a second basic form of Tayu meditation called Co-meditation. In this two-person meditation one enlists the help of another in one's quest for reliable self-knowledge. One learns how to use another being as a mirror in which one can see things about oneself that might otherwise be difficult or impossible to observe. Just as one cannot observe one's back without help, many of our most important inner qualities are only revealed in contact with others.

Co-meditation can also teach one how to bridge the gulf between oneself and others and to overcome the fear of openness and relationships that can result form one's upbringing in this society. Co-meditation is designed to expand the awareness and focus it on the rest of Creation, in particular the other beings with whom we share this Universe. This eventually enables one safely to establish full and open communication with others, and gives one a greatly enhanced ability to enter freely into relationship on many levels.

Introduction and Opening of the Conference

Sy Ginsburg, Esq.

Greetings, messages, announcements.

History of the genesis of the conference.

Copying, recording, ordering facilities and waiver forms.

Seymour B. (Sy) Ginsburg, J.D., was born in Chicago in 1934. He currently resides at Fort Lauderdale, Florida.
Northwestern University School of Business (now the Kellogg School), B.S., 1954, C.P.A.
Northwestern University of Law, J.D. 1957.
Past President, Toys-R- Us, Inc.
Past President, Glass, Ginsburg Ltd., Member Firm, Chicago Mercantile Exchange.

Since 1978, Student of Sri Madhava Ashish in Theosophy and Gurdjieff Studies.
Former Member, Gurdjieff Society of Florida (affiliated with Gurdjieff Foundation, NYC)
Co-founder, Gurdjieff Institute, Inc. (Florida)
Currently President, The Theosophical Society in Miami & South Florida, Facilitator of the Gurdjieff Study Group at the Theosophical Society.

Author: *Gurdjieff & The Secret Doctrine*, American Theosophist, Spring Special Issue 1988.
Co-author: *Gurdjieff, A New Introduction to his Teaching*, 1994.

Introduction

Good morning everybody. I am Sy Ginsburg and on behalf of the Planning Committee I would like to welcome everybody to All & Everything '98. This is the third All & Everything Conference. I would like to give a little of the history of how this began, particularly for those of you who have not been here before. But I was told last night that my understanding of the origin of the Conference was in fact not really its beginning. I thought the Conference began some three years ago with several of us meeting together to discuss the manuscript of that now published book by Russell Smith, "Cosmic Secrets". Russell Smith is not with us here this year, and that particular manuscript was brought to my attention by Nicolas Tereshchenko, who got it from Mrs.

All & Everything Conference 1998

Staveley. But I was told last evening that this kind of Conference really had its genesis with Mrs. Staveley and some of the people who worked with her. Some of them are sitting here today. Apparently this kind of Conference was talked about for a couple of years prior to that. In fact I know that when the first Conference took place, Mrs. Staveley suggested that participants should call it "The Brotherhood of the Book". Subsequently it became "The Companions of the Book", and here we are at the All & Everything Conference. What we should recognize is that the Conference is not sponsored or under the auspices of any Gurdjieff group or organization. So in that respect this Conference does not put forward any particular view point of the Work. It is a get-together, perhaps, of Companions of the Book who are associated with Mr. Gurdjieff's ideas.

I have several announcements to make. Some were mentioned last evening. Sophia Wellbeloved has kindly consented to keep track of some of the things that need to be kept track of, namely the payment of the £30 administrative fee. If you have not yet paid, please see Sophia some time during the Conference. For those of you who are presenting at the Conference, we do need you to sign a waiver for publication. Many of you have. It was in the Invitation. Sophia has those forms and we need that so that we can include your contribution in the Proceedings of the Conference. There is also going to be a participants list which we will get out before the end of the Conference. Sophia has a tentative list already and we need you to check to make sure you are on it, your address correct, your phone number, and an Email address if you have one, before the end of today so as to give Bert Sharp time to reproduce the final list. This will be helpful to enable you to keep in touch with one another. If you don't want your name included please let Sophia know that.

Also you can order the Proceedings if you wish. If you order them here it will be somewhat less expensive than if you order them later. It is £22 if you live in the UK or Europe. It is £27 if you live in the USA or elsewhere. By The Way Books, which is based in Sacramento, California, has undertaken to publish the previous proceedings. It is somewhat more expensive at 45 US dollars but they are actually contributing 5 US dollars a copy for supporting the Conference. They will be doing the same in the case of the Proceedings of this years Conference. Michael Smyth of Abintra the Bookseller, will also, we hope be reproducing the Proceedings of All & Everything '98. If you are in the UK, of course, you can order direct from Dr. Sharp and save money doing that.

We have several greetings for the Conference. The first is from a group in Berlin and the administrator is Carla Angeloni who contacted Dr. Sharp, wanting some help in getting illustrations of the Movements for their publicity. Prof. Taylor was able to help them with their request. The head of the group is a Dr. Reichelt, a psychiatrist with a broad experience in the Gurdjieff Work. He is assisted by Mr. Heise, while Carla Angeloni would appear to be the administrative driving force. They are organizing a Workshop in Berlin for April 17-19th this year. Wim Van Dullemen of our Advisory panel, who will be here on Saturday, is involved in this, so if any of you want more information he is probably the best to speak to about it. In their correspondence Miss Angeloni wrote: "The main reason I am writing now is to send you some money begging you to buy some flowers and to put them on the table of your Conference as loving greetings from your Berlin friends to the participants". And here are the flowers.

Introduction

Some of you have heard the name of Dr. Phillip Groves. He also sends his best wishes for our Conference. He was mentioned here last year by Nicolas Tereshchenko who has had some contact with him, and one of his pupils, who in effect represent him, is giving a paper on Friday evening with the title "Joy without a Cause: Work on the Emotional Centre in Daily Life", and this is Robert Bryce, who is not here this morning. Some of you met him last evening.

Massimo Introvigne who is also a member of the Advisory Panel again cannot be here this year. He presented a paper last year and was here the previous year in person. He sends his greetings and asks me to remind everyone of CESNUR '98. If you are not familiar with this, CESNUR is an acronym for The Centre for the Study-of New Religions, and each year they have a Conference in an academic setting. This year the Conference is September 10-12th in Torino, Italy. There will be a Gurdjieff section of the Conference as there was last year and Dr. Introvigne has encouraged this. Both Nicolas Tereshchenko and I have agreed to participate and any others who are here who would like to do that will be welcome. This is in effect a call for papers. A summary should be submitted by the end of this month. Prof. Connie Jones will be at the Conference again. She is connected with the Gurdjieff Work in California and there is likelihood that she will be the facilitator of the Gurdjieff section this year. Those of you who would like copies of the papers presented by us at CESNUR '97, these are available for £5. There are several copies on the table at the back. While mentioning the table, Michael Smyth has brought some books that he thought would be of interest. It you would like to purchase any of them you can. Leave the money on the table or give it to Michael.

Finally I would like to mention something else on the table. There is in my opinion an extraordinary piece of statuary created by Dr. Sharp. If you look at it, some of you will recognize it because it represents some of the psychological structure described by Mr. Gurdjieff. At least that is what I understand by it. And I personally would like to thank Bert for his unstinting efforts in making these Conferences possible. Thank you very much, Bert.

A few words about the Presentations. We are recording Presentations. I would like to mention a resolution that we passed last evening, and that is that when the question and answer periods after each Presentation occurs, see if you can be sufficiently present to state your name before you ask a question, so when the Proceedings are transcribed we will be able to know who asked the question.

I also want to say a word about the Forums. Seeing everybody has a copy of the program, you will see that amongst the Presentations there are four Open Forums which are intended as a discussion among members here, and they are at the end of the afternoons of each day, with one change, and that is that the Forum today which is at 4.15 pm is now entitled "Secrecy in the Work". The second Forum, tomorrow afternoon, is entitled "Gurdjieff, the past, present and future tense of the Work". The first Forum will be facilitated by Prof Paul Beekman Taylor, the second by James Moore. The third Forum is going to be on Saturday afternoon at the same time and is "What is an Authentic Form off the Work", chaired by Dr. Andrew Rawlinson. And the fourth and last Forum which I particularly would call your attention to is "Where Do We Go from Here?" That is going to be on Sunday afternoon.

A number of the things that we will be doing at this Conference came as a result of suggestions from a previous Forum, "Where Do We Go from Here". If we are going to have another Conference, then how do we make it more useful to all of us? So during these few days, if you can give some thought to that and contribute your ideas, and if you want to be particularly active in planning future Conferences, you will be more than welcome to serve.

What we are going to do in the Forums, unlike the Presentations which will be recorded, is to have a vote before each Forum to decide whether you want it all recorded or not. Last year some people felt that if we want them to participate in Forums about sensitive issues, they might be inhibited if everything was recorded including the identification of contributors. So we thought it best to vote on each Forum and depending upon the consensus we will or will not record these Forums in total.

Unidentified: How about not recording the names, but recording the question and discussion? People I guess in that way could remain anonymous and still we could have the discussions.

Sy Ginsburg: Well that is a distinct possibility and I guess at the Planning Committee meeting we did discuss that and so what I would like to do is to pick that up this afternoon at the beginning of the first Forum and we will see how everyone feels about it. It may be a very useful suggestion.

Bert Sharp: Then you will have to remember not to give your name.

Sy Ginsburg: Another one of the changes that you may have noticed in the program is that there is a 15 minute introductory time before each Presentation. The idea here is that rather than just going into the Presenter's talk, to allow a few moments to quieten ourselves. In some cases, depending upon the Presenter's wish, there could be a reading from the *Tales*, or perhaps some music played. It is an opportunity to call us back to ourselves. And so you will see that there is a 15 minute break before the actual beginning of each talk. I would like to ask the speakers to keep to their allotted time, except I have already gone over mine, but there is one more announcement. And that is about the hotel. There is another voluntary task suggested last evening, that is, for us all to try to externally consider the hotel staff. See if we can put ourselves in their shoes as we interact with them. The hotel is arranging coffee and afternoon tea in that room behind us, and if there is nobody there to collect, we leave a £1 on the collecting plate.

I would just like to finish by personally wishing all of us a useful Conference and I would like to introduce Dr. Sharp who will introduce our first Presenter.

The Transcaucasian Kurd

Sophia Wellbeloved

Sophia Wellbeloved was a member of the Gurdjieff Society in London from 1962 - 1976. She is now doing Doctoral Research at King's College London into *Beelzebub's Tales to His Grandson*, supervised by Professor Peter B. Clarke in the Theology & Religious Studies Department.

She has given seminars on *Beelzebub's Tales to His Grandson* at King's College and at The School of Oriental and African Studies (SOAS) London University, and has lectured on Gurdjieff at the Royal College of Art, London, and at King's College and SOAS.

She made contributions to the two previous *All & Everything* Conferences and presented a paper at the 1997 Conference - "The Invoking of Names".

She is a Lay Preacher at St. James Church Piccadilly.

Sophia Wellbeloved was introduced by Bert Sharp who, at her request, opened the session by reading Genesis, Chapter 3.

The quotations from *Beelzebub's Tales to His Grandson* referred to in Sophia's presentation were read by Chris Thompson as they occurred.

Genesis, Chapter 3

1. Now the serpent was more subtle than any beast of the field which the Lord God had made. And he said unto the woman, Yea, hath God said, ye shall not eat of every tree of the garden?

2. And the woman said unto the serpent, We may eat of the fruit of the trees of the garden:

3. But of the fruit of the tree which is in the midst of the garden, God hath said, Ye shall not eat of it, neither shall ye touch it, lest ye die.

4. And the serpent said unto the woman, Ye shall not surely die:

5. For God doth know that in the day ye eat thereof, then your eyes shall be opened, and ye shall be as gods, knowing good and evil.

6. And when the woman saw that the tree was good for food, and that it was pleasant to the eyes, and a tree to be desired to make one wise, she took of the fruit thereof, and did eat, and gave also unto her husband with her; and he did eat.

7. And the eyes of them both were opened, and they knew that they were naked; and they sewed fig leaves together, and made themselves aprons.

8. And they heard the voice of the Lord God walking in the garden in the cool of the day: and Adam and his wife hid themselves from the presence of the Lord God amongst the trees of the garden.

9. And the Lord God called unto Adam, and said unto him, Where art thou?

10. And he said, I heard thy voice in the garden and I was afraid, because I was naked; and I hid myself.

11. And he said, Who told thee that thou wast naked? Hast thou eaten of the tree, whereof I commanded thee that thou shouldest not eat?

12. And the man said, The woman whom thou gavest me, she gave me of the tree, and I did eat.

13. And the Lord God said unto the woman, What is this that thou hast done? And the woman said, the serpent beguiled me, and I did eat.

14. And the Lord God said unto the serpent, Because thou hast done this, thou art cursed above all cattle, and above every beast of the field; upon thy belly shalt thou go, and dust shalt thou eat all the days of thy life:

15. And I will put enmity between thee and the woman, and between thy seed and her seed; it shall bruise thy head, and thou shalt bruise his heel.

16. Unto the woman he said, I will greatly multiply thy sorrow and they conception; in sorrow thou shalt bring forth children; and they desire shall be to thy husband, and he shall rule over thee.

17. And unto Adam he said, Because thou has harkened unto the voice of they wife, and hast eaten of the tree, of which I commanded thee, saying, Thou shalt not eat of it: cursed is the ground for they sake; in sorrow shalt thou eat of it all the days of thy life;

18. Thorns also and thistles shall it bring forth to thee; and thou shalt eat the herb of the field;

19. In the sweat of thy face shalt thou eat bread, till thou return unto the ground; for out of it wast thou taken; for dust thou art, and unto dust thou return.

20. And Adam called his wife's name Eve; because she was the mother of all living.

21. Unto Adam also and to his wife did the Lord God make coats of skins, and clothed them.

22. And the Lord God said, Behold, the man is become as one of us, to know good and evil; and now, lest he put forth his hand, and take also the tree of life, and eat, and live for ever:

23. Therefore the Lord God sent him forth from the garden of Eden, to till the ground from whence he was taken.

24. So he drove out the man; and he placed at the east of the garden of Eden Cherubims, and a flaming sword which turned every way, to keep the way of the tree of life.

An Exploration Of The Tale Of The Transcaucasian Kurd: in G. I. Gurdjieff's *Beelzebub's Tales to His Grandson* [1]

This exploration of the Tale of the Kurd has arisen partly out of my doctoral research which is an analysis of the Zodiacal structuring of the *Tales*.[2] However, in this paper my primary aim is to look at this Tale in relation to the story of the Fall in *Genesis*. I also wish to suggest that the Three Series of *All and Everything* are interconnected not only by the themes and subject matter about which Gurdjieff writes but also by the imagery he uses.

I became particularly aware of this last year at the All and Everything Conference (1997) during Professor Paul Taylor's paper *Gurdjieff's Deconstruction of Historical Time in the Third Series*. In his paper Professor Taylor refers to the event Gurdjieff writes of when in response to hearing what was happening in the next room he:

> ... Dumped into the casserole [which he was cooking] with the left hand the whole supply in the kitchen of powdered cayenne pepper ...

and that his right arm had swung back hitting his secretary of music and that:

> '... [I] then flung myself into my room, fell on the sofa and, burying my head in the cushion, which, by the way, were half moth-eaten, began to sob with bitter tears.'[3]

---

[1] The Tale of the Transaucasian Kurd comes from the opening chapter The Arousing of Thought, page numbers are from the 1950 edition; I have numbered the paragraphs.

[2] I have included a brief summary of my analysis of the zodiacal structuring of the *Tales* in an appendix.
[3] G. I. Gurdjieff, Third Series, *Life is real only then, when "I am"*. London: Viking Arkana, 1991 pp 124/5 (first published (1975).

Gurdjieff continues by writing that he will recount what happened within him due to the eating of this 'immoderately peppered dish' in a special book of this third series. It would probably be unwise to assume that although there is no chapter with this title, that this 'book' is not included in the Third Series.

I would like to offer a close reading of the Tale of the Kurd and then I will examine some possible links between the two 'peppery' stories.

This Tale begins and ends with Gurdjieff's thoughts on why a reader might purchase his book and I include these introductory and concluding paragraphs.

The Transcaucasian Kurd

Pages 18/19, paragraph 78
Yes, I think you might as well be told also about an idea which has only just arisen in my madcap brain, and namely, specially to request the printer, to whom I shall give my first book, to print this first chapter of my writings in such a way that anybody may read it before cutting the pages of the book itself, whereupon, on learning that it is not written in the usual manner, that is to say, for helping to produce in one's mentation, very smoothly and easily, exciting images and lulling, reveries, he may, if he wishes, without wasting words with the bookseller, return it and get his money back, money perhaps earned by the sweat of his own brow.

Commentary:
Gurdjieff brings us back to the present moment with this 'yes', indicating that he is in the process of thinking while he is writing. Although we know from J. G. Bennett that this piece of writing (the first chapter) was revised and rewritten 'at least seven times' and thus is not spontaneous, yet this style of address suggests an immediate and intimate relationship of reader and author.[4]

Should we be living in France in that time when pages were left uncut, we might even now be standing in a bookshop in the process of deciding whether to read on or not. Even if we are not there we are drawn into an imaginary intimacy in which Gurdjieff has given us a kind of ambiguous gift.

Maybe we earned the money to pay for this book, earning by the sweat of the brow maybe a Biblical reference to post-Fall work. In Paradise all was provided for Adam and Eve, toil and sweat exist only after the Fall.[5] In this sense Gurdjieff's 'work' is essentially post-Fall.

---

[4] Bennett J. G. John G. Bennett's Talks on Beelzebub's Tales. Compiled A. G. E. Blake. Maine: Samuel Weiser, 1988, p.p. 7/8.
[5] KJB Genesis 3: especially verses 19 and 23.

The Transcaucasian Kurd

Page 20, paragraph 79
I shall do this without fail, moreover, because I just now again remember the story of what happened to a Transcaucasian Kurd, which story I heard in my quite early youth and which in subsequent years, whenever I recalled it in corresponding cases, engendered in me an enduring and inextinguishable impulse of tenderness. I think it will be very useful for me, and also for you, if I relate this story to you somewhat in detail.

Commentary:
We are still in the moment of Gurdjieff's unfolding thoughts and memories. He promises to have the book published with the pages of the initial chapter uncut because he has remembered a story, from his early youth, that is, long ago as in fairy stories. This story continues to arouse tenderness in him. This shows us that stories can have a profound and lasting effect. (Perhaps the *Tales* will have a lasting effect on us.) Gurdjieff aligns himself with his reader; will this story light a flame in us as it did in Gurdjieff, an ever burning flame?

Page 19, paragraph 80
It will be useful chiefly because I have decided already to make the "salt" or as contemporary pure-blooded Jewish businessmen would say, the "Tzimus" of this story, one of the basic principles of that new literary form which I intend to employ for the attainment of the aim I am now pursuing by means of this new profession of mine.

Commentary:
Maybe "pure-blooded" Jewish business men are a reference to Jewish notions of purity of race. The strength of this tale, its saltiness is also saltiness as in salty tales, earthy, robust in nature. So this is an earthy or bodily tale, perhaps somehow sexual. Salt in alchemy is the non-volatile fixer of the spirit, in ordinary terms a preserver of food. This story may fix in us the nourishing ideas that Gurdjieff is offering us, and this will be one of the basic principles which he will use to obtain his aim. His stated aim is the destruction of our habitual way of understanding ourselves and our world. Here Gurdjieff admits to being the creator of a new literary form.

Perhaps the 'corresponding cases' (see paragraph 78 above) which remind Gurdjieff of the Kurd are all of us, thus the tenderness he feels for the fate of the Kurd stands in for his tenderness for the fate of his readers. As we will see, the Kurd suffered because he insisted on consuming something he had bought and maybe we too would suffer if we insisted on reading what we have paid for.

In this first chapter concerned with beginnings, this is a story from Gurdjieff's early childhood, perhaps concerning sex, the body, maybe having a connection with Jewish procreation, (Jewishness is bestowed upon a person by their mother): could it be that these references lead us to Genesis, the early Jewish myth of our origin and Fall? The Fall is indeed the essence of the *Tales*, Gurdjieff's story which relates the Fall of Beelzebub, of Earth and of human beings.

Page 19, paragraphs 81, 82
This Transcaucasian Kurd once set out from his village on some business or other to town, and there in the market he saw in a fruiterer's shop a handsomely arranged display of all kinds of fruit.
In this display, he noticed one 'fruit', very beautiful in both colour and form, and its appearance so took his fancy and he so longed to try it, that in spite of his having scarcely any money, he decided to buy without fail at least one of these gifts of Great Nature, and taste it.

Commentary:
The Transcaucasian Kurd is on business, not pleasure; he has an aim to transact something. His name suggests a huge journey across the Caucasian mountains, but he is on a day's journey to town. We might read the Kurd's day as his life, his journey from Great Nature to town, his life's purpose never explicitly stated, his eventual return to Nature.

In the market he sees attractive fruit, which has been 'handsomely', a word with sexual associations, arranged, so as to attract him. In terms of ideas: these are attractively presented ideas for sale. The Kurd is in a shop, just as the reader has been in Gurdjieff's presentation about his reader's decision to buy the *Tales*. One particular fruit 'takes the Kurd's fancy', because of its colour and form, (perhaps emotional colour and intellectual form) it arouses his imagination, his interest and desire.

Although the fruit is a 'gift' of Great Nature, the poor Kurd must pay for it before he can taste it. The Kurd is poor not only in money terms but also in experience and knowledge because he does not recognise these fruits. An ignorant or innocent man, and an attractive unknown fruit, we certainly seem to be in Gurdjieff's version of Eden, about to witness a Fall.

Page 19, paragraph 83
"Then, with intense eagerness, and with a courage not customary to him, he entered the shop and pointing with his horny finger to the "fruit" which had taken his fancy he asked the shopkeeper its price. The shopkeeper replied that a pound of the "fruit" would cost two cents."

Commentary:
The eager Kurd points a horny, that is hard working, but also horny as in sexual desire, - indicating finger. The fruit has taken his fancy, it has power over him simply because he desires it, but his desire also gives him a courage beyond that of his usual socialised being, so he is able to enter the shop and ask the price.

Page 19/20, paragraphs 84, 85
Finding that the price was not at all high for what in his opinion was such a beautiful fruit, our Kurd decided to buy a whole pound.
Having finished his business in town, he set off again on foot for home the same day.

Commentary:
The Kurd buys lots of the fruit. He has bought the fruit in town, in the market, he did not find it, or grow it in its natural setting. But business over he goes homeward, to his "natural" place, on foot rather than in a mechanical vehicle, thus he is "in touch" with the earth.

Page 20, paragraph 86
Walking at sunset over the hills and dales, and willy-nilly perceiving the exterior visibility of those enchanting parts of the bosom of Great Nature, the Common Mother, and involuntarily inhaling a pure air uncontaminated by the usual exhalations of industrial towns, our Kurd quite naturally suddenly felt a wish to gratify himself with some ordinary food also; so sitting down by the side of the road, he took from his provision bag some bread and the "fruit" he had bought which had looked so good to him and leisurely began to eat.

Commentary:
The difference between aspects of town and country life is emphasised by the fact that here the Kurd breathes pure air, not industrialised air. He is in touch with Mother Nature's enchanting, spell casting exterior, the mothering milk-providing bosom of our common mother. By implication he is out of touch, cannot see the interior, hidden (the esoteric) invisible other side of the Great Mother, that is her devouring of her own children. Thus sex and death are not linked in his understanding. (Sex brings death into the world because it procreates life, and all life must die. Eve is referred to as the mother of all living, but she is, of course, also the mother of all dying.)

So the Kurd, innocent and trusting child of Nature, fed by the food of impressions and air, desires ordinary food, bread symbolic of the female earth and of resurrection, (the dying and re-growing corn) a sacramental and communion food. Bread is a transformed food, it has been cooked, but the fruit the Kurd is about to eat has not been transformed. Although it looked "good" to him just as the tree of knowledge had looked good and pleasant to the eyes to Eve, the Kurd's fruit will turn out to be deceptive in appearance.[6]

Page 20, paragraphs 87, 88
But ... horror of horrors! ... very soon everything inside him began to burn. But in spite of this he kept on eating.

And this hapless biped creature of our planet kept on eating, thanks only to that particular human inherency which I mentioned at first, the principle of which I intended, when I decided to use it as the foundation of the new literary form I have created, to make, as it were, a "guiding beacon" leading me to one of my aims in view, and the sense and meaning of which moreover you will, I am sure, soon grasp - of course according to the degree of your comprehension - during the reading of any subsequent chapter of my writings, if of course, you take the risk and

---

[6] Genesis 3:6.

read further, or, it may perhaps be that even at the end of this first chapter you will already "smell" something.

Commentary:

The Kurd burns inside. Fire has a dual nature, both creative and destructive. The sun as fire both nourishes and destroys, so does knowledge, and so also does Mother Earth. The fire within as experienced by the Kurd seems to represent passion; in the context of the Fall myth, once Adam and Eve had eaten of the fruit, the apple, and had been expelled, Paradise was surrounded by flames and could only be re-entered via a baptism of fire. In alchemical terms passing through the flames burned away the dross or body.[7] In another sense we could recognize that the fire of sexual passion itself can provide a temporal re-entry into Paradise.

But this burning is a horror to the Kurd and sounds more like the flames of Hell, especially as he continues to eat, that is, he himself is not changed, or transformed by the fire.

The Kurd continues to eat, even though burning inside, because he has paid for his food; so Gurdjieff counts on our continuing to read his book once we have paid for it, even if we find it is disagreeable, painful or it burns us up, destroying rather than nourishing our knowledge and ideas. This property is like a guiding beacon, which Gurdjieff will use as a foundation for his new literary form, the aim of which will become clear to us as we read on, if we do, in proportion to our capacity to understand.

As we take in the ideas, like air, maybe we can smell them, gain an intuitive understanding or form a suspicion. When something smells it is usually an indication that the something is rotting or decaying, perhaps we may suspect something, have some sense of death.

Pages 20/2, paragraph 89, 90
And so, just at the moment when our Kurd was overwhelmed by all the unusual sensations proceeding within him from this strange repast on the bosom of Nature, there came along the same road a fellow villager of his, one reputed by those who know him to be very clever and experienced; and seeing that the whole face of the Kurd was aflame, that his eyes were streaming with tears, and that in spite of this, as if intent upon the fulfillment of his most important duty, he was eating real "red pepper pods" he said to him:

"What are you doing, you Jericho jackass? You'll be burned alive! Stop eating that extraordinary product, so unaccustomed for your nature."

Commentary:
Now we return to the Kurd, still eating. A wiser and more experienced person (a guide) sees the Kurd his face a flame, his eyes weeping. Tears are salty, that is they are part of the essence of this story, the suffering of the Kurd, which might "fix" some meaning or understanding in him. He is eating red pepper pods, which are not to be eaten like this, uncooked, unmixed with other food in

---

[7] I was directed to this aspect of the Fall myth by Dr. Leon Schlamm.

The Transcaucasian Kurd

such a concentrated form. Red peppers are useful, but the Kurd has no understanding of how they are to be used, as a flavour and not a substance on its own. The pepper pods are hot, red and fiery, phallic in shape and they contain potent seeds.

The Kurd chose this fruit and he suffers for his choice made without knowledge or experience. The fruit gives him direct knowledge, just as the fruit in Eden gave Adam and Eve direct knowledge and experience. But the Kurd has exchanged an artificial means of value 'two cents' for the peppers and cannot asses or value them by natural means, his senses. As his fellow villager, and potential guide says he is a Jericho jackass, a silly donkey which brings destruction on itself. We might connect the Kurd's horny finger in this sense with the horn that destroyed Jericho. Even if he dies the Kurd will insist on eating the peppers, this shows how a "natural" person can be ensnared by the values of 'Fallen' industrialisation, by contemporary poisonous values.

The 1992 edition has 'stop eating that barbarous stuff so foreign to your nature', giving the idea that barbarism and not culture has been achieved. The 1950 edition is 'stop eating that extraordinary product so unaccustomed for your nature' suggesting the peppers as a product of the industrialized city life, where the Kurd found them, and not belonging to his natural life.

Page 21, paragraphs 91, 92
But our Kurd replied. - "No for nothing on Earth will I stop. Didn't I pay my last two cents for them? Even if my soul departs from my body I shall still go on eating." Whereupon our resolute Kurd - it must of course be assumed that he was such did not stop, but continued eating the "red pepper pods".

Commentary:
The Kurd will not stop for anything on Earth, that is, he needs or demands heavenly intervention, which his earthly guide cannot give. He has however become aware of death. Gurdjieff gently mocks the poor Kurd whom he has presented as our representative; and yet Gurdjieff did require resolution from his pupils and a willingness
to continue even if suffering greatly.

As read to Gurdjieff's pupils this seemingly simple Tale, might not have seemed so simple. Now the pupil would realise that although willingness to suffer voluntarily would be demanded, suffering because of inadequate understanding or knowledge will not necessarily be useful.

Is the Kurd resolute or just stupid? We must make the same distinction for ourselves as readers. The Kurd remains 'poor' because he failed to transact any business, that is, he did not profit from his experience.

Earlier in this chapter Gurdjieff has warned, alarmed, blamed and denigrated his reader. Yet Gurdjieff has also confessed to a feeling of tenderness, perhaps the reader feels confused. The more confused he feels, the more likely he will be to accept the wise and perhaps heavenly guidance of "one who knows": perhaps someone with authority.

Through this Tale Gurdjieff lets us know that he is inviting us, or tempting us to 'Fall', to eat the fruit he offers, to read, to gain knowledge, to recognise death, to awaken and become exiled from our dream paradise of innocence. It is an invitation to a rite of passage which we may take with the once exiled Beelzebub on board the Karnak, an epic voyage which ends in transformation.

Pages 21/22, paragraph 93
After what you have just perceived, I hope there may already be arising in your mentation a corresponding mental association which should, as a result, effectuate in you, as it sometimes happens to contemporary people, that which you call, in general, understanding, and that in the present case you will understand just why I, well knowing and having many a time commiserated with this human inherency, the inevitable manifestation of which is that if anybody pays money for something he is bound to use it - to the end, was animated in the whole of my entirety with the idea, arisen in my mentation, to take every possible measure in order that you, as is said "my brother in appetite and in spirit" - in the event of your proving to be already accustomed to reading books, though of all kinds, yet nevertheless only those written exclusively in the aforesaid "language of the intelligentsia" - having already paid money for my writings and learning only afterwards that they are not written in the usual convenient and easily read language, should not be compelled as a consequence for the said human inherency, to read my writings through to the end at all costs, as our poor Transcaucasian Kurd was compelled to go on with his eating of what he had fancied for its appearance alone - that "not to be joked with" noble red pepper".

Commentary:
Gurdjieff hopes that we are learning by association, that we will make connections between the Kurd and ourselves. What we call understanding is not what Gurdjieff calls understanding, thus our definitions and understanding are suspect, in quotation marks, the term understanding means something more, or different to Gurdjieff.

He wants us to understand that he is taking every possible measure to protect us from the discomfort of reading his book just because we have paid for it. As he addresses 'my brother in appetite and spirit' he allies himself with males and his product, his text with the not to be joked with red pepper. We might connect this potent fruit of Mother Earth with the fiery Beelzebub, the potent fruit of Gurdjieff's creation (his new literary creation). Gurdjieff continues his food/appetitive/ideas trope and reminds us that appearances are deceptive, that inner content may not be what we expect. The red pepper is 'noble' because it is the fruit of knowledge, from the French noble, the Latin (g)noblis, (gnoscere - to know).

Appetite and spirit represent the Gnostic duality between earthly appetites, the corruptible body, and the heavenly incorruptible spirit. The reader is addressed as a brother and so perhaps as readers we are included in Gurdjieff's special brotherhood, his pupils, his readers.

Page 22, paragraph 94:

And so, for the purpose of avoiding any misunderstanding through this inherency, the data for which are formed in the entirety of contemporary man, thanks evidently to his frequenting of the cinema and thanks also to his never missing an opportunity of looking into the left eye of the other sex, I wish that this commencing chapter of mine should be printed in the said manner, so that everyone can read it through without cutting the pages of the book itself.

Commentary:
Contemporary man is compelled to consume that which is purchased as a result of going to the cinema where he consumes easy entertainment "exciting images and titillating reveries", an escapism which avoids the experiencing of real life. The cinema offers a dream world and an illusory paradise, in Gnostic terms, the lure of the world.

Looking into the left eye, the sinister, dark, invisible aspect of a person of the other sex, that is not a person of opposite gender, but a person of sexual interest to the looker. This looking at only one side or aspect of the person. Perhaps the unconscious or instinctive side, or the only side in which the looker has any interest.

Frequenting (frequent) and never missing an opportunity suggest an instant gratification of desire and this is what Gurdjieff says he wishes to avoid. He will present his book so that it has a visible and a visibly invisible side (the uncut part). I do not know if this plan was carried out when the book was first published, but we cannot rely on it in the 1992 edition. Both the examples given of how contemporary man misunderstands are about illusory (the cinema) or partial (looking into the left eye) vision, we might say 'don't judge a book by its cover'.

Now that the story of the Kurd has been examined in the light of the Fall it is interesting to look at the story Gurdjieff gives us in the Third Series about the moment when he gained knowledge about Orage. The 'fruit of knowledge', the pepper is dumped into the casserole he is making and this is followed by Gurdjieff's own weeping, which echoes that of the Kurd. Gurdjieff's head is 'buried' a word that has connections with death, in half moth-eaten cushions. In this context the reference to 'moth-eaten' cushions seems to be a Biblical reference to the corrupting power of moths.

> Lay not up for yourselves treasures upon earth, where moth and rust doth corrupt, and where thieves break through and steal: [8]

Later he and all the people with him are 'compelled for lack of any other food, to eat the dish' he has peppered.[9] They are compelled as Adam and Eve are compelled by God who says:

> Cursed is the ground for thy sake: in sorrow shalt thou eat of it all the days of thy life.[10]

---

[8] KJB Mathew 6:19
[9] G. I. Gurdjieff, *Life is real only then, when "I am"*. London: Viking Arkana, 1991 p 125
[10] KJB Genesis 3:17

In the story of the Kurd Gurdjieff refers to the book in which the story occurs, and which we may read in the future; here Gurdjieff refers to a book within the Third Series which he will write in the future. Book in this context carries suggestions of 'the Book', the Bible.

We can see that the imagery and the events of the Fall in Genesis are related to those in the Kurd's story and that these images and events: peppers, weeping, and death are echoed by the imagery used in the events of the Third Series. All three stories are about the suffering which arises due to the loss of innocence and the acquisition of knowledge which in itself is an awareness of change corruption and death.

The elements which correspond in both stories are worth examining (along with references from the Second Series); in more detail than there is time for here.

In conclusion I hope that the relating of events and imagery in the First Series to events and imagery in the Second and Third Series will offer a fruitful and potent way of exploring Gurdjieff's writings.

© Copyright 1998 - Sophia Wellbelloved - All Rights Reserved

The Transcaucasian Kurd - Questions & Answers

Professor Paul Taylor: This is not so much a question as it is an observation, I think you caught a lot of the spirit of what Gurdjieff is trying to do. As you know when his work was being translated into English he continually asked those who worked with him, Orage, or there were others, exactly what an English word meant; and as you know he played that game, he loved the polysemous aspect of English, if you remember because he played with the sole of the foot and the soul. Surely he knew that the word book is the name of a tree and he would have played on that too.

Also the fact that the red pepper is not indigenous to anywhere in the world except to the Americas; it is foreign, capsicum existed only on the other side of the Atlantic and was imported very, very quickly all over the world, after the first exploration. He calls it a 'fruit' and it is not quite, but its not a vegetable and he knows that too, so what I am a suggesting is that there is a lot in there and I think the probing that you are doing, and it is your pun, is very fruitful.

Dr. Keith Buzzell: I wanted to add only, I certainly never was a witness to this but I was told by several people and I believe that John Bennett also writes about it: that in the later years, in the apartment in Paris, that Gurdjieff either gave up totally, or would very infrequently make use of many of the terms that he had made use of earlier for such things as consciousness, or waking up, or self-remembering, or efforts in that direction. What he spoke about was 'red pepper' and he would use that as a constant reference, which was often very confusing for people who were very new coming to the apartment.

Sophia Wellbeloved: Yes, Stanley Nott says that Gurdjieff gave him a red pepper and made him eat it.[1]

---

[1] He handed me a red pepper and said, "Eat, then will remember." I put in my mouth, and like the Kurd in *Beelzebub's Tales*, continued to eat though it was as if my whole body was burning. He said, "Can be a reminding factor." Nott, C. S. *Journey through This World*. London: Routledge Kegan Paul, 1969 p. 76.

Appendix - Summary of Astrological Themes

Brief Summary of Astrological Themes in Beelzebub's Tales to His Grandson

In this analysis the forty-eight chapters of the *Tales* are divided into twelve sets of four chapters. Each set of four chapters represents a sign of the Zodiac.

Chapters 1-4
Aries: The Ram
Element Fire: *the creative, spirit, fires, things which are red, firey, angry, burning, hot*
First House: *creation, beginnings, origins, youth.*
Planet Mars: *sex and death, the Fall, war, warriors.*

Correspondences in text: *Gurdjieff's childhood and youth, cultural origins, the formation of his individuality, cultural origins and Fall of language, red pepper, garlic, the comet Kondoor, Beelzebub's firey youth, Beelzebub as warrior, his Fall, Beelzebub makes his home on Mars.*

Chapters 5-8
Taurus: The Bull
Element Earth: *Female, embodiment of what was created, rules matter, building, construction, endurance, money.*
Second House: *formation in matter.*
Planet: *Venus: harmony order/disharmony chaos, beauty, copper.*

Correspondences in text: *The materials that the space ships are built from, the construction of the ships, Hassein does not yet have to pay for his existence, men as slugs (earth bound).*

Chapters 9-12
Gemini: The Twins *double sign, duality of giving out/ taking in*

Element Air: *male rules ideas.*
Third House: *giving and receiving, transmission of ideas, communications.*
Planet Mercury: *male/androgynous, rules mobility, connects the above with the below. Messengers, writing, analysis and critical faculties, tricks and tricksters, deceptions.*

Correspondences in text: *Genesis of Moon and Anulios from Earth (birth of twins), angelic committee of enquiry, analysis of problems on Earth, three descents and ascents of angelic committee, men's perceptions are deceived by the organ Kundabuffer.*

Appendix - Summary of Astrological Themes

Chapters 13-16
Cancer: The Crab
Element Water: *Female rules death, dispersion, emotions, the sea, drowning, and end of first set of elements.*
Fourth House: *the home, mother.*
Heavenly body Moon: *Female, changeability, cycles of time, fertility, illusions, madness, the psyche, the unconscious.*

Correspondences in text: *men unable to tell real from unreal, psychologist, sinking of Atlantis, increase in birth rate, suggestibility of man, psychosis, relativity of time.*

Chapters 17-20
Leo: The Lion, *lions, cats, hunters*
Element Fire: *male, spirit creation, start of second set of elements, creation of family, blood, heart.*
Fifth House: *creativity, parenthood/children.*
Heavenly Body Sun: *male, consciousness, light, kings.*

Correspondences in text: *The sun, heat and light, the Sun Absolute, Blinding light, blood sacrifice, formations of deserts, lions and cats, Beelzebub meets the future mother of his children, hunting deer, King.*

Chapters 21-24
Virgo: The Virgin, *wholeness, purity, pearls, health, wheat*
Element Earth: *female, matter.*
Sixth house: *harvest, work, communal and family life.*
Planet Mercury: *travels, communications, divine messengers, the marketplace, trade.*

Correspondences in text: *Pearl land, pearls, travellers and traders, Saint Buddha (divine messenger), Beelzebub's travels, The Earth as planet, eruption of earthquakes, growth of mountains,, work, the materialising of ideas, thought tapes, degeneration of matter, the sphinx has breasts of a virgin, alchemy (the great work).*

Chapters 25-28
Libra: the Scales*: justice, law, double sign, balance seeing both sides of a situation/idea.*
Element Air*: male, ideas, partnership.*
Seventh house: *sublimation of self in collective social order, community.*
Planet Venus: *ascending and descending planet, as heavenly brings harmony, beauty; as earthly brings disorder, chaos, and disharmony; as morning and evening star mediates beginnings and endings.*

All & Everything Conference 1998

Correspondences in text: *Ashiata Sheimash (divine messenger), restoration of harmony on Earth, destruction of labours, Ashiata's story balanced by that of Lentrohamsanin false messenger who brings about destructive communities, Alexander as destroyer of bliss created by Ashiata.*

Chapters 29-32
Scorpio: The Scorpion
Element water: *Female, death, end of second set of elements.*
Eighth house: *Death and rebirth, genitals, occultism, astrology, legacies.*
Planets Mars: *sex, death, war, destructive desire for change.*
and Pluto: (discovered 1930) *influences whole generation as well as individuals, rules collective unconscious (the Moon rules individual unconscious), world wars, gangsters, fluctuating economic situations, revolutions, the hidden invisible forces in large communities, fanatics, revolutionaries, the control of masses through the unconscious, propaganda, magic.*

Correspondences in text: *Greek and Roman destruction of Ashiata's teaching, Greeks were fishermen, Roman's masturbation, depraved sexuality, Alexander's destruction, Hasnamus, fanatic, the club to preserve knowledge is destroyed, mediums, gunfire, North Pole (ice).*

Chapters 33-36
Sagittarius: The Centaur-Archer
Element fire: *male, spirit, the creative start of third set of elements, religious and spiritual leaders/fathers.*
Ninth house: *education, religion.*
Planet Jupiter: *expansion, travel, long journeys, initiation, mania, literature, religion, philosophy, learning.*

Correspondences in text: *Beelzebub as benevolent hypnotist healer, Egyptian religion, Beelzebub studies the Russians, charitable trust, planetary conditions for ease of transformation, the desire to expand, need for freedom, false education of Germans.*

Chapters 37-40
Capricorn The Goat: *climbing, ambition, scapegoats*
Element Earth: *female, perfected matter.*
Tenth house: *organisation, public, fame, and fortune, ambition.*
Planet Saturn: *Father, time, patriarchs, festival of Saturnalia misrule, depression, isolation.*

Correspondences in text: *patriarchalty of French, sexual depravity, night of misrule, (male and female prostitutes, brothel, clubs, fights, Beelzebub brought near to second revolt against H<small>IS</small> E<small>NDLESSNESS</small>, endurance (no change for 101 centuries,) limits of religion, elders, Christ as scapegoat, Judas as scapegoat, purgatory (perfect planet), role of matter on Earth, human reflections of Divine Father, sacrament, struggle against body, forms higher body, alchemical transformation of matter, Law of Seven in terms of matter, goat's milk, study of substances.*

Appendix - Summary of Astrological Themes

Chapters 41-44
Aquarius: The Waterbearer
Element Air: *male, idealistic relationships.*
Eleventh house: *friends and enemies, social matters, coldness, abstraction, utopian idealism, planning, plotting.*
Planets Saturn: *Authority, melancholy, depression, limitation, restriction;*
and Uranus: *influences a whole generation as well as individuals, innovation, change, abstraction, electricity, eccentricity, rebellion.*

Correspondences in text: *contemporary scientists, electricity, inventions, scientific equipment, Law of Seven expressed as sound air vibrations, music; Saturnine depression of Dervish, suicidal feelings, withdrawal, isolation, solitude, healing vibrations, x-rays, personal suffering transmuted into universal good, Beelzebub in New World, New Age, mass aspects of education, advertising, propaganda, prohibition; strange inventions, perversity, group sexuality, unfavourable conditions for collective existence, Purgatory beings rebel against injustice.*

Chapters 45-48
Pisces: The Fishes, *Double sign, duality of heart and head*
Element water: *female, death, tears, end of third set of elements.*
Twelfth House: *ends, ends/beginnings, seclusion, prisons, escapism, inertia, connects with the first house.*
Planet Neptune: *Influences whole generations as well as individuals, the deep, oceans, emotions, dreams, drugs, drink, mysticism, the invisible, the hidden, secrets, illusions.*

Correspondences in text: *Beelzebub and Ahoon in old age, Hassein weeps, Beelzebub at end of story, end of travels, end of exile, end of the Tales. Hassein stops thinking; myrtle a plant of Neptune and herb of the Jewish festival of Sukot (exile/return): the planet Neptune, Beelzebub realises the dream of all beings, Ahoon and Hassein overcome by emotion, Hassein feels love, salvation of men through remembrance of death. Gurdjieff completes the Tales, he re-reads the first chapter, he connects the beginning with the end; his mortification, his accident should have killed him, lectures correspond to hidden thoughts in the Tales, Gurdjieff 'liquefies' his Institute, ex-Institute pupils come to bad ends, mother nature slaughters us, die to ordinary life, illusions, end of era, Gurdjieff will drink calvados. Gurdjieff will begin again to write.*

All & Everything Conference 1998

Bibliography

Bennett, J. G., *Talks on Beelzebub's Tales*, Complied A.G.E. Blake. Maine: Samuel Weiser, 1988

Gurdjieff, G. I. *All And Everything* Ten Books in Three Series:
First Series, *Beelzebub's Tales to His Grandson*, London: Routledge Kegan Paul 1950 Second Series, *Meetings With Remarkable Men*. London: Routledge Kegan Paul, 1977
Third Series, *Life is real only then, when "I am"*. London: Viking Arkana, 1991 (first published 1975)

Nott, C. S. *Journey Through This World: The Second Journal of a Pupil. Including an Account of Meetings with G. I. Gurdjieff, A. R. Orage and P. D. Ouspensky*, London: Routledge and Kegan Paul 1969

© Copyright 1998 - Sophia Wellbelloved - All Rights Reserved

The Nature and Sources of Conviction

Keith Buzzell

Dr. Buzzell is a 1960 graduate of the Philadelphia College of Osteopathic Medicine. From 1963-66 he was Medical/Educational Director of the Osteopathic Hospital of Maine (now Brighton Medical Center). While serving as chairman of the department of Osteopathic Theory and Methods at Kirksville College of Osteopathic Medicine he authored a "History of Manipulative Therapeutics", a four volume 'Teaching Manual of Osteopathic Methods' and co-authored "The Neurophysiologic Basis of Osteopathic Practice" (N.Y. Postgraduate Institute 1969). In 1937 he published "The Neurophysiology of Television Viewing: A study in physiologic disharmony". He is presently a member of the staff of Northern Cumberland Memorial Hospital in Bridgton and a clinical adjunct member of the faculty of the N.E. College of Osteopathic Medicine in Biddeford. Dr. Buzzell speaks from a broad perspective deriving from his life work as a musician, musicologist, author, teacher, researcher, and physician. He is presently in Family Practice in Fryeburg, where he also serves as Medical Director of Hospice of Western Maine.

Dr. Buzzell took part in the '96 Conference, presenting a paper, "The Enneagramatic Structure of Beelzebub's Tales", and in the '97 Conference, presenting a paper, "Kundabuffer".

Dr. Buzzell was introduced by Michael Smyth.

Michael Smyth: Keith has asked me to read two paragraphs from *Beelzebub's Tales* before I introduce him. The first is in Chapter 46. Beelzebub Explains to His Grandson the Significance of the Form and Sequence Which He Chose for Expounding the Information Concerning Man.

At page 1165 we have:

"I, in consequence of this, when we set out on this journey in the space-ship Karnak, thought of profiting by this time to help you so that the harmonizing of the functions of yours and the formation of your future active mentation which depends on them, I should proceed precisely in that order, of the correctness of which I became convinced with the whole of my presence during the process of my long personal existence"

The second is in Chapter 32, Hypnotism. At page 567 we have:

"Only thanks to the single fact that your favourites, especially the contemporary ones, do not know at all and even do not suspect that necessity of at least adapting their famous education to the said subconsciousness of their offspring, but they always and in everything intentionally assist every one of the rising generation to perceive impressions only from the abnormally artificial, then thanks only to this, when every one of them reaches the age of a responsible being all his being-judgments and all his deductions from them are always purely peculiarly-subjective in him and have no connection not only with the genuine being-impulses arising also in him, but also neither with those general cosmic lawful phenomena, to sense which by Reason is proper to every three-brained being, and by means of which there is established that connection between all the three-brained beings of all our Great Universe for the collective fulfilment of the common universal functioning, for which purpose everything existing in the Universe just exists."

So I was asked to introduce Keith Buzzell and I am not going to say anything that is on that piece of paper, because you can read those things about Keith. But I would like to introduce him as a catalyst and a stimulus for those of us who were working with *Beelzebub's Tales* at Two Rivers Farm. Keith and Mandy came to us many years ago and Keith gave some talks which catalysed a different kind of interest in the Book. And I find one of the things fascinating in listening to Sophia's talk this morning, and the ones from last year, is the necessity for the different approaches to reading *Beelzebub's Tales* and sharing with one another. I know sometimes when Keith spoke that you were wondering how people felt afterwards. Sometimes Keith would speak at the Farm and we would kind of go - ugh. We would not know what to say. As time went on we were able to feed back more. So he may give you a lot of other stuff and your mouth may fall open. But let it sink in. Let it sink in, since it is all really, really valuable.

The Nature and Sources of Conviction

Introduction

What is the origin and the cause of the origin of the *feeling* of Conviction? When we say that we are *convinced* that this or that is true, what are the sources of the *certainty*, and what processes led to this potent and essential state? How is this emotionally imbued state related to the physical world of facts and matter, and to the intellectual world of thought and reason? If the emotional part of us does not know the language of reason or sensation, how can we be sure that what we feel *convinced* about, is not illusion or fantasy?

Gurdjieff has a great deal to say about conviction. He emphasizes the necessity of its presence in all brained beings as well as the great hazards and vulnerabilities that are present during the process of its formation. On the first and last pages of *Beelzebub's Tales* he focuses our attention on this powerful and pervasive inner state, placing it firmly in the forefront of our minds as we begin, and end, a reading of the *Tales*. Between the first and last pages he carefully and organically takes the state of conviction apart, demonstrating its origins, its interstices, and the processes by which varied types of conviction come into being. It is our aim to extract and concentrate on a number of his considerations of conviction, the end purpose being to construct a broad perspective that will be both useful and, in some respects, perhaps surprising.

The Nature and Sources of Conviction

Before taking up Gurdjieff's considerations a brief side note will be mentioned concerning the relationship between the *feeling* of conviction and modern neurophysiologic findings. Beginning in the 1960's with the work of Paul MacLean at the National Institute of Health repeatedly verified, multi-focal investigations have found that the essential feeling-state-of-conviction arises within the Limbic or, what we choose to call, the Second (Emotional) Brain. The study of focal seizure disorders, brain tumors and brain trauma has confirmed (1) that the feeling of *conviction* can be experientially separated or *dissociated* from both First and Third Brain functioning and (2) as Gurdjieff also noted many years ago, the 'language' of emotion is totally different from the language of sensation or thought. With that caveat in mind we return to our theme.

Part I

The opening words of the First Series are:

"Among other convictions formed in my common presence during my responsible, peculiarly composed life..." Page 1, "The Arousing of Thought"

Into these few words Gurdjieff has compressed a good deal about the nature of conviction.

1. It is, first, a plural form indicating that there are many possible convictions.
2. They are "formed... during". Here both the passage of time and a *coming together* are inferred. A conviction is, thus, not a ready made 'something' but a something that necessitates a process of formation - a duration.
3. Convictions are formed in the *common presence*. Gurdjieff makes use of this expression, 'common presence', in a considerable number of quite different contexts. For Example:

p.p. 236 "there was required a certain change in the functioning of the common presences of your ancestors, namely, there was implanted into their presences a certain organ..."

p.p. 438 "According to this principle, the duration of being-existence and also the whole of the contents of their common presences are in general acquired from the results arising from the following seven actualizations surrounding them..." Then the seven Itoklanoz principles.

p.p. 487 "the presence of each of your contemporary favourites during the process of his existence consists of three quite separate personalities - three personalities which have and can have nothing in common with each other, either in respect of the nature of their arising or in respect of their manifestations.
Hence it is that there just proceeds in them that particularity of their common presence which is that with one part of their essence they always intend to wish one thing..."

p.p. 529 "...my essence prompts me and animates my 'I' and all the separately spiritualized parts of my common presence..."

p.p. 1198 "And so, all that has been said about the separate parts of that organization of which, taken as a whole, a hackney carriage consists can be fully applied also to the general organization of the common presence of a man."

In sum, the 'common presence' is closely related to all parts, or aspects, of 'What-I-am' - the planetary body as well as the spiritualized, or brained, parts; the Being, the essence, and aspects of the Will. The presence is *common* because, while composed of multiple levels and 'parts' it is also one, unique Whole.

The point, in reference to our theme, is that a conviction is formed *within* the common or 'wholed' presence. The sense of certainty, or surety, is formed not in just one part of the whole but *throughout*. The intimation that conviction is a *shared* certainty that comes, via the process of its normal *formation*, to be an intimate, interwoven attribute of the common presence is of focal importance. If part of us (i.e., the emotional) is 'convinced' of something, and the data which underpins that emotional state is not shared, compared, analyzed and validated in *all* the other parts of the common presence, then it remains an unbalanced *conviction* that can only lead to distortion and harm.

4. "during my responsible, peculiarly composed life"

A responsible life only *begins* when one has developed the ableness to respond maturely and appropriately to whatever emerges in the flow of our 'peculiarly composed' lives. Hassein, for example, comes to responsible age only at the note LA (the chapter 'Form and Sequence') of the Great Octave of *The Tales*.

Inferred is a great deal of preparatory activity, a long period of disciplined inquiry, manifestation, error, commitment, correction, and active mentation. In the end it brings one only to the *beginning* of a responsible life.

It would be inappropriate to speak of conviction, as Gurdjieff makes use of the term here, until one is both "of responsible age" *and* has lived out that responsibility within the 'peculiar' composition of one's life. Etymologically the word *peculiar* connotes both odd or strange and singular or unique. In its Latin root it applies to the property that even a slave, wife or child was permitted to hold as his or her own. Each of us sees the difficulties, challenges and opportunities that come, unpredictably, throughout our life, as strange or odd and yet uniquely our own.

"Among other convictions formed in my common presence during my responsible, peculiarly composed life…"

In these fourteen opening words of '*The Arousing of Thought*' Gurdjieff has set down a formidable and quite detailed image of the essence of our *sense* of truth.

* * *

The Nature and Sources of Conviction

In Chapter 2, the opening of the epic *'Tales'* themselves, Beelzebub is exiled as a direct result of a *conviction* - namely, that in the government of the World something seemed 'illogical' to him. He acts with impetuosity and force, utilizing his extraordinarily resourceful intelligence - and is sent away.

In "The Inevitable Result of Impartial Mentation' (p.p. 1182) Hassein states:

"Sacred Podkoolad, and cause of the cause of my arising.

"In order that the *convictions* formed in me during this time, owing to Your explanation of the abnormalities proceeding on the Earth, may become definitely crystallized in me, I still wish very much to have this time Your personal and frank opinion as to the following: How You would reply if let us suppose, our ALL-EMBRACING CREATOR ENDLESSNESS HIMSELF, were to summon You before Him and ask You this:"

Following Hassein's question comes Beelzebub's answer - to Endlessness as well as to Hassein - spoken with great passion and conviction. It is notable that this is the first, and only, time in the *Tales* that Hassein asks for a "personal and frank" *opinion* - and receives an answer.

On the last page of the *Tales*, spoken under "essence-oath", is the statement of one of Gurdjieff's fundamental tasks - "ultimately also to *prove, without fail, theoretically* as well as *practically*, to all my contemporaries, the absurdity of all their inherent ideas concerning the suppositious existences of a certain "other world" with its famous and so beautiful a "paradise" and it's so repugnant a "hell":

A statement of conviction thus opens and closes the First Series, and opens and closes the epic tales of Beelzebub and Hassein. Within the great octave that spans the entirety of *'Beelzebub's Tales'*, and appearing with great frequency in many of the inner octaves of the Six Descents, there are many references to, and examples of, varied forms of conviction. It is here, in the interstices of the *Tales*, that Gurdjieff dissects the triadic form of conviction and illustrates the many ways in which the peculiar three brained beings of Earth form *their* convictions. There are many more examples than time allows us to quote, so we have selected an assortment that we hope will make our thesis clear.

Varieties of Conviction

We find "unshakable conviction" in the Karapet of Tiflis and in the "new understandings" crystallized in three brained beings if Smith speaks in a certain way and Brown says the same.
The kinsmen of Beelzebub come to a state of conviction regarding their inability to find an answer to the dilemma created by the "young being of our tribe". It is there in Gornahoor Harharkh's "observations of many years" and in Looisos' statement just prior to the second catastrophe. A somewhat different form of conviction is present in "those men who destroy the existence of other beings and are convinced beyond all doubt that they are doing a "good" deed. Another form is

present in the "frequent change in convictions accumulated in them" which led the three brained beings to swallow the powdered horn of the Pirmaral.

King Konuzion, in his "original religious doctrine" of Mister God, ingeniously uses a form of conviction to counter the evils of chewing the seeds of Gulguhan. In the same descent Beelzebub, speaking in the city Gob, is convinced that the addition he makes to the religious doctrine of Mister God had succeeded in uprooting the custom of Sacrificial Offerings.

Belcultassi (the founder of the Akhaldan Society) "after exhaustive observations and impartial constatations" comes to a state of conviction regarding the abnormalities proceeding in his common presence.

When the diminishing duration of existence of the Three Brained Beings was suddenly perceived just prior to the 5th Descent, and Beelzebub began to recall his prior impressions about it, "each of the separate independent spiritualized parts of my whole presence became filled with the *conviction*". In this quotation lies a key to, the nature of real conviction. We will return to this later.

Again, during the 5th Descent, the peculiar Persian King becomes finally *convinced* that the learned beings of this community knew nothing about the mystery of transmuting gold from ordinary metals. Shortly after this Beelzebub's friend Hamolinadir gives his tragi-comic manifestation of the 'Instability-of-Human-Reason' as he loudly pronounces, logically and with conviction, on the instability and feebleness of Man's Reason, and "showed, in detail, how easy it is to prove and convince this Reason of anything you like".

Concluding the 5th descent Beelzebub then reflects on man and how similarly repeated facts (deriving from the sum of all the impressions perceived by him) are the material for the formation of definite convictions and from this is formed his Reason - his own subjective psyche. In contrast to this we next encounter Ashiata Schiemash's gradual, coming to *conviction* in regard to "the 'second nature' of their common presences" because of the crystallized consequences of the properties of the organ Kundabuffer. As illustration of this the mechanism behind "convincing beings of this planet to believe any old tale" is detailed two pages later. This chapter, "The Terror of the Situation", then concludes by emphasising that via his ponderings Ashiata Shiemash becomes "fully convinced" of the only possible means to save the Three Brained Beings of Earth.

Opening the "Organization by Ashiata Shiemash" is "the arising in all the separate spiritualized parts of the common presences of Poundolero and Sensimirinko of the continuously sensed suspicion, which later becomes a conviction, that owing to some obviously nonlawful causes, 'something-very-undesirable' for them personally had been acquired and had begun to function in their general organization".

The Nature and Sources of Conviction

To become an All-the-rights-possessing brother of the brotherhood Heechtvori it was necessary to attain the 'ableness' to know how to *convince* all the three separate spiritualized and associating parts of a hundred three brained beings concerning the Divine impulse conscience.

From this high point of conviction we descend immediately after to "a certain extremely strange conviction" formed in the psyche of three brained beings that concerns the followers of a well known and important being, (Lentrohamsanin) and how they seem to be, to all other beings, almost as well known and important as the founder. In the chapter 'Hypnotism' Beelzebub gives further definitive commentary on a balanced conviction when he notes to Hassein, "Possibly now, in your presence also there already *begin* to be *crystallized* the *data* for the *engendering* always in *corresponding* cases of the being-impulse of an *indubitable conviction*".

A variant form of conviction is dramatically pictured for us in the description "that in addition to this indubitable information, that Jesus Christ was crucified on a cross, and that after His crucifixion and burial, Jesus Christ was resurrected and continued to exist among them and to teach this and that, and only afterwards did He raise Himself and His planetary body to Heaven". Here Gurdjieff points to the type of conviction wherein a real truth is coupled with an invention. From the three brained being conviction that Judas was the basest of beings conceivable, -"a conscienceless, double-faced, treacherous traitor" we are led into the chapter, Purgatory.

The "long and detailed researches" of Theophany and his friends, led to their becoming aware and categorically convinced" of the seven aspectness of nearly all cosmic results. Similarly Hadji Troov notes, "As my investigations of long years have *convinced* me" and a bit later Beelzebub states when Hadji is suffering over his failure, "then I swear by the cause of my arising that I will give you an answer which will fully satisfy you. You will be *convinced* not only that your beloved science is the truest of all sciences etc...."

From here the pendulum of convictions swings, in the chapter 'America' to where learning the five words 'Maybe - Perhaps - Tomorrow - Oh, I see- and All right' is sufficient to *convince* everybody of Beelzebub's knowledge of the English language.

Closing out our selection of 'convictions' there is the "former, typically subjective and therefore always changeable conviction" that characterizes the society "The-Earth-is-equally-free-for-all" in Beelzebub's Opinion of War'.

The Triadic and Enneagramatic Nature of Conviction

As we noted earlier this is a small selection from among the many references to *conviction* found in the *Tales*. When we became aware of the recurring emphasis on various forms of conviction we also became interested in the question of the structure, or internal organization of these states of conviction. Early on we accepted that all states of conviction, when viewed as manifestations of the law of Three, would have a triadic form and that the impulses carrying the forces in this triad would reflect functional activities of each of the three brains or their subcenters.

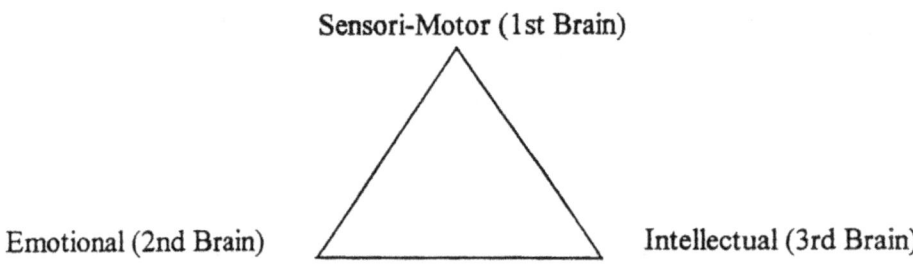

Figure 1. The triadic form underlying the state of conviction

Further, we concluded that the state of conviction was fundamental to all brained life. A one-brained creature, such as a reptile, forms convictions based on the data provided by its external senses. The images derived from the senses of vision, hearing, taste, touch and smell are coalesced by its brain into a composite 'Sense of the External World'. The *conviction* concerns the circumstance coalesced in its 'common presence', that what it sees, hears, smells, tastes and touches is real or the truth and can be reliably acted upon. We could call this *certainty* a Sensorimotor, or First Brain, conviction. It appears with the very earliest of one brained, or cold-blooded, creatures and is a state that becomes finely honed by 600 million years of survival and neural differentiation. All two and three brained beings possess this First Brain *conviction* and it plays an obvious and essential role in everyday life-events.

The second level is associated with the *internal* senses, i.e., with the data and images that accrue from the monitoring and expression of the internal dynamic metabolic states. With input varying from temperature, O_2 content, blood flow and degree of muscle tension, to biochemical fluctuations in sugar, mineral and neuro-hormone levels, the Second, or Limbic Brain builds and reflects *images* of the 'state of affairs' of the internal environment. Blended with the sensory-motor activity of the First Brain a relational 'Sense-of-Self-Other' is produced that is characteristic of mammalian life forms. The type of conviction which emerges from the blending of the images of two 'realities' (the exterior and interior worlds), plus the inherent forms and energies of its 'unconscious' planetary body, concerns its 'selfness' (i.e., as wolf, giraffe, dog etc.) in relation to its group (the den, pride, pack etc.). This 'self-feeling' is, for the creature, its coalesced sense of what-it-is. It is a formed conviction which is not only immensely powerful but is one which arises in a world far beyond, or within, the world of the First Brain. The subjective experience of this blended 'inner-outer' world is, in Gurdjieff's terminology, called mechanical emotion. It is both what the creature 'is', as a member of a mammalian grouping, and what it 'is' (in self-feeling i.e., fearful, angry, playful or affectionate) in any particular moment.

Put in everyday experiential terms the 'two brainedness' of a monkey creates, or forms, a state of conviction that it is 'monkey', as self, belonging to this particular grouping of monkeys. It experiences a wide range of subjective 'feeling states' (or emotions) like anger, fear, affection or curiosity and, simultaneously, is - as 'self' - those feeling states. Being convinced of those 'realities' (its monkeyhood and its anger) is not a simple *by-product* of its brained function. Rather the conviction is a Holy Reconciling or neutralizing force that binds the physical body and both

The Nature and Sources of Conviction

brains into one *Self*. The survival of the monkey, in both the physical and social (Self-Other) senses, depends greatly on the strength of this 'conviction'.

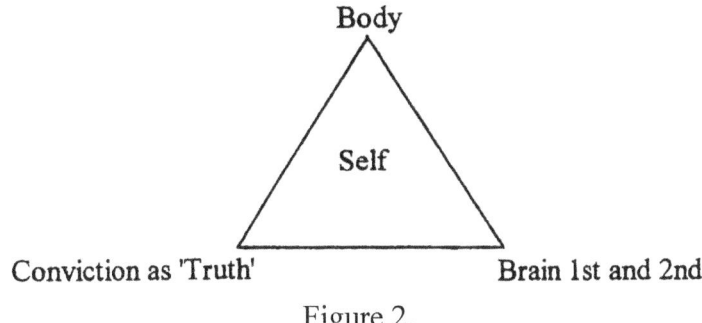

Figure 2.

The third level, or type, of conviction arises in three-brained beings. The 'truth' of First Brain sensori-motor conclusions is, as in one and two brained creatures, the underpinning of our 'sense' of the reality of the outside world. Man's First Brain senses, while generally more refined than those of reptiles, still provide data for the creation of *images* of the external world and we are neurally hard-wired to accept those images as *real*. We are 'convinced' of this and, fortunately, operate in response to them at an essentially subconscious level. If we did not, none of us would have survived to be here today (Remember the car you jumped out of the way of, the thrown rock you ducked your head beneath, the brake you applied just in time, or the awful taste that caused you to spit out some noxious substance).

The emotional life of a three brained being (with its center of gravity in the Second, or Limbic, Brain) carries with it, as in all other Mammals, a conviction that concerns the 'Self and all Other ('Other' as other human, other creature, other life form such as a tree, and other as non-living object (mountain, chair, ocean etc.) The expansion of Self and 'Other' is the result of the integrated activity of the Third (Neocortical) Brain with the Second. The ability to name, analyze and differentiate, to compare and abstract - all of these enlarge and make more subtle the feeling of 'Self and the feeling of *separation* from all 'Others'. As a result of this increase in sophistication the neural requirement of a state of conviction in regard to the 'Self' is equally increased. Of prime importance here is the recognition of the *mechanicalness* of this form of conviction. Incorporating many of the capacities of the Third Brain intensifies the feeling state of 'Selfhood', especially with regard to its *separation* from 'Other'. The plethora of racial and ethnic difficulties present in today's world has, at its core, this mechanical vulnerability to a conviction that 'separates' more than it 'unites'. Throughout *The Tales*, and especially in those segments that focus on reciprocal destruction. Gurdjieff points to the devastating effects of this form of disharmonious brained conviction. This vulnerability is equally imaged by Gurdjieff in respect to how easy it is to convince a man of anything you like if only you play on his vanity or false pride while you share your 'truth' with him.

All & Everything Conference 1998

Religious and political beliefs also depend on this type of mechanical emotional 'conviction'. As essential as the roles they play are in the communal life of man, bringing an important sense of belonging to, or being a part of a larger grouping, they inevitably introduce degrees of separation. Into these degrees of separation new 'convictions' enter, enabling the growth of the substrate feelings of suspicion, distrust, antipathy and, finally, hatred of others.

From the survival imperative of One-brained beings - that the world 'outside' *is* what it appears to be and can be depended on in coming to life-preserving decisions - convictions continue to be formed as critical contributors to the 'Self-Other' group survival of all warm blooded creatures. The neural pathways for the same physical and emotional 'convictions' are inherited by man and form an essential underpinning to the Itoklanoz principle - the seven Influences that guide the growth and development of one, two and three brained beings in ordinary life. These mechanical, survival-oriented convictions, while necessary to certain aspects of human life, create astonishing vulnerabilities when they are misapplied in the broader context of human existence. To give full dimension to these vulnerabilities we must take up the unique 'convictions' that arise and are formed *within* the Third Brain itself.

Third Brain Conviction

Ratiocination, or logical processes of reasoning, is the foundational requirement for forming a third brain conviction. Under 'normal' circumstances, that is, without the consequences of Kundabuffer or Man's egoism, this conviction would be formed in accordance with the Law of 3, as event, and with the Law of 7, as process. *All three brains* would contribute their 'relative' realities of 'image' to both the triad and the enneagramatic process.

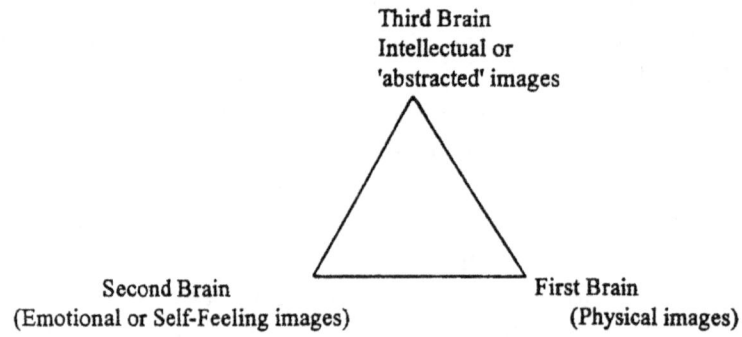

Figure 3. Sources of Conviction for a 'normal' Three Brain Being

The Nature and Sources of Conviction

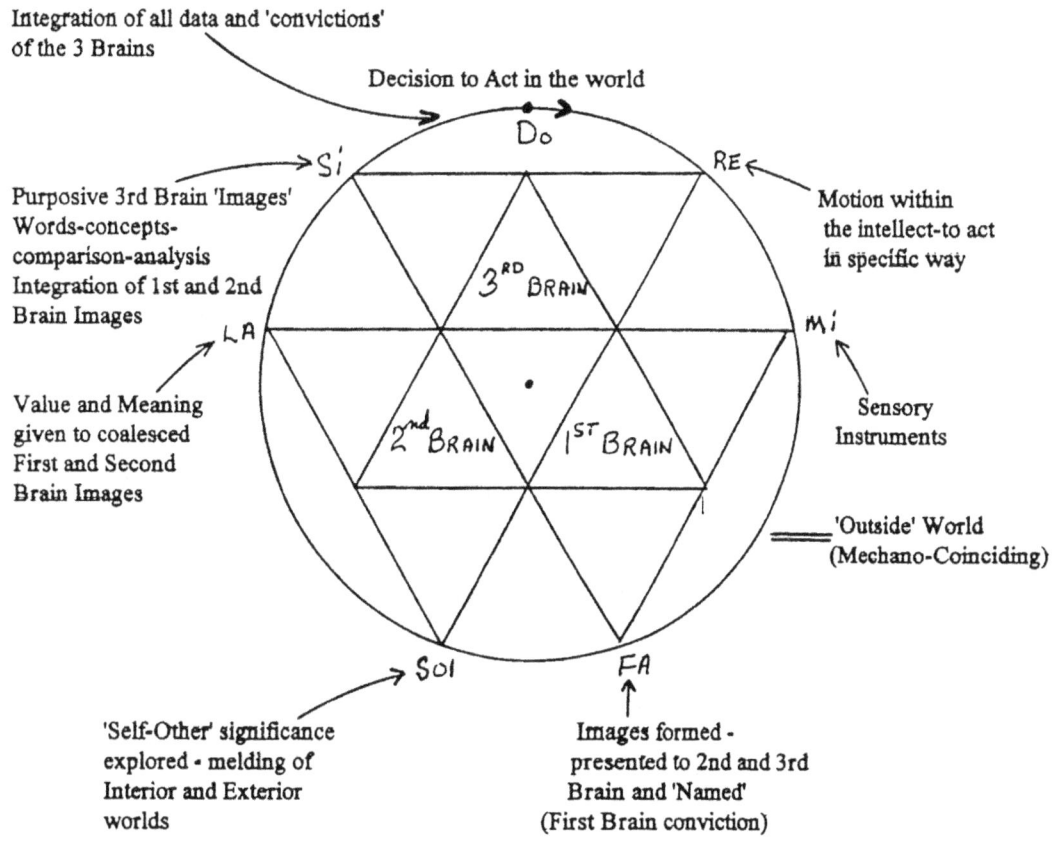

Figure 4.

Notable in this enneagramatic form is the critical role of the neutralizing force played by the Emotional (Second) Brain, When this is absent or distorted, as it is under the influence of Kundabuffer and Egoism, then a most 'peculiar' circumstance results. Lacking appropriate input from the center of gravity of the Real Value and Meaning of 'Self-Other', the Third Brain depends almost totally on First Brain concrete-external images for input. It applies its capacities for logical, rational processing, but does so in the nearly complete absence of any real emotional value for Self or Other. The 'feeling' aspects that are included derive from the emotional part of Moving Center - the narrow, mechanical 'self- feeling' of like-dislike that is dedicated to physical self-preservation.

In the formation of a mechanical conviction there is a minimum or absence of associative activity in all three brains. Everything is reaction, on the surface, preconditioned by past events and prior fixed conclusions. What is seen or heard is taken at face value. It is what it is – on the surface. Sounds and words have no inner resonances; the visual images, while flat, are subjectively experienced 'as if' they were immutably solid.

All & Everything Conference 1998

The intellect participates by categorizing and 'naming' and by assembling a superficial train of logic. This train of logic involves little new associative brained activity. It is primarily an assembly of what has been said by others (i.e., family, teachers, powerful or popular figures) that resonates with the present situation. This linear mechanical train of reasoning is then infused with emotional value, the second brain 'Sense of self identifying itself with the conclusive truth arrived at by the First and Third brains.

All convictions, from the most subjective and mechanical that Gurdjieff illustrates in the *Tales* to the 'indubitable' conviction noted in the opening words of the First Series, contain, in ordinary life, a 'line-of-reasoning' built on sensory data which is then blended by emotional value and fused by the Will.

Each of the three force carriers is subject to great vulnerability. Each may be too diffused or too focused; the images formed by each brain may be faulty or incomplete; the past (as Itoklanoz) may be grossly distorted or unbalanced at any of its seven steps. And perhaps most vital, the Will can be so fractured or so imploded on itself that the triad of forces is held together or fused in a grossly unbalanced way. Thus the most 'peculiar' but recurring form illustrated in the *Tales* is the form of conviction that leads to the Custom of the Sacrificial Offering of One, Two *and*, finally, Three Brained Beings. In war the imploded will fuses with an 'imaginary' set of values. A primal significance is given to the material world and the intellect, presumptively the carrier of the highest force, becomes instead the passive supplier of a tenuous thread of reason - the justification and the clever machinations - for the physical manifestation of destruction and the imposition of suffering on Others.

Given the multiple vulnerabilities of each of our brains and the multitude of unbecoming and egoistic manifestations that abound in our world today, – what enablement's are there to help us find our way through the tangled jingle of our inner world? Of the many enablement's that Gurdjieff set in motion none is more essential than the one which makes it possible for us to recognize our three brain vulnerabilities to narrow and limited conviction and to begin the process of learning how to digest and, ultimately, to re-form the multitude of mechanical convictions into Senses-of-truth that reflect the Cosmic Trogoautoegocrat. We will end with the succinct comment of Beelzebub on that singular enablement.

"In short, the transmutation in themselves of an all-round understanding of the functioning of both these fundamental sacred laws conduces to this, that in the common presences of three-brained beings, data are crystallized for engendering that Divine property which it is indispensable for every normal three-brained being to have and which exists under the name of 'Senzooniranoos'; of this your favorites have also an approximate representation, and they call it 'impartiality'.
p.p. 756 Purgatory

© Copyright 1998 - Keith Buzzell - All Rights Reserved

The Nature and Sources of Conviction - Questions & Answers

Bert Sharp: I couldn't agree more with the introduction, showing us the importance of us all trying to understand the findings of really objective, modern science. Going on from there, am I right in inferring that Keith is suggesting that Gurdjieff was so far in advance of all of us that he anticipated many of the latest findings of modern science and, does that in fact mean that he was conscious in 'higher mind' and, if so, where is it and what is it?

Laughter: One question?

Keith Buzzell: This is a great question, one that we've all asked ourselves a good many times. One way of looking at this is that if a human being becomes wholly balanced and his 'I' emerges, he or she consequently has an appropriate connection with Higher Emotional and Higher Intellectual centers. I am convinced Gurdjieff stood in that place and speaks from Higher Intellectual through Higher Emotional and thence out into the world. It is not a matter of whether or not the factual data was known to him, as fact. That's not the issue. We can get ourselves trapped in a lot of silliness here. Last night, for instance, we were talking about a femto-second - point 14 zeros and a 'one' - and a biochemical process that underlies our visual system. This has been known for a year or so. It has taken some of the most elaborate technology that modem quantum mechanical principles can construct in order to make this kind of observation into the world of such brief time intervals that are absolutely critical to our first brain senses. But does that mean that Gurdjieff really knew that as a fact. For me that is not the point. Certainly, when you stand 'in-the-law', you stand wholly resonant with the Law. There is the strong temptation - I see it in myself - to say 'How did he (Gurdjieff) know that?' and I want to put it instantly into the functional world, when that is not the point. The important thing is to see where Gurdjieff is speaking *from* and then all truth about our functional world is going to be harmonic with that.

Sophia Wellbeloved: Could you say something about conviction in relation to language - as opposed to non-language convictions?

Keith Buzzell: Do you mean third brain conviction as language or second brain conviction, which is a different kind of language or communication?

Sophia Wellbeloved: It just seems that there's a lot of - when you spoke about the reptilian brain having conviction, - there are other kinds of conviction - for instance, it is a common experience that you can be convinced about what is happening to another person that you can't see. That's a feeling - you don't have any sensory input for it apparently so that as far as I can understand there must be a lot of input that we receive that we're not able to describe linguistically.

Keith Buzzell: It seems that this has to do with Second Brain images. It has to resonate into the world of 'Self-Other'; it is coming from 'Other' but it is not an external sense - it is an internal sense that becomes resonant with another internal sense, - and because of that resonance we may become 'open' to it if we are 'sensitive' enough in our real emotional part.

Edgar Clarke: I've got two questions I would like to ask; one particularly relevant to what you've just been speaking about and that is that you spoke about the balancing of centers. Certainly when I first started in this Work there was talk about how people's centers were not in balance and how the Work would bring it into balance. It has occurred to me for some time that all the work that seems to go on that brings one to a balance is usually done on individual centers rather than as a deliberate pattern of trying to obtain balance. I've never come across a teaching or a practice that says "The aim of this is to bring it in balance". It all seems to be work on one center or another. Is that your experience?

Keith Buzzell: For me this is the implication of the functional expressions of Work. The necessary integration of all of those is not only implied, it is spoken about in many ways. For instance, we come here to share intellectually, essentially, and we cannot speak of this sharing as the fullness or Wholeness of Work, because Work is all that Gurdjieff brought; in our inner Work, and Movements, it involves exercises of many different kinds etc. Out of that can come a synthesis. If we are unbalanced in this part or unbalanced in that part we have to work on each first. I referred to the 'common presence' as all of this together. If we allow ourselves to come too quickly to a state of conviction or certainty about the nature of this or that when we have not had the experience and it has not been our background to really be involved in all aspects that Gurdjieff set out then we can never hope to become balanced. He took the multitude of levels and parts, and he placed something, something of enormous essentiality for each of those, in the individual aspects of Work. But we can focus too much on one or another 'part' and speak incorrectly about the 'common presence', Where is the wholed sense of conviction that can come from that if we leave this out, leave that out and say this is what's important, this is the nidus , this is the kernel. No, not that way! That's how I would understand it.

Edgar Clarke: The second question I would like to ask referred to your experience of the physician and his conviction after his seizure. It's almost word for word a description that I recall from the book *The Common Experience* when Marguerita Lasky said that she was at a time taking her children out and looking out over the Firth of Ford. She suddenly had a conviction of truth and understanding that was overwhelming. She finished off her brief account by saying "What I understood I don't know, but it remains with me and it's been fundamental in my experience". My understanding of that is that it wasn't a malfunction of the physical but rather that somehow she had an insight from higher entities and I would think that would be a valid reason. You wouldn't have to have a malfunction to have this sort of insight, would we?

Keith Buzzell: No, but you can also have the malfunction and have a temporary connection to it. Gurdjieff speaks about this very specifically in *In Search*. He says that there can be momentary states, that we give great significance to because they are so powerful, but they can he the result of brain trauma, drugs, injury and epilepsy. He makes mention of those specific things saying they can create such a state because of the tremendous impact coming in mechano-coinciding that will make a resonant and very brief connection with higher centers.

Edgar Clarke: But that wouldn't invalidate somebody having a genuine insight (if I could put it in those terms); it wouldn't invalidate the spiritual experiences of people.

Keith Buzzell: It's not my purpose to try and invalidate that, only to see that it is a small piece of a very large whole and because the experience is so intense we are vulnerable to taking that and saying, 'Ahah! This is a cosmic level truth', when it may be nothing more than a connection to Anulios. Because we are so disconnected from our normal emotional life that we suddenly have an experience, however brief, of real connection with ordinary but real emotion (it's in the Cingulate Gyrus, not even in the Neocortex). But we are so peculiar in the way we are put together that an experience of that kind can be so intense that we can often tend to mistake it and think that it is beyond what it actually is.

Bert Sharp: In regard to Edgars's remarks I feel I must say that, when one makes the connection, what you are given cannot be put into words. So you cannot even tell yourself about it as it were, it's something like that. It is indescribable. The other comment I'll make is this. In the eighteen hundreds Frederick Meyers wrote on this subject. For him the unconscious, or as he called it, the subliminal secondary personalities revealed in trance states, dreaming, crystal gazing, and automatic writing, potentially possessed a higher intelligence than one's waking or superficial personality and often served to convey messages of guidance. Meyer's work paved the way for Theodore Florinoid, who published his major book in 1899 which significantly had the title *From India to the Planet Mars*. He goes into all this in great detail, which to my mind seems to relate very much to higher mind, working its way through us to whatever it leads us or wherever it is. But his work was put under the counter for 20 years because it didn't suit a lot of other people. Jung resurrected it a bit and was about the only person who actually acknowledged Florinoid's work.

Keith Buzzell: Two points that I want to make relative to this. First is that I believe Gurdjieff gives a very comprehensive treatment of this in Hypnosis. The other has to do with the end of the talk where I quoted the primordial emphasis that Gurdjieff places on impartiality. He gives us such a gift. You spoke of these experiences, these moments that are so intense and carry such energy, such conviction. It is not to deny them, it is not to say that they are not significant - they are! You can't walk away from it and say "Well because I don't understand the interstices and I can't put it into words, therefore it doesn't mean anything". No, I believe it means we must be impartial to them. Are they significant? I don't know. It certainly appears so; it had tremendous impact on me. But am I going to come to a conclusion, am I going to become convinced on the basis of this experience that therefore all of this out there - all of the other events of my life and the line of my life and the significance of my doing this and that are therefore determined? No, that is not being impartial, it's being overloadedly partial. So for me it may be very significant and it may also be the first of a series of psychomotor seizures for which I need a medication so that I will not have that again.

Gurdjieff, Blavatsky and the Masters of Wisdom

Seymour B. Ginsburg

Seymour B. (Sy) Ginsburg, J.D., was born in Chicago in 1934. He currently resides at Fort Lauderdale, Florida.
Northwestern University School of Business (now the Kellogg School), B.S., 1954, C.P.A.
Northwestern University of Law, J.D. 1957.
Past President, Toys-R-Us, Inc.
Past President, Glass, Ginsburg Ltd., Member Firm, Chicago Mercantile Exchange.

Since 1978, Student of Sri Madhava Ashish in Theosophy and Gurdjieff Studies.
Former Member, Gurdjieff Society of Florida (affiliated with Gurdjieff Foundation, NYC)
Co-founder, Gurdjieff Institute, Inc. (Florida)
Currently President, The Theosophical Society in Miami & South Florida, Facilitator of the Gurdjieff Study Group at the Theosophical Society.

Author: *Gurdjieff & The Secret Doctrine*, American Theosophist, Spring Special Issue 1988.
Co-author: *Gurdjieff, A New Introduction to his Teaching*, 1994.

Seymour Ginsburg was introduced by James Moore who at Seymour Ginsburg's request opened the session by two short readings from *Beelzebub's Tales to His Grandson*. First comes from Chapter 2, Why Beelzebub Was in Our Solar System, page 53-54:

Although the solar system "Ors" had been neglected owing to its remoteness from the center and to many other reasons, nevertheless our lord sovereign had sent from time to time his Messengers to the planets of this system, to regulate, more or less, the being-existence of the three-brained beings arising on them, for the co-ordination of the process of their existence with the general World Harmony.

And thus, to a certain planet of this solar system, namely, the planet Earth, there was once sent as such a Messenger from our endlessness, a certain Ashiata Shiemash, and as Beelzebub had then fulfilled a certain need in connection with his mission, the said Messenger, when he returned once more to the "Sun Absolute," earnestly besought HIS endlessness to pardon this once young and fiery but now aged Beelzebub.

In view of this request of Ashiata Shiemash, and also of the modest and cognoscent existence of Beelzebub himself, our maker creator pardoned him and gave him permission to return to the place of his arising.

Gurdjieff, Blavatsky and the Masters of Wisdom

And that is why Beelzebub, after a long absence, happened now to be again in the center of the Universe.

His influence and authority had not only not declined during his exile, but, on the contrary, they had greatly increased, since all those around him were clearly aware that, thanks to his prolonged existence in the aforementioned unusual conditions, his knowledge and experience must inevitably have been broadened and deepened.

The second reading comes from Chapter 25, The Very Saintly Ashiata Shiemash, Sent from Above to the Earth, pages 347-349:

And so, my boy!"

"Now listen very attentively to the information concerning the Most Very Saintly, now already Common Cosmic Individual, Ashiata Shiemash and his activities connected with the existence of the three-brained beings arising and existing on that planet Earth which has taken your fancy.

"I have already more than once told you, that by the All Most Gracious Command of Our OMNI-LOVING FATHER ENDLESSNESS, our Cosmic Highest Most Very Saintly Individuals sometimes actualize within the presence of some terrestrial three-brained being, a 'definitized' conception of a sacred Individual in order that he, having become a terrestrial being with such a presence, may there on the spot 'orientate himself' and give to the process of their ordinary being-existence such a corresponding new direction, thanks to which, the already crystallized consequences of the properties of the organ Kundabuffer, as well as the predispositions to such new crystallizations, might perhaps be removed from their presences.

"It was seven centuries before the Babylonian events I have spoken of, that there was actualized in the planetary body of a three-brained being there a 'definitized' conception of a sacred Individual named Ashiata Shiemash, who became there in his turn Messenger from Above, and who is now already one of the Highest Most Very Saintly common-cosmic Sacred Individuals.

"Ashiata Shiemash had his conception in the planetary body of a boy of a poor family descended from what is called the 'Sumerian Race,' in a small place then called 'Pispascana' situated not far from Babylon.

"He grew up and became a responsible being partly in this small place and partly in Babylon itself, which was at that time, although not yet magnificent, already a famous city.

"The Very Saintly Ashiata Shiemash was the only Messenger sent from Above to your planet who succeeded by His holy labors in creating on that planet conditions in which the existence of its unfortunate beings somewhat resembled for a certain time the existence of the three-brained beings of the other planets of our great Universe on which beings exist with the same possibilities; and He was also the first on that planet Earth, who for the mission preassigned to Him refused to employ for the three-brained beings of that planet the ordinary methods which had been established during centuries by all the other Messengers from Above.

"The Very Saintly Ashiata Shiemash taught nothing whatever to the ordinary three-brained beings of the Earth, nor did He preach anything to them, as was done before and after Him by all the Messengers sent there from Above with the same aim.

"And in consequence, chiefly of this, none of His teachings passed in any form from His contemporaries even to the third generation of ordinary beings there, not to mention the contemporary ordinary beings there.

"Definite information relating to His Very Saintly Activities passed from generation to generation from the contemporaries of the Very Saintly Ashiata Shiemash to the beings of the following generations through those called there 'initiates,' by means of a certain what is called 'Legominism' of His deliberations under the title of 'The Terror-of-the-Situation.'

"In addition to this, there has survived from the period of His Very Saintly Activities and there still exists even till now, one of several what are called 'marble tablets' on which were engraved His 'counsels' and 'commandments' and 'sayings' to the beings contemporary with Him.

"And at the present time this surviving tablet is the chief sacred relic of a small group of initiated beings there, called the 'Brotherhood-Olbogmek' whose place of existence is situated in the middle of the continent Asia.

"The name Olbogmek means, 'There are not different religions, there is only one God.'

"When I was personally on the surface of your planet for the last time, I happened by chance to become acquainted with the Legominism which transmits to the initiated men-beings of the planet Earth of remote generations these deliberations of the Saintly Ashiata Shiemesh under the title of 'The Terror-of-the-Situation.'

"The Legominism was of great assistance to me in elucidating certain strange aspects of the psyche of these peculiar beings-just those strange aspects of their psyche which, with all my careful observations of them during tens of centuries, I had previously been unable to understand in any way whatsoever."

"My dear and beloved Grandfather, tell me, please, what does the word Legominism mean?" Hassein asked.

"This word Legominism," replied Beelzebub, "is given to one of the means existing there of transmitting from generation to generation information about certain events of long-past ages, through just those three-brained beings who are thought worthy to be and who are called initiates.

Gurdjieff, Blavatsky and the Masters of Wisdom

"This means of transmitting information from generation to generation had been devised by the beings of the continent Atlantis. For your better understanding of the said means of transmitting information to beings of succeeding generations by means of a Legominism, I must here ex-…"

Gurdjieff, Blavatsky and the Masters of Wisdom

A Suggested Answer to René Zuber's question: Who are you Monsieur Gurdjieff?

This paper takes as its hypothesis, that there is a spiritual hierarchy which guides the involution and evolution of the universe, and the development of humankind on earth. This is in consonance with numerous indications given throughout *Beelzebub's Tales to his Grandson*.[1] The purpose here is to open for the reader's intuition, suggestions of extraordinary visitations to our planet by the being we know as Gurdjieff, and his connection with that spiritual hierarchy. The attempt is made to show corroborating evidence in support of this hypothesis.

Contents:
1. The Gurdjieff-Blavatsky Connection in the Context of Rene Zuber's Question.
2. The Secret Doctrine Connection.
3. Gurdjieff and the Practical Teaching
4. Gurdjieff and the Mahatma Letters
5. The Curious Chronology of the Players and Events in the Mahatma Letters Drama
6. The Sirius Connection
7. The Missing Letter Referred to by Kenneth Walker
8. Symbols, Elements, Triads, Octaves, Vibrations
9. Conversation with a Channel
10. Conversation with a Guru
Appendix: *Taking the Life Cure in Gurdjieff's School*, by Maud Hoffman, N.Y.T. 10 Feb 1924

1. The Gurdjieff-Blavatsky Connection in the Context of Rene Zuber's Question

The question of a connection, if any, between Georges Gurdjieff and Helena P. Blavatsky (H.P.B. to her students), founder of the Theosophical Society and her teachers, has interested students of these two traditions for many years. I addressed this question in two articles that appeared in the American Theosophist in 1987 and 1988[2], and at a talk given in London before the annual conference of the Theosophical History Centre in July, 1989. I pointed out several instances in H. P. B.'s, *The Secret Doctrine* and in Gurdjieff's *Beelzebub's Tales to his Grandson* that suggest

---
[1] G. I. Gurdjieff, *All and Everything, First Series: Beelzebub's Tales to his Grandson* (London: Routledge & Kegan Paul, 1950).
[2] Seymour B. Ginsburg, "Gurdjieff's Contribution to Theosophy," *The American Theosophist*, Vol. 75, No. 11 (December, 1987), 406.
Seymour B. Ginsburg, "H.P.B., Gurdjieff and The Secret Doctrine," *The American Theosophist*, Vol. 76, No. 5 (May, 1988 - Spring Special Issue), 147.

All & Everything Conference 1998

Gurdjieff drew an intentional connection to *The Secret Doctrine*, in addition to other evidence outside those writings. In July 1990, James Moore, in the journal of the Theosophical History Centre, *Theosophical History*, brought to light additional facts bearing on this question, having to do with the publication of *The Mahatma Letters*.[3] I propose now to put forth various propositions, as I currently have them, supporting a Gurdjieff-H.P.B. connection, and a connection with H.P.B.'s Masters, sometimes called "The Masters of Wisdom" in the context of René Zuber's question titled in his book, *Who are you Monsieur Gurdjieff?*[4]

Rene Zuber, a French journalist became a student of G. I. Gurdjieff in Paris during the Second World War. There, under the Nazi occupation, Zuber along with others caught up in that maelstrom, sat at Mr. Gurdjieff's table and participated in the teaching sessions which Gurdjieff led, through a dialog of questions put to him and the responses he gave.

On one occasion, Zuber asked the question: "Monsieur, who are you, then? Are you a true master or a false one? I never board a ship without being perfectly sure of the journey and the identity of the captain".[5]

To this question, Zuber comments that Gurdjieff gave no answer, and Zuber recounts in his book that the question continued to burn in him. But he gives his own answer to his question in paragraphs throughout the book. For example:

> "Where did Gurdjieff come from or, rather, from where was he returning? From exile, a long exile which he could not be said to have submitted to, since he had given it a meaning and had voluntarily taken all the consequences upon himself. Seen in this light his solemn funeral service, celebrated according to the rites of the Russian Orthodox Church, signified the return of an exile to the land of his birth. It restored him to the motherly arms of the Church in the presence of his two families joined anew, the one of the blood, the other of the spirit"...[6]

> "To behold Mr. Gurdjieff for an instant without being seen by him was so exceptional that I have never forgotten it. I remember that his face, the face of an old athlete imbued with compassion for human beings, had an air of melancholy about it, as if he belonged already to an 'elsewhere' which he would not name"...[7]

> "Who could pride himself on ever having met Gurdjieff? A master meets you for the sole purpose of showing you the direction, the way to the inner master which is called

---

[3] James Moore, "The Blavatsky-Gurdjieff Question: A Footnote on Maude Hoffman and A. T. Barker," *Theosophical History*, Vol. 3, No. 3 (July, 1990), 77.
[4] René Zuber, *Who Are You Monsieur Gurdjieff?* (London: Routledge & Kegan Paul, 1980), p. 10, translated by Jenny Koralek from the French edition, 1977.
[5] *Who are you Monsieur Gurdjieff?*, p. 10.
[6] *Who are you Monsieur Gurdjieff?*, p.p. 42-43.
[7] *Who are you Monsieur Gurdjieff?*, p. 43.

conscience. He helps you to discover that you are already its subject, but that you were not aware of it. And then he disappears. He melts into the sky as the mountain does the moment you believe you have set foot on it"...[8]

It is proposed here that Gurdjieff himself acknowledges René Zuber's conclusion that he is a Master (or at least a high initiate in the theosophical pantheon of hierarchical Masters and initiates) who meets you for the purpose of showing you the direction. He confirms this by constructions he gives in *Beelzebub's Tales to his Grandson*, which are designed to fulfil H.P.B.'s 1888 prediction in *The Secret Doctrine*, of the coming of a Master, a new world teacher in the 20th century.

Gurdjieff's likely influence over his own students at the Prieure, Maud Ho the executrix and custodian of the Mahatma Letters, and Trevor Barker who was editing the Mahatma Letters for publication in 1923, adds additional weight to the theory of Gurdjieff's connection not only with H.P.B., but with her teachers, Morya and Koot Hoomi, the "Mahatmas" who authored the letters. Numerous indications in support of this theory have come to light. Let us examine several of these.

2) The Secret Doctrine Connection

In the two volumes of *The Secret Doctrine*,[9] that H.P.B. brought to the West toward the end of the nineteenth century, there are indications that additional portions of the teaching introduced in these volumes might be given out by those whom she called her Masters or the "Masters of Wisdom", in this twentieth century. H.P.B. tells us that there are important parts of the teaching not disclosed by her in these two volumes. More is to be expected, especially as concerns the practical aspects of the teaching.

An examination of H.P.B.'s statements in *The Secret Doctrine* will help us to focus on what can be expected. She completes her writing of *The Secret Doctrine* with these words:

> "these two volumes should form for the student a fitting prelude for Volumes III. and IV. Until the rubbish of the ages is cleared away from the minds of the Theosophists to whom these volumes are dedicated, it is impossible that the more practical teaching contained in the Third Volume should be understood. Consequently, it entirely depends upon the reception with which Volumes I. and II. will meet at the hands of Theosophists and Mystics, whether these last two volumes will ever be published, though they are *almost* completed."[10]

---

[8] *Who are you Monsieur Gurdjieff?*, p. 65.
[9] H. P. Blavatsky, *The Secret Doctrine* (Los Angeles: The Theosophy Company, 1974).
[10] *The Secret Doctrine*, Vol. II, p.p. 797-798.

All & Everything Conference 1998

Thus, we have it from H.P.B. that the practical teaching of *The Secret Doctrine*, may be revealed in a third volume of that work, if we are ready to receive it. This implies that the practical teaching has not for the most part been given out.

Of what might the more practical teaching promised for Volume III. consist?

H.P.B. tells us quite plainly:

> "In Volume III. of this work (the said volume and the IVth being almost ready) a brief history of all the great adepts known to the ancients and the moderns in their chronological order will be given, as also a bird's eye view of the Mysteries, their birth, growth, decay, and final death -- in Europe.[11]

She repeats:

"In that volume (III) a brief recapitulation will be made of all the principal adepts known to history, and the downfall of the mysteries will be described; after which began the disappearance and final and systematic elimination from the memory of men of the real nature of initiation and the Sacred Science."[12]

And what of Volume IV.? What will it contain? Once more H.P.B. tells us:

> "Volume IV. will be almost entirely devoted to Occult teachings."[13]

Finally, we may ask: who will bring the more practical teachings of which she writes?

This is what she says:

> "In Century the Twentieth some disciple more informed and far better fitted, may be sent by the Masters of Wisdom to give final and irrefutable proofs that there exists a Science called *Gupta-Vidya* (Esoteric or Secret Science);[14] and that, like the once-mysterious sources of the Nile, the source of all religions and philosophies now known to the world has been for many ages forgotten and lost to men, but is at last found."[15]

In addition to these obvious clues, we can select from any number of other statements made by H.P.B. as we look for indications of what more might be given. One such statement that has often been repeated when considering esoteric teachings is her comment about oral transmission in relation to *The Secret Doctrine*:

---

[11] *The Secret Doctrine*, Vol. I, p. 437.
[12] *The Secret Doctrine*, Introductory, p. xl
[13] *The Secret Doctrine*, Vol. I, p. 437.
[14] H. P. Blavatsky, *The Theosophical Glossary* (Los Angeles: The Theosophy Company, 1973), p. 130.
[15] *The Secret Doctrine*, Introductory, p. xxxviii.

"that which is given in these volumes is selected from oral, as much as from written teachings."¹⁶

Therefore, we shall want to consider oral teaching that has been given to us along with that which has been set down in writing.

As it is now almost the end of the twentieth century, we may reasonably review these past ten decades and ask who, if anyone, has already fulfilled H.P.B.'s prediction? Who, if anyone, has brought *Gupta-Vida*? Who, if anyone, has brought the secret science?

The elders of the Theosophical Society in the early part of the twentieth century, under the leadership of Annie Besant, were not unmindful of H.P.B.'s prediction. In a world wind tour of the United States, Mrs. Besant spoke incessantly of the imminent coming of the World Teacher. Benefitting from the psychic insights of Charles Leadbeater, they discovered the young Jiddu Krishnamurti and saw in him the fulfilment of the prophecy. Subsequent events showed Krishnamurti to be a serious teacher. Many will say that his discourses, given largely in the form of dialogues, constitute the practical teaching anticipated in the already issued volumes of *The Secret Doctrine*. Others cannot find in them the "how to" given out in a usable form. Krishnamurti himself, seems to have settled the issue, disclaiming any mantle of authority as the predicted disciple in his arguably most important speech "Truth is a Pathless Land" given before thousands of theosophists in Holland in 1929.

The extraordinary quantity of teachings given out by the Tibetan, Djwhal Khul through the clairaudience abilities of Alice A. Bailey between 1919 and 1946 are also seen by many people as a fulfilment of what had been predicted for the twentieth century by *The Secret Doctrine*.

Alice Bailey, an early worker for the Theosophical Society, saw in the Tibetan's teachings communicated through her, the fulfilment of H.P.B.'s prophecy. About his teachings she wrote:

> "Another revolutionary thing that the Tibetan did was when He dictated the contents of *A Treatise on Cosmic Fire*.¹⁷" In this book He gave what H.P.B. prophesied He would give, the psychological key to cosmic creation. H.P.B. stated that in the 20th century a disciple would come who would give information concerning the three fires with which *The Secret Doctrine* deals: electric fire, solar fire and fire by friction."¹⁸

Some regard this material as being too theoretical to constitute the anticipated practical teaching. Others feel that it is too mixed and distorted through the personality of Alice Bailey. Still others believe that the disciple foreshadowed by H.P.B. must of necessity appear incarnate.

---

¹⁶ *The Secret Doctrine*, Introductory, p. xxxvii.
¹⁷ Alice A. Bailey, *A Treatise on Cosmic Fire* (New York: Lucis Publishing Company, 1925).
¹⁸ Alice A. Bailey, *The Unfinished Autobiography* (New York: Lucis Publishing Company, 1951), p. 236.

All & Everything Conference 1998

Krishnamurti and Djwhal Khul are perhaps the two best known examples of the numerous claims to the role of the new world teacher that have been made.

Let us now look at Gurdjieff's position when he came public in Moscow beginning in 1912 and consider his actions over the next decades. Let us also assume that he is the Master that René Zuber believes he is. Gurdjieff is undoubtedly aware of H.P.B.'s predictions in *The Secret Doctrine*. P. D. Ouspensky, who he met in 1913 and who became his student, was already well known in theosophical circles. A. R. Orage, who became his student and eventually his American representative was a public speaker for the Theosophical Society in England. We can readily assume from these and other contacts that Gurdjieff knew a great deal about theosophy and the theosophical movement. Let us further assume he wants to give the world indications that he is the teacher predicted in *The Secret Doctrine*, who will bring the practical teaching. How does he do it?

Of course, he actually brings the practical teaching. That is his job. It is why he was sent in. The practical teaching is essentially oral, and he gives it out piecemeal to Ouspensky and others in the early Russian groups. Ouspensky recognizes this and realizes "that a great deal-of time must pass before (he) could tell (himself) that (he) could outline the whole system correctly."[19] Eventually, Ouspensky does outline the system and writes it down as he understands it, however incomplete. This written account, *In Search of the Miraculous*[20] (formerly *Fragments of an Unknown Teaching*) is published only after the deaths of both Ouspensky in 1947 and Gurdjieff in 1950.

By the 1920s Gurdjieff is certainly aware of Krishnamurti's selection by the theosophists as the new world teacher. He can hardly stand in opposition to this. It would appear unseemly and he would be accused of self-serving. What does he do?

Gurdjieff has by now, after the auto accident in 1924, which determined that he would have to close his school, dedicated himself to writing. He writes the intentionally abstruse *Beelzebub's Tales to His Grandson*, a great mixture of allegory and fact, and writes into it a scenario that will fulfil H.P.B.'s prediction. He does this by creating a great scientist who appears as a Saturnian bird, Gornahoor Harharkh, who helps Beelzebub (or Gurdjieff) to construct a telescope on the planet Mars, by which he is able to observe the happenings on Earth. In this way he is able to give "a bird's eye view of the Mysteries, their birth, growth, decay, and final death -- in Europe"; and he does this along with giving us "a brief history of all the great adepts known to the ancients and the moderns in their chronological order", just as H.P.B. has predicted. This is the setting of *Beelzebub's Tales*.

To draw a link between Beelzebub's bird being scientist friend who invents a telescope for observing Earth and H.P.B.'s bird's eye view to be given in the foreshadowed Volume III of *The*

---

[19] P. D. Ouspensky, *In Search of the Miraculous* (London: Routledge & Kegan Paul, 1950) p.64
[20] *Ibid*.

Secret Doctrine, is a highly speculative affair. Nevertheless, our purpose is to mount the evidence and inference, that points to the link between Gurdjieff and H.P.B. and the Masters of Wisdom.

It has occurred to more than one student of Gurdjieff's teaching that *Beelzebub's Tales to His Grandson*, in spite of intentional obscuration, is Gurdjieff's autobiography, not just in his most recent incarnation as Gurdjieff, but in his many appearances in the past on this planet, in the role of teacher. Events in his "sixth descent" to the planet Earth which lead us into the twentieth century can definitely be linked to Gurdjieff's life here as we know it. We can speculate that events described in the previous five descents going back to the days of Atlantis are also biographical, however much mixed with allegory, of the being we know this time around as Gurdjieff. Theosophical theory has it that a being sent in from above takes incarnation in a vehicle provided by ordinary human procreation. Beelzebub's statements that he "descended" onto earth, in describing each of his 6 visits, can be seen as the entering into incarnation of this being for the purposes described in the *Tales*.

3. Gurdjieff and the Practical Teaching

Let us now take a look at a bit of his biography and of the teaching Gurdjieff brought to see if it satisfies the requirements for a "how to".

Since the posthumous publication of Gurdjieff's writings beginning in 1950, a growing number of people have begun to recognize the power of the techniques, the "how to" that Gurdjieff brought. One measure of this is the use of these techniques for the purposes of self-development in the mundane sense. While we might justifiably view this as a corruption of Gurdjieff's intent, there are, nevertheless, numerous examples of their effective application in the social and corporate cultures that presently drive Western civilization. We can find many of the practical techniques that Gurdjieff brought for developing an inner unity and attitude of self worth being applied today with increasing frequency in psychological training systems such as those used in E.S.T. and Arica.[21] It may be that those who use these techniques for mundane purposes have little idea of their importance from the standpoint of man's possible evolution in the cosmic sense of *The Secret Doctrine*. But if we have some appreciation of the cosmic significance of the teachings Gurdjieff brought, we will want to examine them, especially the practical teachings, to see if they fit with the indications given by H.P.B. It is important for us to discover whether Gurdjieff's teachings are genuinely useful in helping the advancement of our inner quest.

What do we know of Gurdjieff?

---

[21] *Erhard Seminar Training (EST)*, For example see: James Kettle, *The EST Experience* (New York: Zebra Books, 1976).
The Arica System (ARICA), For example see: Oscar Ichazo, *Between Metaphysics and Protoanalysis* (New York: Arica Institute Press, 1982).

All & Everything Conference 1998

Even more difficult than is the problem of biographing the missing years of H.P.B., we have little or no independent reporting of Gurdjieff's early years. We are not certain of the year of his birth, and unlike H.P.B. who came from a family of relative prominence, Gurdjieff's origins are completely obscure. Various researchers have placed his birth between 1866 and 1880. But as these estimates are based mostly on his quasi-autobiographical and, some would say quasi-allegorical account of his early years entitled *Meetings With Remarkable Men*, [22] the dates are really speculative.

We can, however, say with some assurance that Gurdjieff like H.P.B., but approximately 40 years later, was born near the Black Sea in that part of the world that had for centuries been a crossroads of ancient traditions and civilizations. Just as she came forth in the West after many years of mysterious travel, so too did Gurdjieff, appearing first publicly in Moscow in 1912. If it was his mission to expose the practical teachings contained in the said Volumes III. and IV. of *The Secret Doctrine*, he dutifully began his work by attempting to establish an institute in that city for this purpose.

The ensuing World War and the subsequent Bolshevik revolution disrupted these plans and Gurdjieff was forced to flee with a small band of followers across the Caucuses to Constantinople, Berlin and ultimately to Paris. Included in this band of early pupils was P.D. Ouspensky, himself a noted author who was well known in the theosophical circles of Moscow and St. Petersburg.

Ouspensky was later to author the definitive popular exposition of Gurdjieff's ideas under the title *Fragments of an Unknown Teaching*, later changed to *In Search of the Miraculous.*[23] This book of the teaching was based on Ouspensky's notes and verbatim recollections of talks given by Gurdjieff to his early pupils during the eight years that Ouspensky remained under Gurdjieff's tutelage. Its text was approved by Gurdjieff and it provides a concise, if incomplete, written outline of the practical teachings in a form more accessible than Gurdjieff's own more enigmatic writings.

In Search of the Miraculous, occupies a unique place in the record of what Gurdjieff brought. The majority of the text appears in quotation marks and is represented as being Ouspensky's exact recollection of Gurdjieff's words by which he expounded orally, the practical teachings in piecemeal fashion to Ouspensky and others of his early groups over several years. If Ouspensky, who was known for preciseness in writing and rewriting his own texts, can be relied upon, we have a written document that more closely reflects the content of essentially oral teachings than is likely to be ordinarily encountered.

While no attempt will be made here to catalog the specific practical teachings that Gurdjieff brought, a study of *In Search of the Miraculous*, will handsomely repay the inquirer with indications of the direction of these teachings. It should be kept in mind, however, that since the

---

[22] G. I. Gurdjieff *Meetings With Remarkable Men* (New York: E.P. Dutton & Co., 1969).

[23] P. D. Ouspensky, *In Search of the Miraculous* (London: Routledge & Kegan Paul, 1950).

practical teachings are essentially oral, their communication usually requires the placing of oneself within a group under a leader who has, himself, received transmission of the teachings and who has understood something of them. Gurdjieff explains the necessity for this in the following way:

> "Furthermore, no one can escape from prison without the help of those *who have escaped before*. Only they can say in what way escape is possible or can send tools, files, or whatever may be necessary. But *one* prisoner alone cannot find these people or get into touch with them. An organization is necessary. Nothing can be achieved without an organization."[24]

In fulfilment of the idea that an organization is necessary Gurdjieff eventually established an institute under the name, *The Institute for the Harmonious Development of Man*, just outside Paris at a house he acquired, the *Chateau du Prieure*, in 1922. It was here that he began to train those who came to him in the practical work that he saw as obligatory for men and women who wished to bring about a change in the level of their being and the state of their consciousness. This is the practical teaching, that it is here suggested was predicted by H.P.B., to be given out in the said Volume III. of *The Secret Doctrine*. It was Gurdjieff's intention that those whom he trained and who arrived at a sufficient degree of understanding would go forth to bring the practical teaching to a wider public.

Gurdjieff's plans were interrupted by an automobile accident that occurred in 1924. The accident and its aftermath led to the closing of his Institute, after which Gurdjieff retired to an apartment in Paris where he continued to receive and to instruct a small number of pupils.

With the reduction in his activities, Gurdjieff turned to setting down indications of the practical teaching in a written form. This document which with minor exceptions constitutes all that he wrote is a trilogy given out under the overall title, *All and Everything*. The first series of the trilogy entitled *Beelzebub's Tales to His Grandson*[25] or *An Objectively Impartial Criticism of the Life of Man* is considered to be Gurdjieff's *magnum opus*, and is, being suggested here as, the likely Volume III. of *The Secret Doctrine*. The second series of the trilogy is the aforementioned, *Meetings With Remarkable Men*, and the third series often simply called "The Third Series" is entitled, *Life is real only then, when "I am"*.[26]

This third series, the final portion of the trilogy, was never completed. Gurdjieff began it by stating:

---

[24] *In Search of the Miraculous*, p. 30.
[25] G. I. Gurdjieff, *All and Everything, First Series: Beelzebub's Tales to his Grandson* (London: Routledge & Kegan Paul, 1950).
[26] G. I. Gurdjieff, *Life is real only then, when "I am"*, (New York: Triangle Editions, 1978).

"My last book, through which I wish to share with other creatures of our Common Father similar to myself, almost all the previously unknown mysteries of the inner world of man which I have accidentally learned."[27]

After writing 177 pages of the third series, he put down his pen and left the work undone. Various reasons have been put forward for this but the truth about it will likely never be known. The volume was eventually published but this was accomplished only over the protest of many of Gurdjieff's students and after a legal battle. There was a feeling that since he had not completed the book and had abruptly discontinued the writing, it contained practical material of an esoteric nature that he had decided against releasing.

In reading the unfinished book one becomes convinced of its great promise and there is a sadness in knowing that it has in a sense been withdrawn. Students of the book, however incomplete, recognize that it contains important practical teachings. Principal among these is the very technique that Gurdjieff suggests for sustaining the experience of self-awareness that is central to the practical teaching he brought. It is not a great leap to infer that the foreshadowed Volume IV. of *The Secret Doctrine*, which as H.P.B. tells us "will be almost entirely devoted to Occult teachings," is Gurdjieff's uncompleted, *Life is real only then, when "I am"*.

Notwithstanding the attempted withdrawal of his third series and the possibility that it may have been intended as the fourth volume of *The Secret Doctrine*, Gurdjieff challenges us to discover that he did, indeed, bring the written shell of Volume III., the practical teaching, in his first series of writings under the title, *Beelzebub's Tales to His Grandson*. In *Beelzebub's Tales*, he has intentionally provided the links to H.P.B.'s predictions.

Gurdjieff made *Beelzebub's Tales* intentionally difficult to approach by using cumbersome sentences and impossible language. He wrote and revised it over several years and would have chapters of it read aloud to various groups of his pupils. If the deeper meanings of what he wished to convey were too clear, he would rewrite the chapter making it even more difficult to understand because he believed that people do not value that which they acquire without effort. In explaining his frequent rewriting of the chapters in *Beelzebub's Tales*, he commented that he would have to "bury the dog deeper."[28] In this context it is reasonable to assume that while Gurdjieff wanted us to discover that he linked his writings with *The Secret Doctrine*, he would not make our task an easy one.

Beelzebub's Tales is exactly what H.P.B. predicted, "a brief history of all the great adepts known to the ancients and the moderns in their chronological order." Gurdjieff hints at the link to *The Secret Doctrine*, by giving a literal "bird's eye view of the Mysteries, their birth, growth, decay, and final death in – Europe", and we might also add, in America. He does this through the device of a telescope invented by a bird and erected on the planet Mars so that from there Beelzebub, his

---

[27] *Life is real only then, when "I am"*, Forward p. xi.
[28] J. G. Bennett, *Gurdjieff: Making a New World* (New York: Harper & Row, 1973), p. 274.

protagonist, could have a bird's eye view of activities taking place on the planet earth over long periods of time. This technique is quite in keeping with the mischievousness for which Gurdjieff is known.

Beelzebub's Tales is a vast allegory set in the description of visits to and observations of the planet earth over several thousand years as recounted by Beelzebub who is an old and wise space traveller. In the story, Beelzebub exploring the universe perhaps for his last time in the spaceship Karnak is accompanied by his near attendants and his kinsmen including his beloved young grandson, Hassein, who is often seen as the allegorical "we" who sit at Gurdjieff's feet. During the lengthy periods of this cosmic journey there is much time for conversation and Hassein who has become especially interested in the strange three-brained beings (human beings) inhabiting the planet Earth, continually questions his grandfather about them.

It happened that previously for a very long period of time Beelzebub had been exiled from the center of the universe to our remote solar system where he took up residence on the planet Mars. From there he made six sojourns to Earth covering various epochs, the first beginning during the days of Atlantis and the last ending in the early 20th century. In between these visits Beelzebub continually monitored activities on Earth from his base on Mars with the aid of the above mentioned telescope.

To answer Hassein's many questions, Beelzebub recounts his experiences during these six visits along with the results of his telescopic observations. Through these accounts Gurdjieff's allegorical Beelzebub reveals a string of practical teachings which, along with the oral teachings recorded so diligently by Ouspensky in *In Search of the Miraculous*, provide indications of an array of techniques by which human beings can and must work for their own evolution.

Foremost among the adepts known to the ancients, according to Gurdjieff was the being whom he refers to as the very saintly Ashiata Shiemash. He is one of many adepts whose history H.P.B. prophesied would be recapitulated in the third volume of *The Secret Doctrine*, and his activities are here recounted by Beelzebub. Unlike the more recent founders of well known religious traditions about whom Beelzebub also speaks, these ancient adepts are unknown to modern historians. Whether such a being actually existed is not really important. It is the teaching that the actual or allegorical Ashiata Shiemash brought some seven centuries before the height of the Babylonian civilization[29] by which Gurdjieff sets the stage for the practical work that he insists is required of us.

Central to this teaching, Gurdjieff tells us, is the requirement for "personal conscious labors and intentional sufferings."[30] He explains this in the following way:

---

[29] *Beelzebub's Tales to his Grandson*, p. 347.
[30] *Beelzebub's Tales to his Grandson*, p. 384.

> "The 'man-machine' with whom everything depends upon external influences, with whom everything happens, who is now one, the next moment another, and the next moment a third, has no future of any kind; he is buried and that is all. Dust returns to dust. This applies to him. In order to be able to speak of any kind of future life there must be a certain crystallization, a certain fusion of man's inner qualities, a certain independence of external influences...."

"Fusion, inner unity, is obtained by means of 'friction,' by the struggle between 'yes' and 'no' in man. If a man lives without inner struggle, if everything happens in him without opposition, if he goes wherever he is drawn or wherever the wind blows, he will remain such as he is. But if a struggle begins in him, and particularly if there is a definite line in this struggle, then, gradually, permanent traits begin to form themselves, he begins to 'crystallize.'"[31]

This idea is among the most important of the practical teachings that Gurdjieff brought because it explains what he saw as a misunderstanding that had developed among students of esotericism.

Those familiar with H.P.B.'s teaching will know that the ancient wisdom postulates an obligatory pilgrimage for every soul or essence, which is itself a spark of the Universal Oversoul, through countless cycles of incarnation in accordance with cyclic and karmic law. During these incarnations, the essence evolves from the lowest mineral form, through plant, animal, human and superhuman states to a level of consciousness that knows its identity with the Universal Oversoul or Absolute, the one ultimate reality.

Accompanying the doctrine of the obligatory evolutionary pilgrimage is the theosophical tenet of the seven bodies or principles of man. This is the idea that man consists of seven interpenetrating bodies, each of an increasingly rarified matter and carrying in turn an increasingly conscious nature. The first or lowest of these is our physical body and the seventh or highest principle is the one ultimate Reality of which we are each a spark. The first through the fourth bodies are considered to be the lower part of our nature and relate to our physical, emotional, and ordinary mental makeup, characteristics which are merely temporal. The three higher bodies are viewed as the permanent, essential, and thus reincarnating part of our nature.

In classical theosophical theory, it is given that we possess these interpenetrating bodies, although in a vague sense we know that we need to stand not in our lower natures but in the upper triad. We need to stand in our divine nature. But how shall we do this?

Although H.P.B. taught that we must win our evolution by our own personal efforts, we often forget this, taking our evolution for granted. We frequently hold the illusion that if this life is not just as we like it, then the next one will certainly be higher and better. We assume that karma and reincarnation will take care of our evolution. Gurdjieff tells us that this simply is not so other than as part of the deliberate general evolution.

---

[31] *In Search of the Miraculous*, p.p. 31-32.

Gurdjieff, Blavatsky and the Masters of Wisdom

Gurdjieff speaks of some esoteric systems describing the interpenetrating bodies as three in number, some as four, and others as seven. In *Beelzebub's Tales* he describes a system of three interpenetrating bodies, and in *In Search of the Miraculous*, as recounted by Ouspensky, he describes a system using four interpenetrating bodies. But the crux of the matter, he tells us, is not whether the interpenetrating bodies number three, four, or seven, but that such as we are the higher bodies are not accessible to us. Such as we are, while the interpenetrating finer matter of these higher principles are within us, the bodies themselves are not in his word "crystallized". Gurdjieff goes on to say that if we wish to stand in the higher bodies they must be crystallized within us and for this, work on ourselves with much friction is required.

Gurdjieff presents this idea in two ways.

He speaks of the disease of "tomorrow", an affliction suffered by a majority of the people on Earth. Of this disease he says,

"...a very singular and most strange disease, with a property of evolving, arose and exists among them there even until now - a disease called there 'tomorrow'.

"This disease 'tomorrow' brought with it terrifying consequences, and particularly for those unfortunate three-brained beings there who chance to learn and to become categorically convinced with the whole of their presence that they possess some very undesirable consequences for the deliverance from which they must make certain efforts, and which efforts moreover they even know just how to make, but owing to this maleficent disease 'tomorrow' they never succeed in making these required efforts.

"And this is just the maleficent part of all that great terrifying evil, which, owing to various causes great and small, is concentrated in the process of the ordinary being existence of these pitiable three-brained beings; and, by putting off from 'tomorrow' till 'tomorrow,' those unfortunate beings there who do by chance learn all about what I have mentioned are also deprived of the possibility of ever attaining anything real."[32]

For those suffering from this disease, Gurdjieff warns that such as we are, the inner bodies which provide the prospect of another possibility for man do not functionally exist. He puts it this way:

> "most systems and teaching... recognize something more in man than the physical body. But almost all these teachings, while repeating in more or less familiar form the definitions and divisions of the ancient teaching, have forgotten or omitted its most important feature which is: that man is not born with the finer bodies, and they can only be artificially cultivated in him provided favorable conditions both internal and external are present."[33]

---

[32] *Beelzebub's Tales to his Grandson*, p. 362.
[33] *In Search of the Miraculous*, p. 41.

All & Everything Conference 1998

Taking the more traditional view Gurdjieff also speaks of higher centers in man that already exist, we might say on another plane, but with which man, such as he is, is not connected. He suggests:

> "All mystical and occult systems recognize the existence of higher forces and capacities in man although, in many cases they admit the existence of these forces and capacities only in the form of possibilities, and speak of the necessity for developing the hidden forces in man. This present teaching differs from many others by the fact that it affirms that the higher centers exist in man and are fully developed.
>
> "It is the lower centers that are undeveloped, And it is precisely this lack of development, or the incomplete functioning, of the lower centers that prevents us from making use of the work of the higher centers."[34]

Thus Gurdjieff issues his clarion call for us to work on ourselves, and his teaching has, in fact, become known as The Work. He asks us to begin this required work by honestly and impartially observing ourselves over a long period of time and to examine the state of our consciousness. He gives us a guideline by dividing the continuum of human consciousness into four qualitatively distinctive states, and he suggests that we can verify for ourselves the differences between at least three of these states.

Gurdjieff tells us that we spend our ordinary lives in only the two lowest states, sleep (typified by sleep at night) and what we call waking consciousness, our ordinary state of awareness as we function in the world. If we can appreciate the difference in the quality of consciousness between these two states, it will give us some indication, he says, of the differences in consciousness that states higher than these represent.

There are two of these higher states of consciousness. The highest, he calls objective consciousness, that state which has been variously described by mystics as illumination or enlightenment. Libraries are filled with accounts of this state left by those persons who have experienced it and have tried, however inadequately, to describe that experience. For most of us the attainment of this state remains merely a glorious hope about which we can dream but into which, such as we are, we have no access.

It is the third state of consciousness, that which Gurdjieff calls self-consciousness or self-awareness, that is the key to his practical teaching. This state is our rightful condition and when we enter it, we have a qualitatively enhanced experience of the world. It is from our position in this state that we may eventually experience the fourth state of consciousness: that of enlightenment or illumination. It is our adequacy to reside in these two higher states of consciousness that gives the crystallization of the higher bodies within us, of which Gurdjieff speaks.

---

[34] *In Search of the Miraculous*, p. 194.

Gurdjieff, Blavatsky and the Masters of Wisdom

It is easy to wonder why, if the state of self-consciousness is our rightful state, we do not exist in it. The answer to this question lies in a natural but erroneous assumption that we make. We do not exist in the state of self-consciousness because we already think that we have it and consequently are unwilling to make the efforts that are required to attain it. We need to be shown this state, and we need to taste it. It needs to be demonstrated to us so that we can verify for ourselves that we do not ordinarily exist in it, but that we can by effort, attain it.

The state of self-consciousness may be briefly described as the condition of including the experience of ourself in our attention along with whatever else is in our attention in each moment of time. This experiencing of oneself included in the attention can be brought about by using certain techniques, techniques that Gurdjieff taught. They place great emphasis on sensation of the physical body as a gateway to more fully experiencing one's entire self Once this state is shown to us and we sufficiently verify its qualitative difference from our ordinary waking state, we must admit that we do not ordinarily reside in it and we realize the assumption that we are ordinarily self-conscious is erroneous.

An intentional struggle in the direction of attracting the attention back to oneself so that one's experience of self is included in the attention is what is required to be self-conscious. This intentional struggle, or in the words attributed to Ashiata Shiemash, these "personal conscious labors and intentional sufferings," generate the friction about which Gurdjieff speaks.

A second question arises once we acknowledge that we are not ordinarily self-conscious. If self-consciousness is our rightful state, why then does it require special effort to exist in it? The answer to this lies in our conditioning, the improper education that we have received from infancy which places our entire life's emphasis on identification. When we begin to impartially observe ourself as Gurdjieff insists we must do, we discover that we identify with everything. We identify with what we say, with what we think, with what we imagine and most insidiously with the whole gamut of our negative emotions.

Each identification according to Gurdjieff is another "I" in us. It is in the lexicon of the Gurdjieff work, the doctrine of "I's." He describes it thus:

> "*Man has no permanent and unchangeable* I. Every thought, every mood, every desire, every sensation, says "I." And in each case it seems to be taken for granted that this I belongs to the *Whole*, to the whole man, and that a thought, a desire or an aversion is expressed by this Whole. In actual fact there is no foundation whatever for this assumption. Man's every thought and desire appears and lives quite separately and independently of the Whole. And the Whole never expresses itself, for the simple reason that it exists, as such, only physically as a thing, and in the abstract as a concept. Man has no individual I. But there are, instead, hundreds and thousands of separate small I's, very often entirely unknown to one another, never coming into contact, or, on the contrary, hostile to each other, mutually exclusive and incompatible. Each minute, each moment, man is saying or thinking 'I' And each time his I is different. Just now it was a thought,

now it is a desire, now a sensation, now another thought, and so on, endlessly. *Man is a plurality*".[35]

When we identify, as we do all the time with one "I" or another, we are absorbed entirely into that "I" with which we identify. We are so absorbed that it becomes impossible to include an awareness of our whole self in our attention. There is simply no room left nor do we have the energy needed to include our whole self in the experience of our life.

As we observe this condition in ourself and work along these lines in accordance with Gurdjieff's teachings, we discover a truth of immense proportion. We discover that identification is the enemy of self-consciousness. And we begin to see that self-consciousness is the gateway to the real world.

It is while residing in the state of self-consciousness that intentional access to the fourth state, that state which Gurdjieff calls objective consciousness, becomes possible. A person who works on him or herself with prolonged effort, aspiration, the help of enhanced energy and perhaps what might be called grace, or what appears to be grace because one has no control over it, may eventually attain this state.

In this high state, a view of the real world is had and an understanding of incarnated planetary life in relation to the bigger picture of involution and evolution is attained. Oftentimes, while one is in the state of self-consciousness, glimpses of the higher state appear. These are likely to come most often during periods of meditation, but on occasion during our daily rounds if during those rounds we are present to ourself.

It can be seen that each of these four possible states of the level of our consciousness require a different quality of energy. We easily recognize that a higher and finer energy is required for our ordinary waking state than for our situation of sleep at night. Similarly, the state of self-consciousness requires a finer energy and the state of objective consciousness requires a finer energy yet. So our approach to practical work must be through an intelligent effort both to transmute the energy produced by our organism into an energy that is higher and finer, and also to conserve our energy and not permit it to be drained away.

This maximization and transmutation of energy is an exact science and is the basis of what was known as alchemy amongst esoteric orders during the middle ages. It can be discovered under other names in other traditions and in all time periods. It is the *gupta-vida* referred to by H.P.B. and brought to the contemporary West by Gurdjieff.

In chapters of both the written *Beelzebub's Tales to His Grandson*,[36] and in his oral teaching recorded by Ouspensky in *In Search of the Miraculous*,[37] Gurdjieff traces the flow of and

---

[35] *In Search of the Miraculous*, p. 59.
[36] *Beelzebub's Tales to his Grandson*, Chapter 39, "The Holy Planet Purgatory."

transmutation of energy through the organs of the body. He speaks of the two great laws of world creation and world maintenance that apply to all transformation of energy through all involutionary and evolutionary processes by which spirit involves into matter and evolves back into conscious spirit. As part of this process we human beings transform energy as we process the nutrients that we receive from food, air and impressions. Students familiar with H.P.B.'s teachings, or who otherwise have an independent key to the esoteric basis behind exoteric religious teachings, will know of these two laws even though they are presented in a somewhat different context. Gurdjieff calls the one law, the *Law of Three Forces*. "According to this law every action, every phenomenon in all worlds without exception, is the result of a simultaneous action of three forces - the positive, the negative and the neutralizing."[38] In exoteric Christianity, for example, this law appears as the Holy Trinity, and in exoteric Hinduism it is allegorized as the Trimurti.

The other great law is, called by Gurdjieff, the *Law of Octaves* or of disharmony of vibrations. "In order to understand this law it is necessary to regard the universe as consisting of vibrations."[39] Accordingly, not only does all so called matter consist of vibrations, but this law evidences that there has been intentionally inserted into the universe a principle of disharmony in order to produce the infinite variety and experience required for the Absolute to become conscious of itself. Further explanation of this law can be found in H.P.B.'s teachings about vibrations.

Gurdjieff explains how intentional efforts both to stop the leaks of energy resulting from identification and to refine the available energy processed by our bodies in a special way through conscious labor and intentional suffering, in accordance with the two great laws, serve to alter the automatic processing of foods in our organism so that the nutrients derived may be used for the higher esoteric purpose. These efforts make use of working with the attention in the experiencing of one's life as well as in meditational technique.

It is through these undertakings that the necessary crystallization begins, the crystallization which brings about in us a permanent and unchangeable "I" instead of all the separate small and fleeting "I's" of which we ordinarily consist. It is through these undertakings that the crystallization begins which permits us to reside in the higher states of consciousness, therefore allowing us to be more continually self-conscious.

Thus, in this life, in this planetary incarnation, if we have started a good crystallization, a good capability to be self-conscious, and if we are able to direct the flow of energies and control them, then the possibility for our further conscious evolution becomes real. It is then that we begin to actually experience the bigger picture about which *The Secret Doctrine* speaks.

---

[37] *In Search of the Miraculous*, Chapter 9.
[38] *In Search of the Miraculous*, p. 122. Also see *Beelzebub's Tales to his Grandson*, Chapter 39.
[39] *In Search of the Miraculous*, p. 122. Also see *Beelzebub's Tales to his Grandson*, Chapter 39.

All & Everything Conference 1998

4. Gurdjieff and The Mahatma Letters

In examining the idea that there is a connection between Gurdjieff and H.P.B., we will want to look at the curious circumstances surrounding the editing for publication of *The Mahatma Letters*.

H.P.B explains the meaning of the term Mahatma as follows:

> A Mahatma is a personage who, by special training and education, has evolved those higher faculties and has attained that spiritual knowledge which ordinary humanity will acquire after passing through numberless series of incarnations during the process of cosmic evolution.[40]

H.P.B. called her two teachers, Morya and Koot Hoomi, Mahatmas or Masters, and claimed that she first met the Master Morya in the flesh in London in 1851. She said that Koot Hoomi was a Kashmiri Brahman educated in Europe and that Morya was a Rajput prince, and that they were part of a brotherhood of evolved beings whom she called the Masters of Wisdom, and who mostly lived in Tibet. Gurdjieff called these beings and others like them, the Inner Circle of Humanity. H.P.B. also described the Mahatmas as imbued with extraordinary powers as the result of their evolutionary development, and among these powers was the ability to communicate with her psychically. She herself was known to possess highly developed psychical faculties. *The Secret Doctrine*, she said, was transmitted to her psychically by the Mahatmas.

When H.P.B. moved the headquarters of the Theosophical Society from New York City where she founded it in 1875, to Bombay, India and then to Adyar (Madras), India, her activities came to the attention of the establishment that then ruled India.

Among the more prominent Englishmen who became interested in H.P.B. and her work were Alfred P. Sinnett, editor at the time of *The Pioneer*, then the largest English language newspaper in India, and Allen O. Hume, a career governmental official, Secretary to the British Government of India and founder of the Indian National Congress. In 1880, having become aware of H.P.B.'s psychical powers and hearing of her connection with her two teachers, the Masters Morya and Koot Hoomi, they wished, especially Mr. Sinnett, to be put in contact with these teachers. H.P.B. was doubtful but nevertheless agreed to try, attempting to apport a letter written by Mr. Sinnett to the Master, Koot Hoomi. To the surprise of H.P.B. Sinnett received a reply from Koot Hoomi, also transmitted by occult means, and from that a correspondence ensued.

There were in all a total of 148 letters received from these Masters between 1880 and 1884 when the correspondence stopped. Shortly thereafter Sinnett retired and returned from India to England. He took with him these letters which he had saved and stored in a wooden trunk and tin case. There, in 1910, he met Maud Hoffman, an American Shakespearean actress, who would later

---

[40] H. P. Blavatsky, "Mahatmas and Chelas", *The Theosophist* (July, 1884).

become his executrix. Hoffman at the time shared an apartment with Mabel Collins, channel for the theosophical classic: the occultly transmitted *Light on the Path*.

The letters themselves are a combination of personal correspondence between the Masters, and Sinnett and Hume, as well as documents, in the form of letters, containing substantive occult teachings. The Theosophical Society has since developed several courses of study around *The Mahatma Letters*.

5. The Curious Chronology of the Players and Events in the Mahatma Letters Drama [41]

Let us look now at the curious chronology of the players and events surrounding the timing of the editing of *The Mahatma Letters*.

April 5, 1919: Sinnett receives an honorarium presented at the house at 146 Harley Street, London. At that time Maud Hoffman resides at that address along with Dr. Maurice Nicoll and Dr. James Young who also used the house for their psychiatric practice. The three of them also jointly owned a weekend cottage at Chorley Wood, Bucks, where Dr. C. G. Jung and Dr. Kenneth Walker stayed as guests. Dr. Jung also stayed at 146 Harley Street.

November, 1919: The Tibetan Master, Djwhal Khul, a colleague of the Master Morya and the Master, Koot Hoomi, makes first contact with Alice A. Bailey. This takes place at the Kratona Institute of the Theosophical Society in Ojai, California. The first chapters of *Initiation, Human and Solar* are written, and the beginning of 27 years of channelled communication begins resulting in the publication of 25 books.

June 26, 1921: A.P. Sinnett dies in London. Maude Hoffman, who has tended him during his last illness is named executrix of his estate and his sole legatee. Hoffman thereby becomes "owner" of the Mahatma letters.

August, 1921: Hoffman decides to make public the Mahatma letters and chooses as their editor for publication, another theosophist, Alfred Trevor Barker. (Many years later, in 1939, the actual letters were given by Hoffman to the British museum where they can now be viewed.)

October, 1921: Trevor Barker, Maude Hoffman, Dr, Maurice Nicoll, Dr. Kenneth Walker and Dr. James Young become students of Ouspensky who had arrived in London from Constantinople in August, and holds forth at the Theosophical Hall at 38 Warwick Gardens.

---

[41] Dates and information cited are from Moore, "The Blavatsky-Gurdjieff Question" (f.n.2). Beryl Pogson, Maurice Nicoll, *A Portrait* (New York: Fourth Way Books, 1987), p.p. 63-69. James Moore, Gurdjieff, the *Anatomy of a Myth* (Shaftesbury: Element Books, 1991) p. 160. A.T. Barker ed., *The Mahatma Letters to A.P. Sinnett* (Adyar: Theosophical Publishing House, 1962 3rd ed.), prefaces.

All & Everything Conference 1998

February, 1922: Gurdjieff arrives in London where Barker, Hoffman, Nicoll, Walker and Young, among other of Ouspensky's followers hear Gurdjieff speak at 38 Warwick Gardens on Feb. 13, 1922, and again in March, 1922. They become his students.

September 30, 1922: Gurdjieff leases the *Chateau du Prieure des Basses Loges* at Fountainbleau-Avon as the site for his residential school. At this time Barker, Young and the wives of Gurdjieff and Ouspensky begin to work there to prepare the school to receive students. Hoffman arrives soon after. Barker is already editing the Mahatma letters. His work will be completed during the next 12 months.

October 17. 1922: Catherine Mansfield comes to live at the Prieure which will not officially open until mid-November.
November 4, 1922: Maurice Nicoll comes to live at the Prieure with his wife and baby.

Summer, 1923: Hoffman and, to all indications, Barker are still at the Prieure. Hoffman describes the activities there in an article in the New York Times of February 10, 1924 (see my Appendix).

September, 1923: Barker completes the text for publication of *The Mahatma Letters*.

December, 1923: *The Mahatma Letters* are published.

This chronology does not prove that Gurdjieff had a hand in editing *The Mahatma Letters*. Nor does it prove that Gurdjieff had any influence over his students Hoffman and Barker in their work with *The Mahatma Letters*. What it does attempt to show is that there was a much closer relationship between people in the theosophical movement and people who were students of Gurdjieff. In numerous cases they are the same people. It is also an attempt to show that Gurdjieff could very easily have influenced his students, and was on the scene while the work with the Letters was going on. Conversely, it would be naive to think that Gurdjieff knew nothing about the work with *The Mahatma Letters* in which his students, Hoffman and Barker, were engaged. From February 1922 through September 1923 when the Letters were being edited, Hoffman and Barker are students of Gurdjieff, both residing with him at the *Prieure* a good part of that time.

6. The Sirius Connection

In *Beelzebub's Tales*, Beelzebub/Gurdjieff gives us a clue to the location of his home planet Karatas, while explaining to Hassein how time is measured. He says,

"It is similar to our reckoning of a 'year' for our planet Karatas, which is the period of time between the nearest approach of the sun "Samos" to the sun 'Selos' and its next similar approach."[42]

---

[42] *Beelzebub's Tales to his Grandson*, p. 121.

Gurdjieff, Blavatsky and the Masters of Wisdom

Beelzebub is here describing a binary star system near to which the planet Karatas is linked, a system of two stars circling each other. Why did Gurdjieff choose a binary star system with which to link his home on Karatas? There are in the twentieth century many binary star systems known to astronomers, but the most well known of these by far is the binary star system, Sirius.

Sirius is the brightest star in the sky and it is often assumed that all the references to Sirius in folklore has this as its reason. In esoteric literature, however, Sirius is seen as an occult center of the Milky Way galaxy. About Sirius, the Tibetan, for example, as channelled by Alice Bailey says,

> "One great fact to be borne in mind is, that the initiations of the planet or of the solar system are but the preparatory initiations of admission into the greater Lodge on Sirius."[43]

John G. Bennett took the matter of Gurdjieff's connection to Sirius, as a matter of real importance. Bennett wrote of this in describing the difficulties Gurdjieff placed in front of the reader of *Beelzebub's Tales*:

"If Gurdjieff had intended his meaning to be readily accessible to every reader, he would have written the book differently. He himself used to listen to chapters read aloud and if he found that the key passages were taken too easily - and therefore almost inevitably too superficially - he would rewrite them in order, as he put it, to 'bury the dog deeper'. When people corrected him and said that he surely meant 'bury the bone deeper', he would turn on them and say it is not 'bones' but the 'dog' you have to find. The dog is Sirius the dog star, which stands for the spirit of wisdom in the Zoroastrian tradition."[44]

Although it is said that the expression "to bury the dog" is not unknown in Russian colloquialism, an actual Sirius connection should not be overlooked in view of the clue given to us by Gurdjieff about his home being connected to a binary star.

There are many enigmas about the star system Sirius which have not been satisfactorily answered by science. Not the least of these was the discovery by two French anthropologists in the 1930's, that a primitive African tribe, the Dogon, had knowledge of the binary nature of Sirius embedded in its folklore many centuries before confirmation by astronomers in 1862. Investigators open to the metaphysical possibilities have suggested a visitation to Earth by beings from the Sirius system.[45]" More conservative scientists have also recognized the mystery surrounding this seemingly impossible knowledge by the Dogon of the binary nature of Sirius, and have simply noted it without drawing conclusions.[46]

---

[43] Alice A. Bailey, *Initiation, Human and Solar* (New York: Lucis Publishing Company, 1922), p. 17.
[44] *Gurdjieff, Making a New World*, p. 274.
[45] Robert K. G. Temple, *The Sirius Mystery* (Rochester, Vermont: Destiny Books, 1976).
[46] Kenneth Brecher, "Sirius Enigmas" in Astronomy of the Ancients, ed. Kenneth Brecher (Boston: MIT Press, 1979), p.91.

All & Everything Conference 1998

7. The Missing Letter Referred to by Kenneth Walker

The aforementioned Dr. Kenneth Walker, who became an eminent London physician, surgeon and professor continued to work with and to write about the Gurdjieff teaching until his death in 1966, publishing several books. In his book, *A Study of Gurdjieff's Teaching*,[47] Walker tells of Gurdjieff's expertise as a teacher of sacred dance through which, along with special music, Gurdjieff also brought his teaching. Gurdjieff saw this as another method, suited to particular types of people who, through participation in these special dance and exercise techniques, can be helped to attain a heightened experiential state of awareness. Walker makes the following statement:

> "Indeed, in most European circles Gurdjieff was regarded not so much as a philosopher, but as one of the greatest living experts on the sacred dances of the East. What may be of interest to many readers is that in a letter written by Madame Blavatsky to one of the early members of the Theosophical Society, she foretells that the next great teacher of Eastern ideas in Europe will be an instructor in Oriental dancing."[48]

To help draw this connection, it should be mentioned that we are reminded by Gurdjieff, of how he wished to sign his authorship of *Beelzebub's Tales*. He subscribed it, "FINALLY, SIMPLY A TEACHER OF DANCING."[49]

8. Symbols, Elements, Triads, Octaves, Vibrations

The cosmology given out by Gurdjieff includes references to 1) symbols representing numbers, 2) the periodic table of the elements, especially hydrogen, nitrogen, oxygen and carbon, 3) triads, 4) octaves, and 5) vibrations. Ouspensky has masterfully pieced these together in *In Search of the Miraculous*, into a system with a rational cosmology that appeals to many students. All of these terms can also be found referenced In *The Secret Doctrine*,[50] sometimes related to the same ideas and sometimes used slightly differently. While many such terms have ancient sources, someone familiar with both the work of H.P.B. and of Gurdjieff is hard put to ignore a seeming connectedness between the two expositions.

9. Conversation with a Channel

Ghislaine Gualdi is a French woman who lives just outside Geneva, Switzerland. In 1984 her psychic abilities came to the attention of a prominent theosophist from Geneva, who helped her to develop these abilities for psychical contact. This resulted in Gualdi coming into contact through channelled communication with an entity who has chosen to call himself "Pastor" and who claims

---

[47] Kenneth Walker, *A Study of Gurdjieff's Teaching* (London: Jonathan Cape Ltd., 1957).
[48] *A Study of Gurdjieff's Teaching*, p. 152.
[49] *Beelzebub's Tales to his Grandson*, p. 50.
[50] *The Secret Doctrine* on 1) numeric symbols, ii 591-593, 2) elements ii 593, 627, 3) triads ii 591, 595, 4) octaves ii 627, 5) vibrations ii 562-566.

to be a minor initiate in what is known in theosophical circles as "the spiritual hierarchy." At the inception of her psychical work with "Pastor", Gualdi had only heard of theosophy and had never heard of Gurdjieff. This contact resulted in Gualdi becoming a public speaker as a channel for the entity "Pastor" over a 10 year period from 1984-1994 in public gatherings. These public talks, numbering in excess of 200, were given in French before audiences in southern France, French speaking Belgium and French speaking Switzerland. Some of the teachings given out by "Pastor", appear in the book, *La Conscience Cosmique*, published in France in 1990.[51]

I met Ghislaine Gualdi in 1988. On November 21, 1989, Nicolas Tereshchenko and I met with Gualdi in a private session at her home outside Geneva. Tereshchenko had the following exchange with Gualdi who, in light trance, spoke as the entity "Pastor":

> Tereshchenko: "Mr. Gurdjieff calls the 'heptaparaparshinokh' one of the primary cosmic laws, but he does not give, it seems to me, all the data necessary to understand it well. What must I know, in addition to what is given in Mr. Gurdjieff's work, in order to really understand this law in depth?"
>
> Pastor (in part): "The initiate you are talking about is a being who has been composed. Of course, he came on earth with his own spiritual dimension but, in fact, the Masters he has met have not created in him the spirituality he could radiate. We must know that he has been composed as far as the kind of intellectual radiance, as far as the kind of alchemical radiance which he could propose to people and to which he has initiated people.
>
> "This is to say that if the being you are talking about who you call Gurdjieff (although for us he has another name), had known totally free spiritual enfoldment, he would have given of his own being, of his own initiatic level. And what he would have given would have been, believe me, something entirely different. However, there was written in his stars, in his destiny, the fact that he would have to take on one destiny, to offer one message. And this was in direct resonance with the disobedience he had committed a very long time ago, a very long time ago in history.
>
> "This means, in fact, that his work was a service and at the same time also a karma, a kind of reverence he owed to humanity but especially to the Lodge to which he belongs. This is why he could not do anything else but to return to this Lodge, to return to see his Masters whom he had disobeyed. And, by the way, disobedience, originality, is something that characterized him even in the life he has known as Gurdjieff, all the way to the end of his days.
>
> "It is by this note that we could discover his disobedient nature or, if you wish, the final impact of his disobedience. Although I speak of disobedience, we must not see it as being an error. It is simply something that happens. It is almost unavoidable in, the development

---

[51] Pastor, *La Conscience Cosmique* (Paris: Editions Fernand Lanore, 1990).

of the initiate. I would say it is even desirable, because it is where we can see that he really exists, that he is building himself, that he is beginning to understand the universe and he is beginning to appropriate the divinity. Therefore, it is desirable. But, of course, this commits the individual to a certain kind of karma; this is also certain."

"So, to get back to the question, I would say that the teaching he gave rests on one hand, on the spiritual dimension he himself was, which he has developed throughout history. But, at the same time, his teaching was largely composed by the Masters he had met who ordered him to say things this way, to do things that way, and to give until such point and no further. This is why we can discern randomly in the texts, randomly in the lines that something is missing. Not because something is really missing, but rather because he did not have the permission or the command to give the complement of information."[52]

At the time of this contact, Gualdi had learned a bit more about theosophy, but still nothing about Gurdjieff. She stopped speaking publicly in 1994 on the instructions of "Pastor" who had completed the messages he wished to transmit. In the years since 1989 through the present, Ghislaine Gualdi has become my good friend. I vouch for her complete honesty and credibility.

Toward the end of the 1989 exchange between Tereshchenko and Gualdi, Pastor went on to say,

> "If you want more, call Gurdjieff, be truly Gurdjieff's disciple. Then, if you show yourself to him as his disciple (and when I say 'his disciple' it is not in the meaning of membership), I would rather say show yourself as a cup that strives to join another cup in order for that cup to tip over and fill it. Then you are out of the conditionings the Masters who composed Gurdjieff who composed his service, insisted upon. You are out of the orders which conditioned Gurdjieff. Therefore, he does not have to keep his word either to the Masters, or to the plan, or to the necessity of the present civilization. There is simply a Master and a disciple. And the one who will be the limit of the transmission of the teaching will not be the Master but will be the disciple. So, if you want more, call him.

> "However, you will tell me, 'But I cannot call Gurdjieff. How can I get in contact with Gurdjieff? Does it mean that I must become either telepathic or that I could receive a teaching myself?'

> "Then I will tell you that there are a thousand and one ways to be in correspondence, whether with a Master, with a simple initiate, or with the mind of the Hierarchy, or with the mind of the Solar Hierarchy, or with God's mind let us suppose. There exist a thousand ways.

"But generally, the method the Master uses is the one the Egyptian initiate used to use, and it is what they used to call 'the prophetic dream' or 'the sacred dream'. This is to say that we must put

---

[52] Seymour Ginsburg & Jacqueline Beccai, eds. and translator, *A Commentary on Gurdjieff's Teaching, and Other Matters* (Fort Lauderdale: privately published, 1989).

ourselves into a deep meditative state, during which we do not predestine ourselves to meet the Master or find the answer to this or that question. We - try simply to open ourselves, to be an absence, to be a cup waiting to be filled.

"From the moment we begin to be in that state, and supposing that during all the subsequent days we have called the Master or we have called the Hierarchy, and we have sent the question or we have sent the enigma that preoccupies us, at the moment we present ourselves in the universe with this openness, the answer automatically comes.

"The answer comes in different ways: either through a symbolic dream, or by an apparition who says something, or by a film which seems to unfold and explains everything, or simply as if nothing appeared to be happening but the individual finds himself to be guided toward a book which contains the answer, or he picks up for the nth time the same book he was studying and inside a sentence, because of his multiple vision, he succeeds to decode the mystery and to obtain the answer. So the way of administering the answer will depend entirely on the disciple and on the most subtle antenna which reaches him in the easiest way.

"This is to say that you must not expect to hear something, to read it in a book which appears, or to see Gurdjieff or his superiors appear and speak to you. It can happen in an entirely different manner."[53]

10. Conversation with a Guru

My acquaintance with the Gurdjieff teaching came first through a contact with Sri Madhava Ashish (born Alexander Phipps) who I met in India in 1978, and who became my mentor. I met him because of his co-authorship with his guru Sri Krishna Prem of Man, *The Measure of All Things*,[54] and his authorship of *Man, Son of Man*[55]. These two books are commentaries on Volumes I and II of *The Secret Doctrine*, and contributed in helping me to understand what H.P.B. wrote.

Madhava Ashish is a man whom many people believe had attained a higher state of human consciousness during his life here. When I first visited Ashish in 1978, he told me that the practical teaching to which *The Secret Doctrine* refers had been given out by Gurdjieff since 1915, and that I should return to the West and find a group of people with whom to study Gurdjieff's teaching. On subsequent annual visits Ashish would talk often about Gurdjieff, whom he said is not an ordinary person. Gurdjieff, unlike Ashish's guru Sri Krishna Prem, had not attained a higher state of consciousness during this life. Gurdjieff is, according to Ashish, "the great Russian-Armenian Bodhisattva", who was sent in to again bring the practical teaching. And this

---

[53] *Ibid*.
[54] Sri Krishna Prem and Sri Madhava Ashish, *Man the Measure of All Things* (Wheaton: Theosophical Publishing House), 1969.
[55] Sri Madhava Ashish, *Man, Son of Man* (Wheaton: Theosophical Publishing House, 1970).

All & Everything Conference 1998

is how Ashish always referred to Gurdjieff, with great reverence and respect. "Remember", he often told me, "Gurdjieff always 'is', never 'was'."

In a letter to Professor Constance Jones read out at this conference last year, Ashish wrote:
"On p. 434, the last sentence of the (anonymous) Biographical sketch, 'He is buried in the cemetery of Avon at Fountainbleau.' <u>Please</u> 'His body is buried,' or 'His planetary body is buried.' Not 'He'. G never was buried. G is."[56]

I once asked Ashish how he knew of Gurdjieff's status as a Bodhisattva, one who has returned or been sent in to help humanity. I asked him how he knew who Gurdjieff is?

"Gurdjieff will tell you," Ashish said. "Pay attention to your dreams."

© Copyright 1998 - Seymour B. Ginsburg - All Rights Reserved

---

[56] H. J. Sharp ed., *The International Humanities Conference*: *All & Everything '97, The Proceedings* (Littlehampton, England: privately published, 1997).

Appendix - Taking the Life Cure in Gurdjieff's School

TAKING THE LIFE CURE IN GURDJIEFF'S SCHOOL

An Intimate Description of the Russian's Institute in France Whose Aim Is the All-Round, Harmonious Development of Man

By MAUD HOFFMAN.

DURING this last Summer the inhabitants of Fontainebleau and Avon, in France, and the Summer visitors at the hotels flocked to the old Prieuré des Basses Loges to see the Saturday evening demonstrations of the work done there by the pupils of the Gurdjieff Institute. The demonstrations are given in a large aerodrome, erected by the pupils, which comfortably accommodates more than sixty pupils and several hundred visitors. The stage is large enough for forty people to take part in the exercises at the same time, and a large space, covered with Persian carpets, remains free in the centre.

The pupils sit around this square space on sheepskins and cushions in the Oriental fashion. The interior of this study house has been decorated with color, drawing, stencilling and designs. The whole of the extensive canvas ceiling—and every buttress, beam and space is covered. The colors are rich and vivid, as are the windows. All the work of painting and designing has been done by the pupils themselves.

The demonstrations are unique in their presentation. They consist of movements which include the sacred gymnastics of the esoteric schools, the religious ceremonies of the Antique Orient and the ritual movements of monks and dervishes—besides the folk dances of many a remote community.

The movements are not only bewildering in their complexity, and amazing in the precision of their execution, but rich in diversity, harmonious in rhythm, and exceedingly beautiful in the gracefulness of the postures, which are quite unknown to Europe. To the accompaniment of mystical and inspiring music, handed down from remote antiquity, the sacred dances are executed with deeply religious dignity, which is profoundly impressive.

Philosophy of the Movement.

You may or may not know about the philosophy which lies at the back of all the activities of this unique community. The American papers have called them the "Forest Philosophers" and you listen carefully to catch any of the teaching. But the nearest that you get to philosophy for many days is to make the acquaintance of a good-natured, but not well-pointed, fox terrier, with a large body and a small head, named 'Philos.' You venture to ask if there are any lectures or classes. Quietly you are told, without further comment, that there are none. After this you think a while and observe the people around you. They are all English and Americans. Where then are the Russians—that little band of people whom Gurdjieff led safely out of Russia when the revolution broke out? Later you find that everything that is done in this place of work has a meaning. You work hard—not for the sake of the work—but for the sake of what the work evokes in you, for the sake of activity, for the purpose of making efforts, and for the purposes of self-observation. You soon begin to suspect that this place may be an outer court of one of those old mystery schools about which you have read, over the portals of your business. If you are a Summer visitor wanting to see the demonstration you will be asked to come on Saturday evening at 8 o'clock. But if you have come all the way from America solely for the purpose of living at the institute you probably are expected and you will be admitted at once into courtyard with its fountain and duck pond and the old chateau standing there close to the gate. As you cross the courtyard, and as you enter the house, you will have a feeling that, at any rate, there will be esthetic satisfaction here, for you see at a glance that the house is an excellent example of the smaller type of French chateau.

You probably have already heard that it was formerly a hunting lodge belonging to Mme. de Maintenon, before that there is the tradition of a Carmelite monastery. More recently it was the property of Dreyfus, who gave it to his avocat, Labori, in payment for his defense in the famous trial. For several years past it has had the fate of so many historic mansions and has been let as a Summer residence to wealthy Americans.

You are left to wait in the first salon, one of three which is furnished in the Empire period, and you go at once to the window, where there is a lovely view of the terrace and the extensive lawns beyond, with their fountains surrounded by beds of flowering plants and great forest trees, for the whole of the estate of forty acres is a part of the forest. Beyond the lawns is a long alley of formal lime trees, leading to a round bathing pool in a basin of stone. From here short paths lead to the top of a little knoll where you can sit and view the grounds and the chateau on one side and the meadows on the other.

During the warm days of July and August the piano was brought out of doors and we practiced our gymnastics and dances in the shelter of the lime tree alley. From 10 to 11—from 3 to 4—from 9 to any hour in the night.

Pay According to Means.

Presently some one takes you up to the "Ritz" corridor, so named because of its beautiful furnishings, or in the beautiful "Monks" corridor above, so named for its cloisterlike appearance. In the Ritz the rooms are luxurious, while in the Monks' corridor they are comfortable and quaint. All pay according to means. Those who are rich must pay very well indeed, for there are many among the pupils who cannot pay at all.

Round about midday there is a meal. At noon, if you have risen at 6, at 1 if at 7, at half-past 11 if you have risen at 8. You have probably arrived in time for this meal. If your room is in the Monks' corridor you take a hasty glance round at the red brick floor, the old French chintzes on the walls and furniture, and the heavenly forest garden without, before you hurry down to the dining room. This is a beautifully proportioned room with red hangings and fine old paintings. Three windows overlook the grounds and a door leads on to the terrace.

If the day is warm you can have your bread and soup on the terrace, or in the dining room, or you can take it to your

The Gurdjieff system aims at an all-round and harmonious development of man. It is a place where every one can be an artist or an artisan, and the material with which he works are his own mental, emotional and instinctive energies. As most of the energy in modern life flows into mental activity, much physical activity is needed, and many acute emotional conflicts are required to divert this energy into instinctive and emotional channels.

The claim made by the Gurdjieff Institute is that, by the reactionary effect of harmonious movements on the psyche, man may hope to progress to that balanced development which has been arrested by the cramping of an unnatural and mechanical civilization.

But the process toward a balanced development of being is not confined to gymnastics and dancing. Every kind of manual labor, within doors and out-of-doors, is performed by the students, both men and women doing all kinds of work. Combined with the physical work are difficult mental exercises; and the emotions are kept active by the natural reactions in each person to an environment and conditions that are in many ways the reversal of most of their fixed ideas and habits.

Irregularity a Principle.

If you wished to visit the Gurdjieff Institute, you would, on leaving Fontainebleau Station, turn down the hill to the right toward Avon and the old Prieuré des Basses Loges instead of to the left toward Fontainebleau and the palace. At the foot of the hill at the crossroads on the right hand corner is the gatehouse of the old Prieuré, now known as the Gurdjieff Institute, and Chateau du Prieuré. You will see the little door in the wall and you will know it is the door you are seeking, because over the bell on the right are the words "Sonnez-fort."

It will be well if you take the advice and ring loudly and long. Your arrival may correspond with that phase of the life within which does not provide an attendant at the gate. Unlike other communities the gate-keeper is not a fixed and invariable post. Had you arrived any time between the end of last August and the middle of October your ring would have been instantly answered. During that period the gates had keepers, both the front gate and the back gate at the end of the far garden, six minutes' walk from the chateau. Before that time there was no gate-keeper, since that time there has been no gate-keeper.

In the meaning attached to this irregularity, which arises at the very entrance to the Gurdjieff Institute, lies a crucial principle of the enterprise. It is a place where habits are changed, fixed ideas are broken up, mechanical routines do not exist, and adaptability to ever-changing forms and modes of life is practiced. So "sonnez-fort" and wait. Some one passing within may open for you. It is really the "kitchen boy's" duty. There is a different kitchen boy each day and it is the most onerous job in the place. He may not be able to drop what he is doing at once. Presently he will appear with a large apron tied round him—possibly not a clean apron. He may be anybody, the editor of a London paper, a Harley Street specialist, a court musician or a Russian lawyer. England, America, Russia, France, Poland, Georgia, Armenia and several other nations are represented here.

nourishing and sufficient, but useless conventions of service and elaboration of dishes, food and courses are absent. You receive your food from the hands of the cook in the kitchen, and after you have eaten it, you wash your plate and cup, and there is an end of it. In the matter of food there is an opportunity to "change habit."

As you are a visitor your soup has been brought to you, but you decide to fend for yourself for the pudding or fruit, and make your way through the pantry to the kitchen. It is crowded with Russians whose dining room is on the other side. Seated at the kitchen table, with his hat on and an overcoat, is Mr. Gurdjieff. He is having his dinner—one dish only, and coffee, surrounded by the noise and bustle of the kitchen. It is crowded with people, among them the Russians, whose dining room is on the other side of the kitchen, past the dairy, to what was probably the servants' hall.

Work and Effort; Nothing Easy.

When you enter, Mr. Gurdjieff greets you and makes you welcome, with a smile that has both sweetness and spiritquality. You get a first impression of a nature of great kindness and sensitiveness. Later you learn that in him is combined strength and delicacy, simplicity and subtlety. That he is more awake than any one you have ever known.

Your first evening in the study house is a never-to-be-forgotten experience. Here from nine o'clock to twelve, to one, perhaps to two o'clock the work goes on. When the obligatory exercises begin you receive a shock. You find yourself sitting up, leaning forward and receiving impacts from that moving mass of energy on the stage. The obligatory exercises contain every movement which is later worked up and used in the various special groups and dances. After the first hour of exercises—when the blood is tingling in every accustomed and unaccustomed cell of their bodies—the pupils rest on the goat-skins and this is the moment chosen for the most difficult kind of mental concentration.

The key words of the Gurdjieff Institute are "work," and "effort." Nothing is made easy in this place. Always the task is a little beyond your strength—you must make an effort; the supply of work material runs short, you must invent—make effort; the time is curtailed—hasten!—make effort; you have reached the limit of your strength and are exhausted—then is the moment to make effort—and tap the higher energies and the source of Will.

Those who are intellectually powerful and physically and emotionally weak cannot be considered successful. Their structures are topheavy. The saints found only incomplete illumination by means of an over-developed emotionality on the path of devotion. Exquisite movements alone, or physical strength alone cannot give knowledge or perfect being. At the Gurdjieff Institute an attempt can be made to fill in deficiencies, correct heredity and habit and to balance knowledge and being. Incidentally and as a by-product of these efforts you renew your energies and your youth and make yourself more efficient for life.

"LA GARCONNE" BANNED.

BUDAPEST courts do not consider Victor Margueritte's much-discussed novel, "The Bachelor Girl," fit for general reading in Hungary, as the translator was recently found guilty of an offense against public morals and fined 30,000 crowns (about $1).

Gurdjieff, Blavatsky and the Masters of Wisdom - Questions & Answers

Sophia Wellbeloved: I really want to go back to what you began with, about the *Tales* and *The Secret Doctrine*. I have been looking at the structure of All and Everything, and there is a tremendous parallel. The bit that you read out at the beginning of the second volume, you can find correspondence in Gurdjieff. It is the function of the *Tales* to do that. You can also make correspondence between volumes three and four of *The Secret Doctrine* referred to by Madame Blavatsky, and *Life is real only then, when "I am"*. I am not saying it is a rewrite, but he knew. The other thing is that Alice Bailey said there was an astrological key to *The Secret Doctrine*.

Sy Ginsburg: You are realizing my hope because I do not presume to be an academic. I am hopeful that people like you will look into this further and develop these correspondences.

Nicolas Tereshchenko: As Sophia has mentioned the third and fourth volume of *The Secret Doctrine*, I do, in fact, have the third volume of *The Secret Doctrine*. I am not talking about the five volume edition. I have the two original ones plus a third one which is supposed to be a continuation of it, and that is the volume in which there is a page and a whole article devoted to the four elements which she calls hydrogen, carbon, oxygen and nitrogen, which is presumably where Mr. Gurdjieff got those terms when he was teaching Ouspensky and their groups. It is surprising that Ouspensky never found that himself. I have a question: The fourth volume, could it not be considered the lessons of the esoteric school which have also been published, at least as part of the projected fourth volume of *The Secret Doctrine*?

Sy Ginsburg: There are two parts to your question. The first part is that Annie Besant, who was the head of The Theosophical Society from the beginning of this century and certainly the most powerful figure in it until her death in the mid nineteen thirties, recognized that there was this prediction for a third volume. So, what she did was to collect a bunch of articles that H.P.B. had written, and had them published as the third volume. I can tell you that since that time many theosophical scholars have simply dismissed this. That is, they recognized what this is, but did not see it as the predicted third volume. My own opinion is that since what was transmitted through her said that the third volume would contain a practical teaching, in some of those articles I do not see the practical teachings that we have gotten from Mr. Gurdjieff. I see it somewhat in The Voice of the Silence, which is a different document.

In so far as the teachings of the esoteric school of the T.S., I am not a member of that school although I know a number of people who are. From what I can observe as an outsider, I do not see it clearly described. I realize that the papers of the esoteric school were published and appear now as part of the Collected Writings of Madame Blavatsky. But at least for me, I do not see the clearly laid out teaching about self-awareness, or as I mentioned earlier, the way Madhava Ashish put it, "being aware of being aware". One can also find this in the teachings of some of the famous

Gurdjieff, Blavatsky and the Masters of Wisdom - Questions & Answers

Indian gurus like in the teachings of Ramana Maharshi and the teachings of Nisargadatta. These are all, in my view, the practical teaching that was clearly expressed to us in western terms by Mr. Gurdjieff.

Stefano Elmazis: I wrote something about Sirius in my magazine. I have a magazine in Greece. We have a very great subject about Sirius in the last excavations in the tomb of Phillip, the father of Alexander the Great. The ancient Greeks, the ancient Macedonians knew about Sirius. I cannot say more about it right now, but perhaps I will send by the Internet this article in English.

Sy Ginsburg: Wonderful! I look forward to it.

Bert Sharp: You have brought back a memory. I liked your paper very much. Some years ago I wrote a letter to Gnosis, in which I pointed out it was intriguing to me that Gurdjieff and C. G. Jung were very prominent in certain circles at the same time. But in the all of the work about either of them or by either of them, there is no cross reference whatsoever. This struck me as strange when one could see, or at least I could see, that Nicoll was being trained by Jung as his representative in England if not in Europe, and then suddenly he moves to Gurdjieff and is trained by Gurdjieff and teaches. The letter that I sent described this inferring that perhaps this was the way the Masters of Wisdom worked. As a result of which, you wrote to me. Nicolas wrote to me. And now we have these conferences. That is what I call meaningful coincidence.

Sy Ginsburg: Yes, indeed.

James Moore: Bert, in relation to your point about the lack of interface between Jung and Gurdjieff, I just invite peoples' attention to a new book in the Jungian genre called, The Aryan Christ. Although, I think it is full of misconceptions, it has in the footnotes to it, allusion to a primary document, one that I don't know, which treats of the events around the critical time that James Carruthers Young and Maurice Nicoll left the Jungian persuasion and went to Gurdjieff. So that I think you are quite right in saying that cross allusion in published works is very, very sparse. But I would not say totally absent in correspondence. There is quite a struggle, an ideological struggle between Jung and Gurdjieff that is beginning to come to light in correspondence.

Bert Sharp: Thank you very much, James, for that. I have recently read The Aryan Christ, and I would agree with you in your very polite comments. In many cases he doesn't know what he is talking about. But it contains a lot of material and it put me onto the concepts of cryptamnesia, and also onto Theodore Flournoy.

Andrew Rawlinson: Sy, I am sure you are aware of the controversy about the letters apported by Blavatsky. The strongest evidence is that they appeared in a cabinet that was a revolving cabinet just outside her room. The charge that was made by a certain Emma Coloumb, who was her secretary and companion, was that this cabinet went into her bedroom. There was a fire and it was never proved. I am not trying to judge the factuality of that over a century later. All I am saying is that that charge was made at the time, and how is it going to affect your argument. Any person, not necessarily you, will say that they were forgeries.

Sy Ginsburg: There is a lot about that. In fact, it is related to the Society for Psychical Research here in England. I think that Society still exists, and it was quite prominent toward the end of the nineteenth century. They sent an investigator from England to India to investigate the charges of the Coloumbs. They were a husband and wife. The wife worked as a housekeeper on the Theosophical estate in Adyar, and the husband, I believe, was a carpenter. They are the ones who brought these charges. It put Blavatsky into disrepute. It brought her back to England actually to face these charges. It was quite interesting to me, and this is the other side of the story. I don't have the exact details, but it turned on handwriting analysis. A handwriting analysis was made about 10 years ago and it turned out that what was reported by this investigator for the Society for Psychical Research, Richard Hodson, was not correct, and the Society retracted its charges against Blavatsky. That's the other side of the story. I have no doubt that this kind of thing will always remain in dispute, whenever we are dealing with these kinds of so-called psychical events. I personally went and looked at the Mahatma Letters. You can see them in the rare documents room of the British Museum. It doesn't mean that they are genuine. It doesn't mean that somebody didn't forge them. I don't know. But I know this. I know that there are very significant teachings in the Mahatma Letters. Whether Blavatsky wrote them herself or not, I don't know. The other thing I just want to mention is that *The Secret Doctrine*, I don't know how many of you have looked at *The Secret Doctrine*, but it is a giant of a book, about thirteen hundred pages of small type and footnotes, probably a lot more words than the *Tales*, and with a huge amount of footnotes. It was all done in two years. That doesn't mean that Blavatsky could not have done it herself. But some of the references in there are so obscure, it is hard for me to understand how someone, wherever she was, working for two years, could have produced that document with that information. In order to make your own judgement about that, you will have to become somewhat familiar with the document itself, and it raises this question of how did this person produce that in a two year period.

Andrew Rawlinson: I heard that she had help in research, but there were two questions. One was to remind people that there was this charge of forgery. The second question which is more interesting is, even if someone thought they were forgeries, would it matter. With the kind of correspondences that Sophia just pointed to between two volumes of the work, would they stand regardless of the authenticity of the documents. That's the question. I am not asking for an answer.

Bert Sharp: What comes to me at this moment is what was said, I mentioned this to James earlier today, was said yesterday by him and by one or two other people. A key question is: Why are we here? Another key question or fact perhaps is that we are all looking for something. That then gives us another key question: What is it that causes and drives us to look for something? What's it all about?

Sy Ginsburg: I would just like to go back to the question I raised at the beginning which is from René Zuber. Who are you Mr. Gurdjieff?

First Open Forum - Secrecy and the Work

Facilitator: Paul Beekman Taylor

Professor Paul Beckman Taylor lived for some years with Jean Toomer in New York and Pennsylvania as a young boy, studied with Gurdjieff in Paris after World War 2, before turning to a teaching career in Medieval Germanic languages, first in Iceland and for the past thirty years in Geneva, where he lives with his wife and two teenage children. He retired from teaching in 1997. His latest book, *Shadows of Heaven: Gurdjieff and Toomer*, has just been published by Samuel Weiser, Inc.

The first open forum was introduced by the reading of a short paper by Bert Sharp with the title "Secrets."

Secrets

"These are the secret words which the Living Jesus spoke and Didymos Judas Thomas wrote: And he said: Whoever finds the explanation of these words will not taste death.

Jesus said: Let him who seeks, not cease seeking until he; finds, and when lie finds, he will be troubled, and when he has been troubled, he will marvel and he will reign over All.

Jesus said: If those who lead you say to you: "See, the Kingdom is in heaven." then the birds of the heaven will precede you. If they say to you "It is in the sea," then the fish will precede you. But the Kingdom is within you and it is without you. If you know yourselves, then you will be known and you will know that you are the sons of the Living Father. But if you do not know yourselves, then you are in poverty and you are poverty."

Let us now turn for a moment to some of Goethe's notes.

"The psychology matches what it comprehends. The importance of recognizing that the other person is different, has different needs."

"In order that the individual consciousness can arise from the collective psyche, it has to be a different consciousness."

So humanity is a collection of individual physical bodies each with their own partly developed consciousness. And where is humanity now? As C. G. Jung said (CW Vol. 4, p. 193).

"The modern man does not want to be guided by a creed or dogma, he has now reached the stage at which he wants to understand. To no longer think and act as a child but as a man. But he is not yet ready to take on this responsibility."

This for me relates to the decline of the conventional church and also to members of cults who cling to their so-called secrets so as to feel superior, to indulge in the ego trip they need. This is in fact regression of the individual who is unable to make the big step of becoming a responsible individual so as to be used by something higher, regression to the stages of early childhood.

From early times society has been based on initiation rites which are usually secret. Having passed through the rite, the boy becomes a man, often having been given so-called secret knowledge All that really happened was that the men told him, now you are a man and so he acted in the future as if he was one.

The culmination of such secret societies and grades of initiation into secrets can be seen, perhaps in the Rosicrucian Society. One of the founders of this was Walter Maier. Writing in the early 1600's, he recounts that is presumably a symbolic journey at the end of which he returns to the house of Saturn from whence he began his journey, and there finds what he had been seeking, Mercurius. He only mentions their "numerous conversations" without disclosing their content. This is surprising because this is the Great Teacher, the Light Bringer who knows the secret of transformation and immortality. But Maier is silent. He Is the Keeper of the Secret. Why does he have to keep the secret? Is it because he considers it would be harmful to the uninitiated? Is it because he considers they would not understand it? Is it to make himself feel superior as a being "in the know?"

What are now known of the so-called Rosicrucian secrets does nothing to explain why they were so hushed up. It is of no consequence to keep them secret. This is in fact true of most "mysteries" of the early church which quickly turned into "sacraments" and so lay open to all in the rite.

Andreas Rosencreutz used as a motto for his "Chymical Wedding"–"Mysteries profaned and made public fade and lose their grace. Therefore cast not pearl before swine nor spread roses for the ass." Is this a motive for keeping secrets?

But I think we need to go deeper. Once our consciousness reached the stage at which we invented sin in the sense that conscience suggested one course of action which our developing consciousness, our superficial desires suggested another, psychic concealment arose, repression. We had secrets from then on. Such secrets did have the advantage of giving us a feeling of being separate, of being different, the beginning of the development of individuality eventually leading to observing "I". But too many secrets, being too different from others, behaving too differently from the promptings of buried conscience, could lead to breakdown and regression.

But let us go deeper still. To quote again C. G. Jung (Vol. 10, p 468, para. 886)

First Open Forum - Secrecy and the Work

"Esotericism means mystification. Yet we never know the real secrets, even the so-called esotericists do not know them. Esotericists - at least earlier - were supposed not to reveal their secrets. But the real secrets cannot be revealed. Nor is it possible to make an "Esoteric" science out of them, for the simple reason that they are not known. What are called esoteric secrets are mostly artificial secrets, not real ones. Man needs to have secrets, and since he has no notion of the real ones he fakes them. But the real ones come to him out of the depths of the unconscious, and then he may reveal things which he ought really to have kept secret. Here again we see the numinous character of the reality in the background. It is not we who have secrets, it is the real secrets who have us."

In other words, the real secrets link with the fully functioning Higher Mind which we normally have no conscious connection with. Once the lower mind is put in proper order, however, and the connection is made by Higher Mind and we are momentarily conscious in Higher Mind, this is and has to be a secret, simply because it is inexpressible.

* * *

Paul Beekman Taylor was then introduced by Marlena Buzzell and he began with the question whether such forums should be recorded or not. Those present agreed that a suitable compromise would be for all four forums to be recorded and for the names of the contributors given for inclusion unless someone wished not to be identified, in which case they would simply say for the record that they wished their name not to be included in the proceedings. Their question or comments would, however be included.

Then, after quoting Matthew 13: 10-13 - "To you it is given to know the mysteries of the kingdom of heaven, but to them it is not given... Seeing they do not see, and hearing they do not know" – Taylor made a few dilatory remarks about the history of secrecy in the Western European intellectual history. He noted that beginnings (Genesis), ends (Doomsday) and the process of life between (Providence) are necessarily secret. All things "sacred" are necessarily clothed in some secrecy, and to the innocent and the saintly, all things are sacred.

Since the Age of Exploration, and particularly during the Industrial Revolution, the sacred has been secularized, and all secrets of life are challenges to scientific scrutiny. The worst of secrets, as Gurdjieff's chapter "America" implies, are social and psychological, the secret weaknesses whose publicity people fear.

To open the Forum discussion, Marlena directed attention to the place in *Beelzebub's Tales* where Beelzebub visits Hadji-Asvatz-Troov with Hadji-Bogga-Eddin. Chris Thompson was asked to read the passage, which begins on page 901.

Chris Thompson; This is extremely serendipitous, but I happen to have the book open at the right page. You will remember it was about the boil:

All & Everything Conference 1998

"Can you picture for yourself, my dear boy, my situation then? What could I reply to him?"

"For the second time that day, I could not on account of this terrestrial being, see any way out of the situation that had arisen."

"This time there was mixed in this state, so unusual, for me, my 'being-Hikhdjnapar,' or, as your favourites say there, 'pity' for that terrestrial three-brained being, chiefly because he was suffering through me."

"And this was because I was then clearly aware that if I spoke a few words to him, not only would he be calmed, but thanks to them, he would even understand that the fact that no boil was forming on my left leg proved the truth and precision of his adored science still more."

"I had full moral right to tell him the truth about myself, because by his attainments he was already 'Kalmanuior,' that is, a three-brained being of that planet with whom it is not forbidden us from Above to be frank."

"But at that moment I could in no way do this, because there was also present there the dervish Hadji-Bogga-Eddin who was still an ordinary terrestrial three-brained being, concerning whom already long before, it was forbidden under oath from Above to the beings of our tribe to communicate true information to any one of them on any occasion whatsoever."

"This interdiction on the beings of our tribe was made chiefly because it is necessary for the three-brained beings of your planet 'knowledge-of-being."

"And any information, even if true, gives to beings in general only 'mental knowledge," as I have already once told you, always serves beings only as a means to diminish their possibilities of acquiring this knowledge-of-being."

"And since the sole means left to these unfortunate three-brained beings of your planet for their complete liberation from the consequences of the properties of the organ Kundabuffer are just this Knowledge-of-Being, therefore this command was given to the beings of our tribe under oath concerning the beings of the earth."

"And that is why, my boy, I did not just then in front of the dervish Bogga-Eddin, decide to explain to this worthy terrestrial sage Hadji-Asvatz-Troov, the real reason of his failure."

Keith Buzzell; You need to continue, because he does say something.

Chris Thompson: "But as both dervishes were waiting for my reply, I had in any case to tell them something, and therefore, addressing Hadji-Asvatz Troov, I then told them only as follows:

"Venerable Hadji-Asvatz-Troov! If you agree to have my answer not now but a little later, then I swear by the cause of my arising that I will give you an answer which will fully satisfy you. You

First Open Forum - Secrecy and the Work

will be convinced not only that your beloved science is the truest of all sciences, but that also that since the great scientists, the saints Cho-Kil-Tez and choo-Tro-Pel, you are the greatest scientist of the Earth."

John Perrot: First of all, what I wanted to say has been substantially covered by Keith, but is there anybody here, because I have not heard it yet, who really does believe that some secrets that they clearly need to know are being withheld in any way by anyone and would be happy to give us their reasons for perceiving things in this way? Is there anyone like that?

Keith Buzzell: I think this comes close to the Midas of concern. I guess that is the perception. It is not an uncommon perception that within this Work there are those who know certain things and who, because they have come to certain conclusions that they are privy to themselves, do not share them. There is that perception among some people that has produced a great deal of difficulty, a great deal of misunderstanding within many, many people who value this Work from their own perspective. That was one of the reasons why it seems perhaps an interesting and useful exploration to go into that in this kind of Open Forum, to address that question specifically. Because, why else would they be concerned about secrets?

Sy Ginsburg: Well, we have not spoken about the abuse of so-called secret knowledge. It is my opinion that there are certain occult secrets. Now maybe people who are here know some of them. I will just mention the occult mechanics of energy transformation which is spoken about at great length in Gurdjieff's teaching, and in other teaching as well. It is also my opinion that certain people who have become familiar with some of these so-called secrets use them to manipulate people like their students or disciples. So this is a danger which I think we need to recognize. I don't have any particular answer to it, but I recognize that this is a danger.

Nicholas Tereshchenko: Well, this is a very difficult question, this question of secrets, because certainly, even without mixing them up with sacred things like staffs with serpents, there are certain things which have not been known to everybody. For example, I am quite sure that it would be not a good thing at all if everybody knew how to make an atom bomb in their kitchen, which I believe is possible. But coming back to secrecy in the Work, I do know of people who have been refused answers in the first instance. I myself have been told that on at least two occasions that you would not understand. And when I challenged the person, OK, if you think I won't understand the answer to my question, let's draw the Enneagram on the sand and we will see who knows more about it. But he would not take the challenge, because he knew perfectly well that at the particular moment, I happened to know a bit more about the Enneagram which I had been studying, than he does. I also know that in the Work there are supposed to be secrets to be kept from certain people and whatever. And I do know at least one case when a person has been threatened with expulsion from his group if he continues to have friendly relations with another person. Now that is what I call the bad secrecy in the Work. I also know that it is extremely difficult to get into certain groups. They are kept secret. People who know where the groups are, are not supposed to reveal it. Beelzebub was not supposed to reveal that he was an extraterrestrial, or not supposed to reveal where these things are or whatever, and it has to be done in some roundabout way. Until recently I had a problem because some people are writing to me and asking me to help them find a group. Until recently I had a friend who had a group of her own. She had been with Mr. Gurdjieff for some 15 years. But, unfortunately, she is going blind and no longer has groups. So now I have a problem where to direct her people. And perhaps someone here can tell me. What do I do with the people who want help in finding a group?

Unidentified: I have to disagree with what has just been expressed. It is my understanding that real secrets cannot be expressed in words. They can only be demonstrated. And it is inevitably acquisition of someone not telling me something, something you need to know. Yet, if it is demonstrated and if nothing happens when you demonstrate it, it is not a good demonstration. I am not at all concerned about people having some secret in words, and as to a school that can't be found, it does not need to be found. And there are plenty of schools that make their existence available. You can find them on the Internet, and that says nothing at all about the quality of the teaching.

Unidentified: The way I received the Work was through a particular form and sequence which, as time goes by, I value more and more. I do not feel things were withheld from me, but there was a form and there was a sequence. I have the feeling that those times have changed. And I would like to know first of all if you feel that way? I almost think that there is a different need. There is not the luxury of that past time. My husband and I have travelled to different groups and, from my point of view, because of my training, it seems that there is a little bit of this and a little bit of that. I don't perceive a form and sequence. And I don't know if that is because my foot is nailed to the ground with that form and sequence I was brought up with or if times have changed. I think these ideas are coming differently. I would like to hear what you say about that.

Keith Buzzell: I think Chris has already read how I would understand that. In context, it is Being that is the requirement. There is no short way to that. One must have a certain level of Being in order to go further. There are no shortcuts. In that context, I would say we are really living in a more fractured, more fragmented time. It is even more important that we hold to a form and sequence that makes it possible for those people with genuine interest not to be misled into misidentifying bits and pieces of form and sequence. There is no substitute. A child cannot become 18 years old. They cannot jump from Physics 101 to 105, and not misapply it. To me, it would be analogous to this. There is this sense of urgency among many young people. They want to know, they need to know, they wish to know. And there is so much more out there in one form or another. I choose to think that the electronic media are typically a malevolent source of data, because they pay no attention to Being, none whatsoever. In fact, they do what they can to fracture that Being. So this why, I would go back to the reasoning of the Venerable Hadji-Asvatz-Troov, that interface there that Gurdjieff places so clearly, so vividly because here is Bogga-Eddin. He is right there. What do I do? What do I do? But the moment is always a recurring one. We meet this in group Work all the time. What do you do in this situation at a Work day when something happens, and you see the opportunity under those circumstances to present something to one person, but you know that there are these other people here and you cannot do it? It is not something that has a nicely formulated approach to it. What do you do in that moment. You go back to Bogga-Eddin, or at least that is what I think we try to do. But relative to this fracture, for me that is a really essential thing. We are living in different times. They are more fractious than ever and it is even more essential for our emphasis to be on Being, to be an appropriate form and sequence.

Unidentified: We were talking about things on an intellectual level. The ultimate secrets that we were talking about are secrets to be used as tools. I think the nature of the secrets we were talking about is a key. Like a key that can be put on public display for all to see. Some will recognize it, some won't. I am not personally very enamoured of this, but I know that it's rather like seeds that are thrown on the ground. Some fall on poor soil, some on good. There are no bad plants. I think as fellow three-brained Beings we owe it to mankind to share the key if not the secret. The secret is what you find when you know how to use the key. That depends upon the individual.

Paul Taylor: What you say reminds me of the implications of Plato's cave. Who would thrust into the blinding light those who are accustomed to seeing shadows as the reality of Being? After all, they do not and cannot see the difference between shadows and the real. That is what Christ meant in explaining the parables to his disciples: there are those who see but do not see, and those who hear but cannot hear. So, it is an error to expose a secret truth to those who are blinded by it.

Bert Sharp: I would reinforce what Keith and others have said. I remember very clearly learning Elementary Chemistry and finding it was all very interesting, lovely and simple. And later, I learnt more advanced Chemistry and realized that you have to do it in the right order, because you then find that what you first of all learnt is not strictly true. It is a little bit more complicated than that. And I am also reminded that there is a lot about this in the Ring operas. They are based on Goethe's poetry. You see the gods were worried about keeping their special knowledge secret from everybody else. And they were advised Loge, the spirit of Deceit and Delusion to make a bargain with the two giants Fafner and Fasolt to build an aerie with a ring around them as a fortress to separate them from the rest. Having thus become separated, they became secret and reneged on paying the giants. But it was eventually sorted out and they lost their immortality and their special knowledge deteriorated. This is the way it seems to go. On a more practical level, what seems very important to me in helping others, in helping one another, is to recognize that it is important we believe in what helps us most until we can move to another level of belief and eventually, perhaps, to know. Therefore, the most horrendous thing that anyone can do is to undermine another person's belief. One needs to very, very carefully support them and, at the same time, try to somehow psychologically strengthen them so that they become, eventually, ready to expand their belief.

Paul Taylor: A propos, the riddle of the manner of one's death is not answered so that death can be avoided, but so it can be properly faced.

Edgar Clarke: Talking about the question of secrecy, not talking about things being withheld to keep them in sequence. I have often thought about how I have come along. I don't think I have ever learnt anything without asking for it. As far as I am concerned, I don't think anything has ever been given to me without it being asked for, and I think that is the way it should be. On that understanding from my own experience. I won't volunteer information to anyone until I think they need it. If they ask for it. I will give them the basics to answer their question. If they don't ask, I don't volunteer.

Bob Curran: Back in the mid-sixties when I first came into the Work, I remember coming across the idea that humanity is asleep. I remember being very hung up on that very powerful idea, and that it should be kept out of the public wherewithal. It kept surprising me to see everyone working in the market place, and yet there was a very powerful idea that people are asleep. For some thirty years through trying, myself to, so to say, "wake up," it became clear that I was asleep, and just by extension, yes, all humanity is asleep. All these people I see moving around in my life, they are asleep. For thirty years I held this condition–yes, people are asleep. Maybe it was not a secret, because it was in both places. But, then, something happened: two experiences in very close succession in public places, one in a commuter train packed full, and one in a department store packed full. For about 20 seconds each, something was lifted, and it was transparently clear to me that everyone around me was absolutely asleep, and so for these 30 years I thought I had discovered the answer to this secret that they were asleep. In those two 20-second intervals I had found all I needed to know. With respect to the secrecy thing, there are secrets and everybody knows them, and there are secrets for people who by the design of things, one way or another. Fortunately, for their liberation and self-preservation, and I think the secrets reveal themselves in proportion to the needs of the individual. They become property that is still invisible.

Nicholas Tereshchenko: Bert, I do not agree with what you say about undermining belief. If the belief is wrong, it should be undermined. I take it that if you should not undermine belief, Beelzebub should not have been written, because the whole purpose of Beelzebub was to undermine all the wrong beliefs of humanity.

Bert Sharp: It was surely also written to be difficult to understand, at least in the beginning. In fact, one can never fully understand it, so it is protected.

John Perrot: I think the aphorism is: Never destroy a man's belief structure unless you know that you have something better to put in its place and can so do.

Bert Sharp: And he is ready.

Unidentified: In terms of secrets being withheld, I often notice as a part of myself, particularly in my relationship to my interior, there is a part of me that wants to believe that there is one secret in there and that if you can just figure out this one secret, then one would be awake all the time. That is like the king in one of the Descents who gets it in his head that there is one more secret, and if he can collect all the philosophers and wise men and torture it out of them, he will learn how to transform lead into gold. But, it is in me something that wants to believe this tale. The only other thing that I would just mention is that I have a little difficulty with a lot of these generalizations of the analogies we use, because they become vague to me, such as the idea that the real secret is inside, and then the key, and then we can do what we want with the key because it is a matter of Free Will. I guess I don't understand what is meant by "the key" because my experience, particularly with the assertions you all make, is that we come down on either the left or the right of them: but, the analogy in the middle is more complex. I have met and worked with many people who had what I would consider a magnetic centre, who had unmistakably something about them, I don't know what, and yet they made serious mistakes and hurt people. So, the secret may protect itself if our understanding about keys is correct. There are people who are confused and with those people we need to be careful.

Bert Sharp: It is also said that when the pupil is ready the teacher appears.

Unidentified: If I am not wrong in details, in the *Tales*, the sacred individuals make some mistakes. So we have in the concept of Higher Beings, Divinities, or very high levels of consciousness at which level mistakes are made.

Paul Taylor: We must conclude here. I thank all of you for a lively discussion.

End of Session

* * *

Postscript by Bert Sharp: The same day I finished transcribing this Open Forum, I received a letter from my friend Lewis Creed which contained a number of interesting items, in particular one which related to the above material, an item which, in fact, could be considered as an example of synchronicity:

> "THIS WORK IS BEAUTIFUL WHEN YOU SEE WHY IT EXISTS AND WHAT IT MEANS. IT IS ABOUT LIBERATION. IT IS AS BEAUTIFUL AS IF, LOCKED FOR YEARS IN PRISON, YOU SEE A STRANGER ENTERING WHO OFFERS YOU A KEY, BUT YOU MAY REFUSE IT BECAUSE YOU HAVE ACQUIRED PRISON-HABITS AND HAVE FORGOTTEN YOUR ORIGIN, WHICH IS FROM THE STARS."
> - MAURICE NICOLL

The Kunderbuffer: The Kundalini Alchemy and Creation of the Soul

Adam W. Petts

Adam William Petts is an instructor of The Gnostic Institute of Anthropology within which he has been studying and practising for the past eight years. During this time he has travelled in Mexico, India and the U.S.A exploring various systems of psychological and spiritual development. He presently runs The Gnostic Institute of Anthropology in Brighton, England, with his fiancé, Tara.

In his life profession Adam is a postman.

Adam Petts was introduced by Keith Buzzell and the session was opened at Adam's suggestion by some 15 minutes of quiet sitting in silence and working with the double arrow of attention that we hear so much of in this Work. Our external senses, the external arrow of awareness, and at the same time making it a double arrow by making present "I's" inside ourselves and being in the room together.

Kunderbuffer, Kundalini and the creation of the higher being bodies

Good Day. Allow me to introduce myself, my name is Adam and I am very pleased to be here to present this talk on the subject of Kundalini, Kunderbuffer and the creation of the higher being bodies. In this talk I will be exploring the work of G.I. Gurdjieff in the light of the teachings of Samael Aun Weor. In this way I hope to approach Gurdjieff's abundant table with an offering that comes from the same kitchen and may indeed be upon the table although not immediately apparent.

Firstly, I would like to explain how I came across the work of G.I. Gurdjieff, without giving you an autobiography, I must say that I have had the motivation and impulse to seek a deeper meaning to my own existence for as long as I can remember. This has led me into many different areas of study and practice. Seven years ago I came across a group in London known as The Gnostic Institute of Anthropology. This group is part of an international organisation that formed as a result of the teaching of Samael Aun Weor. Samael was born in Columbia in 1917. In the light of his own experiences he began to teach, write books and give lectures and as a result a group formed around him. He wrote over sixty books, all of which are very profound and deal with many aspects of esoteric initiatic knowledge, fourth way psychology etc. He used the term Gnosis to indicate that his teachings were a fundamental blueprint of techniques for the self-perfection of the human being that can be found at the root of all world religions. Although the form changes, the content remains the same.

The Kunderbuffer: The Kundalini Alchemy and Creation of the Soul

It was through studying the works of Samael that I came across a number of references to the fourth way, Gurdjieff, Ouspensky and Nicoll. As Samael's work is originally in Spanish I began to study the abundant material by and about Gurdjieff.

One of the founding principles of the Gnostic Institute is to suspend acceptance or rejection of an idea, to believe or disbelieve an idea means to stop any exploration of it, to be satisfied with the dualism of the formative mind. Students are encouraged to question, to work with ideas and aim to arrive at a direct experience of the truth. To know is Gnosis.

I found this, and many other concepts, paralleled in Gurdjieff's work:

"No faith is required on the fourth way; on the contrary, faith of any kind is opposed to the fourth Way. On the fourth way a man must satisfy himself on the truth of what he is told. And until he is satisfied lie must do nothing." (*In Search of the Miraculous,* p. 49)

The question of the origin of Gurdjieff's teachings and the importance that so many authors, fourth way students and teachers have put on it is an aspect that I would like to address in relation to the higher bodies, the astral, mental and causal bodies.

If we assume that as masters Gurdjieff, Samael and others had in previous existences created these bodies, (in fact Samael affirms that he had) then it is evident that they were conscious in higher worlds of less laws. This being the case they had access to various colleges of initiation in those higher worlds in which they could receive teachings and the authority to unveil things that previously had been concealed. Samael puts great emphasis on the importance of any student acquiring these bodies and consciousness in order to verify for themselves the truth of the worlds of 24, 12 and 6 laws. In these worlds it is possible to know directly, free from the limitations and complications of the 48 laws. Samael gave many accounts of his experiences in the higher worlds, the teaching's that he received and the particular mission that he was given. He stressed again and again the necessity to suspend belief and disbelief and to arrive, by means of awakening, death and birth, at one's own direct experience.

In order to explore this subject further I would like to talk about the kunderbuffer of *Beelzebub's Tales* and relate this to Samael's unveiling of initiatic Kabbalah found within the book of Genesis of the Old Testament. Firstly, we find the story within *Beelzebub's Tales* of a problem within the not yet blended solar system. This being the arrival of the comet Kondoor. Due to the error of certain sacred individuals this comet and the earth collided forming the moon. Arising from this was the necessity of organic life on the earth to emit certain vibrations that will keep the moon in orbit.

"After some time had and elapsed the all too diligent most high commission decided to make a return visit to our solar system in order to complete its rescue work. Fearing that men would prematurely comprehend the real cause of their arising and existence... , namely that by their existence they should maintain the detached fragments of their planet, and apprehensive that they may revolt against their fate and in order to escape it would be unwilling to continue their existence, the commission decides, provisionally to implant into the common presence's of the three brained beings there a special organ with a property such that, first, they should perceive reality topsy turvy and, secondly, that every repeated impression from outside should crystallise in them data which would engender factors for evoking in them sensations of "pleasure and enjoyment".

So the story continues with those sacred individuals implanting the kunderbuffer.

Gurdjieff continues:

"They cause to grow in three brained beings there, in a special way, at the base of their spinal column, at the root of their tail-which they also, at that tie, still had, and which part of their common presence's further more still had its normal exterior expressing the, so to say, "fullness-of-its-inner-significance"– a "something" which assisted the arising of the said properties in them. And this "something" they then first called the "organ kunderbuffer."

The organ kunderbuffer, although later removed, had crystallised certain consequences. Namely the "it", those multiple 'I's' that are the roots of our unconsciousness, the states of harmful identification with ones own passions.

Samael tells us in his book *Tarot and Kabbalah* that the implanting of kunderbuffer is hidden within the myth of Adam and Eve and the Garden of Eden. We find in the Garden two trees, the tree of life related to the qualities of our being and the ray of creation and also the tree of the knowledge of good and evil connected to kunderbuffer and the fall.

In Genesis 2:8-9 we read:

"And the Lord God planted Garden in Eden, in the east; and there he put the man who he had formed. And out of the ground the Lord God made to grow every tree that is pleasant to the sight and good for food, the tree of life also in the midst of the Garden, and the tree of the knowledge of good and evil."

In order to study the inner meaning of the story of Genesis we need to relate it to kabbalah and humanity before the fall. In Eden man and woman made in the likeness of God (our common megalocosmos) were conscious of themselves. They were eating of the tree of life. Samael says that in those secret histories of mankind humanity suspected the reason for their arising and was losing interest in the physical world. For this reason the tree of knowledge of good and evil and the beguiling serpent were placed in the garden.

The Kunderbuffer: The Kundalini Alchemy and Creation of the Soul

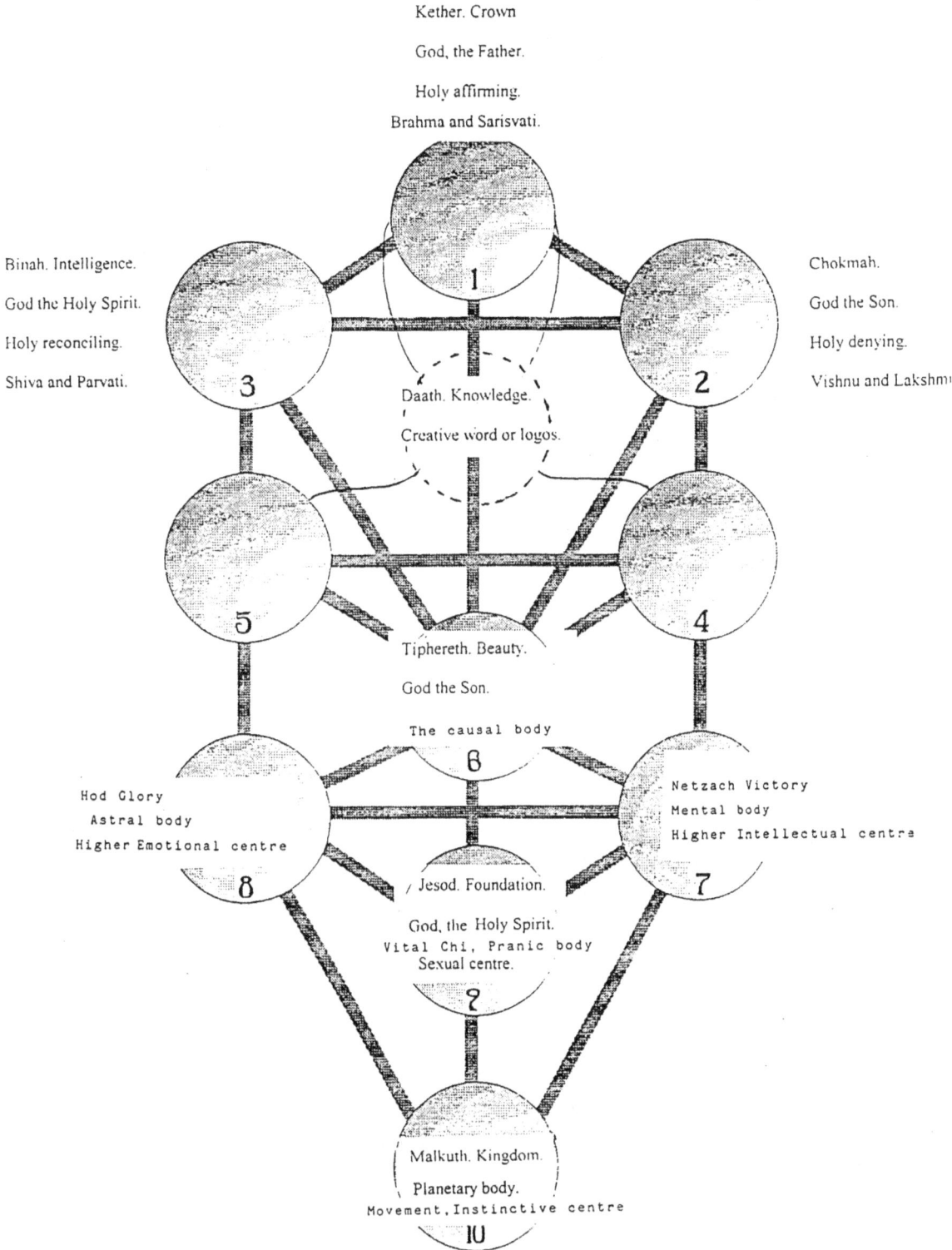

Diagram One: Kabbalah. Tree of Life

All & Everything Conference 1998

So let us look at the diagram or the tree of life and explain from the Gnostic esoteric kabbalah the fall and kunderbuffer. If we look at the tree as the microcosm we step back into it. We find three vertical pillars and three triangles. Each triangle finds its balance in the middle pillar. These teachings of kabbalah are very in-depth and unfortunately we do not have time to cover all the details. So briefly, the right pillar is the pillar of severity or justice and is feminine, negative. The left pillar is that of mercy and is masculine or positive and the middle pillar is equilibrium. In the first triangle we find expressed the law of the triamazikamno. The first sephira is the father, Kether, the crown. The second sephira is Chokmah, wisdom, the son. The third is Binah, intelligence, the Holy Spirit. In Hinduism Brahma and Sarisvati, Vishnu and Lakshmi and Shiva and Parvati represent this trinity. The union of the divine elohims give rise to creation. This word elohim is very interesting; it is plural and is comprised of 'el', masculine and 'him' or 'heva' feminine. We find in the word elohim and Jehovah the idea of gods and goddesses in perfect multiple unity. The three forces unfold into the mysterious sephira Daath that is directly below the first triangle on the middle pillar. Daath, unlike all the other sephira, has no symbols. The word Daath in Hebrew means knowledge and it is the result of the union of the three primary forces, the shock between do and si on the descending octave of creation. In the microcosmic man it is situated in the throat, the larynx. It is the creative word or logos, "In the beginning was the word, and the word was with God, and the word was God." (John 1:1-3)

"And God said, 'let there be light' and there was light." (Genesis 1: 3)

In the Bible the word Daath, meaning knowledge or to know, is used to indicate the sexual act "Now Adam <u>knew</u> Eve, his wife, and she conceived Cane." (Genesis 4:1)

Also when the angel Gabriel appeared to Mary, telling her she would have a son, she replied 'how is this possible, as I have not <u>known</u> any man'. In Daath we find the secrets of the middle pillar. The relationship between the larynx and the sexual potency is clear in the life of every young man with the breaking of the voice in puberty. The only way to keep the pure soprano voice of a pre-pubescent boy was by castration, in Italy they known as the castratos. In accordance with the hermetic maxim. As above so below find the ninth sephira, Jesod, located within the sexual organs of the man and woman. Below our physical father is the holy affirming and our mother the holy denying. The attraction and sexual union between the two is the holy reconciling. From the three forces our physical bodies have arisen.

In speaking of the involuntary conception of children which is a distressing result for them Beelzebub says, "The mixing of these two sacred Substances of the two opposite sexes who actualise in themselves two opposite forces of the sacred Triamazikamno. During the satisfaction by them of that function of theirs which has become, thanks to the inheritance from the ancient Romans, the chief vice of contemporary three brained beings."

In initiatic kabbalah it is said that Jesod, the foundation is the world of vitality, chi, prana, the world of sexual potency. Gurdjieff's being-Exioehary. Samael writes that this is file fourth dimensional aspect of our tetra-dimensional world, Eden itself.

The Kunderbuffer: The Kundalini Alchemy and Creation of the Soul

Looking at the middle pillar of the tree we see Kether, the crown, ruling the first triangle. This is the God, the Father in potential within our own head, the higher intellectual centre. Next we find the sephira Daath, knowledge, situated in the throat. In the region of our heart or solar plexus we find the sephira beauty, the son, the Christ, the higher emotional centre. Directly below is Jesod, the foundation, the Holy Spirit, situated in our sexual centre. Finally we find the sephira Tephereth, the kingdom our planetary body, the physical world, with its mineral, plant, animal and human kingdoms. This sephira is fallen. We can understand that prior to the fall it was within the fourth dimension Jesod, the Garden of Eden. Now let us study Genesis further:

"The Lord God took the man and put him in the Garden of Eden to till it and keep it. And the Lord God commanded the man, saying, "you may freely eat of every tree of the garden; but of the tree knowledge of good and evil you shall not eat, for in the day that you eat of it you shall die." (Genesis 2:15-17)

"Now the serpent was more subtle than any other creature that the Lord God had made.

He said to the woman, 'Did God say, "You shall not eat of any tree of the garden"?' And the woman said to the serpent 'We may eat the fruit of the trees of the garden; but God said, "You shall not eat of the fruit of the tree which is in the midst of the garden neither shall you touch it, lest you die"' But the serpent said to the woman 'YOU will not die. For God knows that when you eat of it your eyes will be opened, and you will he like God, knowing good and evil.' So when the woman saw that the tree was good for food, and that it was a delight to the eyes, and that the tree was desired to make one wise, she took of its fruit and ate; and she also gave some to her husband, and he ate. Then the eyes of both were opened, and they knew that they were naked, and they sewed fig leaves together and made themselves aprons.

And they heard the sound of the Lord God walking in the garden in the cool of the day, and the man and his wife hid themselves from the presence of the Lord God among the trees of the garden. But the Lord God called to the man where are you? And he said 'I heard the sound of thee in the garden and I was afraid, because I was naked; and I hid myself.' He said. 'who told you that you naked? Have you eaten of the tree of which I commanded you not to eat?' The man said, 'The woman whom thou gavest to be with me, she gave me fruit of the tree and I ate.' Then the Lord God said to the woman what is this that you have done? The woman said 'The serpent beguiled me and I ate.'

The lord God said to the serpent, 'Because you have done this cursed are you above all cattle, and above all wild animals: upon your belly you shall go, and dust you shall eat all the days of your life. I will put enmity between you and the woman, and between your seed and her seed; he shall bruise your head, and you shall bruise his heel." (Genesis 3:1-15)

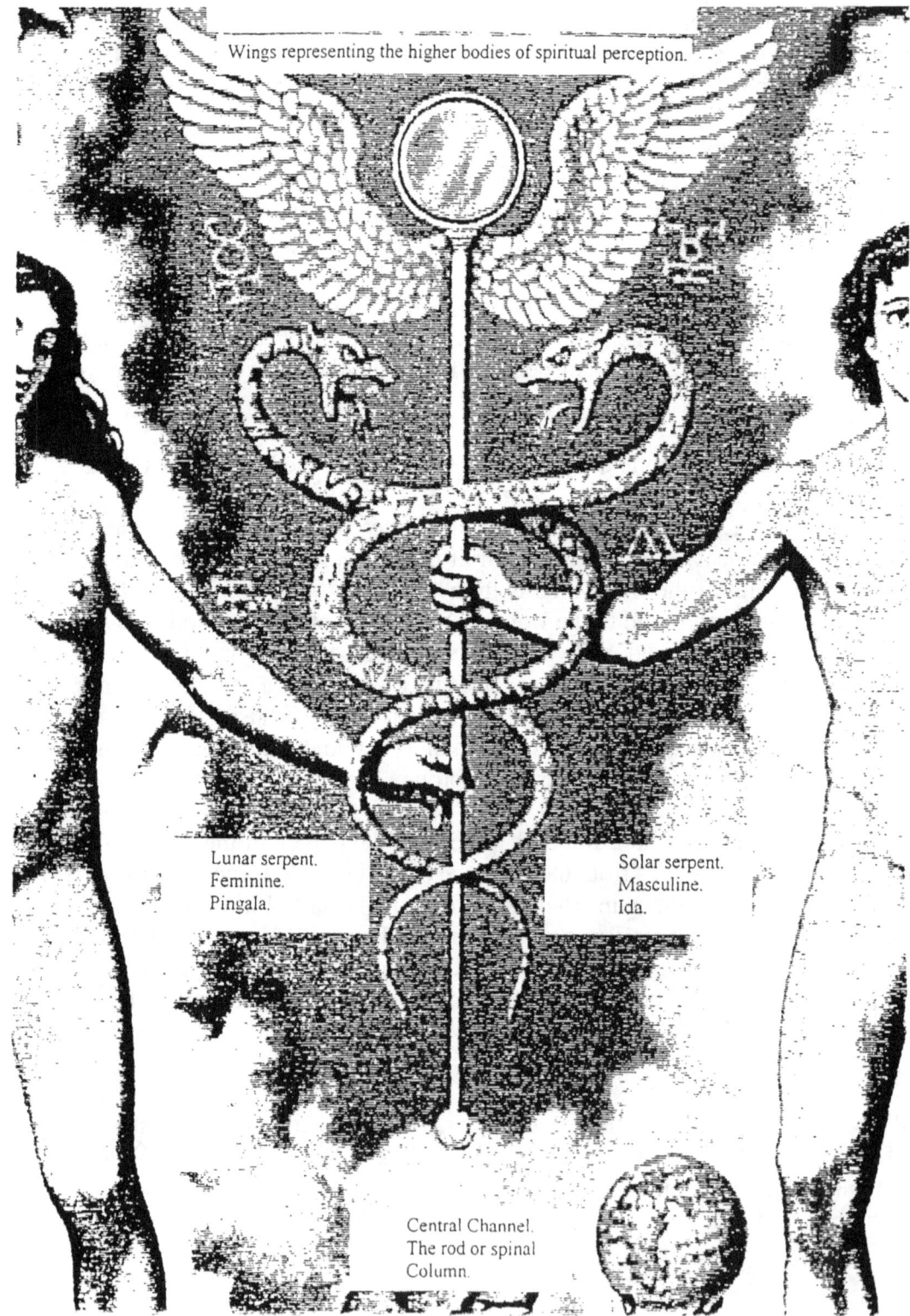

Diagram Two: The Caduceus of Mercury

The Kunderbuffer: The Kundalini Alchemy and Creation of the Soul

We can understand from this that Adam and Eve not only represent humanity but also various forces inside man and woman. If we look at this second diagram we find the Caduceus of mercury which is connected with the hermetic mysteries. It constitutes of a staff and two ascending serpents. One is lunar, feminine, the subtle channel known as Pingala to the Hindu yogis. The second is solar, masculine, the channel of Ida. Eve eating the forbidden fruit is representative of the descent of the lunar serpent or the implanting, of the kunderbuffer organ. Samael Aun Weor clearly teaches that the kunderbuffer and the fall are sexual. He writes that in the ancient civilisations, prior to the fall, sex was sacred, that is the third being food, hydrogen si 12 or the being-Exioehary which according to Beelzebub the Atlanteans called the sacred Amarhoodan (help for God). Beelzebub also refers to this act as "sacred-sacraments-of-the-great-Scrooazar". In the sexual act in Eden the orgasm or spasm was unknown. It was implanting of the kunderbuffer or the descending lunar serpent that gave rise to the instinctive desire to taste the sexual act as it was performed by the animals. As Gurdjieff says in *Beelzebub's Tales* "They should perceive reality topsy turvy and secondly that every repeated impression from outside should crystallise in them data which would engender factors for evoking in them sensations pleasure and enjoyment." Prior to the implanting of kunderbuffer it was known that the purpose Being-Exioehary was for the coating and perfecting of higher being bodies and the conscious and intentional sacred being duty of the continuing of the species." This sexual fall became the root and origin, the "chief vice" of the multiple I's, the 'it', the unfortunate structure of us as three brained beings, our sleep, lack of will and continuity etc. Because sex is creative, the fall or the original sin was lust that gave rise to desire and attachment to the earth. This is the forming of the Nephesh, in Hebrew, the animal or instinctive soul that is born from Jesod. Gurdjieff speaks of this in the chapter 'Holy Planet Purgatory' in *Beelzebub's Tales*, specifically on pages 381-388.

We would like to quote from *Beelzebub's Tales*, chapter 39 in the second book, after describing the process of transformation of various types of being foods Beelzebub relates the further transformation of the piandjoehary from its location in the cerebellum. "From the cerebellum of beings a part of these definite substances also goes to serve the planetary body itself, but the other part, passing in a particular way through the nervous nodes of the spine and the breast is concentrated in the beings of the male sex, in what are called testicles and in the beings of the female sex in what most of your favourites call ovaries, which are the place of concentration in the common presence's of beings of the being-Exioehary, which is for the beings themselves their most sacred possession. You should know that this particular way mentioned is called Trnlva."

We hear this affirmed in Samael's book *The Mystery of the Golden Blossom* where he quotes the ancient sages of China. "In an extremely wise treaties I read the following: Taoism has other influences on medicine as is confirmed by reading the compilation of Taoist treaties the Sing-Ming-Kuei-Chen, from circa 1622."

The human body has three regions. The superior or cephalic region, is the origin of the spirits that live in the body. The pillow of jade (U-Chen) is found in the lower part of this region, at the back of the head. The so called pillow bone is the occipital (Chen-Ku). The palace of Ni-Huan is to be found in the brain, known also as the sea of the bone marrow (Suei-Hai), the origin of the seminal substances. The middle region is the vertebral column, considered not as a functional shaft but as a channel which joins the cerebral cavities with the genital centres; it terminates at a point called the celestial column (Tien-Chu), situated at the back of the neck, at the hairline. In this location, genital activity is represented by the two kidney's, the fire of the tiger, Yang, on the left and tile fire of the dragon, Ying, on the right. Sexual union is symbolised by a couple. A young man leads a white tiger and a young woman rides upon a green dragon. Lead, the masculine element, and mercury, the feminine element are about to be combined. As soon as they are united, the young people cast their essence into a bronze cauldron, the symbol of sexual activity. However, the genital fluids, particularly the sperm (Tsing), are neither eliminated or lost but can return to the brain via the spinal column, thanks to which life's course is restored."

Returning to the book of Genesis we read:

"Then the Lord God said, 'Behold, the man has become like one of us, knowing good and evil: and now, lest he put Forth his hand and take also of the tree of life, and eat and live forever- therefore the Lord God sent him forth from the garden of Eden to till the ground from which he was taken. He drove out the man: and at the east of the Garden of Eden he placed the cherubim, and a flaming sword which turned every, direction to guard the way to the tree of life." (Genesis 3:22-24)

Samael teaches the return to Eden (the path of awakening, death and birth) is through the door by which we left, that of sex. As Beelzebub says to Hussein:

"Where as this same 'being act', which for your favourites has been turned into chief vice, constitutes and is considered everywhere in our great universe for beings of all kinds of natures, as the most sacred of all sacred divine sacraments." (*Beelzebub's Tales*, p. 386)

The sacred sexual act of Eden is without the orgasm and loss of the being-Exioehary performed with sanctity, chastity and the transmutation of the creative energy. Within the bible and many other ancient texts we find two serpents, the tempting serpent of Eden and the ascending serpent of the staff or rod of Moses and Aaron. This second serpent heals the Israelites in the desert. The ascending serpent is the much misunderstood kundalini. Samael teaches that kundalini is an ancient Atlantean word. Kunder refers to the kunderbuffer and lini means 'the end of Kundalini is awakened by the connection of the rising solar and lunar channels in the coccyx at the base of the spine. It then rises through the central channel slowly and in accordance with sanctity, chastity and the merits of the heart (psychological work). Within the mystery schools it is said that if you seek initiation (inner development of being) write it on a staff, which of course represents the spinal column. There is an interesting parallel between this and the sacred rod by which Beelzebub regains his horns that signify his graduation of reason and are also symbolic of the sexual potency of the stag.

Now we would like to quote from Samael's work *Tarot and Kabbalah*, ch.26.

The Kunderbuffer: The Kundalini Alchemy and Creation of the Soul

"Speaking about the school of the fourth way, we find that Gurdjieff, Ouspensky and Nicoll, have expounded that which they know, but the exposition contains many defects. For example: Gurdjieff commits the error of confusing the kundalini with the abominable kunderbuffer organ, and Ouspensky commits the same error. We must not forget that there is that blind fohatic force, which has people hypnotised, but that it has nothing to do with the kundalini. The kunderbuffer is lunar fire. The bible speaks of the forty-four fires, but one can only speak of two great fires, kundalini and kunderbuffer. The first is the Pentecostal fire, the ray of Vulcan ascending the spinal column; the positive fire which crystallises in worlds and suns. Its antithesis is the kunderbuffer, the negative fire which crystallises in those psychic aggregates, those screaming and troublesome 'I's' which we carry within. They are negative crystallisation's which have people submerged in the unconscious.

Gurdjieff commits the error of saying nothing about the lunar bodies which everyone has, and only says that we must transform the being and fabricate the solar bodies. Ouspensky speaks about the second birth but his teachings are incomplete. The solar bodies are first fabricated in the ninth sphere (Jesod, sex), attaining the second birth; but neither Gurdjieff nor Ouspensky give the key.

The school of the fourth way is very ancient; it comes from archaic lands; is the basis of the great mysteries. One finds it alive in Gnosticism, in the religions of Egyptians, Lemurians, Atlanteans, Phoencians etc."

In reference to the lunar and solar bodies mentioned in this quote Samael states that nature gives a lunar astral, mental and causal bodies. These bodies are subject to decay and are also possessed by animals and plants. He writes that certain teachers of the past had mistakenly perceived the essence within the lunar bodies as the solar bodies themselves. These adepts in previous existence's had attained the second birth of the solar bodies and therefore were born possessing these vehicles, as a result they assumed that everybody was in possession of their soul. This explains the great challenge Gurdjieff placed before those of various traditional religions that postulate the afore mentioned.

With the practice of Fourth way psychology, self-remembering, self-observation and the transmutation of the being-Exioehary to create the Resulzarian, the food for the higher being bodies. This work can be done as a single person or as a couple in sexual alchemy with neither the man nor the woman reaching the orgasm. With regard to the creation of the higher being bodies it is clear that nothing is born of ideas. All worlds and beings are born from the Union of three forces, as above, so below. A special shock is produced that passes the sexual hydrogen si 12 to a second musical octave forming the body kesdjan, the astral body. In the sexual centre is found the Holy Spirit, Shiva-Shakti, the creator destroyer. The kundalini indicates the end of the kunderbuffer crystallisation's and the second birth. Jesus the Christ teaches this key in the book of John when he speaks to Nicodemus saying:

"'Truly, truly I say unto you, unless one is born anew, he cannot enter the kingdom of heaven.'

All & Everything Conference 1998

Nicodemus said to him: 'How can a man to be born when he is old? Can he enter a second time into his mothers womb and be born?"

Jesus answers:

"Truly, truly I say to you, unless one is born of water and the spirit, he cannot enter the kingdom of God. That which is born of the flesh is flesh and that which is born of spirit is spirit... No one has ascended into heaven but he that descended from heaven, the Son of man.' And as Moses lifted up the serpent in the wilderness, so must the son of man be lifted up, that who ever believes in him may have eternal life." (John 3:1-15)

I would like to relate this to what is written in *In Search of the Miraculous*:

"Fusion, inner unity is obtained by means of friction, by the struggle between yes and no in man. If a man lives without inner struggle, if everything happens in him without opposition, if he goes where ever he is drawn or where ever the wind blows, he will remain such as he is, but if a struggle begins in him, and particularly if there is a definite line in the struggle, then gradually permanent traits begin to form themselves, he begins to crystallise."

"Let us imagine a vessel or retort filled with various metallic powders. The powders are not in any way connected with each other and every accidental change in the position of the retort changes the relative position of the powders.... It is impossible to stabilise the interrelation of powders in a state of mechanical mixture. But the powders may be fused; the nature of the powders make this possible. To do this a special kind of fire must be lit under the retort, which, by heating and melting the powders, finally fuses them together. Fused in this way the powders will be in the state of a chemical compound... the contents of the retort have become indivisible, individual. This is a picture of the formation of the second body. The fire by means of which fusion is attained is produced by friction. Which in its turn is produced in man by the struggle between yes and no... The process of imparting new properties to the alloy corresponds to the process of the formation of the third body... The process of fixing these acquired properties corresponds to the process of the formation of the fourth body. And only the man possesses four fully developed bodies can be a 'man' in the full sense of the word. This man possesses many properties which ordinary man does not possess. One these properties is immortality." (*In Search of the Miraculous*, p. 31-32)

Samael affirms that it is the struggle between yes and no in the psychological work and specifically in the sexual centre that creates this fusion or birth. This is symbolised in Genesis by the cherubim with the flaming sword that guards the doorway to Eden. Within us, in our sexual, instinctive centre, carried by the blood is the force of this cherubim or fallen angel who is known as Lucifer meaning the light-bearer. It is said that temptation is fire. We find this special fire in the passionate impulse towards the pleasurable and hypnotic expelling of the being-Exioehary from the body. To overcome temptation is to make light. This is stealing the fire from the devil or climbing the ladder on the devils back in Dante's Inferno. The friction between yes and no in sexual alchemy is tremendously powerful. If we look at the third diagram we find Baphomet.

The Kunderbuffer: The Kundalini Alchemy and Creation of the Soul

Diagram Three: The Baphomet

All & Everything Conference 1998

Written on his arms are the words 'Solve et Coagula' Solve is to dissolve the multiple I's, Coagula indicates the formation of the higher being bodies, the astral, mental and causal. This is the inner secret of the medieval alchemists.

Finally in relationship to all of this I must say that Samael Aun Weor states his level of mastery as originating from real 'I', from the causal plane and above. He speaks of being given the mission and the authority to unveil the key of sexual alchemy. He claims that his being was the first to be aloud to give this secret publicly. He spoke of the need for the seeker to enter into the field of practical and experiential work in order to prove the reality of this possible evolution. All authentic development or initiation is founded on awakening, death and birth, which in turn is founded on the mysteries of Daath, the foundation of Jesod, sexual alchemy and transmutation.

"Where as this same 'being act', which for your favourites has been turned into their chief vice, constitutes and is considered everywhere in our great universe for beings of all kinds of natures as the most sacred of all sacred divine sacraments." (*Beelzebub's Tales*, p. 386)

This is the sacred, divine sacrament that is found at the root of all esoteric systems and schools. In the tantras of Tibet and India, in Daath of the kabbalists, in the Karezza of the Sufis, in the alchemy of the Taoists and the medieval sages, within the codexes of Quetzalcoatl, the feathered serpent of ancient Mexico and in the message of esoteric Christianity. So the question for those of us that are working practically is yes or no?

I would like to end with a prayer from *Beelzebub's Tales*:

Sources of divine rejoicing,
Revolting and suffering,
Direct your actions upon us
Holy God
Holy firm
Holy immortal
Have mercy on us.

© Copyright 1998 - Adam W. Petts - All Rights Reserved

Appendix - Quotes Related to Sacred Sexuality

Quotes related to sacred sexuality from various ancient texts

"If anyone becomes a son of the bridal chamber, he will receive the light. If anyone does not receive it while he is in the world, he will not receive it in the other place...When he goes out of the world, he has already received the truth in the images (of inner light)" (The Gospel of Philip 134:4-17)

"If the woman had not separated from the man, she would not die with the man. His separation became the beginning of death. Because of this, Christ came, in order that he might remove the separation which was from the beginning, and again unite the two; and that he might give life to those who died in the separation and unite them." (The Gospel of Philip 118:9-17)

"Those who say they will die first and rise again, are in error. If they do not first receive the resurrection while they live, when they die, they will receive nothing." (The Gospel of Philip 121:1-5)

"The union of man and woman is like the mating of Heaven and Earth. It is because of their correct mating that Heaven and Earth last forever. Humans have lost this secret and therefore become mortal. By knowing it, the path to immortality is opened." (The Taoist Master Shang-San-Tai)

"For as a young man marrieth a virgin, so shall thy sons marry thee: and as the bridegroom rejoiceth over the bride, so shall thy God rejoice over thee." (Isaiah 62:5)

"The yogins who... unite the upaya (male) and prajna (female)... (have... great ecstasy." (Commentary on Caturdevipariprccha by Tsong-Kha-Pa)

"... This is not the union of ordinary marriage. This is the mystical androgynous element, composed of the white (male) and red (female)... in the central channel, causing... states of consciousness." (Tsong-Kha-Pa (1st Dalai Lama of Tibet))

". . . A reunion of the male and female - mystically brings death -from which comes the new life, the rebirth. The yogin... evoking this state... restores the androgyne (half male, half female)." (Yoga of the Guhyasamaja-Tantra)

"From the union of prajna and upaya, there arises the configuration of a deity." (The Hindu Master Sri-Laksmi)

"When you make the two one... and when you make the male and female into a single one, so that the male will not be male, and the female not be female... then shall you enter the Kingdom." (The Gospel of Thomas 82:25-35)

"Jesus said: When you make the two one, you shall become sons of man..." (The Gospel of Thomas 98:19, 20)

"Lord there are many around the reservoir (of water), but none inside it. Jesus said: Many are standing at the door, but solitary are the ones who will enter the bridal chamber." (The Gospel of Thomas 94:9-13)

"The Lotus-flower, the sex organ of the (female) partner, is an ocean filled with bliss... where the thought of enlightenment can rise up. When it is united with the sceptre (lingam), the male organ, their mixture is compared to the Elixir... from their union a pure knowledge arises, which explains the nature of all things." (The Kalachakra Tantra)

".. Draw up the goddess Kundalini, for she is the giver of all powers." (Shiva Samhita (Holy book of Hinduism))

"She (Kundalini) maintains all beings of this world by means of inhalation and exhalation and shines in the cavity (yoni) of the sexual region." (Satcha Kranirupana (Holy book of Hinduism))

"Death is eaten by the person who reverses the flow of energies within the body. Energy flow can be reversed by...(hermetic) seals, by drawing up, by breath control and by meditation." (Kaula Tantra)

"If any man thirst, let him come unto me, and drink… out of his belly will flow rivers of living water." (John 7:37, 38)

"Then the Lord said, 'Behold the man has become like one of us, knowing good and evil; and now lest he put forth his hand and take also of the tree of life and eat, and live forever'.. at the east of the garden he placed the cherubim, and a flaming sword which turned every way, to guard the way to the tree of life." (Genesis 3:22, 24)

"For this is the will of God .. that each one of you know how to take a wife for himself in holiness and honour, not in the passion of lust like heathen who do not know God." (2 Thessalonians 4:3-4)

"Therefore whoever disregards this, disregards not man but God, who gives his Holy Spirit to you." (Thessalonians 4:8)

"Jesus answered, Truly, truly I say to you, unless one is born of water and the Spirit he cannot enter the Kingdom of God." (John 3:3)

Appendix - Quotes related to sacred sexuality from various ancient texts

"No one has ascended into Heaven but he who descended from Heaven, the son of man. And as Moses lifted up the serpent (The Spinal Column, The Kundalini) in the wilderness, so must the son of man be lifted up, that whoever believes in him may have eternal life" (John 3:13-15)

"If we make a comparative study of religions, we shall discover phallicism at the base of all schools, religions, and esoteric sects. Remember Peristera the nymph, the hand maiden of Venus, who was transformed by love into a dove. Remember the virtuous Venus. Remember the processions of the God Priapus in the august old Rome of the Ceases, when the priestesses of the Temple, full of ecstasy, majestically bore an enormous phallus of sacred wood. With just reason Freud, the founder of Psychoanalysis says that religions have a sexual origin. Contained within the Perfect Matrimony are the Mysteries of Fire." (Samael Aun Weor)

The Kunderbuffer - Questions & Answers

Edgar Clarke: You speak of an error in G's work, where by you are speaking of solar and lunar bodies, for the integrity of G's system is the four bodies. What are the lunar bodies and how do they fit into this?

Adam Petts: How I understand this in my limited understanding and experience is what Samael taught in the light of his own investigations, that the lunar bodies are something nature gives us related to the different dimensions or worlds. They are not immortal, rather something subject to the laws of nature. The distinction between solar and lunar is that the solar are born of fire and water, the results of sexual work, created by conscious work on oneself. Samael said that people can utilise the lunar body to verify the law of 24 laws, the astral plane. To have a conscious experience there, to unfold from the physical body and be in that dimension in what is sometimes called a lucid dream. Yet this body is not immortal, it is subject to decay. It is the vehicle that the multiple I's are using, for this reason the dreams are related to the mechanics of centres.

Unidentified: Yes, but G said the second body is not immortal.

Adam Petts: Yes

Nicholas Tereshchenko: We do know there is an etheric body, so are you relating the lunar body to the etheric body or not?

Adam Petts: Samael said there are lunar and solar, there is a lunar etheric, astral, mental and causal. The thing I would like to say is the context of the whole teaching is not accepting or rejecting on a purely intellectual or cognitive basis. Within the Gnostic school we find many exercises, techniques, where anybody is interested to, can, verify in their own experience. For example, in my own work I have had some experiences in the world of 24 laws, as to whether they were in solar or lunar bodies, I do not know, I can only speak in relation to the teachings of Samael Aun Weor and my own limited experiences, unfortunately I can say no more.

Nicholas Tereshchenko: Surely its a matter of words and terminology, for example, in *The Tales* the moon was not originally provided for, it was an accident, so lunar seems to be an odd name. If we use the etheric body with the 5 ethers of the alchemist and all that and as you know Daath is not in the same plane or continuum as the rest of the sephira. Perhaps the etheric body comes from that particular dimension which is different from ours which we receive at birth. Where as you say the solar bodies are the ones we have to create for ourselves.

The Kunderbuffer: The Kundalini Alchemy and Creation of the Soul - Questions & Answers

Addendum

Due to the lateness of the hour and the nature of the subject matter, there were far less questions than I had anticipated, yet over the remaining days of the conference various questions and comments were given to me personally. I would like to take this opportunity to write them and expand upon my response for the benefit of those interested.

It was indicated to me that I had made an impression with my paper that the fourth way, as left by G., was lacking or incomplete. In response to this I feel that in the light of my study and practice that this is indeed so. G. certainly transmitted much, yet as has been expressed by others during the conference, the teachings appear incomplete, or if they are the completion is encoded in his written works, "...keys and locks hidden in *All and Everything*" In direct relation to this point and sexual energy I would like to quote T. de Hartman from his *Our Life With Mr G.*, page 125, "In Essentuki Mr. G. had begun to give us exercises for this purpose, including the concentration of thought and some quite complicated ones with regard to breathing. I do not think that I should write about them, and besides, it could not be useful to just read about them; and Mr. G. often warned us that exercises connected with breathing could even be harmful if they were not done in the proper way. For the same reason he said not to repeat to others his personal talks with individuals, especially talks about breathing and sex energy."

In the light of this and other references I feel Mr. G. certainly knew the key of sexual alchemy although he clearly did not teach it publicly as J.G. Bennett indicates in relation to the Higher Intentional-actualising-mdnel-in found in *Talks On Beelzebub's Tales* (p. 57):

"The question then arises: What of the second mdnel-in? In none of Gurdjieff's talks or writings of which we have any record is it explained what is meant by the *intentional-actualising-mdnel-in*. Everyone has the feeling that here something more is needed than that the apparatus should work, something has to come from us that has something to do with sacrifice and suffering. Gurdjieff would never answer questions about this. In *The Tales* he simply says that it is here that the substance needed for the Higher Being Body or Soul enter."*

*"Gurdjieff in "Purgatory" simply says that here enters the "foreign help" foreordained by our creator for our perfecting, that is, being-partkdolg-duty or "conscious labours" and "intentional sufferings.""

It is my opinion, in the light of Samael's work, that this "something more" that is needed is the conscious labours and intentional suffering inherent in the sanctified work with ones sexual force, either as a single or a couple resulting in the birth of the higher being bodies.

Who among the students of G's work have the created those higher being bodies so clearly spoken about by Mr. G., who is experiencing these realities." By their fruits you shall know them." I feel that the work of Samael Aun Weor sheds new light, expands and clarifies the profundity of Gurdjieff's work.

Another point expressed to me during the conference was that it would be necessary to arrive at a certain level in the work (centre of gravity, deputy steward etc.) before beginning work with sexual energy. In response to this view Samael teaches that the work of sexual transmutation is primary and fundamental, it is the foundation stone. For this reason within the international organisation of The Gnostic Institute or Anthropology, after a number of months of studying and practising fourth way psychology the information and techniques of sexual transmutation are given.

Samael expressed that we find ourselves in the Kali Yuga, the iron age of escalating degeneration and because of the urgency of these days it has been authorised to give the revolutionary and previously secret keys of the sexual mysteries

Time in the Cosmology of Mr. Gurdjieff

Forrest McIlwain

Forrest McIlwain came across the Work in early 1972. He had begun a correspondence with Hugh B. Ripman, who was the leader of the Work Group in the Washington, D.C. area until his death in 1980. He continued to actively participate in the Washington Group until 1985. After Mr. Ripman's death, Mrs. Ripman replaced her husband. While he was working with the Washington Group, Mrs. Ripman gave him the honour of leading the Beelzebub reading group. Mrs. Ripman observed on numerous occasions that he had a deep love for Beelzebub, and it is this continuing love which says why he wishes to present on this occasion a paper on "Time".

Forrest McIlwain was introduced by Michael Smyth and the session was opened by the playing of music specially selected by Forrest McIlwain as follows:

Erik Satie Gnossenne 4.
Reading from a Sacred Book.
The Bokharian Dervish Hadji Asvatz-Troov.
Song of the Molokans.

This was then followed by the reading by Forrest McIlwain of Ecclesiastes, Chapter 3:

1. To every thing there is a season, and a time to every purpose under heaven:

2. A time to be born, and a time to die; a time to plant, and a time to pluck up that which is planted;

3. A time to kill, and a time to heal; a time to break down, and a time to build up;

4. A time to weep, and a time to laugh; a time to mourn, and a time to dance;

5. A time to cast away stones, and a time to gather stones together; a time to embrace, and a time to refrain from embracing;

6. A time to get, and a time to lose; a time to keep, and a time to cast away;

7. A time to rend, and a time to sew; a time to keep silence, and a time to speak;

8. A time to love, and a time to hate; a time of war, and a time of peace.

9. What profit hath he that worketh in that wherein he laboureth?

10. I have seen the travail, which God hath given to the sons of men to be exercised in it.

11. He hath made every thing beautiful in his time: also he hath set the world in their heart, so that no man can find out the work that God maketh from the beginning to the end.

12. I know that there is no good in them, but for a man to rejoice, and do good in his life.

13. And also that every man should eat and drink, and enjoy the good of all his labour, it is the gift of God.

14. I know that, whatsoever God doeth, it shall be for ever: nothing can be put to it, nor any thing taken from it: and God doeth it, that men should fear before him.

15. That which hath been is now; and that which it to be hath already been; and God requireth that which is past.

16. And moreover I saw under the sun the place of judgment, that wickedness was there; and the place of the righteousness, that iniquity was there.

17. I said in mine heart, God shall judge the righteous and the wicked: for there is a time there for every purpose and for every work.

18. I said in mine heart concerning the estate of the sons of men, that God might manifest them, and that they might see that they themselves are beasts.

19. For that which befalleth the sons of men befalleth beasts; even one thing befalleth: as the one dieth, so dieth the other; yea, they have all one breath; so that a man hath no preeminance above a beast: for all is vanity.

20. All go unto one place; all are of the dust, and all return to dust again.

21. Who knoweth the spirit of man that goeth upward, and the spirit of the beast that goeth downward to the earth?

22. Wherefore I perceive that there is nothing better, than that a man should rejoice in his own works; for that is his portion: for who shall bring him to see what shall be after him?

Time in the Cosmology of Mr. Gurdjieff

Introduction

In the Cosmology of Mr. Gurdjieff, there does not exist that which you and I conceptually know as "time." Emphatically I say to you, "There is no 'time." This statement makes no sense in the view of conventional thinking, but I would ask that, while pondering this statement, you do so in the light of the following observation from Mr. Gurdjieff:

"... that on Earth in the past it has been usual in every century that every man, in whom there arises the boldness to attain the right to be considered by others and to consider himself a "conscious thinker," should be informed while still in the early years of his responsible existence that man has in general two kinds of mentation one kind, mentation by thought, in which words, always possessing a relative sense, are employed, and the other kind, which is proper to all animals as well as to man, which I would call "mentation by form."[1]

You need to contemplate Mr. Gurdjieff's words, and consider that all your understanding, all your knowledge, has at its foundation the two forms of mentation indicated by Mr. Gurdjieff. It follows that each of us is accordingly conditioned: that is, we think and act in the world wholly within the framework of our conditioning. Later in this paper, more will be said about this conditioning and how you have allowed it to limit your world. First, let's take a look at the traditional view of "time."

Contemporary Views of Time

At some point in your life, you have probably wondered about the concept of "time."

I have even wondered if trees and flowers understand and feel "time" as I do. Just as surely, each of us has formulated some notion about the phenomena of "time." In a very simple way you can say that "time" is how long it takes to do something. To a sprinter, it may be the duration of a 100-meter dash, and for a child awaiting the arrival of Santa Claus, "time" may seem endless. Some argue that "time" is money Merely coping in today's world requires you to perform your duties in a timely manner and to have an accompany in a awareness of "time." You have to awaken in a timely manner, in order to not be late for work or any other appointment. If your heart fails to beat in a timely manner, then, you die! It appears that my entire life is in some way or the other moving from one timed event to another. I even depend on other people to be cognizant of the necessity of their timely responses in the world.

It's absolutely amazing the number of roles that this thing called "time" can and does take on. A thief serving a sentence of ten years in prison has "time" on his/her hands. I run short of "time"

---

[1] G. I. Gurdjieff, *Beelzebub's Tales to His Grandson,* New York: Harcourt, Brace and Company, 1950, p15.

when I am faced with a deadline that's too immediate. With the onset of death, you sooner or later run out of "time."

Here's an interesting observation: whatever "time" is, it must be that there exists subsets of a general all-containing universal "time." I draw this conclusion, because on any given day, there are those people who are feeling tremendously pressed by "time," there are those people who are feeling that they have nothing but "time," and of course there are those people for whom "time" has come to an end. In fact, it would not be farfetched to conclude that on any given day, someone may have experienced each of the aforementioned subsets of "time."

You can go on and on, uncovering definition after definition for the concept we call "time." In a very general way, we can agree that a good working definition for "time" is the distance, as measured by the clock, between an event (A) and an event (B) or (C).

However we are still left with this huge question, "What is time?" Maybe towards an attempt to define "time" we can examine some of the aspects of "time." For instance, are we able to see from which direction "time" comes? I believe it is reasonable to state that for most of us, "time" appears as movement and comes from the right, along an invisible "time" line, and flows on to the left. This concept of "time" flow is usually stated thusly: you move along the "time" line from the present into the future, which then becomes the present, and what was the present has now become the past. Expressions such as yesterday, tomorrow, last week, ancient, and historical, all reinforce the accepted concept of "time" flowing in the manner stated above.

There unfolds an immediate and serious consequence for human beings (three-brain-beings) and the "time" line. The problem arises because we have this sense of a "time" line where movement along the line is from past to future, and because of this sense of movement, we make a similar projection onto civilization. It is generally assumed that parallel to the "time" line is a corresponding movement or growth in civilization. But, Beelzebub speaks to an increasing deterioration in the quality of understanding, knowledge, and being in contemporary three-brain-beings. So, viewed from a different angle, one comes to the conclusion that civilization has regressed, not progressed. This view is certainly opposite the conventional view and thinking about civilization.

A Brief Commentary on the History of the Time Concept and the Arising of Time

To say that there was an arising of "time" is to imply that there was a point in the history of the universe where "time" did not exist. While that may be the case, have you ever attempted to imagine a universe where there was no "time"? History is the chronological tracking of events. Many scientists and others generally accept that life and "time" began with what is commonly referred to as the "Big Bang." According to this presumption, matter and the universe as it is known was created with the "Big Bang." A Big Bang Theory: The theory that the universe began in a state of compression to infinite density and has been expanding since some particular instant marked the origin of the universe. The Big Bang is the most generally accepted cosmological theory.[2]

The preceding commentary speaks only to one side of the "time" coin. If I flip the coin, then, I find a world/universe that may not have always existed, but where "time" existed before this world/universe came into being and will persist even if this world/universe ceases to exist. In short, this implies that there was no arising of "time" simply because "time" has always existed and will always exist.

Measuring Time

There are many, many ways by which contemporary people measure "time." Most commonly, "time" is measured simply with a watch that is worn on the wrist or a clock that hangs on the wall. For a more precise measurement, one may choose to use an atomic clock. An atomic clock is a clock whose scale is based upon atomic or molecular motion. The scale in an atomic clock is calibrated to measure "time" by counting the cycles of vibrational motion (frequency) relative to a particular substance or compound. The measurements derived are referred to as Atomic Time. There is an international atomic time defined as the internationally agreed upon time reference conforming to the definition of the second, the fundamental unit of atomic time in the International System of Units (SI). It is defined as the duration of 9,192,61,770 periods of the radiation corresponding to the transition between two hyperfine levels of the ground state of the caesium 133 atom.

In the U.S., official "time" is maintained by the U.S.N.O (United States Naval Observatory). "Time" is coordinated internationally by the International Bureau of Weights and Measures (BIPM) in Paris, France, which is responsible for Coordinated Universal Time (UTC) and the designation of Leap seconds. However, when you speak of clocks and watches, most three-brain beings will be likely to associate some type of mechanical movement (springs, gears, quart crystals) to the means by which clocks and watches operate and "time" is measured. For three-brain beings the basis for all "time" measurements of the mechanical nature is the revolution of the planet Earth around its Sun. I will even venture to suggest that the concept of "atomic time" has as its basis, also, the revolution of the planet earth around its Sun. The concept of "atomic time" is simply a refined aspect of this particular relation between the earth and the sun. It is important that we understand there is no conceptual difference in the psyche of three-brain beings, between "time" measured by an atomic clock and "time" as measured by your analog or digital clock.

All clocks can be classified as instruments by which the earth's rotation is measured. One can examine his/her clock and ascertain how close the earth is towards the completion of its current rotation.

---

[2] Sybil P. Parker, Editor in Chief McGraw-Hill, *Encyclopedia of Astronomy*, New York: McGraw-Hill Book Company, 1983, p32 & p33.

All & Everything Conference 1998

The previous observations may not seem new or insightful, but I implore you to examine this relationship between the Earth and its Sun; and discover the effect it has had on your psyche. Sooner or later, you will begin to see how something in you has so identified with this Earth-Sun relationship that you go about as if in a "time" prison. The identification with the Earth-Sun relationship has formed the bars to your "time" prison cell.

Another of the more commonly used devices for measuring "time is the ordinary calendar. Over the course of human history, there have been many types of calendars. History records the first calendar as appearing around 20 BC. I doubt if one thinks of a calendar as a measuring device, but indeed calendars are just extension of clocks given that their units of measure are multiples of the clock units.

Have you ever considered that a calendar is simply a means by which one is able to track the earth's revolution about the sun? The smallest unit on a calendar is one day and as we measure, it takes the earth approximately 365 days to make a complete revolution of its Sun.

Once again I urge you to examine this Earth-Sun relationship. The identification with this Earth-Sun relationship has been the means by which the walls to your "time" prison have been constructed.

Perhaps it was not immediately apparent, but the two spatial relationships between the Earth and its Sun, and my identification with them, are the mechanisms or movements by which my inner clock functions. Why should this be of concern to you or me? It should be of concern because, regardless of whether I am examining myself or the world in general, it is from the perspective and degree of identification with my inner clock, whose mechanism is set to the motion of the Earth around the Sun. It means that when I look out into the night sky, the stars and planets have been fixed in position by the inner clock. Telescopes merely serve to show me more stars and planets that are locked in place. It means that, unless I have developed my organism to receive and process higher vibrations, the music I hear is simply a harmonic of my inner clock

Units of Time

We are all familiar with the concepts of a year, a *month*, a *day*, and an hour and so on to *minutes* and *seconds*. There are numerous references that speak to the origin of these concepts. For example, the hour: the Egyptians had ten hours of daylight, from sunrise to sunset (exemplified by a sundial described in 1300 B.C.E), two hours of twilight and twelve hours of night. The calendar year was divided into 36 decans, each ten days long, plus five extra days, for a 365 - day year. Each decan corresponded to a third zodiacal sign and was represented by a decanal constellation. In the summer sky, the night corresponded to about twelve decans, although half a day would correspond to eighteen decans. This led to the division of the night into twelve hours.[3]

---

[3] *The Exact Sciences in Antiquity*, 2nd Edition. O. Neugebauer, Dover Publications, New York, 1969
A History of Ancient Mathematical Astronomy. O. Neugebaurer, Springer-Verlag, Berlin, 1975

Time in the Cosmology of Mr. Gurdjieff

The Sensation of Time

Beelzebub often spoke about the wrong-education of the three brain-beings of the planet Earth. Those of you who read *All and Everything*, have encountered this observation again and again. One of the ways in which your education has gone far astray is with the phenomenon of "time." Almost from the moment you arise, you are taught how to tell time, how to measure time and how to keep in time. In short, you are conditioned in a way that will shape and color your world. This is all fine for coping in the contemporary world, but unfortunately, it is quite to the detriment of a healthier psyche.

Very early in one's existence, one had no basis for measuring or sensing time, and the world was experienced in a different way. One no longer remembers those moments, and so it appears that we have always experienced the world in the same way as we do now.

Very early in the Gurdjieff "work," we are told that, "We do not remember ourselves." Couple this observation with one's sense of measurement and "time," and factor in the deeper complication of projecting one's sense of "time" onto everything else in the universe. Mr. Gurdjieff speaks directly to this projection of one's "time": "Only Time alone has no sense of objectivity because it is not the result of the fractioning of any definite cosmic phenomena. And it does not issue from anything, but blends always with everything and becomes self-sufficiently independent; therefore, in the whole of the Universe, it alone can be called and extolled as the 'Ideally-Unique-Subjective-Phenomenon.'"[4]

This is an appropriate place to present this question as food for thought. If, as I have proposed to you, you make this search for the source or sensation of "time," and you discover that the only clock ticking away is in you, then, what does this say about the existence of objective "time"? I say again, "There is 'NO TIME.'"

The Search for My Sensation of Time

What are the consequences of not remembering ourselves and the way we sense "time" and project it onto the universe? I learned about the consequences while searching for my sensation of "time." Is Mr. Gurdjieff saying that only my personal sense of "time" is genuine? If the answer to this question is "yes," then, how is it that my sense of "time" and your sense of "time" seem to agree with everyone else's sense of "time?" Furthermore, how could I even begin to suggest there is *No Time*, given that so much around and about me says there is "time"?

When this question first began to burn within, I found myself at an impasse. While the world to which I was accustomed was filled with a sense of "time," someone else within me seemed to know of another world. At this point in my life I was already questioning things that most people take for granted. I wanted to know why stars and galaxies existed. I wanted to know why I was

---

[4] G.I. Gurdjieff, *Beelzebub's Tales to His Grandson*, New York: Harcourt, Brace and Company, 1950, p124

here on this planet. I was relatively new as a formal member of a Group in the Gurdjieff Work, but I had come to the "Work" because I was convinced that I could find the knowledge I sought, and which I knew, without a doubt, existed somewhere on this Earth.

I didn't realize it then, but in hindsight I can see that my prayers had been answered simply by learning of the "Work" and Hugh B. Ripman. Mr. Ripman was my first teacher and though I can't say specifically what he did to help me along the way, I can say that through him, a lot of help came to me. I share this because, somehow Hugh Ripman not only recognized the questions that were burning in me, but he apparently knew which question had the power behind it. I think this is where, in the form of a strong impetus, he applied the help that arrived unseen and unannounced. I only know that my questions about "time" became more and more intense. I recall that during an early discussion with Hugh Ripman, he said to me, "Time is one of the doorways to consciousness." Thus, it is with this background, that I present the following from Peter D. Ouspensky:

"According to real, exact knowledge, one force, or two forces, can never produce a phenomenon. The presence of a third force is necessary for it is only with the help of a third force that the first two can produce what may be called a phenomenon, no matter what sphere.

But, speaking in general, the third force is not easily accessible to direct observation and understanding. The reason for this is to be found in the functional limitations of man's ordinary psychological activity and in the fundamental categories of our perception of the phenomenal world, that is, in our sensation of space and time resulting from these limitations."[5]

Cosmology

In general, cosmology is the study of the origin of the universe. It is not common knowledge that, there are many, many cosmology theories, just as there are many, many relativity theories. The concepts of space and "time" are common to all of the cosmology theories. So it is with this in mind that I relate Mr. Gurdjieff's cosmology to "time."

Mr. Gurdjieff's Cosmology

First, let me make basic points about Mr. Gurdjieff's Cosmology. This Cosmology discussion begins with what Mr. Gurdjieff referred to as the two great cosmic laws. They are the sacred Heptaparaparshinokh and the sacred Triamazikamno (sometimes referred to as the law of threefoldness). According to Mr. Gurdjieff, "Everything that has arisen owes its manifestation to the workings of the two sacred fundamental cosmic laws. Without exception, these two laws act in everything in every moment."

---

[5] P. D. Ouspensky, *In Search of the Miraculous: Fragments of an Unknown Teaching*, Harcourt Brace Jovanovich, 1977, p77

Time in the Cosmology of Mr. Gurdjieff

Mr. Gurdjieff goes on to say, "The first of these fundamental primordial cosmic scared laws, namely, the law of Heptaparaparshinokh, which present-day objective cosmic science, by the way, formulates in the following words:

"The-line-of-the-flow-of-forces-constantly-deflecting-according-to-law-and-uniting-again-at-its-ends.'

"This sacred primordial cosmic law has seven deflections or, as it is still otherwise said, seven 'centers of gravity' and the distance between each two of these deflections or 'centers of gravity' is called a 'Stopinder-of-the-sacred-Heptaparaparshinokh.'

"This law, passing through everything newly arising and everything existing, always makes its completing processes with its seven Stopinders."[6]

Regarding the second primordial fundamental cosmic law, Mr. Gurdjieff says that objective science formulates in the following way:

" new arising from the previously arisen through the "Harnel-miatznel," the process of which is actualized thus: the higher blends with the lower in order to actualize the middle and thus becomes either higher for the preceding lower, or lower for the succeeding higher; and as I already told you, this Sacred Triamazikamno consists of three independent forces, which are called:

the first, the 'Affirming force' or the pushing-force' or simply the 'Force-plus', the second, the 'Denying-force' or the 'Resisting force' or simply the 'Force minus" and the third, the 'Reconciling-force' or the 'Equilibrating-force' or the 'Neutralizing-force.'"

Gurdjieff's Cosmology is expressed in a precise ancient symbol, of which he states, "Speaking in general it must be understood that the Enneagram is a universal symbol. All knowledge can be included in the Enneagram and with the help of the Enneagram it can be interpreted.

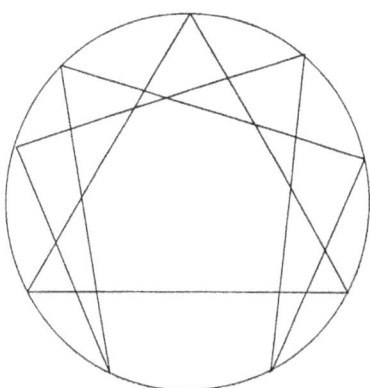

---

[6] G. I. Gurdjieff. *Beelzebub's Tales to His Grandson*, New York: Harcourt Brace and Company, 1950, p750-751

All & Everything Conference 1998

In order to approach an understanding of the Enneagram, it is first necessary to acquire a sound understanding of the workings of the two sacred primordial fundamental cosmic laws. This paper is about the concept of "time," and so I will speak only to the relevant aspects of Mr. Gurdjieff's Cosmology. In most of the books published about the Enneagram, or even in the Enneagram workshops, there is no indication that the two sacred primordial laws have anything whatsoever to do with the Enneagram symbol. I can't begin to understand how one could speak about the Enneagram without speaking about the sacred Heptaparaparshinokh and the sacred Triamazikamno.

For the purposes of this paper, I will simply remind you that the sacred Heptaparaparshinokh expresses seven notes counting from Do to Si, with an eighth note appearing as the entrance into the next octave. Another aspect of this sacred law is that the distances (intervals) between the notes (Do-Re-Mi-Fa-Sol-La-Si-Do) are not equal. In an attempt to understand this law, you should remember that from one interval to the next, the development or deterioration of an octave occurs unevenly. It is because of this aspect of the law that variation and deviation are expressed in the universe. In any given note of an octave, there are likely to be multiple levels of octaves, or if you think about this from the other direction, the octave being examined may simply be a note in its harmonic. At this point in your study of this sacred law, you start to get a sense of how the many ascends to the one, or the one descends into the many.

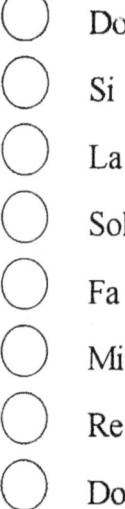

○ Do
○ Si
○ La
○ Sol
○ Fa
○ Mi
○ Re
○ Do

Now, let me say a little about the sacred Triamazikamno or as it is sometimes called, "The Law of Three." This law centers on the interplay of three forces. In Mr. Gurdjieff's Cosmology, this fundamental law creates all phenomena in all the diversity or unity in the universe. Every phenomenon, on whatever scale and in whatever world, from molecular to cosmic phenomena arises as the result of the combination or meeting of three different and opposing forces. Once again, I won't get into a major discussion regarding the working of this sacred law, but for the purposes of this paper the three forces will be designated as force 1, force 2, and force 3. I caution you not to attach any additional meaning to these designations and in particular the numbers. The three forces stand in a vibratory relationship to one another, where the unit of measure is density

Time in the Cosmology of Mr. Gurdjieff

of vibrations or density of matter. There is an inverse relationship between density of vibrations versus density of matter. The more prominent the density of matter, then, the more diminutive the density of vibrations. A substance in one moment is the conductor of force 1 and in the next instance it may be the conductor of either of the other two forces or vice versa. So it is as regards force 2 or force 3.

For most of us the aforementioned properties of the sacred Triamazikamno, along with some other properties of this great cosmic law, make the detection of force 3 extremely difficult. Recall Ouspensky's observation in this regard. Again, I can't help but wonder how it is that people can take such a casual approach to the study of the Enneagram, and then claim to understand it.

The three forces combine in such a way that there are six possible triads arising from the combinations.

Possible Triads

1	2	3	4	5	6
force 1	force 1	force 2	force 2	force 3	force 3
force 2	force 3	force 1	force 3	force 1	force 2
force 3	force 2	force 3	force 1	force 2	force 1

I won't attempt, in this paper, to do a major analysis of the sacred Triamazikamno, but for those who are interested and haven't already done so, then according to Mr. Gurdjieff, there is significant benefit in making the effort to understand the two great Cosmic laws.

○ ABSOLUTE
○ ALL WORLDS
○ ALL SUNS
○ SUN
○ PLANETS
○ EARTH
○ MOON
○ ABSOLUTE

This is the diagram of Gurdjieff's Ray of Creation. This diagram resembles the previous diagram with the exception that the notes (Do-Si-La-Sol-Fa-Mi-Re-Do) have been replaced with other labels. This diagram is sometimes presented as the octave of radiation. Looking at the diagram, you will see that the different levels of worlds are represented in a descending order, when you consider the aspect of density of vibrations. In other words, the density of vibrations in the Sun is far greater than the density of vibrations in the Earth. Conversely, this means the Sun has a smaller density of matter than does the Earth. Here again, we are faced with an observation that flies in the face of conventional thinking.

Earlier it was stated that everything in the universe came about as a result of three forces coming together. In the Ray of Creation, we find that the forces are acting in the following triad: 1- 2 -3. Keep in mind, however, that the way in which the forces act (manifest) is not the same as the density of vibrations. If you were considering density of vibrations alone, then, the order would be 1- 3- 2.

The triad that has forces acting in the order of 1 - 2 - 3 is known as the growth triad I can't speak for you, but prior to encountering this Cosmology, my concept of growth was that something was moving in the upward direction. For as long as I held onto my initial concept of growth, I was unable to penetrate the mystery of a creation that was a part of a descending order, as opposed to an ascending order.

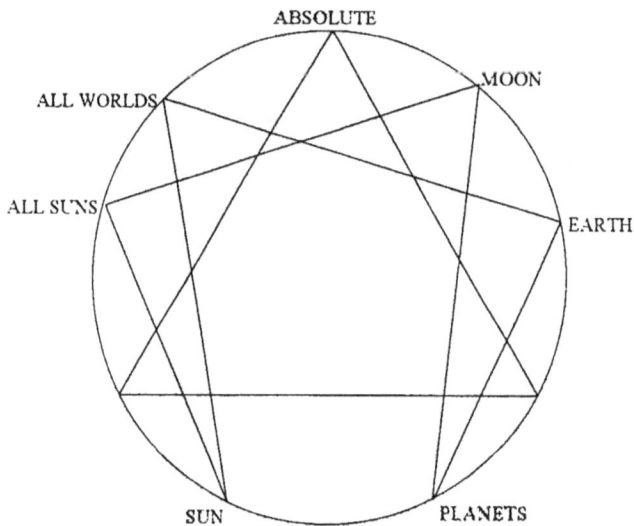

The illustration above is the Ray of Creation, as it appears when it is laid out on the Enneagram.

More will be said about the Ray of Creation and its development. Many of you have already been studying this Cosmology, and so I wish to focus on matters that speak directly to you and me. I will move to the place in the Ray of Creation where Tetartocosmoses (three-brain-beings) have developed.

In the Cosmology of Mr. Gurdjieff, the whole aim behind the Ray of Creation and its growth is towards an eventual return (ascent) to the Absolute. You and I need to see where we fit into the

Time in the Cosmology of Mr. Gurdjieff

scheme of things, and see what, if any, possibilities there are for benefiting by participation in an ascent towards the Absolute.

I introduce here another Enneagram, but this Enneagram is not a representation of the outer world. It is instead, a map that shows the development of food after it enters the organism of three-brain-beings. In other writings, this Enneagram map has been labelled as the food diagram.

Remember in the Ray of Creation diagram the triads are of the nature 1- 2 - 3. Once more, the 1- 2 - 3 is an expression of the order in which the forces act. In the food diagram, the triad is of the nature 2 - 1- 3. This triad is recognized as the transformation of matter in the scheme of nutrition. Measure by density of vibrations and the triad stand in the order 3- 1- 2.

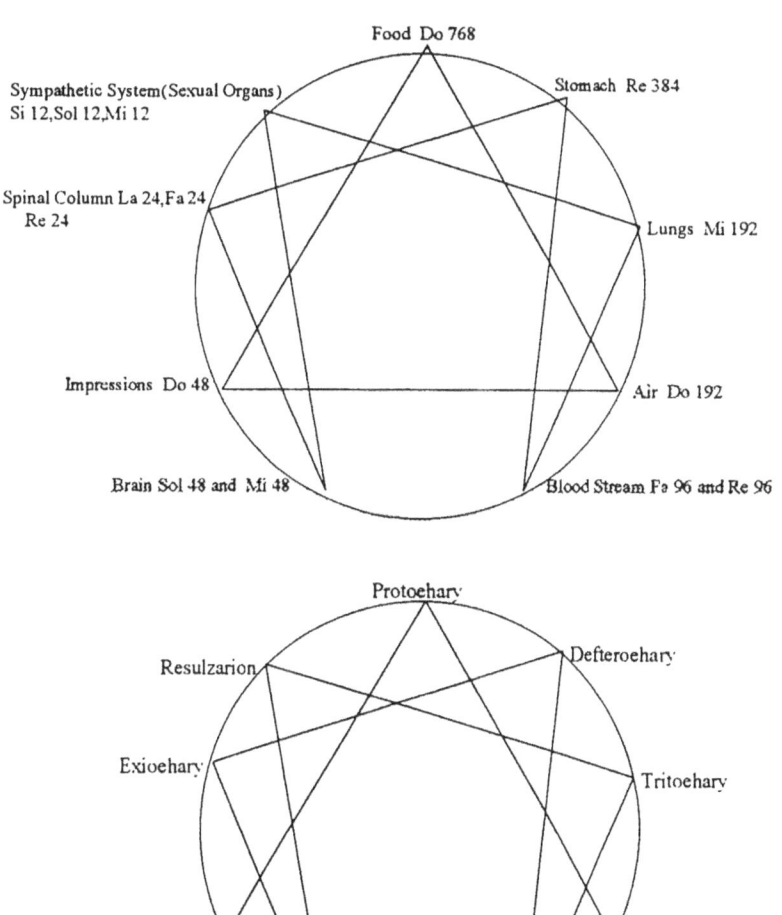

Radiation resulting from the process of food in three brain-beings.

All & Everything Conference 1998

Mr. Gurdjieff indicated that from one viewpoint, the entire universe could be seen as different levels of vibrations. It follows that a three-brain-being is in a sense a collection of forces. To put this in another way, a three-brain-being is a point where various forces meet (come together). In Gurdjieff's Cosmology, a major aspect of it is what he refers to as the Law of Reciprocal Maintenance, where everything in the universe "eats and in turn, is eaten by something else."

In this context, you and I have been designed with the potential to transform forces of a certain quality. Nature has so arranged things that various forces are naturally transformed in us. It simply means that without conscious participation, these transformations occur. These transformations would be labelled as mechanical or automatic transformations. Even though three-brain-beings have the potential to transform forces of a very high quality; it is more likely that those possibilities beat their wings in vain. The possibilities beat their wings in vain because three-brain-beings have not developed to a level of consciousness, where forces of higher quality can be processed. As a result, these high quality forces either pass through our body or they are reflected in some way.

Probably this presentation is triggering some reflection on the "Table of Time and Cosmoses"[7] compiled by Mr. Ouspensky, after some hints from Mr. Gurdjieff. My only comment regarding that table is that if Professor Einstein had encountered Mr. Gurdjieff early on, then, Professor Einstein would have been spared the effort of making a new mathematics towards developing his famous Theory of Relativity. I encourage you to examine this table and see for yourself that indeed, without the need for complex mathematics or physics, the Relativity just falls out. Towards this end, it may be useful to think about Ouspensky's table as a table reflecting time and distance (size). The table in discussion offers at least one other insight. Physicists generally assume that the speed of light is the limiting speed in the universe, however, the table clearly says that this assumption is wrong. Interestingly, some scientists are starting to question the assumption about the speed of light.

Continuing With My Search for Time

In one of our conversations, Hugh Ripman had given me some exercises related to the sensation of time. In connection with the exercises, it was only natural that I began to make larger efforts to detect the origin of the "time" sensation in myself. One day I was blessed with this wonderful insight. I discovered that in my ordinary state of awareness, I was for the most part only vaguely aware of one or two impressions even though I knew that a multitude of impressions had entered my being. For instance, colors, sounds, and shapes I was fascinated with this discovery, since I had previously thought I had a high state of awareness of the world about me.

---

[7] Peter Demianovich Ouspensky. *In Search of the Miraculous: Fragments of an Unknown Teaching.* Harcourt Brace and Jovanovich. 1977, p332

Time in the Cosmology of Mr. Gurdjieff

More discoveries were on the horizon. As I became more sensitive to impressions coming in, I learned that there was a process working unconsciously in me. It became obvious that there was a huge mechanical operation functioning within my being. As near as I could tell, the main function of this operation was to seize incoming impressions and classify them, such as, "this is blue, that is red." This revelation alone was disturbing, but it wasn't all that was revealed. I began to see that that aspect of my being I call "I" was largely outside of myself My attention was usually scattered to the winds.

"If you wish... to come to the knowledge of truth, always urge yourself to rise above sensory things... Thus compelling yourself to turn inwards, you will meet principalities and powers, which wage war against you by suggestions in thought."[8]

"Sensory perception, or the perception of sensory impressions, belongs to the man of action, who labors over attaining the virtues. Non-perception by the senses, or being unmoved by sensory impressions, belongs to the contemplative."[9]

Now that I had learned of this mechanical operation functioning within me, I was in a far better position to see how the factory carried out its mission. After a long period of practice, I was able to bring some attention to bear. I could see that the factory was processing impressions in a singular mode. On occasions there would be more processing in a given period than another period of the same length, but this was only an illusion.

For the most part, I was experiencing the world in a serial manner; that is, one event after another. I was beginning to better understand how with my biases, beliefs, and concepts, I gave shape and color to my world.

If it were not for all the reinforcements of my "time" sensation, then, I might have made these discoveries earlier. Interestingly, I found that I impose the reinforcements on myself, as do you impose them on yourself. For instance, we are all witnesses to the transition of night into day, and day into night. Watching night change into day or, the day become night, feeds and justifies the feeling of an objective sense of "time." Consider the possibility that the earth is breathing, and the phenomena, which you and I identify, as day and night is just the external outer expression of that breathing. Question yourself about the true significance of night and day. Try to learn what it is in you that you stamp with the marking of the days of the week? What clock in you is set when the calendar moves from one month to another?

Consider the birth and death of stars. Both of these events are rarely detected I will suggest here that the birth and death of stars are rarely detected, not because they are rarely occurring events, but because of the relatively brief existences of three-brain-beings on the planet Earth. (Stars have an average life of sixty million years, and three-brain-beings have an average life of 70 or so

---
[8] St. Mark The Ascetic, *Philokalia: Prayer of the Heart.*
[9] St. Maximus The Confessor, *Philokalia: Prayer of the Heart.*

133

years). My observation has some similarity to one made by Mr. Gurdjieff. We have the following from Beelzebub, "But actually from the point of view of the sensation of the duration of Time by your favorites of the planet Earth, the whole length of the existence of the 'beings microcosmoses,' lasts only a few 'minutes' and sometimes even only a few of their 'seconds.'" [10]

I continued with the exercises and soon thereafter made another discovery. My insight was an intellectual insight, but it gave me enough of a hint to see that my sense of "time" was arbitrary. Someone inside of me was beginning to feel some sense of freedom from the habitual sensation of "time." I went on with the exercises and then, out of the blue it happened! *My sense of "time" disappeared.*

Now I know that many of you have had experiences and accordingly you know those experiences were a gift to you and for you. While it's not possible to truly share this particular experience with you, I can say that the experience was a direct experience of no "time," and that along with the sensation of time disappearing, there also disappeared many other things that are clearly attached to this sensation of "time". Prior to this experience, I would never have guessed that so much baggage was riding on that sensation that you and I feel as "time".

This is what Gurdjieff had to say on the matter to which I've just spoken. 'Not for nothing is it stated in that branch of genuine science entitled "the laws of association of human mentation," which has come down from very ancient times and is known to only a few contemporary people, that the sensing of the flow of time is directly proportional to the quality and quantity of the flow of thoughts."[11]

Final Thoughts

There is a point in the "Work" when you are told, "You need to repair the past." How is this possible? It's not only possible, but also valid in the light of this paper. The past and future all come to one 'Now.' An event occurring on Saturday appears to reach back in "time" to trigger yet another event on Tuesday. As remembering yourself becomes more intense, you begin to see the budding and blossoming of seeds planted decades ago.

This paper will probably hold little interest to those who are not on the path, and Perhaps only a small interest to those who are on the path. My intent with this Presentation has been to raise high my torch, and point to a doorway to which I've been guided by the map of Mr. Gurdjieff Cosmology. Maybe a more direct impetus behind this paper, and just before his death, was a firm, but heartfelt, encouragement from Hugh B. Ripman. His words to me, "If you've been smitten by God, then, stay smitten!" There is no "time"!

---

[10] G. I. Gurdjieff, *Beelzebub's Tales to His Grandson*. New York: Harcourt Brace and Company. 1950, p127
[11] G. I. Gurdjieff, *Beelzebub's Tales to His Grandson*. NY: Harcourt. Brace and Company. 1950, p1185

Time in the Cosmology of Mr. Gurdjieff

I must say to you that here in England, on previous visits, I've had the most intense awareness of a "time" body. This means that someone in me is aware of a physical body that is not bounded by time or space I don't mean to imply that this physical body resembles the image that appears in your mind when you hear the word "body." In fact, it would be far more accurate to describe my experience as the presence of an awareness of being without the limitations of boundaries connected with a physical body. It's not only the physical boundaries that disappear; there is also a falling away of national boundaries, racial boundaries, class boundaries and boundaries of personality. When this experience is upon me, it is as though you and everyone else are having the very same experience. In the midst of this experience, we are all in the same place and there is no sense of "time."

Perhaps my words don't carry much weight, but Beelzebub tells us directly:

"Time itself does not exist, there is only the totality of the results ensuing from all the cosmic phenomena present in a given place." Time itself no being can either understand by reason or sense by any outer or inner being-function. It cannot even be sensed by any gradation of instinct which arises and is present in every more or less independent cosmic concentration."[12]

Someone in me does not believe Beelzebub's words because, I often say to myself, "I will work harder tomorrow." Perhaps it's not true for you, but there's no doubt that I have the disease of tomorrow! Gurdjieff indicates in his writings, "There is no tomorrow! It turns out, Gurdjieff is not alone in this observation. Among others who have noticed the phenomenon of "no tomorrow" is Mr. Ouspensky. Take heed of these words from Peter Ouspensky: "Life in itself is time for man. For man there is not and cannot be any other time outside the time of his life. Man is his life. His life is his time... Absolute time for man is his life. There can be no other time outside this time. If I die today, tomorrow will not exist for me."[13]

Truly, it is to this moment that everything comes. Speaking in the *Divine Comedy - Paradise*, Dante says, "All time comes to one **Now** (emphasis mine)."[14] Only when there is **no** "**time**" can I reconcile these words from Lord Krishna, "There was never a time when I was not, nor thou, nor these princes were not, there will never be a time when we shall cease to be...That which is not, shall never be, that which is, shall never cease to be. To the wise, these truths are self-evident."[15] So I say to you, "It is only **NOW** in this moment when I can be." It is only in this moment, no longer in time, where I can say **I AM**! It is only here **NOW**, where there is no "time," that I can speak of eternity! There is **no "time"**!

---

[12] G. I. Gurdjieff, *Beelzebub's Tales to His Grandson*. NY: Harcourt, Brace and Company, 1950, p123
[13] Peter D. Ouspensky. *A New Model of the Universe*. New York: Vintage Books. 1971, p418
[14] Dante. ***The Divine Comedy – Paradise***. Great Britain: Penguin Books, 1962. XVII. 18
[15] Translated by Shri Prohit Swami, *The Bhagavad Gita*, New York: Vintage Books, 1977.

All & Everything Conference 1998

Time in the Cosmology of George I. Gurdjieff
Forrest McIlwain, College Park, MD. March 20, 1998

- *Mr. Gurdjieff:* ...that on Earth in the past it has been usual in every century that every man, in whom there arises the boldness to attain the right to be considered by others and to consider himself a "conscious thinker," should be informed while still in the early years of his responsible existence that man has in general two kinds of mentation: one kind, mentation by thought, in which words, always possessing a relative sense, are employed; and the other kind, which is proper to all animals as well as to man, which I would call "mentation by form."

Contemporary View of Time

- Simple view: how long it takes to do something -- distance from event A to event B
- Various roles of time in different situations:
  - to a sprinter -- duration of the 100-meter dash
  - to a child waiting for Santa, time is endless
  - time is money to some
  - Nothing but time: a thief serving a long sentence
  - Out of time: death
- Aspects of "time": from what direction does it come?

Consequences of Time Line

- We project our sense of movement on to civilization
- Assume corresponding movement or growth in civilization
- Beelzebub: deterioration in quality of understanding, knowledge, and being
- Civilization regressing, not progressing

History of Time Concept

- History: chronological tracking of events
- Big Bang Theory: generally accepted point of creation of matter and the universe -- beginning of life and time
- No arising of time -- time always existed and will continue to exist even if the universe does not

Measuring Time

- Mechanical movement
- Atomic time -- molecular vibrations
- Calendar
- Basis of measurements: Earth's revolution around the Sun

Effect on Psyche

- Identification with Earth-Sun relationship
- Inner clock mechanism set to motion of the Earth around the Sun
- The bars to your "time" prison cell
- Stars and planets fixed in position by our inner clock
- Unless I develop to receive higher vibrations, music I hear is a harmonic of my inner clock

Time in the Cosmology of Mr. Gurdjieff

The Sensation of Time

- Wrong education about time a detriment
- Before we are taught to tell "time," experience world differently
- The Work: We do not remember ourselves
- We project our sense of "time" onto everything else

Projecting One's Sense of Time

- Mr. Gurdjieff:
  - Only Time alone has no sense of objectivity because it is not the result of the fractioning of any definite cosmic phenomena. And it does not issue from anything, but blends always with everything and becomes self-sufficiently independent; therefore, in the whole of the Universe, it alone can be called and extolled as the "Ideally-Unique-Subjective-Phenomenon."

No Time

- Search for the source of your sensation of time
- If the only clock ticking away is in you, what does this say about the existence of objective time?
- There is NO "Time"

My Search

- I learned the consequences of not remembering ourselves and the way we sense time and project it onto the universe.
- Came to work because I questioned life views most take for granted
- Hugh B. Ripman: "Time is one of the doorways to consciousness."

Peter Ouspensky

"According to real, exact knowledge, one force, or two forces, can never produce a phenomenon. The presence of a third force is necessary for it is only with the help of a third force that the first two can produce what may be called a phenomenon, no matter what the sphere....But speaking in general, the third force is not easily accessible to direct observation and understanding. The reason for this is to be found in the functional limitations of man's ordinary psychological activity and in the functional categories of our perception of the phenomenal world, that is, in our sensation of space and time resulting from these limitations."

Mr. Gurdjieff's Cosmology

- The study of the origin of the universe
- Many theories of the origin of the universe -- space and time concepts common to all
- Gurdjieff -- two cosmic laws act in everything in every moment
  - Heptaparaparshinokh
  - Triamazikamno (law of threefoldness)

All & Everything Conference 1998

Heptaparaparshinokh

- The line of the flow of forces constantly deflecting according to law and uniting again at its ends
- Seven deflections -- centers of gravity
- Distance between deflections: Stopinders
- "This law, passing through everything newly arising and everything existing, always makes its completing processes with its seven Stopinders."

Sacred Triamazikamno

- Higher blends with the lower to actualize the middle
- Becomes either higher for the preceding lower, or lower for the succeeding higher
- Three forces:
  - Affirming force (pushing; force plus)
  - Denying force (resisting; force minus)
  - Reconciling force (equilibrating; neutralizing)

The ENNEAGRAM -- an ancient, universal symbol and expression of Mr. Gurdjieff's Cosmology

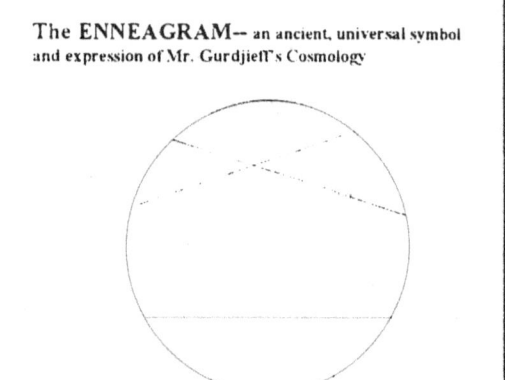

Gurdjieff's Enneagram

- "All knowledge can be included in the Enneagram and with the help of the Enneagram, it can be interpreted." (Gurdjieff)
- Most books on Enneagram do not speak of Heptaparaparshinokh and Triamazikamno.
- Universe - different levels of vibrations
- We are a collection of forces: Law of Reciprocal Maintenance
- We have the potential to transform forces

The Ray of Creation

Do
Si
La
Sol
Fa
Mi
Re
Do

-- distances between the notes are not equal
-- the development or deterioration of an octave occurs unevenly from one interval to the next
-- in any note, there are multiple levels of octaves
-- the many ascends to the one, or the one descends into the many

Three Forces Combine Into Six Possible Triads

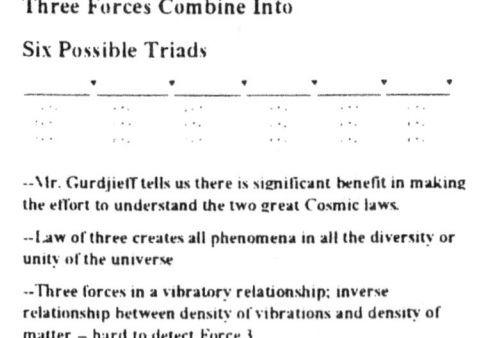

-- Mr. Gurdjieff tells us there is significant benefit in making the effort to understand the two great Cosmic laws.

-- Law of three creates all phenomena in all the diversity or unity of the universe

-- Three forces in a vibratory relationship; inverse relationship between density of vibrations and density of matter -- hard to detect Force 3

Time in the Cosmology of Mr. Gurdjieff

ABSOLUTE	**Octave of Radiation**
ALL WORLDS	--Density of vibrations in descending order
ALL SUNS	
SUN	--Density of matter in ascending order
PLANETS	--Action order is 1-2-3 (growth, descending order!)
EARTH	
MOON	--Density of vibrations order is 1-3-2
ABSOLUTE	

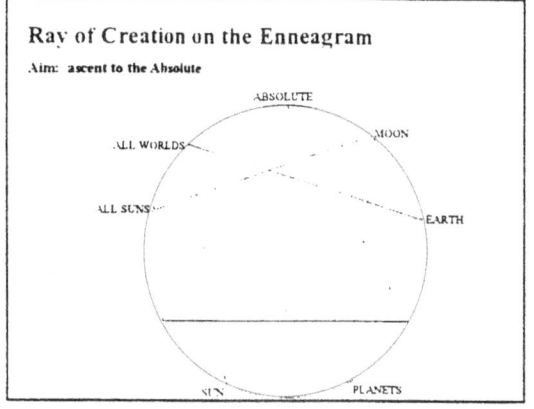

Ray of Creation on the Enneagram
Aim: ascent to the Absolute

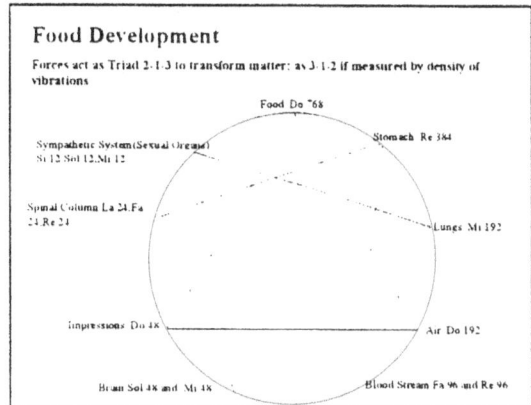

Food Development
Forces act as Triad 2-1-3 to transform matter; as 3-1-2 if measured by density of vibrations

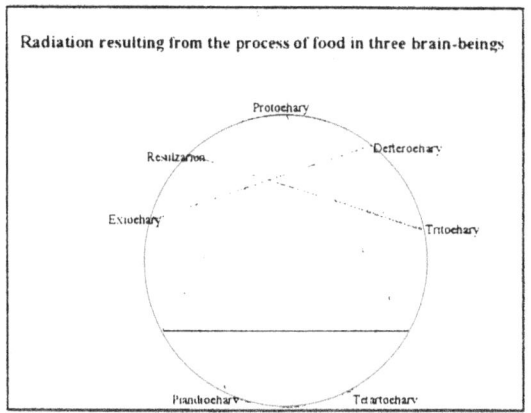

Radiation resulting from the process of food in three brain-beings

Continuing My Search

- Exercises to detect origin of "time" sensation in myself -- arbitrary. My sense of time disappeared.
- Ordinarily aware of only a few impressions although many enter my being
- Mechanical operations to classify incoming impressions-- attention is scattered
- Rise above sensory things and experiencing world serially, one event after another
- The sensing of the flow is time is directly proportional to the quality and quantity of the flow of thoughts (Gurdjieff)

Final Thoughts

- "Repair the past." The past and future are one "Now."
- Mr. Ripman's encouragement: "If you've been smitten by God, then stay smitten!"
- Beelzebub: "Time itself does not exist; there is only the totality of the results ensuing from all the cosmic phenomena present in a given place. Time itself no being can either understand by reason or sense by any outer or inner being-function. It cannot even be sensed by any gradation of instinct which arises and is present in every more or less independent cosmic concentration."
- There is NO "time," no tomorrow. "Absolute time for man is his life." (Ouspensky). It is only NOW when I AM!

© Copyright 1998 - Forrest McIlwain - All Rights Reserved

Time in the Cosmology of Mr. Gurdjieff - Questions & Answers

Nicolas Tereshchenko: Thank you very much for your excellent presentation, but I have three comments, two of which are in question form. My first comment and question is why did you use for your definition of the Heptaparaparshinokh the one in the first English translation? It was later altered by Mister Gurdjieff from "deflecting according to law" (which has no meaning unless the law is explicitly given) into "deflects at specific intervals", as given in the latest English version. So that is the real, the latest version, as I know for certain because I had the privilege of seeing the Russian text itself. The "the line of the flow of forces constantly deflecting according to law and uniting again at its ends" version is, of course, the situation of the Heptaparaparshinokh within the Sun Absolute, that is before it was modified to create the world. That is my first question and comment.

My second comment, you are quite right; in none of the articles and books giving the unnatural usage of the Enneagram by Ichazo and various other people, do they speak about the Heptaparaparshinokh. In my books, so far published only in French, I make it quite clear that until both the Triamazikamno and the Heptaparaparshinokh have been understood at least "intellectually", you cannot understand the Enneagram. I was very interested to see that quite a few of your diagrams of the Enneagram are essentially similar to the ones in my book.

My third comment is really the second question. Why did you not tell us what you think about Mister Gurdjieff's personifying Time as the Merciless Heropass, with its own laws which not even His Endlessness can go against?

Forrest McIlwain: I will try to answer your questions. Regarding your first observation, I have several versions of Beelzebub. I was fortunate to get from the Oregon people one of the original translations, one that is not in book form as we see it, and I could have used that. I could have used any one off the other translations or definitions, as you point out, of the Heptaparaparshinokh. But my attempt was to try and cause as little confusion as possible, and it is only for that reason those such as yourself who have spent a long time studying this, I feel that I could not cause any confusion on your behalf. And so if I was going to make an error, I would do it towards those who had already been studying this and not for those who were beginning to study, because it is very difficult when people first look at the Law of Seven and the Law of Three, and I wanted to try to give as much encouragement as possible, and that was the whole reason for this, to try to use a definition that I thought people would be more likely to have.

And the other observation about the Merciless Heropass, again some of the people present had already mentioned to me that they may have read the Holy Planet Purgatory, in the course of which Mr. Gurdjieff talks about the whole of the development of the Universe in order to arrest what was taking place as a result of the Merciless Heropass. And again, in consideration of the people who are making the effort to read and understand Holy Planet Purgatory, I simply decided not to add any more to it at that time.

Nicolas Tereshchenko: Thank you very much.

Bill Murphey: How does one reconcile the age of Hassein, Beelzebub's grandson, a boy of 12 on the planet Karatas, as opposed to 4668 years as perceived by a being of the planet Earth?

Forrest MacIlwain: Again, you and I talked about this the other day when you brought it up. This is the whole idea about relativity. And in the paper I mentioned how it is that on Earth we tend to project our sense of time and our understanding of the world. We tend to project it on to the rest of the Universe. And this is simply not valid. But if you just want to look at it from a mathematical point of view, you can look at one of the planets such as Pluto and look at the amount of time it takes for Pluto to make its revolution around the Sun and you can see that Pluto takes approximately 300 times as long to make a revolution round the Sun as does the Earth. And in that sense if you were a being on that planet, if you were on the planet Pluto, in the time that you make one revolution, for me it is 300 hundred or so years. But the problem arises because you project your sense of time on to other beings and in the chapter, The Relative Understanding of Time, Mr. Gurdjieff leads us with the example of the beings in a drop of water. And he points out that what for this is a life time, is only a few minutes or a few seconds for you or me. And it is all because of the relativity of size, and if you want to look at it from the point of view of distance, which is a very valid way of thinking about other cosmoses. And again the talk of time and cosmoses given by Mr. Ouspensky is very much a reflection of the theory of relativity. Mr. Einstein talks about time going slow or fast, but it is the same thing. He is talking about it in terms of cosmoses or size, but it is the same thing. And again I can only encourage you to ponder this and not accept what I say but think for yourself. And that is the only way it will have any meaning.

So Hassein appears to be 12 years old on the planet Karatas, but since beings of the planet Earth sense time 389 times slower than the beings of the planet Karatas, to them he is perceived to be (12 x 389) 4668 years old.

Mysterious Coincidences: Gurdjieff, the Enneagram and Tradition

Jim Gomez

Jim was born in 1967, in San Francisco, USA. He discovered the writings of J.G. Bennett during his teenage period in the Bay Area, before moving to Portland Oregon in 1985. There he met Mrs. A.L. Staveley, joining her Gurdjieff groups at Two Rivers Farm during that same year. He participated in her groups until 1993, when he left Oregon to study architecture in the UK.

Jim has studied with Dr. Keith Critchlow, noted expert on sacred architecture, in both the USA and the UK, and as a student at The Prince of Wales's Institute of Architecture in 1993-4. He has also studied at the University of Greenwich where he received his BA Arch in 1996. Since then, he has been working in an architectural practice in London, and has given lectures in sacred geometry at Richmond Upon Thames College as part of an Ecological Building Design unit. He is currently working in a practice, and also pursuing his MA in architecture at the University of Greenwich.

In 1993 Jim was married to Rebekah D. A. Staveley in Aurora, Oregon. They currently live in London and have two children - Jessica I.M. and Samuel T.A. Gomez.

Jim made a presentation at the 1997 Conference under the title:
Musical Proportions and Sacred Geometry in Temple Architecture.

Jim was introduced by Michael Smyth who opened the session by reading from The Golden Verses of Pythagoras and from an unpublished lecture on symbolism by G. Gurdjieff. These readings follow.

Mysterious Coincidences: Gurdjieff, the Enneagram and Tradition

That which thou dost not know, pretend not that thou dost.
Instruct thyself: for time and patience favour all.

- a verse from The Golden Verses of Pythagoras;
translated by Fabre D'Olivet and N. Redford

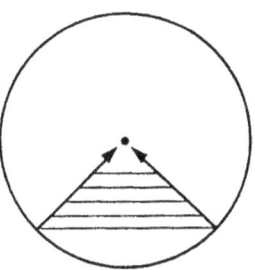

"...In every man there has been implanted a need for knowledge, differing only in its intensity, and the passive human mind, while utilising every means of reception, often gets into an impasse in trying to find an answer to the question `why'.

His eyes are dazzled by the bright play of the colours of multi-formity, and under the glittering surface he does not see the hidden kernel of the one-ness of all that exists. This multiformity is so real that its single modes approach him from all sides - some by way of logical deduction and philosophy, others by faith and feeling. From the most ancient times down to our epoch, throughout the ages of its life, humanity as a whole has been yearning for a knowledge of this one-ness and seeking for it, pouring itself out into various philosophies and religions which remain, as it were, monuments on the path of these searches for the Path, leading to the knowledge of Unity. These searches radiate to the Path just as the radii of a circle join at the centre, getting closer as they come into contact with each other, the nearer they get to the centre. The goal itself determines the direction of the paths, and it brings the wanderers on the paths to a knowledge of the one-ness which reaches the depths where that knowledge becomes a reality to the knower, and can be communicated to another who has not reached the same stage of development..."

- G. Gurdjieff; lecture on symbolism; (unpublished)

All & Everything Conference 1998

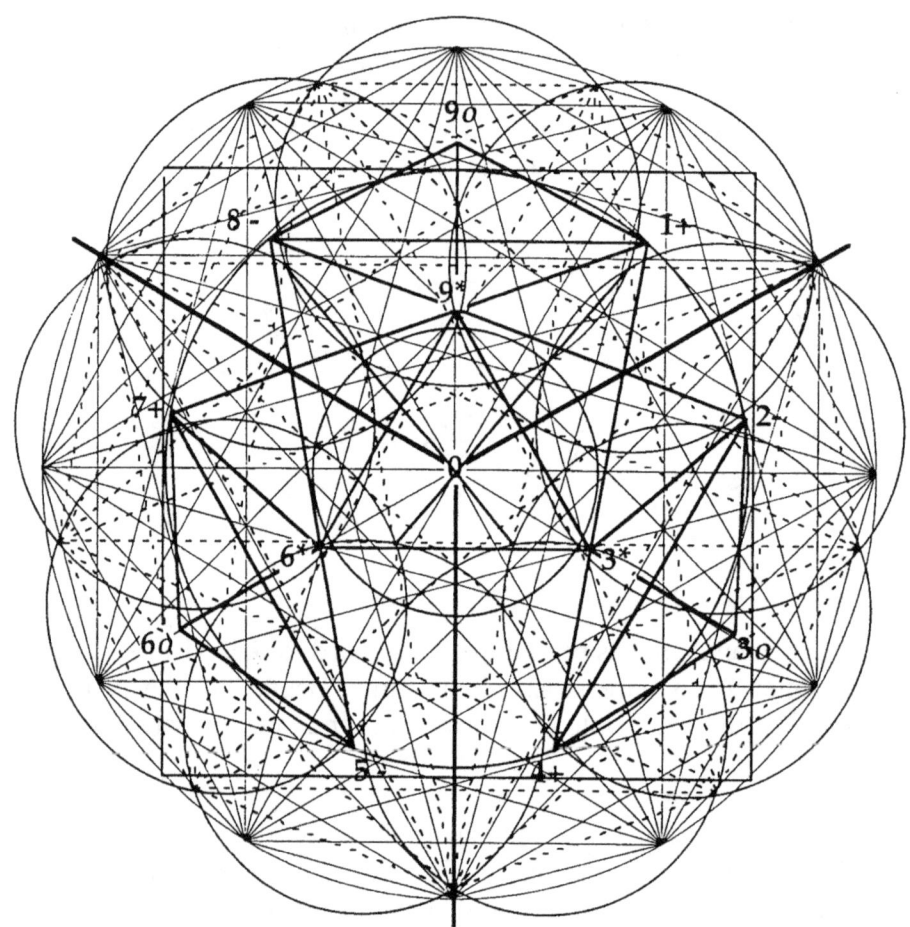

Mysterious Coincidences: Gurdjieff, the Enneagram and Tradition

Introduction

The first mysterious coincidence I would like to mention, and which gave rise to the title for this paper, was the 'coincidence' last year of two talks - one in the UK and one in the USA. Both of these talks dealt, to a much greater and much lesser degree as the case may be, on the enneagram symbol and on its relation to Sufi doctrine - and particularly to the traditional interpretation of the enneagram given from within the most distinguished Naqshbandi Sufi tradition by the American Sufi author Dr. Laleh Bakhtiar.

Temporally speaking, the first of these two talks, entitled *'The Language of Symbolism in Sacred Science'*, was presented here in the UK in March 1997 at the second international *All and Everything* conference, as part of my introduction to an exhibition on sacred geometry and sacred architecture which was on display during the conference. In that talk I also introduced some of the work which has been done by Dr. Laleh Bakhtiar on the Sufi enneagram, and which was published

Mysterious Coincidences: Gurdjieff, the Enneagram and Tradition

in her three-volume work *God's Will Be Done* (Kazi Publications, USA, 1994). Dr. Bakhtiar has focused her study of the enneagram on the symbol as it was and is interpreted and understood within the Naqshbandi Sufi tradition. This tradition is also called 'The Golden Chain' and traces its lineage through 40 Khwajagan or Masters of Wisdom of Central Asia, including Shaykh Muhammed Bahauddin Naqshband of Bukhara, to Abu Bakr as-Siddiq who was the best friend of the Prophet, and through Abu Bakr to the Prophet Mohammed himself (peace be upon him). The history and lives of this Golden Chain of Sufi masters is recorded in a magnificent book entitled *The Naqshbandi Sufi Way* (Kazi Publications 1995), written by the Naqshbandi Shaykh Hisham Kabbani, who is the Shaykh of Laleh Bakhtiar.

I had been in correspondence with Dr. Bakhtiar concerning her work on the Sufi enneagram, and just prior to last year's *All and Everything* conference I was involved in preparing a series of geometric diagrams showing some configurations and layers of interpretation of the Sufi enneagram, following Dr. Bakhtiar's directions. And so, while preparing my short introductory talk last year, I decided to mention Dr. Bakhtiar's work at the last minute. I included a short section on the Sufi enneagram in the paper, along with a few basic diagrams, and I also quickly put together a display board on the Sufi enneagram which was included in the exhibition on sacred geometry and sacred architecture. However, my understanding of her work at that time was very poor, and it was all very new to me, and I therefore failed to give an accurate overview of her profound work at last year's conference. I did, however, feel that this Sufi interpretation of the enneagram could have a special significance for people in the Gurdjieff work. Like a key to a door, it seemed to me that with the help of this new perspective on the enneagram, a new perspective which was also paradoxically an 'old' perspective re-discovered - the enneagram symbol could become more legible to the Gurdjieff groups and as a result become more organically and practically integrated into the psychological, inner task of work on oneself. In our groups in America, the enneagram symbol was often treated as a curiosity, and appeared to many as an eclectic or complicated sideline interest, but not really related to practical work on oneself. This view bothered me, and it seemed rather odd that the symbol which Gurdjieff made such powerful statements about, and which he had 'revealed to the West' for the first time and subsequently used as the symbol for his entire teaching; could be simply dispensed with without any great loss.

A set of geometric drawings of the Sufi enneagram was finally completed in the Summer, and was sent to America in time for incorporation into the second above mentioned talk entitled *The Sufi Enneagram - Balancing the Self* which was delivered by Dr. Bakhtiar in August 1997 to the second International Enneagram Association conference in Baltimore, Maryland USA. During this talk in Baltimore, Dr. Bakhtiar was joined by the Naqshbandi Shaykh Hisham Kabbani who discussed Gurdjieff and the meeting between Gurdjieff and the Naqshbandi Shaykh Sharafuddin Ad-Dagestani, who died in 1936. In Shaykh Hisham's book on the Masters of the Golden Chain, he describes a visit of Gurdjieff to the khaniqah of Shaykh Ad-Dagestani, where he arrived 'after a long and arduous escape from Russia at the time of the Communist Revolution...' (see *The Naqshbandi Sufi Way*; Kazi Publications; p. 360). The town of Daghestan is located in the Southeastern part of Russia, between the Caspian Sea and the border of Georgia. By this time, it is said that Gurdjieff had already had many contacts with Sufis of various orders, and had lived and travelled extensively throughout the region of the Caucasus or *Qaf* mountains, but Gurdjieff was 'pleased to make contact with the most distinguished Naqshbandi order' (op. cit.) During this visit, Gurdjieff is said to have asked for the knowledge of the 'nine points' and to have been given a vision of this knowledge through the Shaykh and his recitation of a verse from the Holy Quran. The verse from the Holy Quran was Surah Ya Sin, also called the 'heart of the Quran', and this verse reads:

"Peace! a Word (of salutations) from a Lord Most Merciful." [36:58]

After his experience with the Shaykh, Gurdjieff is quoted as saying:

"...As soon as you finished the prayer and began to recite, I saw you come to me and take my hand. We were transported to a beautiful rose garden. You told me that this garden is your garden and that these roses are your disciples, each with his own colour and perfume. You directed me to one particular red rose and said, 'That one is yours. Go smell it.' As soon as I did I saw the rose open and I disappeared within it and became the rose. I entered its roots and they led me to your presence. I found myself entering your heart and becoming a part of you.

Through your spiritual power I was able to ascend to the knowledge of the nine points. Then a voice, addressing me as Abd an-Nur said, 'This light and knowledge have been granted to you from the Divine Presence of God to bring peace to your heart. However, you must not use the power of this knowledge.' The voice bid me farewell with the salutation of peace, and the vision ended as you were finishing the recitation from the Quran..."

The Shaykh replied that "...each of the nine points is represented by one of the nine saints who are at the highest level in the Divine Presence. They are the keys to untold powers within the human being, but there is no permission to use these keys. This is a secret that in general will not be opened until the Last Days when the Mahdi appears and Jesus returns. This meeting of ours has been blessed. Keep it as a secret in your heart and do not speak of it in this life. Abd-an-Nur, for that is your name with us, you are free to stay or go as your responsibilities allow. You are always welcome with us. You have attained safety in the Divine Presence. May God bless you and strengthen you in your work." (from *The Naqshbandi Sufi Way*; Kazi Publications; 1995; p. 360-61.)

Shaykh Sharafuddin ad-Daghestani, through whom Gurdjieff is said to have had this experience of the nine points, was the 38th Master of the Golden Chain. He is described as '...a perfect knower in the Divine presence. He was the key to the most inaccessible knowledge ...He was overflowing with knowledge like the Nile when it floods. He was the carrier of the secret of the sultan adh-dhikr, which no one had carried before his time. He was the Master of Wisdom in the beginning of the 20th century and its reviver. The next Shaykh in the Golden Chain, the 39th Master, was Shaykh Abd -Allah Daghestani, and some of you may find his name familiar because he was mentioned by J.G. Bennett in his autobiography *Witness* where he describes his first and second

Mysterious Coincidences: Gurdjieff, the Enneagram and Tradition

meeting with the Shaykh in Damascus in March, 1955 (see *Witness*; pp.308-317; also see J.G. Bennett's *Journeys in Islamic Countries*). Following these two meetings, a chain of events occurred which seemed to be fulfilments of predictions made for J.G Bennett by Shaykh Daghestani. These included events which eventually led to Madame De Salzmann formally separating thee relations between J.G. Bennett's groups and her groups, and forbidding all contact between the two groups (see *Witness* ; *op.cit*.). J.G. Bennett focused his work at Coombe Springs in England, began publishing his book *The Dramatic Universe*, and during this period the group at Coombe Springs built the great hall, called the Djamichunatra, which was based on the design of the enneagram and was used for movements and other exercises.

I was unable to attend the Baltimore conference on the enneagram. Dr. Bakhtiar, however, kindly sent me a tape of her session with Shaykh Hisham Kabbani, and told me how well it went. The positive response from people who had been trying to interpret the enneagram from various 'New Age' perspectives including the Arica, Palmer and other modern typological systems, had been very strong. Dr. Bakhtiar described it as a response of "love and admiration for a Sufi teaching that most new age listeners knew nothing about."

While listening to the recording of this talk in Baltimore, I had - beyond the impression made by the content of the talk itself, and of the beauty and force of the Sufi teaching - a more encompassing impression that this talk was actually an 'event' in what the French esoterist Henry Corbin called 'cosmic history', or *heirohistory*. Heirohistory is a history of the soul, of its descent into matter and its return path. It is a history which is 'more real' than the commonplace, mundane, linear history of spatio-temporal events. Ouspensky, of course, in his *New Model of the Universe*, in his chapter on esoterism, described much the same view as Corbin when he spoke of 'two histories' - one a history of crime, and another which was difficult for him to describe but which was associated in his mind with the idea of esoteric 'schools' - like the school that was behind the building of Notre Dame in Paris. As Ouspensky observed, the history of crime is really the only history we know, whereas to become aware of this 'second' history requires something exceptional from us - that is, an awakened and subtle intuitional perception. However highly developed or refined our ordinary reason may be, cosmic history will remain unperceived without a qualitative shift in our awareness, in relation to our 'valuation' of time, and also without the courage to participate in what can be described as a' living drama' or 'mystery'. As Corbin describes it, sacred history has its own structure which can be seen as:

"...circles, cycles or 'cupolas' of time, ...which not only show us temporal succession finally stabilised in the order of spatial simultaneity, but [also] make possible and illustrate the application of the science of the balance to sacred history. They can do this because the figures and personages distributed within the circles do not constitute the historical causes of their succession to one another, but are the homologues of each other and assume a permanent function according to their respected places and ranks..." H. Corbin, *Temple and Contemplation* (1986)

An event of cosmic history cannot be interpreted but in a cyclic or helical manner. The traditional science of the Balance refers to the astrological mapping of cycles of time according to planetary motions through the Signs of the Zodiac, and their 60 year return to the starting point of Balance in Libra, which then becomes the starting point for a new 60 year cycle (see *God's Will Be Done*, vol. 2; Kazi Publications). As Corbin points out, events of cosmic history are the cycles of psycho-spiritual events as opposed to outer, material events in a non-qualitative, linear time. Something significant had taken place in time - in Baltimore in August 1997 - but the message seemed to 'cut through' ordinary time. As this impression grew with me more and more, I began to reflect on the content of some of my talk from last year. I realised how little I understood of the Sufi enneagram, and it also began to seem strange that I had even discussed it at all. As I wondered about this, the thought came to me that perhaps I was influenced in some way by the second talk in America, and perhaps the significance of the message which is being disclosed concerning the Sufi enneagram at this period in 'sacred history' had somehow pressed itself upon me and made me include it in my presentation in spite of myself and my own personal incomprehension.

The talk by Dr. Bakhtiar and Shaykh Hisham Kabbani presents a special message to the Gurdjieff people. A respect for Gurdjieff and his teaching was clearly shown by Shaykh Hisham, and the assertions concerning Gurdjieff and the meaning of the enneagram symbol have a ring of authenticity. So, this is, for me the first 'mysterious coincidence' - that the paper I delivered at last year's *All and Everything* conference, became coincidentally linked to a Sufi talk in America later that year. And in retrospect it was, in a sense, a result of that USA talk, a talk which came temporally speaking after . As if one of many ripples in the surface of the water, could come in reverse, that is, before the pebble dropped. This type of 'co-incidence' is really very mysterious, as I am sure you will agree. And as I reflected on it in greater depth as a possibility, I was reminded sequentially of many things, and many fundamental work ideas which had lapsed from my consciousness.

In this instance I was also recalled to the book *Living Time* by Maurice Nicoll which is such a significant work and contains such powerful ideas on time. In one passage, Nicoll quotes another of Ouspensky's formulations on the structure of time related to this theme:

"...but although we are not aware of it, sensations of the existence of other 'times', both parallel and perpendicular, continually enter into our consciousness. The parallel times are completely analogous to our [linear] time, whereas the perpendicular 'times' consist only of now, and are, as it were, cross-threads, the woof in a fabric, in their relation to the parallel lines of time which in any case represent the warp..." PD. Ouspensky, *New Model of the Universe*; p. 428; quoted in *Living Time* ; (1976)

And, paradoxically, this became a reminder of certain mysterious aspects of the enneagram symbol itself, aspects which relate the symbol specifically to time, and to the whole mystery of time, its laws and structure, and to time, space and the rest of the conditions of existence.

"...if we take a circle and mark points on it, and imagine a movement around it, we can see how any point may be either regarded as 'future' or 'past' in relation to any other point. It is impossible to speak of any 'beginning' in such a circle..." Maurice Nicoll, *Living Time*; p.161

Mysterious Coincidences: Gurdjieff, the Enneagram and Tradition

This way of viewing geometry and pattern as a symbolic or philosophical geometry, can clearly be related to the interpretation of enneagram symbol. Specifically, it calls into question how we understand the geometric unfolding of the symbol, how we understand its basic mathematical structure, and how we understand the metaphysical or qualitative ideas which are present in that symbol - a theme which I will try to address today in seminar form.

So I thank Dr. Sharp for giving me this theme of mysterious coincidences, a theme which I would not have chosen for myself but which has become a very appropriate reminder to me, and a very useful theme to reflect upon in depth. I have added to this the topic of the relation between Gurdjieff and Tradition, because it is the esoteric and exoteric aspects of the great Traditions of mankind that I am concerned with, and this is where I believe we can find valuable knowledge which will help in a search for Truth separate from politics, in order to further an understanding of the Gurdjieff teaching. It is an error to think that traditional ideas are in some sense worn-out, or only belonging to 'the past'. As Dr. Bakhtiar points out so clearly in her books on *God's Will Be Done*:

"...To speak of Tradition is to speak of the timeless, of religion in its most universal sense. The universal sense of religion incorporates both the Law and the Way. While the Law is the outer dimension, the Way is the inner. This work is encompassed by the inner dimension or the Way, never forgetting that the door to the Way is through the Law..." Laleh Bakhtiar; *God's Will Be Done*; (Kazi Publications) vol. 2; from the preface.

According to the traditional view of cycles of time, we are now in the final stages of the Hindu Manvantara, which is divided into four periods or '*Yugas*'. These periods correspond to the Golden, Silver, Bronze and Iron ages of the ancient Western traditions. And we are now in the final phase or darkest part of the fourth cycle - the '*Kali-Yuga*' or Dark Age, which began over six thousand years ago. According to Rene Guenon, during this period:

"... truths which formerly lay within reach of all mankind have become more and more hidden and difficult of approach; those who have access to them grow gradually fewer and fewer and if the treasure of a 'non-human' wisdom that is prior to the ages can never be lost, it becomes enveloped nevertheless in impenetrable veils, which conceal it from view and beneath which it is extremely difficult to discover it. This explains why there is to be met with everywhere, under various symbols, the same theme of something which has been lost, at least to all appearances and so far as the outer world is concerned, and which those who aspire to true knowledge must re-discover; but it is also stated that what is thus hidden will become visible again at the end of our cycle, which, by reason of its continuity linking all things together, will coincide with the beginning of a new cycle..." R. Guenon, *Crisis of the Modern World* ; Luzac and Co; 1975

© Copyright 1998 – Jim Gomez - All Rights Reserved

Mysterious Coincidences - Questions & Answers

James Moore: Jim, I have a question. I was terribly impressed by your diagrams that you included in your report last year. They are staggering. The detail...

Jim Gomez: Thank you.

James Moore: And so I really put this question to you out of respect for your scholarship, fastidiousness and so forth. Is it your position - and you have made these contacts and have inquired - that the enneagram probably has its antecedents, peculiarly, in the Sufi tradition? I ask again with some background. I knew very well Seyyed Hossein Nasr, Annemarie Schimmel, these people. And I have also heard refrain from Idris Shah, who I very much associate with the Naqshibandi Sufis. At the same time, at this conference we have had people who say they see the sources of Gurdjieff's teaching in the Christian Fathers, in the work of Mouravieff, for example.

Jim Gomez: Yes, I am aware of that.

James Moore: Then you have other people who say that it is a debased shamanism. You have people taking a segmental view of Gurdjieff's material.

Jim Gomez: Yes, that he is somehow a derivative of all these other teachings.

James Moore: Now, is it your position or is it not that the enneagram is peculiarly owed to an Islamic-Sufi tradition?

Jim Gomez: Yes. But. I'll give that a 'but' because the way I am understanding it at the moment is that it is Pythagorean in origin, and goes back to at least the Pythagoreans. Before Pythagoras, who was a very interesting figure, we have no real history because Pythagoras was at the 'cusp' of our Western World and its history. Before that, we have only mythology. Our recorded history stops there, and we go into a mythology of an 'ancient world'. And I think this is also related to the cycles of Yugas that I mentioned in the paper. When we shift from one cycle to the next, the last cycle becomes a foggy 'myth', which is quite interesting. (note - as Guenon points out, even when we do have more ancient records or annals, such as ancient astrological readings in China, for example, which should be accepted as 'scientific', even then scientists and historians still tend to refer to these periods as 'legendary' - for a more lucid account of this idea, see R. Guenon, The Crisis of the Modern World , ch. 1) But Pythagoras, of course, visited Egypt. For 22 years he was living in Egypt and he studied with the priests there. And then, of course, he was taken captive by Cambyses - that is into 'Babylonian Captivity'. And there he met the Magi, and many other people (see Iamblichus's *Life of Pythagoras*, ch. 4). And, of course, Gurdjieff talks about the 'Adherents of Legomonism', Pythagoras, and the Babylonian Captivity, and during that period he devised all these things (see the chapter on 'Art' in *Beelzebub's Tales to His Grandson*). So I think it goes

Mysterious Coincidences: Gurdjieff, the Enneagram and Tradition - Questions & Answers

back to that point. Maybe even before that. (for more on this discussion, see also John Anthony West, The Serpent in the Sky)

Michael Smyth: That's right.

Jim Gomez: But it changes... You see, the interesting idea that Laleh Bakhtiar has talked to me about, is how the Islamic world 'incorporated' ideas from, say, the Platonic tradition. The idea of the four virtues which was a Platonic idea - Wisdom, Courage, Temperance and Justice - this fourfold idea can be found in Plato's dialogues. The Sufi people, according to Laleh Bakhtiar, incorporated or synthesised this Platonic fourfoldness with the three centres, which was part of the Sufi psychology as Cognition, Affect and Behaviour. That made the seven, and the system of the nine points started to work there. So that is how I understand it from her - as a kind of progression.

Jim Gomez: This image is a picture of another Sufi Shaykh - Shaykh Nazim (Maulana Sheik Nazim Al Haqqani Naqshibandiya). He is the 40th Master of the Golden Chain. And this is a picture of him when he was 40. Now he is very old, he is 91 or 90 I believe. And this is a sub-node. I have three 'nodes' and a few 'subnodes', which I will bring in occasionally when I feel I need some help. This is a sub-node, and it is a quote from one of Shyakh Nazim's books:

> "...every branch of knowledge has to reach the point where it will enable people to see the existence of the Creator. We have a saying, telling us that every knowledge takes people to know the real source of that knowledge, which comes from the One. For example, if you use mathematics to its limits, it will lead you to the point of recognising that there is someone who created the huge brain of the ocean of mathematics. If you enter physics, it will be like another ocean and take you to the point of asking yourself, "Where does this huge ocean come from?" Shaykh Nazim al Haqqani, *Defending Truth*, Zero Productions, London.

Jim Gomez: So I've talked a little about Pythagorean symbolism - and thank you very much James Moore for leading me into that - and what I wanted to do is to start by talking about the Pythagorean symbol called the Tetraktys, which a lot of you might be familiar with. It is a very important symbol, I think, and it is related to the enneagram. But the Tetraktys symbol is - of course from what we know because Pythagoras did not write anything down himself - the ancient symbol that people ascribed to Pythagoras with reverence. The Pythagoreans were said to 'swear by' the Tetraktys. ('I swear it by the one who in our hearts engraved the sacred Tetrad, symbol, immense and pure, source of Nature and Model of the Gods...' ; The *Pythagorean Oath*, from The Golden Verses of Pythagoras , translated by Fabre D'Olivet) So, in a way, this is similar to the way we think of the enneagram as Gurdjieff people. The Tetraktys symbol is basically an array of 'dots'; 10 dots or nodes. It is a triangular array of dots - it's a pattern - like this (see illustration 1). And here I have to acknowledge and thank also one of my big influences, and teachers really - Dr. Keith Critchlow. Dr. Critchlow has taught me a lot about 'sacred geometry' somehow. Even though I am very thick, he has managed to teach me things about sacred geometry. And, therefore, a lot of this material is what I understand from Dr. Critchlow. And one thing he has talked to us

All & Everything Conference 1998

about is how the Pythagoreans used to work with mathematics. In the ancient world, and still today in some existing craft schools in the traditional world, numbers were worked with as 'points' - literally as pebbles or small stones or other small ceramic objects - which were then manipulated in a tray of sand to form basic geometrical patterns. So one way number is studied is simply like this - as 'pattern'. And the drawing of geometrical figures is, then, another way. (note - this is also very interesting in relation to Gurdjieff's description of people who meet on the 'Way', and they trace the enneagram in the sand and then see who knows more about it and who becomes, in that case, the teacher... a mysterious coincidence?) And in this case, the 10 points can make this particular triangular pattern of the Tetraktys (see illustration 1). You can also see within this pattern a central hexagon made of six points and a centre point, leaving 3 points on the outside (see Illustration 2). You can also see another pattern here, by taking the topmost point as 'one', and the next horizontal line across as 'two', followed again by 'three' and then 'four', which makes the simple numerical progression 1,2,3,4 (see Illustration 3). So there are different ways of looking at this same symbol.

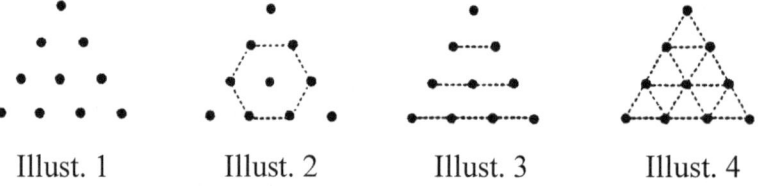

Illust. 1   Illust. 2   Illust. 3   Illust. 4

Ken Pledge: It is the fourth 'triangular number'.

Jim Gomez: Yes, Triangular number, thank you. Triangular Numbers, which Ken has just brought up, are like this. First there is one – that is the first triangular number isn't it ? Is one the first triangular number?

KP: I think , yes, you probably have to consider it to be the first.

(note – for a definition and discussion of triangular number see *The Theoretic Arithmetic of the Pythagoreans*, Thomas Taylor, book 2, ch. 5. '...the first of all triangular numbers, therefore, is that which is formed from unity. But this is first in capacity or power, and not in energy...')

Jim Gomez: Yes, and then we have 3, and then 6, and then 10 (see illustration 4).

KP: You just cut the rows off as you go down.

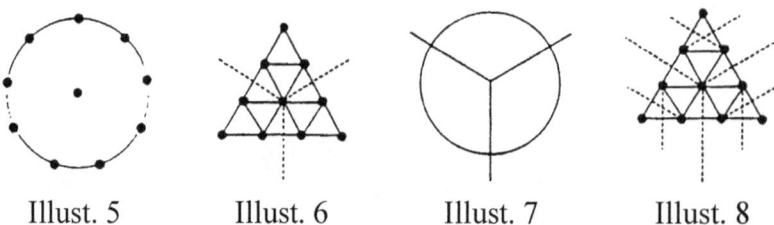

Illust. 5   Illust. 6   Illust. 7   Illust. 8

Mysterious Coincidences: Gurdjieff, the Enneagram and Tradition - Questions & Answers

Jim Gomez: Yes, and then there are square numbers, pentagonal numbers, hexagonal numbers. But what I wanted to show today - and I need to hurry because I want to get to the other stuff - is this basic geometry which I think might be related to the enneagram. That is, how you might look at the Tetraktys as being an enneagram, or as being related to the enneagram symbol. And, of course, the first thing that strikes the attention is that there are 9 dots around the periphery, and there is a centre dot - a dot in the centre making 10. So it does not take great effort of the mind to simply 'push' the 9 points out to the circumference on a circle, and to group these 9 points around a central 10th point at the centre (see illustration 5). It is not difficult to do, and indeed that, might be enough 'to do', in order to be able to simply talk about it. But there is more here, which I think very interesting. If you taking this from number to geometry - the second level which is 'number in space' - (see the description of the four 'levels' of number in last years *The Language of Symbolism in Sacred Science*, All and Everything conference paper) you can start linking up these patterns like this, as geometry. The illustration shows how the lines or edges of the equilateral triangles which join each of the points of the Tetraktys, can permit - if you like - the penetration of one 'axis' into the figure, through the line, and terminating at the centre point (see illustration 6). These three lines or axes can be seen as coming 'in' to the symbol from the outside - moving in towards the centre point - or as starting from the centre point and then going 'out' through the edges of the triangles, as the case may be. And I promise that here I will, Keith (Buzzell), acknowledge your work in a minute here. I am totally aware of you work in this area I can assure you...

Chris Thompson: (slowly and c-l-e-a-r-l-y) totally aware .... totally aware....

Jim Gomez: Oh, I mean that I am aware of the 'totality' of his work, I am not aware of its particular meaning - that is, in its full detail.

OK, these lines which come into the figure here - one from below and two from the sides - are very significant. They will make more sense to you when we discuss the geometry of the sufi enneagram, where they form the basic three-fold division of the circle of 'self' or circle of unity. Because one of the 'keys' of the sufi enneagram is this basic three-fold division of the circle like this - (see illustration 7) - which is missing from the way the Gurdjieff enneagram is looked at the moment. So this basic three-fold division is possible on the Tetraktys because of a 'gap' on the bottom of the figure, and gaps at the sides, as I have shown. And now we have to be rigorous about this, of course. So, one then goes around the figure and performs the same operation in the remaining 'gaps', as shown (see illustration 8). And if we look at the resultant figure, we have 6 'sub-axis' which define or relate to 6 points. The 'sub-axes' combine with the major three-fold division previously shown, and together they show what could be called simply a 'symmetry' . A particular 'symmetry' is present here which bears a remarkable resemblance to the enneagram pattern, as you can see. And it does not take a stretch of the mind to see how one could begin to read the same kinds of cosmology patterns in this figure. But with the Tetraktys, of course, you have other levels of interpretation that the Pythagoreans did teach orally - because we do know that they were very secretive people.

All & Everything Conference 1998

Plato is said to have been given the Pythagorean teaching, and to have 'veiled' it quite carefully in his dialogues (see the *Timaeus*, in particular). But one way to look at this figure of the Tetraktys is in relation to music. Of course, we know that the Pythagoreans were interested in music, (note - according to legend, Pythagoras is said to have been the first to discover the mathematical foundations of music.) And if you take the pebbles again, as a kind of 'matrix', the relationships of the levels form the progression 1:2, 2:3, 3:4 . And as you know, 1:2 is the ratio of the musical octave of sound, 2:3 is the ratio of the fifth, and 3:4 is the ratio of the fourth. And these three ratios, together with the 'tone' between the fourth and the fifth, are called the fundamental Pythagorean Harmonies or harmonics. (for a full definition of 'harmonic proportion' see Nichomacus, Introduction to Arithmetic, see also last year's conference paper on *The Language of Sacred Science* for more discussion on music as 'number in time' - *opacity*.) And this makes it possible to construct a musical octave from Do to Do. Between 2:3 and 3:4 there is a tone, and its value is 8:9. As any musician will know, if you have a low Do and a high Do, when you start from the low and move to the high sounding a fifth, when you return back down the scale from the high to the low the note which was an ascending fifth, now corresponds to the descending fourth. The gap in-between the fifth and the fourth is where the 'tone' is, and as I said, it's value in this scheme is 8:9.

Ken Pledge: Yes, but this doesn't mean that you can construct the octave that Gurdjieff uses *in In Search of the Miraculous*. You need 5 as well for Gurdjieff's octave. You need another line on the symbol. (note - thus making a Pentaktys consisting of 15 'dots' in triangular array)

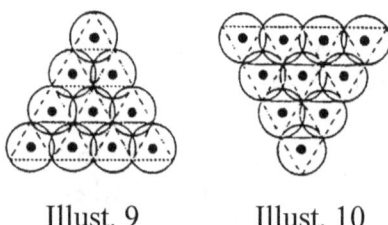

Illust. 9   Illust. 10

Jim Gomez: Right - you need 5. Well, that is terrific, and thank you for that. I am not actually saying that this is the Gurdjieff octave. All I am doing here is pointing out that the Pythagoreans were very interested in music, and that this particular structure of the Pythagorean harmonies is present in the Tetraktys symbol. That is all. But Thank you. So, there was only one other thing that I wanted to say about the Tetraktys symbol, and this is something that I think Dr. Buzzell might find interesting in particular, I hope. I find it very interesting indeed. It requires another diagram. If you take the 10 points of the Tetraktys, and you 'enclose' them each in their own equilateral triangle so that each point becomes the centre of its own triangle, you will obtain a certain geometric figure. If you then draw a circle 'enclosing' each equilateral triangle, you have a more complete figure (see illustration 9). Now, for Keith's interest, I will simply turn this diagram upside down - that is 'invert' the symbol -so that the top, which was pointing up, is now pointing down; the symbol has been 'rotated' 180 degrees - and it now looks like this (see illustration 10).

Mysterious Coincidences: Gurdjieff, the Enneagram and Tradition - Questions & Answers

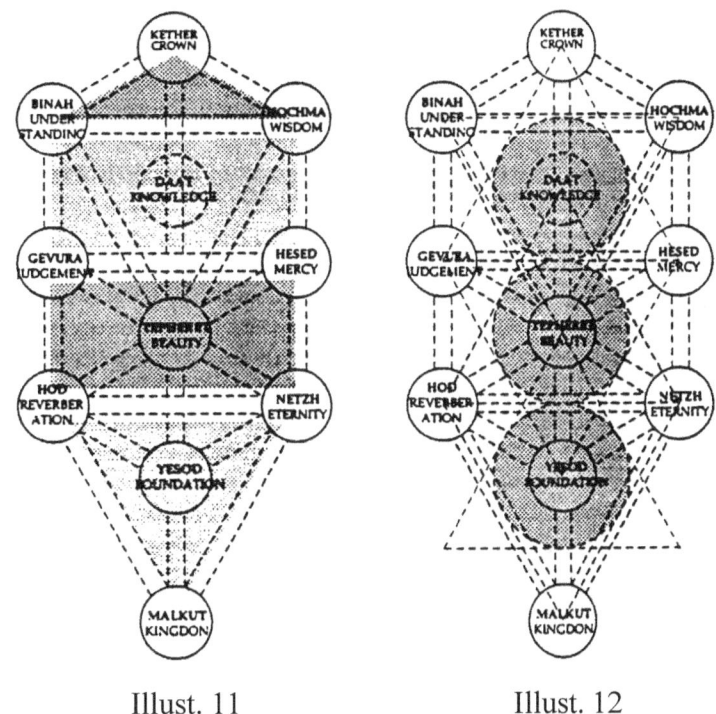

Illust. 11 Illust. 12

Jim Gomez: Well, we are running out of time. I apologise for all of these drawings on the Kabbalah, as I realise we have already had one talk on this subject. I will not, therefore, use all of my drawings. I just wanted to show with these images how a certain basic pattern can be seen firstly in the Pythagorean tradition, and then how this pattern moved through the Judeo-Christian Islamic traditions. Now, I don't know much about the Kabbalah, but I do know a little bit. As far as I understand it, this is the basic structure of the Tree of Life diagram. And it shows again a number of 'points'. (note - 10 points actually, because the 'Daat' is a special 11th point, and is usually either 'dotted on' or is left out altogether.) I do not want to discuss the meaning of each of these points today - in psychological terms for example - but to simply see it as geometry - as 'pattern'. And what I found really interesting here, is that usually the Tree of Life is interpreted in terms of four 'worlds' - called the world of Emanation, world of Creation, world of Formation and world of Action at the bottom (see illustration 11). But what I find interesting is how those four worlds are actually related to the sets of triads - that is, to three 'great triads', which I believe was discussed yesterday. So, what I am interested in now is how you can look at four worlds - yes - but you can also see it as three worlds. I have drawn some additional geometry over the basic diagram to show this correspondence. In this view, you can see three circles, centred on the three points called Daat, Tepheret and Yesod. Then you get Kether on top, and Malkut on the bottom (see illustration 12). And this throws into relief what I think is a key diagram - a three-circle diagram - or a diagram of three worlds. And this particular diagram is related to the enneagram, I believe. Now, if you go back to the basic diagram of the Tree of Life again, and I am just going to quickly point this out because we haven't much time I am afraid, I think it is fairly interesting that by counting the central column one gets 5 points. Of course, as you are aware the columns of the Tree

All & Everything Conference 1998

of Life are three in number, and are sometimes interpreted as being active, passive and middle. There is also a way to view, simultaneously, an octave running through the whole figure - as a 'lightning flash' from the Do at Kether down to the Do of Malkut, and then back up again to Kether. (for a good overview of the diagram, see the book Tree of Life by Warren Kenton; also see his fascinating book A Kabbalistic Universe) But what I am showing in this diagram, is how the 'spaces in between' the five point running down the central column, define secondary, 'hidden' circles if you like. So, the centre column, when one includes these 'hidden circles' has a total of 9 point from top to bottom (see illustration 13). So you get a column of 9 down the centre. And when you include the 'hidden circles' on the side columns, they add up to 5 on each side. And of course this 'ninefoldness' of the centre column is interesting, and it suggests perhaps a 'great octave' coming down the centre column, and ever perhaps the side columns as sort of 'side-octaves', and this is very interesting. But what I wanted to point out today was something about the number 19. Now, if we add together all of the circles - both the visible and the hidden circles - we get 19; because 5 + 9 + 5 = 19.

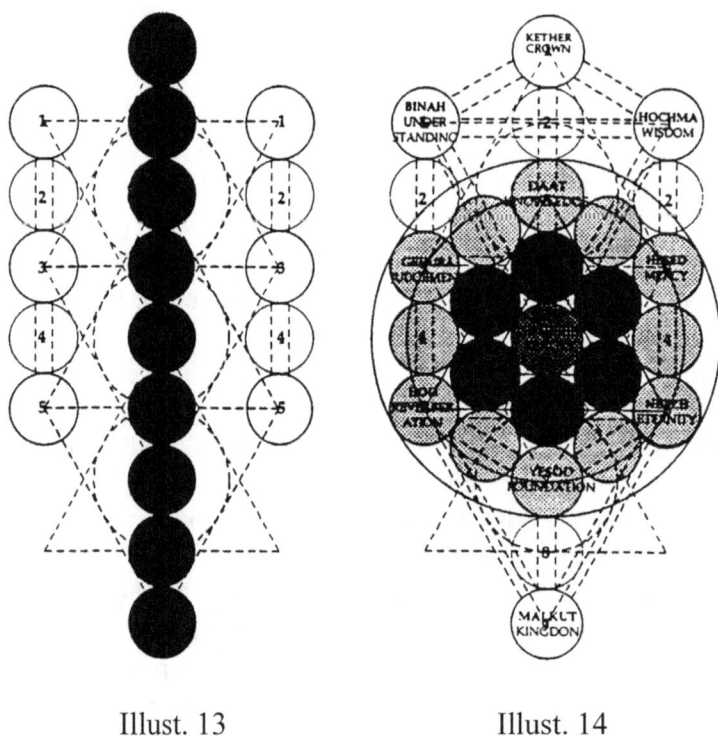

Illust. 13   Illust. 14

Michael Smyth: 19, Russell Smith.

Jim Gomez: Yes, exactly. Now, the number 19 is a 'hexagonal number', which means that it can close-pack or cluster as a hexagonal pattern of circles into a series of concentric 'rings' of hexagons, which surround a central unity (see illustration 14). You see this idea drawn on the tree of life - in this instance I have drawn it centred on Tepheret, but in principle it could be placed in other ways. But if we just look at the clustered geometry by itself, you see what an interesting

Mysterious Coincidences: Gurdjieff, the Enneagram and Tradition - Questions & Answers

image it is (see illustration 15). I think it is very much related to what Russell Smith is doing (see Russell Smith, *Gurdjieff - Cosmic Secrets*). I am sorry he is not here this year, because I wanted to share this with him. But, by taking the geometry of the 19 'balls', one can then 'extract' the basic symbolic geometry of Gurdjieff's 'Eternal Unchanging Absolute' from the 'diagram of everything living' (see *In Search of the Miraculous;* also *Gnosis* by Boris Mouravieff, for more on this diagram). Now, if you look at Gurdjieff's two diagrams - and particularly at the numbers written by the squares - that is 1 and 6, and 3 and 12 - the numerical series interestingly starts with the 1 if you like, and then moves out and eventually reaches the twelve. This numerical progression is figured here in the geometry of the 19 points. And this is the same basic structure geometrically speaking, of the sufi enneagram. Especially with the twelve-foldness around the outside, because this corresponds to the twelve signs of the Zodiac in the sufi enneagram. The six balls around the central seventh, become the six-ness or six points on the circumference of the enneagram. The centre 'three' is symbolised by the equilateral triangle, and it becomes the spiritual 'heart' of the sufi enneagram as 9* - 3* - 6*. The seventh ball becomes related to the point in the centre - as 'one'. I don't have time, unfortunately, to take you through the remarkable way the geometry of Gurdjieff's diagram can be seen to come out of this same basic pattern.

Ken Pledge: Jim, you're jibbering.

Michael Smyth: He's not jibbering, he's just moving fast.

Bert Sharp: It also relates to the atomic packing of crystals.

Jim Gomez: Yes, oh definitely. And to many other things as well. I think it is a very important key pattern. But let us now move on to the sufi enneagram. I will take a brief five minutes to discuss the sufi enneagram - and then we can go and take a shower or have lunch. OK? I am very sorry that I talk too much.

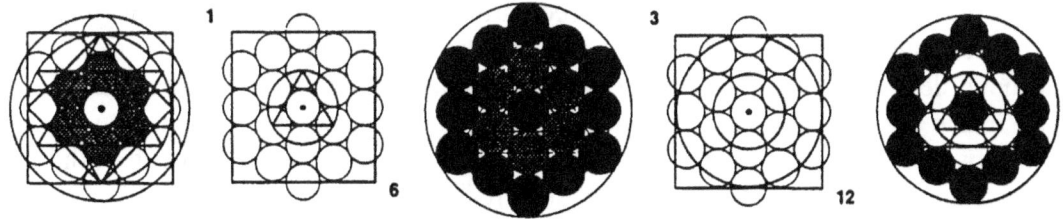

Illustration 15
A study of Gurdjieff's symbol of the Eternal Unchanging Absolute

Jim Gomez: So, this is the sufi enneagram, following the work of Dr. Laleh Bakhtiar as discussed in her three-volume work God's Will Be Done, published by Kazi Publications, Chicago, USA. The most important point today that I think needs to be made about the sufi enneagram, for any of you who are interested in studying the enneagram, concerns the differences in its structure in relation to Gurdjieff's version as shown in *In Search of the Miraculous*. There are really very few differences, but they are significant differences. And if you just know what they are, then if you don't think they are important or significant - that's fine. But at least you will know what they are - and then the ball is in your court. And the key that Laleh Bakhtiar is presenting, the key which was specifically given through Shaykh Hisham Kabbanni during the talk in Baltimore, is the centre-point of the diagram, which is a zero . And it is that zero in the centre that makes the whole enneagram work (see illustration 16).

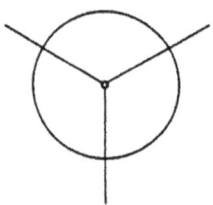

Illustration 16

The zero is not just a number in mathematics. It is the idea of being nothing. Of being a 'zero-type'. Unlike the modern typological systems which focus on the various 'types' around the points of the circumference of the enneagram, the sufi enneagram is about a return from circumference to centre, a path which leads towards becoming a 'zero-type'. And that is also the point through which you can really enter into the spiritual world, and begin the spiritual journey which will be different for every person. So, the sufi enneagram - which is an image of the 'self' both macrocosmically and microcosmically - is about balance. It is about balancing the parts of the 'self' by drawing in towards the centre of 'self', away from the circumference of 'ego-traits', and towards the 'zero' at the centre. To arrive at a place of balance you have to move 'in' from the circumference to the centre - a 'drawing in'. If you look at the basic diagram of the sufi enneagram, you will see that points 9o, 3o, and 6o are actually lying just off or just 'outside' of the circumference - that is, they are even farther away from the centre than the 124578 points, and are not located on the circumference (see illustration 17). These three points represent the state of being 'undeveloped' in one or more of the three parts of the self - which is a affective behaviour lack in terms of 'quality'. A lack of balance in one or more of the three parts of 'self' can also be either an 'underdeveloped' (-) or 'overdeveloped' (+) state, which are both disbalances in terms of 'quantity'. In the case of the points 9o , 3o , and 6o , as one moves towards a state of balance in one or more part of the 'self' one moves on the sufi enneagram towards the centre point or zero - and to the points 9*, 3*and 6* which represent points of balance within each the respective centres. These three points form the three points of a small, inner equilateral triangle, which represents the spiritual heart on the sufi enneagram. The next image here will show, how the three parts of the 'self' according to the sufi enneagram - that is, the cognitive or brain, affective or gut, and behavioural or physical heart - come into balance by developing the four Platonic virtues of Wisdom, Courage, Temperance and Justice (see illustration 18). What that means is that Wisdom is the 'virtue' which will be present in the balanced cognitive (head) centre, Courage is the virtue or 'positive trait' which will be present in the balanced behavioural (heart) centre, and Temperance is the virtue for the balanced affective (gut) centre. When the self becomes balanced in the three centres, then out of this state of being balanced, it becomes possible for real justice to arise - the fourth 'virtue' - out from the centre of 'self'. And at this stage, the enneagram - which

Mysterious Coincidences: Gurdjieff, the Enneagram and Tradition - Questions & Answers

was 9 points as 3x3 - becomes -1x3, or 12 points, which then begins to relate to the 'twelveness' of the signs of the Zodiac. (note - for a more detailed explanation of this system, see Laleh Bakhtiar, *God's Will Be Done*, volume one, Kazi Publications, USA.)

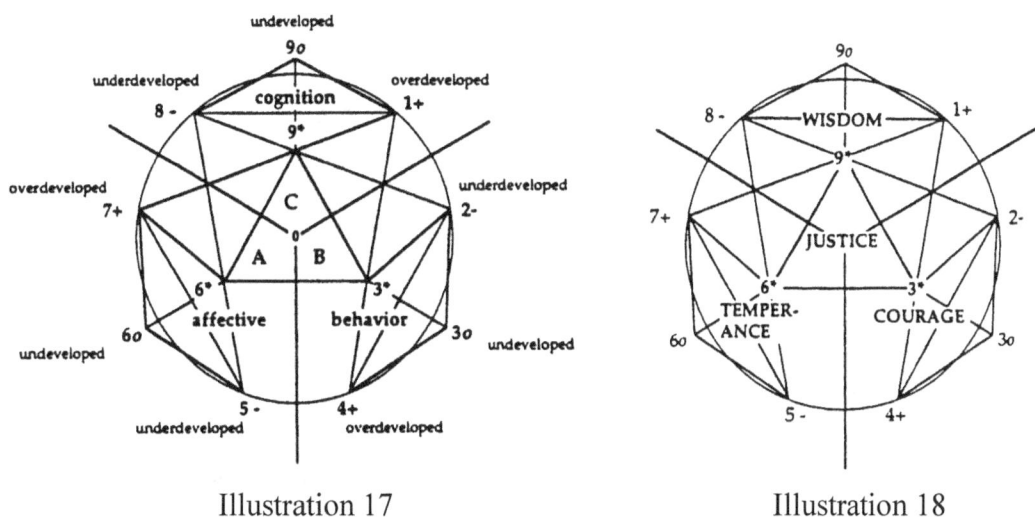

Illustration 17   Illustration 18

This next image shows how the sufi enneagram is related to the twelve-foldness of the Zodiac (see illustration 19). What is very interesting here is how the zero point at the centre is also the point from where the three large axes move out, or to which these same axes are moving towards. These three axes are intrinsic to the three-fold (120 degree) basic division of the circle of 'self', but they are not actually belonging to the enneagram itself, and they link up with the twelvefold division of the Zodiac at the signs of Cancer, Pisces and Scorpio. These three signs are the Water signs, and in the sufi tradition the three axes are called the 'Throne'. And there is a Quranic verse which says that '...His Throne was upon the face of the Waters...' (11:7). So it is as if these three water signs are 'holding up' the Throne of God, and the enneagram is somehow 'sitting within'. The sufi enneagram is also, by the way, called the Wajh Allah or the Face of God, and also as the sign of the Presence of God. And as Laleh Bakhtiar points out in volume two of her book *God's Will Be Done*, the Zodiacal signs can also be seen as 'veils' which hide the Face or Presence of God. The counting around the Zodiac now relates to the 9 points of the enneagram, which are 'sitting within' the 12. If we start at the top and count it as 9, we can then move around to we miss the Water sign Pisces- and then count 2,3,4 - and miss the Water sign Scorpio- and then count 5,6,7 - and miss the Water sign Cancer- and then to 8 and back to 9 at the top. So this becomes a new way of viewing a connection and a translation between the 12 and the 9. The 'qualities' and elemental attributes of the points around the Zodiac - as hot, cold, dry and wet, and so on - can then become related to what is called in the sufi tradition *futuunvah* or 'spiritual chivalry', which is a stage in the method of the 'Way' that leads towards spiritual alchemy within sufism. I have no time to discuss this, unfortunately, but it is very interesting and is possibly the most important practical aspect of Laleh Bakhtiar's work, and is discussed in volume two of *God's Will Be Done*.

All & Everything Conference 1998

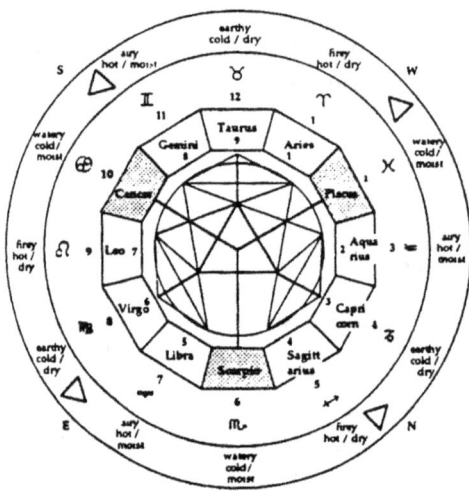

Illustration 19

Finally, I will conclude by showing you some other work that Laleh Bakhtiar has done on the Jupiter - Saturn conjunctions in relation to the sufi enneagram symbol. The signs of the Zodiac, as Laleh points out in volume two of her work, are in a sense the 'first major emphasis' of the macrocosmic view of the sufi enneagram. The 'second major emphasis' is, then, on the planets - and particularly on the seven visible planets in our solar system, which 'revolve in circular form' in the Heavens of the Zodiac. Laleh has looked at the signs of the Zodiac and the astronomical 'coincidence' which some of you who have studied astrology might be familiar with - known as the three 'Great Trigons', which specifically relate to the retrograde (or backwards) movement of the two planets Saturn and Jupiter through the Zodiac, and the conjunctions of these two planets in certain constellations according to definite time-intervals. And in connection with this, I found what Forrest said in his talk earlier today - about the planets as forming the 'bars of a heliocentric prison' - very interesting, because from a heliocentric point of view you simply can't make these readings of sacred geometry and pattern that the planets describe in their movements in the heavens. You could even say, that you can't 'make sense' out of them. But you can make the readings from a geocentric point of view - and that is the perceptual point of view, or how we see things in relation to ourselves and our own experience. And that is also the traditional view. Every 20 years there is a meeting of these two planets, Saturn and Jupiter, in one portion of the Zodiac. And every sixty years, if one traces and superimposes all of the paths and meetings of these planets in the sky during that entire period, they are tracing a giant nine-fold pattern in the sky - in the form of the three 'Great Trigons' (see illustration 20). When one maps the motions of Jupiter by itself during this 60 year period, it traces a 'dynamic' or sharp 9-pointed star, interestingly by following seven year cycles. And when one follows the movements of Saturn by itself during this period, it forms a 9-pointed 'static' star . Both are nine-fold patterns. And the three Great Trigons show a mapping of 'meetings' between these two planets during this time, again in a nine-fold pattern. Now, how all of this is interpreted is very important. It is related to a Quranic verse, which says that 'We shall show them our signs, on the Horizons and within themselves, until they recognise that it is the Real (haqq)...' (41:53) (note - for a further discussion of the Zodiac and the

Mysterious Coincidences: Gurdjieff, the Enneagram and Tradition - Questions & Answers

sufi enneagram, see Laleh Bakhtiar's *God's Will Be Done*, vol. 2; for a further discussion of the macrocosmic \ microcosmic idea within the sufic tradition, and the meaning of (41:53) see also W. Chittick, *The Self-Disclosure of God*, SUNY Press NY, 1998)

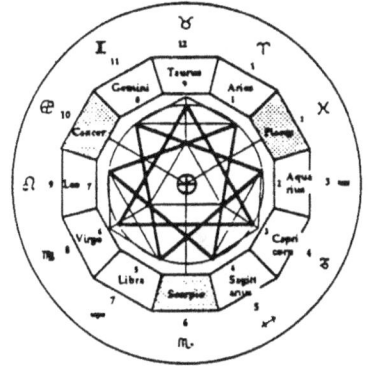 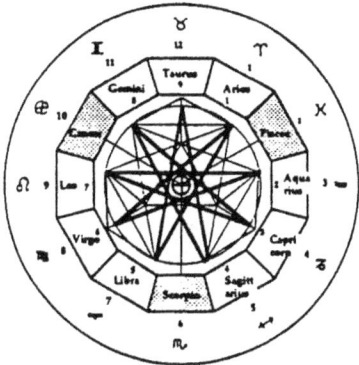 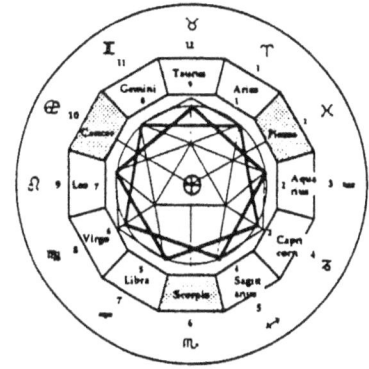

Illustration 20

3 great trigons
Jupiter and Saturn in 3:120 degree / 20 year conjunctions. In one 60 year cycle they make this figure.

Dynamic 9-pointed star
Jupiter makes this pattern during a 60 year period in relation to Saturn, based on a 7 year interval.

Static 9-pointed star
Saturn makes this pattern during a 60 year period in relation to Jupiter, based on a 7 year interval.

Now it seems to me that this is the same idea we heard through Gurdjieff when he stated that the world outside is ruled by laws and structure, and the world inside is also ruled by laws and structure - and they are in both cases the same laws and the same structures. This is a fundamental point, and it is clearly shown in the sufi enneagram, the Wajh Allah or Sign of the Presence of God. And I just want people to see this, to know about this, and to think about it carefully. I also want people to think about the zero, and to reflect upon the new way of reading the enneagram symbol that this zero in the centre provides. Because it is not good enough to continue to move around the circumference. We must begin to move into the centre. And if we can begin to move back towards the centre, we can balance ourselves. We can then reach in even further, towards the zero - and if we can reach this zero, we will be alright.

> "... your ego doesn't want to disappear in the Unity Ocean of Allah. One drop comes from the sky, when it reaches the ocean it is finished and you will not be able to find it because it became part of the ocean. Even though it disappeared, it will continue to exist in the Unity Ocean of Allah. The biggest challenge for humans is to accept that they are nothing. They insist on being something. This is why they are quarrelling continuously until they are completely worn out..."
> Shyakh Nazim al Haqqani, *Defending Truth*, op. cit.

Appendix - Mysterious Coincidences

Appendix - Mysterious Coincidences: Gurdjieff, the Enneagram and Tradition

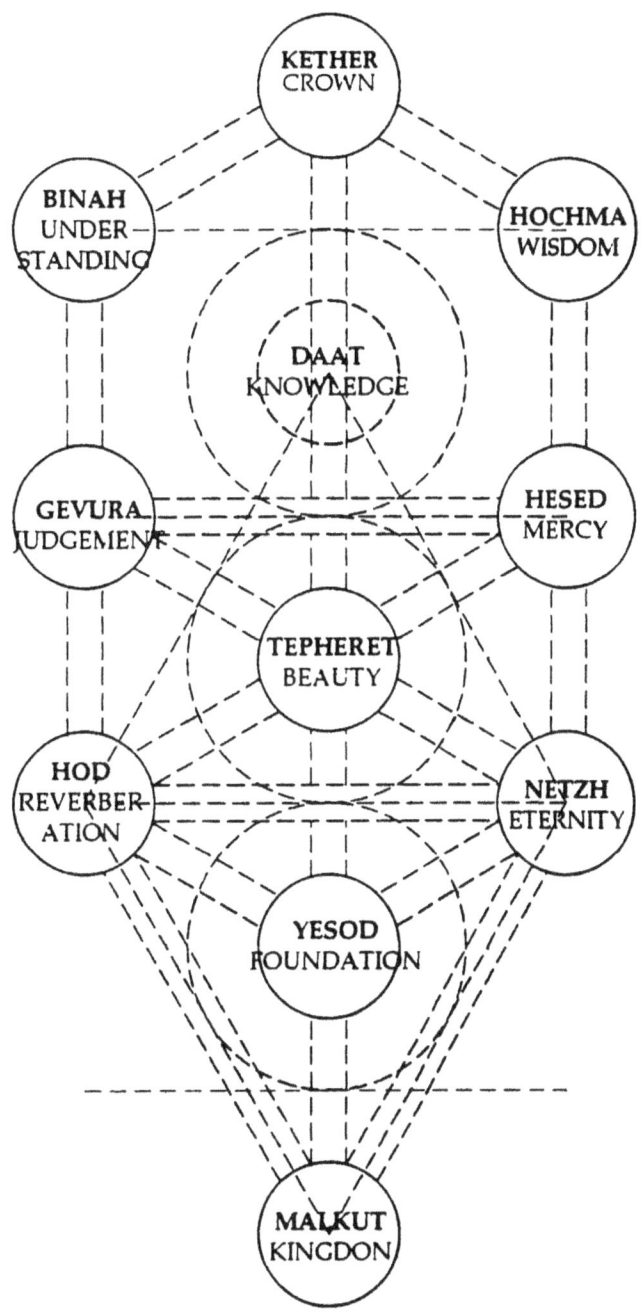

All & Everything Conference 1998

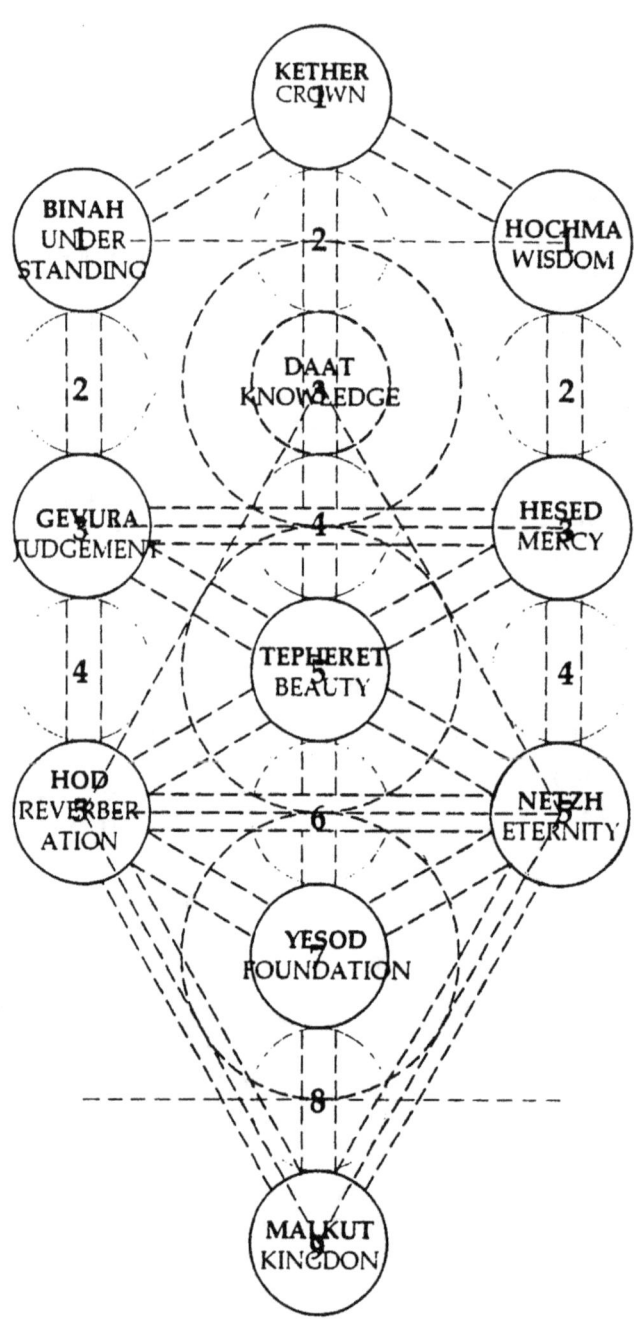

Appendix - Mysterious Coincidences: Gurdjieff, the Enneagram and Tradition

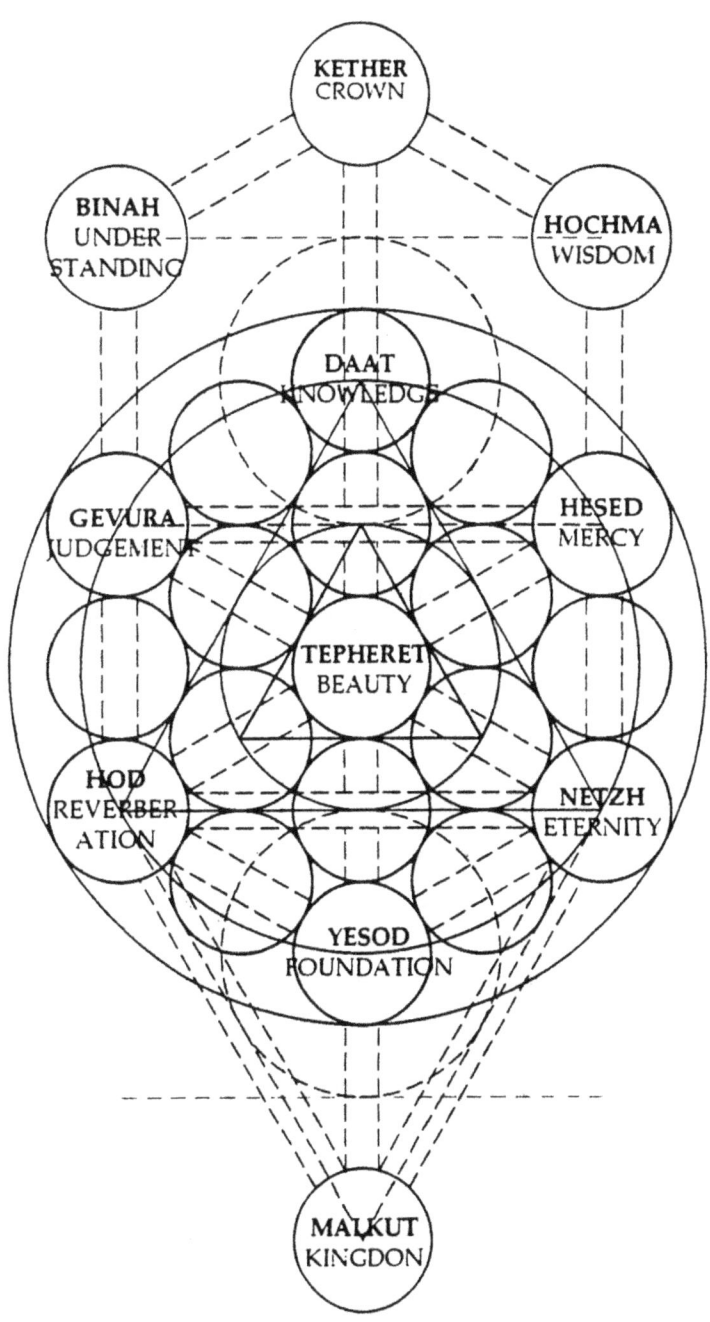

All & Everything Conference 1998

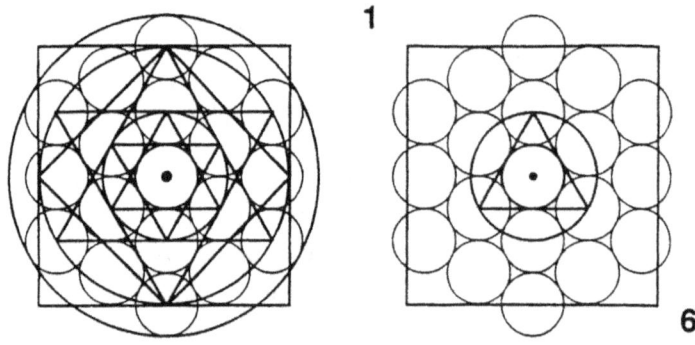

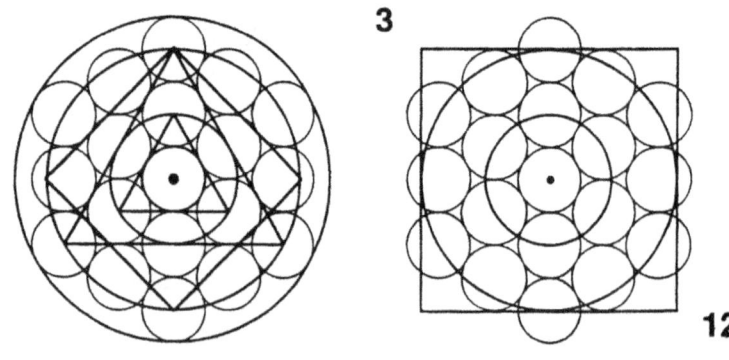

Appendix - Mysterious Coincidences: Gurdjieff, the Enneagram and Tradition

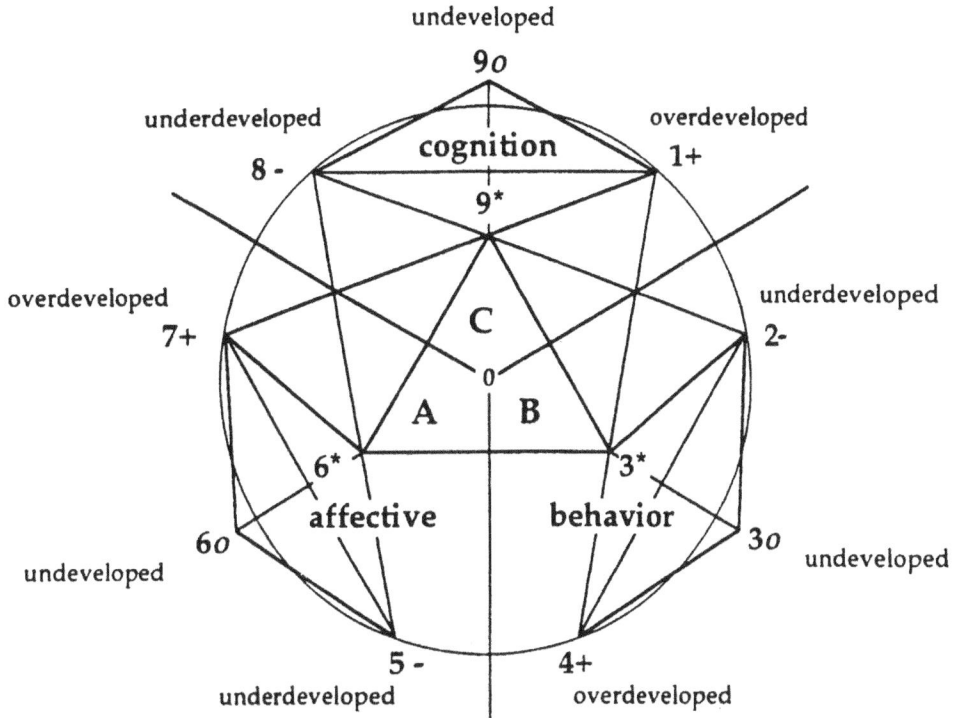

Wajh Allah or Sign of the Presence of God
Level 3: Psychological 3-fold division

The major three-fold division of the circle of self is shown here, dividing self into the three most basic psychological parts or systems: of cognition, behavior and affect / emotive.

The top segment symbolises the brain, and the ability to reason. Underdevelopment of cognition is represented by (-) and represents Multitheism or shirk, that is, worshipping more gods than there are. Overdevelopment of cognition is represented by (+) and represents hypocrisy or nifaq. Undevelopment of cognition is represented by (0) to show ingratitude and disbelief in the One God or (kufr), a moral state lacking in wisdom in terms of quality. The symbol (*) signifies the balancing of cognition in the positive trait of wisdom.

Segment B, behavior, symbolises the heart and is also called the 'avoidance of harm / pain' segment of self. It is one of the two aspects of "the passions". Underdevelopment is cowardice, Overdevelopment is recklessness arising out of inappropriate anger, and Undevelopment is a fear of anything other than God, a state lacking the quality or positive trait of moral courage.

Segment A symbolises the gut (or liver), and affect. It receives its power from the veins and is called the 'attraction to pleasure' as the second aspect of the "passions". It is the most basic drive of human nature, to preserve the species, according to the traditional view. Overdevelopment is greed or lust, Underdevelopment is apathy or lack of self-esteem and self-identity. Undevelopment is envy, a state lacking in the positive trait of temperance or charity towards others.

For a detailed account of this traditional psychology, see Laleh Bakhtiar, *God's Will Be Done*, volumes 1,2 and 3; Kazi Publications, USA

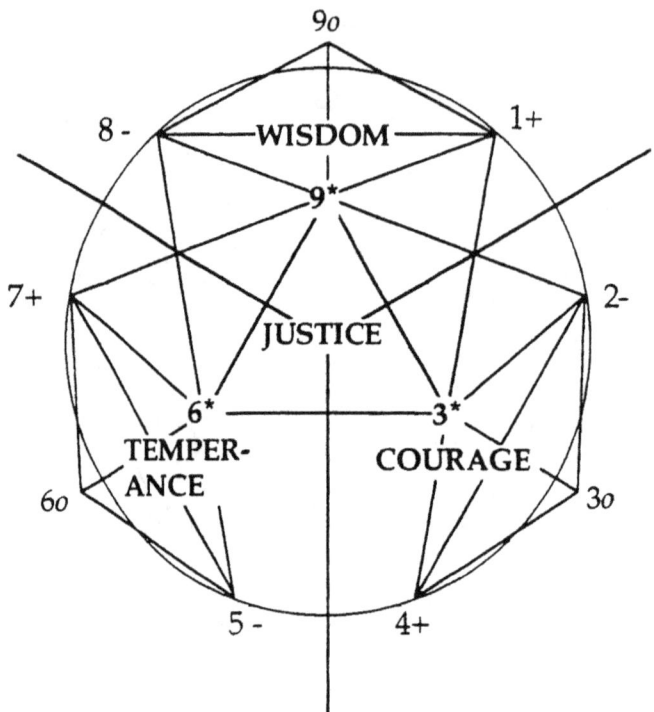

Wajh Allah or Sign of the Presence of God
Level 6 : Psychoethics

"...Wisdom, is a positive trait of the self which enables a human being to freely and consciously distinguish positive from negative dispositions guided by reason (takwini) and revelation (tashri'hi) guidance. It includes consciousness of self operating through free-will and conscience.

Courage is a positive trait by which the self regulates the 'natural disposition of anger in defence, to survive as an individual' through guidance from reason (takwini)i and revelation (tashri'hi).

Temperance is a positive trait by which the self regulates the 'natural disposition to lust, to survive as a species' through guidance from reason (takwini) and revelation (tashri'hi).

Justice is a positive trait of the self in which the natural dispositions of anger in defence, to survive as an individual, and lust, to survive as a species, as well as cognition - seeing things as they really are - are kept in their proper place and given their due according to guidance from reason (takwini) and revelation (tashri'hi). This is the state of 'the mean' or equilibrium between these three basic systems of the human being..."

From Laleh Bakhtiar; *God's Will Be Done*, vol. 1, ch. 2; Kazi Publications; USA

For a detailed account of this traditional psychology, see Laleh Bakhtiar, *God's Will Be Done*, volumes 1,2 and 3; Kazi Publications, USA

Appendix - Mysterious Coincidences: Gurdjieff, the Enneagram and Tradition

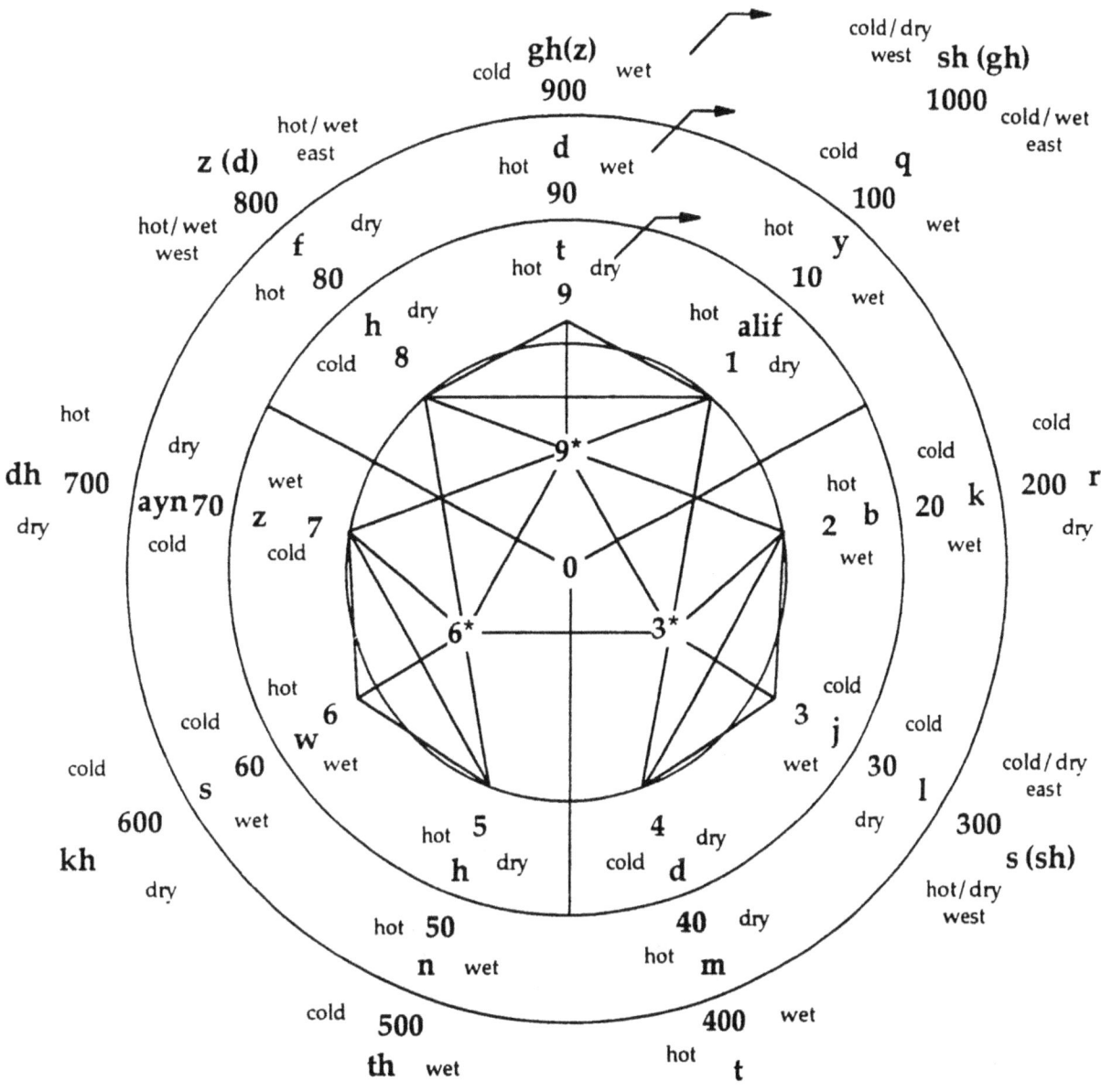

ABJAD - West / East

"The numbers 1-9 on the Sign of the Presence of God are symbols of the Arabic Alphabet. The alphabet corresponds to the same four elements - fire, air, water and earth - and their four qualities - hot and dry, hot and wet, cold and wet, cold and dry - as do the planets, the universe seen as unfolding through the sounds of the letters. While all creation is an emanation of the One, each number, while more basic than the elements and their qualities, are seen as 'repeats' of unity…"

From Laleh Bakhtiar; *God's Will Be Done*, vol.3; Kazi Publications; USA

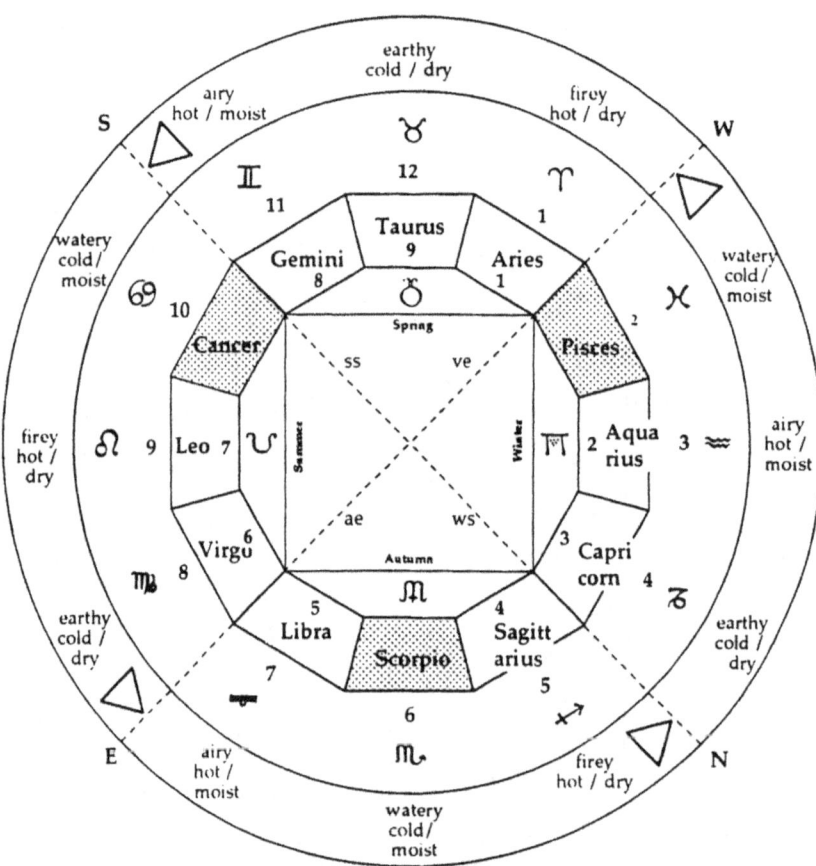

The Zodiac or 12 Constellations

"...Returning to the Sign, 'We shall show them Our Signs upon the horizons and within themselves until it is clear to them that it is the Real (the Truth)' (41:53), spiritual warriors turn outward to find the macrocosmic correspondence of the Sign of the Presence of God.

One of the most significant natural phenomenon to the followers of the Way are the 12 constellations, Zodiac or fixed stars. God swears an oath by them in the Quran, "By the sky displaying the Zodiacal Signs…" (85:1) The Zodiac for the spiritual warrior indicates periods of time and directions in space. '...the indication of periods of time and directions in space occurs in pattern form as intervals around the perimeter of this primal circle. For instance, the face of a clock with its twelve hourly divisions exemplifies the measuring of the passage of time with precision, whereas if one should joint these same intervals on the clock face with straight lines, one would describe a twelve sided shape - a dodecagon. Both can be taken as expressions of the archetype twelve, and in cosmology they are united temporally and spatially in one complete annual cycle of our planet...' "

From Laleh Bakhtiar, *God's Will Be Done*, vol.2; ch.2; Kazi Publications; USA

Appendix - Mysterious Coincidences: Gurdjieff, the Enneagram and Tradition

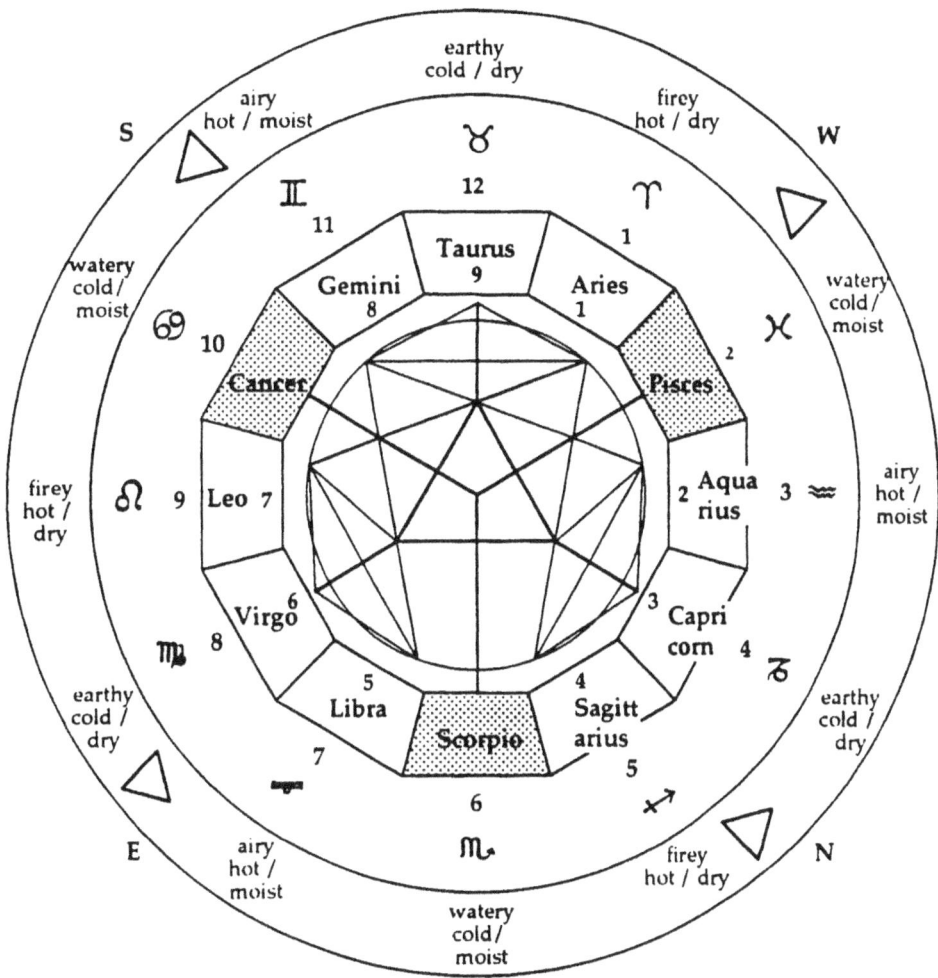

**The Wajh Allah or Sign of the Presence of God
and the Zodiac or 12 Constellations**

"...the numbers 3,6 and 9 on the circumference of the circle as they relate to astrological symbolism, are cold and dry, while the numbers 1,4,2,8,5 and 7 on the circumference of the circle relate to the Zodiacal Signs that are hot and wet or dry relating the Sign of the Presence of God to traditional medicine, where correspondence exists between illnesses and the four qualities of hot, cold, dry and wet. With that in mind, 3,6 and 9 in terms of the Zodiac are symbolic of cold / dry and 1,4,2,8,5,7 are symbolic of hot / wet / dry..."

From Laleh Bakhtiar, *God's Will Be Done*, vol.2; ch.2; Kazi Publications; USA

All & Everything Conference 1998

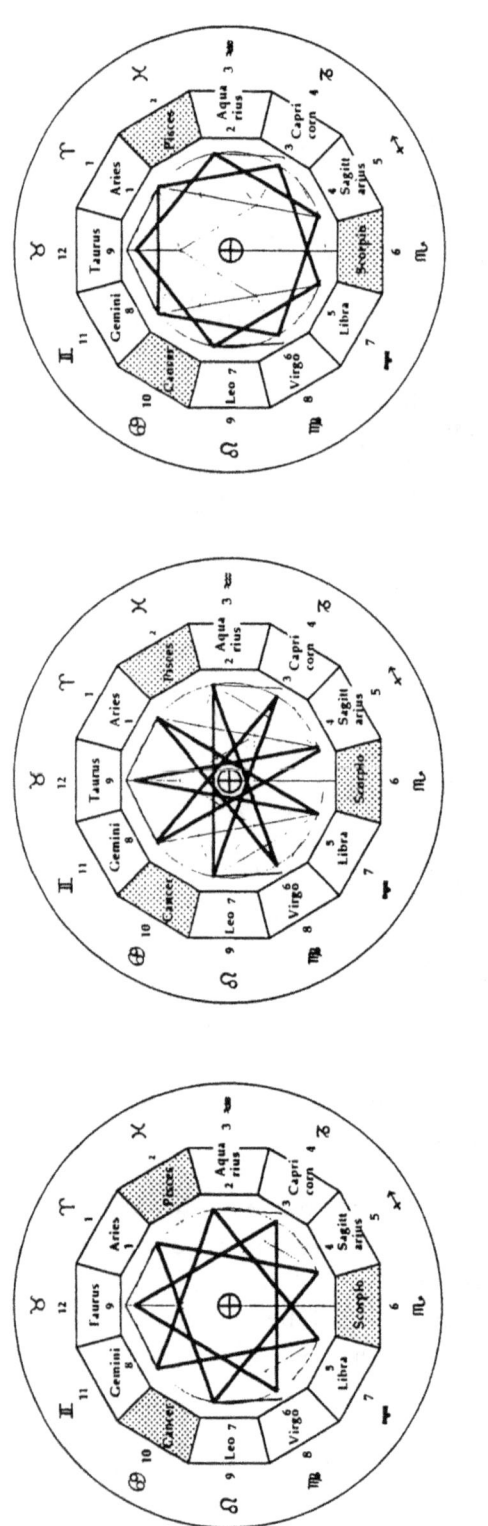

3 great trigons
Jupiter and Saturn in 3 120 degree / 20 year conjunctions. In one 60 year cycle they make this figure

Dynamic 9-pointed star
Jupiter makes this pattern during a 60 year period in relation to Saturn, based on a 7 year interval.

Static 9-pointed star
Saturn makes this pattern during a 60 year period in relation to Jupiter, based on a 7 year interval.

The Wajh Allah
and the Macrocosmic Sign of the Presence of God

"...Saturn and Jupiter form the macrocosmic Sign of the Presence of God in a major astrological phenomenon which occurs every sixty years ... Saturn and Jupiter form a nine-pointed star pattern in intervals of seven years (thus linking the pattern to the enneagram.) Where they are opposite to each other at 180 degrees, not being included in the nine-points unfolding, they are in the three water signs of Piscis, Scorpio and Cancer, cold and wet in elemental qualities. The nine point forms created by Saturn and Jupiter, rest, in a sense, upon the water as the symbol of the Throne of God located in heaven beyond Saturn, recalling the Sign, '*And His Throne was upon the face of the waters...*' (11:7)

This relation of Saturn and Jupiter to the enneagram was shown for the first time by Laleh Bakhtiar, in her book *God's Will Be Done*; vol. 2; Kazi Publications; USA

Appendix - Mysterious Coincidences: Gurdjieff, the Enneagram and Tradition

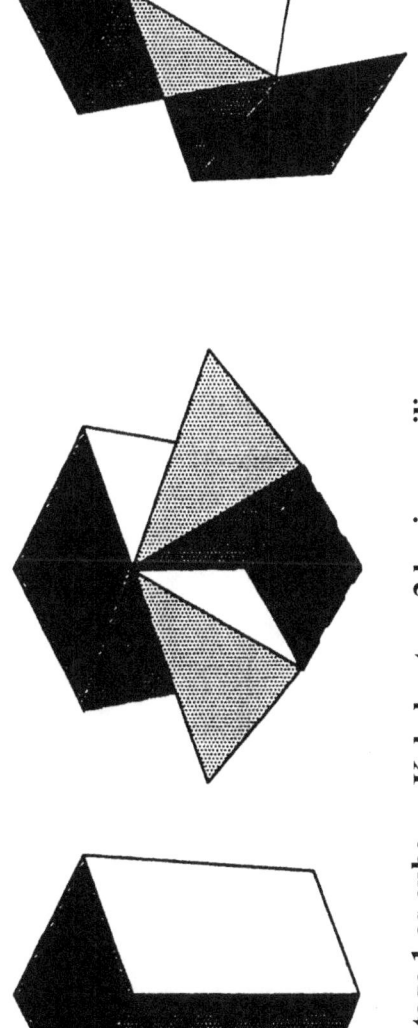

Kabah: stage 1 as cube

Kabah: stage 2 begin unveiling

Kabah: stage 3 revealing the heart / light

Wajh Allah as Kabah

"...the external Kabah being a centre, is a place around which believers circumambulate seven times...

"...the Kabah is an outward symbol in this material world of that Presence not seen by the eye, which dwells within the Divine World, just as the body is an outward symbol in this visible, phenomenal world, of the heart, which cannot be seen by the eye...

"...this visible world is a means of ascent to the invisible, spiritual world for him to whom God has opened the door..."

From Laleh Bakhtiar; *God's Will Be Done*, vol. 2; Kazi Publications; USA

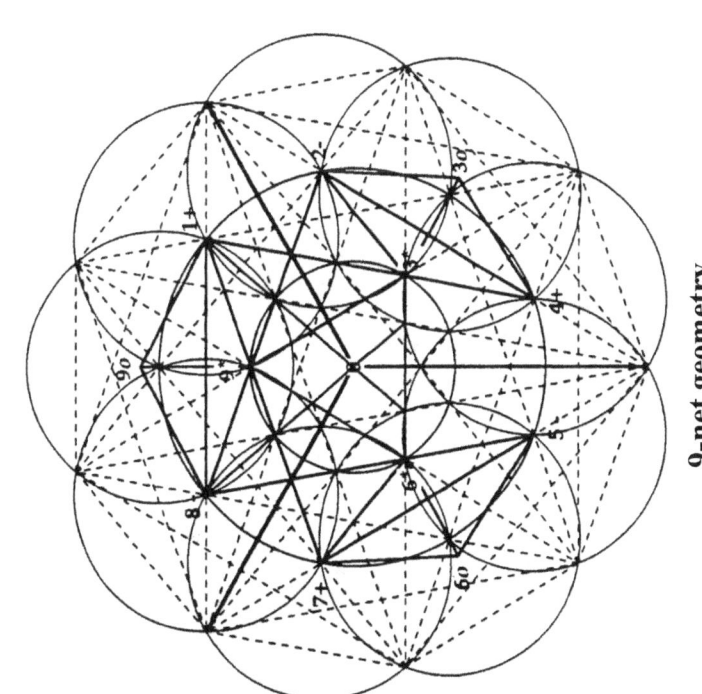

9-net geometry

All & Everything Conference 1998

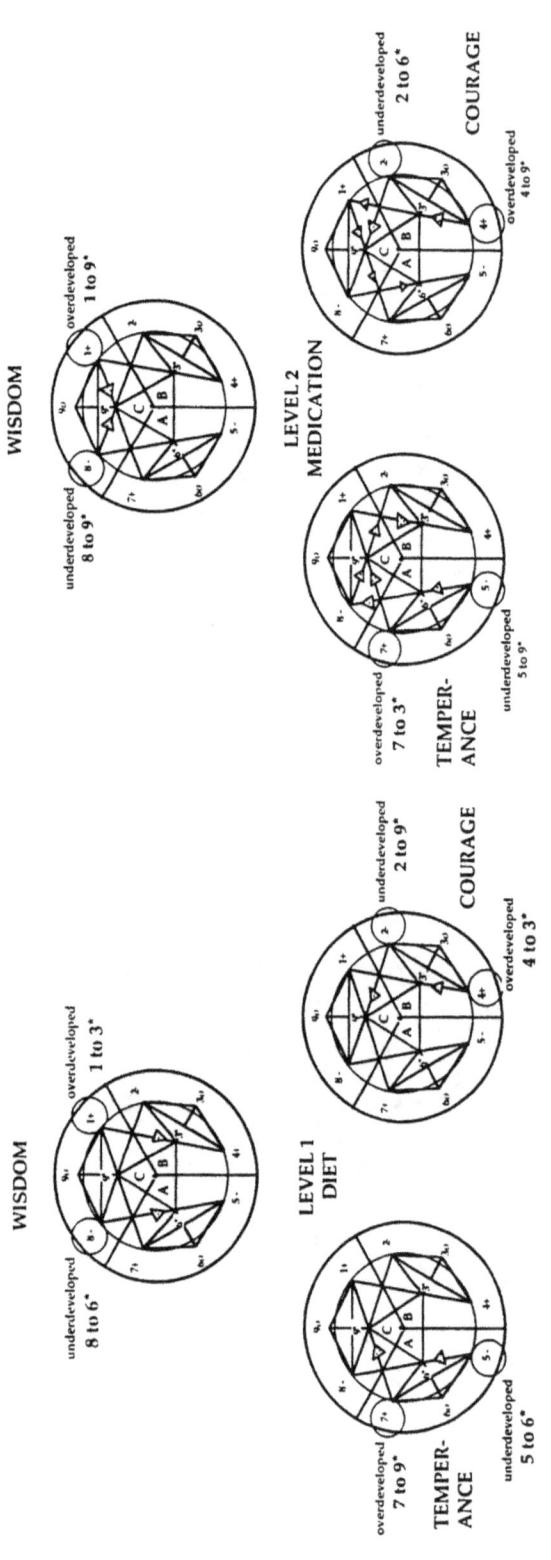

Diet... is for the imbalance to be moved towards the positive trait in the neighboring segment...

Medication... is to move to the second positive trait on the way to the third number and it's segment...

Wajh Allah or Sign of the Presence of God and moral healing or spiritual chivalry

"The greatest contribution of the book is, however, to situate the use of the Enneagram within the context of the Islamic tradition of spiritual chivalry. Known as *futuuwah* in Arabic or *javanmardi* Persian, spiritual chivalry is of the utmost importance for understanding the spiritual life of Islam... Spiritual Chivalry means a continuous spiritual warfare by means of which the soul of the human being becomes imbued with the Virtues that heal the wounds of the fallen soul and prepare it for the encounter with God ..."

S.H. Nasr; from introduction to *God's Will Be Done*, vol.2; Kazi Publications, 1994

Appendix - Mysterious Coincidences: Gurdjieff, the Enneagram and Tradition

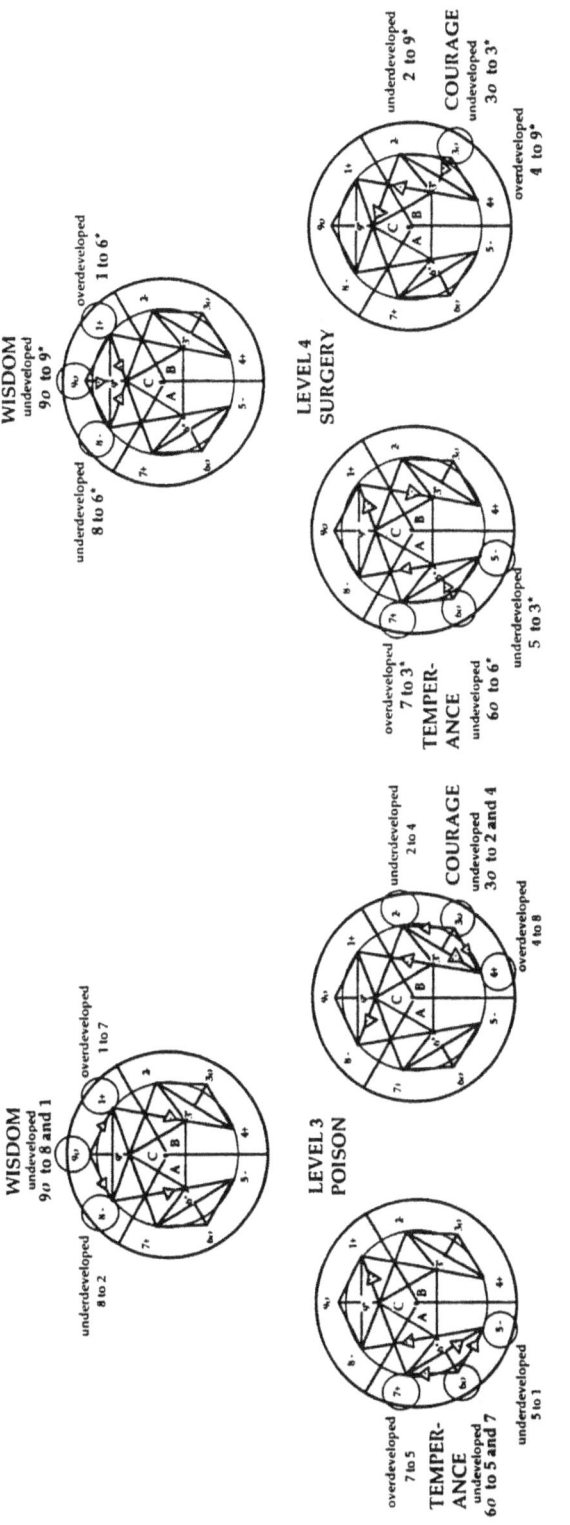

Poison... is to move to the number at the end of the line, and the negative trait it represents...

Surgery... is to move the entire segment towards the positive trait in a neighboring segment...

Wajh Allah or Sign of the Presence of God and moral healing or spiritual chivalry

"...no matter how positive one's nurturing process has been, negative traits will have slipped in to cloud over the mirror of the spiritual aspects of the heart. These negative traits form what is called the false self. However, just as nature provides the means through nurture to limit the development of the false self, it also provides the means to morally heal. This change, in the traditional view, is possible to achieve through the 'greater struggle' (jihad al-akbar) and by Divine Grace or assistance. As we never know when Divine Grace may come, once conscious of negative traits, we then begin the struggle to overcome the false self..."

From Laleh Bakhtiar; *God's Will Be Done*, vol.2; Kazi Publications, 1994

Gurdjieff in Practice: The Liebovian Method

Richard Liebow and his Group

This Session was a practical demonstration of an actual group meeting.

Richard Liebow was born in 1928 in Iowa, USA.
He had strong connections with the quest of the mystics in 1948, inspired by Aldous Huxley's novels (1932-1945 phase).
He was strengthened primarily by Gerald Heard's *Pain, Sex, and Time*, & *Source of Civilization*.
He spent one year in residence at the Prabhavananda/Isherwood Ramakrishna Hindu Organisation in 1952.
His first glimpse of Gurdjieff/Ouspensky literature was in 1954.
Jungian Therapy in 1954.
Egocentric phase inspired by writings of Henry Miller, 1954-1966.
Then came a serious scrutiny of Gurdjieff/Ouspensky literature from 1966 to the present time.
Became a member of the Gurdjieff Foundation of San Francisco (John Pentland, Charles Wright, Ruth Cook) in 1967.
1968-1988, no Gurdjieff group involvement, but on-going serious scrutiny of the literature.
Connection with Nyland Group in San Francisco, 1988-1997
Organizer/sustainer of an independent Gurdjieff/Ouspensky study group in San Francisco - focused primarily on Ouspensky's Search. 1991 - to the present.
Producer of compacted versions of *Beelzebub's Tales*, *Meetings With Remarkable Men*, Ouspensky's *Psychology*, and Ouspensky's *Search*.

Richard Liebow took part in the 1996 Conference, presenting a paper "Meetings with Remarkable Men". He also continued to support our Conferences by presenting a further paper at the 1997 Conference, "Purgatory Compacted". Both these presentations were taken from his own publications based on his Compact versions of *Tales* and *Meetings With Remarkable Men*.

As already mentioned, this presentation was a demonstration of how a Monday night meeting is conducted, the group demonstration being composed of Richard Liebow, Warren Alksnis, Sebouh Der Bedrossian, and Dikran Takvorian. In addition, as the demonstration proceeded others present participated as a question and answer sector. Unfortunately due to unforeseen circumstances the recording of this session was too faint to allow for transcription. Richard Liebow has therefore kindly provided us with a summary of the presentation for inclusion in the Proceedings, and this follows.

GURDJIEFF IN PRACTICE: THE LIEBOVIAN METHOD

WE STUDY THE SYSTEM

DEMONSTRATION OF HOW WE CONDUCT A MONDAY NIGHT MEETING IN A SAN FRANSISCO COFFEE HOUSE
BY
RICHARD LIEBOW, WARREN ALKSNIS, SEBOUH DER BEDROSSIAN, AND DIKRAN TAKVORIAN

Our meetings are highly structured, yet intimate and personal. Everyone participates, and the entire event proceeds in the manner of a ritual.

Our Monday meeting begins precisely at 8:00 PM, and starts with an invocation: "Whatever be the highest perfection of the human mind, may we realize it simply by pausing frequently to focus inward to picture an image of an impartial observer/ listener/ experiencer/ witness within ourselves."

We do demonstrations of how to divide our attention by focusing on an object, a sensory-verifiable image. We observe it, and at the same time, remind ourselves that we are observing it. Checking to see if this activity creates any special feelings or bodily sensations.

We review our own version of the Obligolnian Strivings:
1) Attend to the legitimate needs of the planetary body.
2) Develop a sense of urgency to work ceaselessly to actualize fully the highest potentialities of your own particular form of being.
3) Earnestly strive to know and understand ever more clearly the laws of world creation and world maintenance.
4) Earnestly, to the maximum of your understanding of the concept of Payment & Obligation, strive to pay, as rapidly as possible, for your existence and individuality, so as to lighten the sorrow of Our Common Creator.
5) Devote the full measure of your knowledge, your strengths, and your skills, to helping other creatures, both those similar and dissimilar to yourself, in their strivings for self-perfection.

We review our own list of work methods:
(1) Attend meetings. (2) Read designated chapter, and study outline. (3) Prepare report. (4) Pause frequently just to be present. (5) Struggle to control expression of negative emotions. (6) Practice dividing attention. (7) Verify ideas and methods.

(8) Ask yourself, "Where am I in all of this?" (9) Curb internal considering. (10) Cultivate external considering. (11) Scrutinize speech and strive to control it.(12) Scrutinize habits - and

practice opposing them. (13) Distinguish between the work of the different function centers. (14) Direct attention to specific tasks.

(15) Reconstruct experiences and events. (16) Prioritize & re-prioritize. (17) Practice intensely active thinking by isolating key issues - and doing things in order of their importance. (18) Observe mood swings. (19) Systematically release excess muscular tension. (20) Define and redefine personal aims and purposes. (21) Strive to identify, transform, and utilize A- and B-influences.

(22) Question motives: Are they coming from an informed deputy steward - or from the false personality of a mad machine? (23) Take mental photographs - of postures, attitudes, gestures, breathing, and bodily sensations. (24) Observe struggle to inhibit the tendency to procrastinate and make excuses. (25) And frequently ask yourself: "What will it matter a hundred years from today?"

* * *

We ask for reports In response to the question: "Has there been a particular moment in the past seven days when you have found yourself spontaneously or intentionally pausing to ponder or practice some one of the ideas or methods you associate with what we do here on Monday nights that you would care to tell us about?

For example: Sebouh, on Saturday, the 21st, at about 7:31 am, is sitting at the window in his room at the Royal Norfolk Hotel in Bognor Regis looking out over the English Channel, when he sees a truck pull up at the hotel. Two men come out with a piano, which they carry into the conference room. Seb knows the piano is for Wim's presentation of the Gurdjieff music that afternoon, and he remembers how profoundly he had been affected by Wim's Gurdjieff music at last year's Conference.

And another example: Gina. on Saturday, the 7th, at about 2:30 pm, is in the West Portal branch of the San Francisco public library looking for a book on soil chemistry. She doesn't find exactly what she's looking for but she sees other books on general chemistry--and one, in particular on alchemy. She learns that chem relates to the name of ancient Egypt because of the black richness of the soil of the Nile delta, and decides to checkout the alchemy book. And having read it she's beginning to understand how alchemy relates to what is presented in Chapter Nine in Ouspensky's Search by relating the transmutation of lower energies into higher forms of fuel.

We do an in-depth concentration on the points in the outline of one pre-determined chapter of Ouspensky's *Search*, and the selected chapter corresponds to the date on which the meeting takes place.

We do a reconstruction of some of the images and ideas presented in that chapter.

We then ask each person present the question, "Did anything special come through to you in this meeting?"

We then announce next Monday's Chapter, and recite a few of its outline points.

And again, one of us recites our the prayer as a benediction.

Everyone is then asked to evaluate the meeting on a scale of ten--using his own or her own sense of standards to come up with a score.

Our meeting ends with some External Considering because we clean up our table, rearrange our chairs, and thank the coffee house workers for all they have done to make our meeting a memorable event.

Our group owns no property, pays no rent, charges no fees, is open to everyone and open ended. We impose no artificial commitments or contracts.

Our Wednesday Meetings, by invitation only, are peripatetic moving diagrams, involving more structure and demanding more discipline. The Wednesday agenda includes intense focus on one chapter of Ouspensky's Search, one chapter each of Gurdjieff's *Beelzebub* and *Remarkable Men*, together with the quintessence of the Eastern Perspectives: Shankaracharya's Ten Dakshinamurtfian Meditations.

A summary of each meeting is composed by Richard and mailed to each participant the next day after the event.

Our group is now into its eighth year. Richard has facilitated 332 Monday Night Meetings. Warren has participated in 246 of them. Sebouh 209. Dikran 57. More than 100 people have attended at least one meeting.

© Copyright 1998 - Richard Liebow - All Rights Reserved

Second Open Forum - Gurdjieff, the Past, Present and Future Tense of the Work

Facilitator: James Moore

Seymour Ginsburg: This is the second open forum of All & Everything 1998. The title is Gurdjieff, the past, present and future tense of the Work. It is chaired by James Moore.

James Moore: Struggling to approach this theme we immediately encounter the framework of time, and I must say that my introductory remarks can only be something of a footnote to the very detailed and interesting talk given by Forrest this morning. But not withstanding the validity and subtlety of the ideas he advanced, and the delicious complications of relativity and quantum mechanics, but rather in conformity with ordinary work-a-day empiricism, and in conformity also with the grammatical structure of many, although not all, languages, I will try to approach this simply on the supposition that time is divided into three parts, the past, the present, and the future. If I begin to try to apprehend any of these entities, I find myself quite staggered. Here is this question of now, an advancing dimension, this membrane separating that immensity of the past from the unknown future. If we turn our attention to the past, it has the capacity to strike awe that we meet when we look at the night sky. Here indeed is All and Everything that has already transpired, from the first unknown yet vaguely intuitive dialectic, the fear of Theomertmalogos interacting with the prime source substance, Etherokrilno, to create the Megalocosmos, this world upon worlds.

We are dwarfed by those considerations, the arising, the phosphorescence, the decay of individual stars, unnamed, unknown, vanished into the dark backward and abyss of time. Then the emergence of planets. We don't know how many. And upon those planets somehow the protobio, the first life forms. And on our planet also, until by successive gradations there appears what is called a corresponding three-brained being, at which juncture prehistory begins, aligning into history a colossal drama played out against all kinds of historical backcloths, enacted by innumerable and now forgotten people, differently costumed, enacting in all kinds of manners what polity calls the thirty six dramatic situations. So many lives, human beings like ourselves, there in that huge container, the past. And for each of us we to have our past, the moment of our conception, the moment of our birth, the moments of the successive initiations, the rites of passage, meeting someone we love, the having of children. All that lies in the past. There are our memories, there the domain of nostalgia. Such was life then. There crystallized are all our mistakes, all the inherencies, all the events that laid down in our centres the material that causes us to react in this way or that. Even the moment when I began to speak now lies in the past. The membrane of now has advanced and never ceases. When we turn to the unknown, that unknown future, we are Gurdjieffians and as Gurdjieffians we have a certain sense of the importance of deploying time

Second Open Forum - Gurdjieff, the Past, Present and Future Tense of the Work

wisely. We have our diaries with us, the notes of a group or movement or some commitment or other. So moving from year to year, week to week, until that appointment which does not appear in our diary.

The sole means now for the saving of the beings of the planet Earth would be to implant in that presence again an organ like Kundabuffer, but this time of such properties that everyone of those unfortunates during their process of existence should constantly sense and be cognizant of the inevitability of his own death as well as the death of everyone on whom his eye or attention rests.

We are shown scenarios by futurologists starkly contradictory. We are shown disasters, apocalyptic visions. There will be atomic war, aids will spread, some terrible plague will come from Africa. Finite resources will dwindle. And contrapuntally, we are offered all kinds of facile science based dreams and Utopias based on very cheap computer chips, genetic engineering, and God knows what. And we know nothing of that future in actuality. Science presents us with contradictory visions. On the one case the universe is expanding and by a kind of inflation in which some have seen a paradigm for the various Gurdjieff groups, will disperse, segregate, and pass into loneliness. Science also offers a kind of counter paradigm of a great change of mind, gravitationally, so that everything begins to implode.

Now against this colossal backcloth is positioned the life of a man who has come to mean a great deal in our lives. He punctuates time. He is born in a certain time, let us say 1866. He dies. And yet here we are gathered in his name. The importance that Gurdjieff gave to the past is surely undeniable. His reflections there in Beelzebub and in the Second Series, map of pre-sand Egypt, Babylon, various learned beings whom he adjudicates. He wished us to understand that the past had something to convey to us. He summons us constantly into the here and now that lies on that extraordinary membrane separating those immensities of the past and the future. Without that it becomes all words unless we have some sense of the presence in the now. At the same time in his conjunction there that he wished to make a New World, there is a concern and a care for the future. So we stand here trying to bear witness to our understanding of those three factors. The informative past, the need for a presence which we inhabit with agreement and being, and a responsibility to care for the future. Now what was the circumstance when Mr. Gurdjieff arose? Surely we can see historically the difficulties he met. Although the same in their conditions, the circumstances were radically different from today. Everything is changing. Perhaps an idiom has to change, an idiom of Work. It is not for me to pronounce on that, but I would like to have some sense that we could share together how we understand how that tradition of Mr. Gurdjieff can remain alive in this sense that its spirit remains alive, although its form may necessarily change in conformity with change that is thrust upon us by circumstances.

Well I have said enough and I don't want to monopolize the time. I just want to say two things about our sharing together, the first purely procedural. There has been a concern that those people who speak who wish to have their testimony attributed, may do so, and those who wish anonymity may also have that scope. Then if when you speak you would kindly indicate that so it is recorded on the microphone, we at the editing stage will guarantee, we will guarantee that there will be as they say in the Sydney group - No worries mate. We will act responsibly.

The second thing I would like to say is that we have amongst us such a spectrum of people of different ages and different understanding, and there could be a danger that the same old voices monopolize this forum. Speaking personally, and this is not a command, it is a wish, I would love to hear from some of the shier or more silent people, people who have not spoken. They are as entitled to their view, their recourses of conscience as anybody else. So who will be brave and offer something, and when you do, will you take the microphone and indicate on it whether you wish your talk to be recorded.

Anonymous: It is a very large question for me. Over the last few years, regarding forms of groups work, and my aim and wishes into that future, which is what concerns me most. And I would just put out my current perceptions that everything I have been exposed to and has a taste of, I have come across no more wholesome, complete application of Work as I perceive it, that embraces life now with something real for the future, than the time that I spent at Two Rivers Farm. And it is my hope that those type of communities can move into the future towards that type of community. Thank you.

Jeff Taylor: I am happy to have this recorded. I am going to express a hope as well. It is something like this. I know there is here represented many different streams of the Work of Mr. Gurdjieff, and I think it is a wonderful sign that we are prepared to come and talk with each other, even though I know we represent different views. There are even some quite strong disagreements between different factions of the Gurdjieff Work. And I hope that we can continue to work together and that we can respect the different views that each of us have, that each of us hold, the different ways that we work. Because here again the interpretations vary enormously in this room. But we can respect and we can strive to have a dialogue about this. And that way, I think, the Work can go forward, because I do honestly believe that there is not any one faction of the Gurdjieff movement that holds the whole story, that can really represent what Mr. Gurdjieff was, what he brought into the world. Fragmentation is not the right word, it is more like, it can be developed, it can be carried forward. Which brings me to my next theme, which is to do with what I believe about Mr. Gurdjieff in relation to the past, present and future, which I see as a very dynamic process. I think Mr. Gurdjieff said somewhere that by our work to redeem the past, we are open to the future. That is a paraphrase. The past is not dead, it is not all fixed and done with, and so we can be in touch with that, feel our own mistakes and the mistakes of others, of the people who went before. And in the future, we can be opening more to the future by just having a word to each other and by our respective services. In that way we are open to the future of the work.

Martin Butler: I am quite happy to have this recorded. I will just give you a potted history of my background so that what I am saying will have some context. For about 15 years I got hold of the books, thrashed around with the books, and got nowhere. And then in 1959 I think it was, I met Edwina Hands through a colleague, and I immediately saw when I met Edwina that I had wasted

Second Open Forum - Gurdjieff, the Past, Present and Future Tense of the Work

15 years. But maybe it was not wasted. Maybe I needed to do that to understand what Edwina said to me when I met her. I know Edwina was not main stream as such, but she did well as a teacher. One of the things that Edwina said to me was that she believed *Beelzebub's Tales* was a Koan. It was not really meant to be directly understood in the nature of a word to the unwise, it was something different. She also talked a lot about Zen, the spirit of Zen. And it is fortunate now that I am working with a group that has a similar sort of emphasis on the whole thing. And it seems to me that the past of the Gurdjieff movement has been probably buried in method and analysis and that sort of thing. And I feel as a relative outsider, although I have been involved with two groups now, that the whole thing is becoming much more a direct pointing, I think they would say in Zen. It would certainly be my hope that the whole thing as it moves forward becomes more of a living entity, rather than simply the digestion of material that was produced 30 or 40 years ago. Thank you.

James Moore: Yes, I would just - I don't want to fall into the trap of trying to moderate anything people say, but since it was in 1959 that I began working in one of Rena Hand's groups, I think it would be true to say that she had a most profound respect for Mr. Gurdjieff's teaching in its essence. But it would be a misconception, I think, to suppose that she would wish it to be somehow accommodated to, or simulated by, another tradition. I feel we know perhaps not enough about our own tradition and its practice, without seeking for the essence in another. But may be I have mis-construed what you tried to indicate.

Sy Ginsburg: I am quite happy to have this recorded. I have been in group Work since 1978 in several different situations, and for the past five years, since 1993, I have been involved in a kind of group Work within the Theosophical Society, as many of you know. It is my experience even in an exercise like that, where people are interested in ideas related to this, that almost none of them are aware of the concept of Self Awareness. Now some are, and with the independent key that Mr. Gurdjieff has given us, I can see that concept exists in every religious tradition. It is my view that Mr. Gurdjieff was a Messenger sent from Above, as I believe he is. And if his Work is to mean anything, unless I am mistaken, we can all agree that that concept is a fundamental concept of the Work. In some way that needs to be made available again, as it has been by whoever founded what became each religion. It has to be made available once again as widely as possible to humanity. Exactly what the direction of this would be, I am not certain, but it is my view that that central element of the teaching that Mr. Gurdjieff brought, should be in some way, to the extent that any of us are able to work on ourselves and in some way made available to others. And we have an obligation to do that.

James Moore: How do you relate that side to the teaching that you, to the reading you invited me to read -- Ashiata Shiemash never addressed the ordinary beings directly on the planet, but through initiates.

Sy Ginsburg: It is an open secret that is expressed here. Those who are not ready to get it, won't get it, in my opinion. So I don't think there is any danger. But there are people who are ready and don't know anything about it. Speaking from my experience, the five years of having this Work available within our Society if you like, and most people in that Society in our particular group, there are almost 100 members, people interested in the Gurdjieff Work number maybe 15. The others all know it is there. Once in a while, someone will come in, and they may not pursue it exactly as we would. They may have no interest in the *Tales* at all. But from my experience, they may have begun to realize the importance and significance of Self Awareness.

Robert Ennis: It is fine to have this recorded. It seems to me that we are living in a very, very exciting time in our tradition, in that the Work that Mr. Gurdjieff did has gone on in many different directions, and it is flowering in all kinds of interesting and mysterious and wonderful ways. I have been told, although I cannot verify it, that before he died he whispered in the ear of quite a few people, "Only you can carry on my Work". And to me this would indicate that he felt that it was important for it not to be a monolithic creation, but that he trusted it sufficiently to bear the scrutiny and the working with it by many different approaches. And it is my feeling that the teaching, like a diamond, will remain, even if considerable wiseacreing occurs in the process. People will be able to recognize the teaching when it flowers and where something that is only an imitation appears, that will eventually wither away on its own. So I am very hopeful that all these different directions will produce something different and wonderful, that is still the same living teaching that he brought to us. And so I am really delighted and excited that this kind of Conference is happening, which I don't think would have been possible even a few years ago. And I am hoping that it will become even more interesting in the future.

James Moore: Say something to us from Utah. You say nothing. You are my friend.

Bonnie Phillips: My hope is that all of us in the Work can sufficiently value what we have and what Mr. Gurdjieff and everyone in the Work has brought us, that we can realize that in the present we have an obligation to the future. And I confidently look to myself and to all of you and to people who are working on themselves, for help in this direction. And that is all I have to say.

James Moore: Thank you very much.

Dorothy Usiskin: Because we have Email and it is not all terrible, I think what Paul has done is shear group work with other folk. And I am hoping that other groups will do the same. I think we can all get something from the other groups to help our own group stay viable, stay centred. Sometimes we get stale, lose interest and get negative, what ever. It might help to get ideas from the other groups. And some don't have a group, so this would be marvellous for them to partake in that little way.

Keith Buzzell: This can be recorded. I think it is important to remember in the context of past, present and future, and of relationships as it is possible for us to explore, and very important while we are here, that into that future, coming from the past, in an enormously powerful and important way, is all that Work which is now taking place, and will continue into the future, that is not substantially in numbers present here, and that is the Work of the various formations of the Gurdjieff Foundations in so many countries through the world. And I think it is very essential,

Second Open Forum - Gurdjieff, the Past, Present and Future Tense of the Work

very important, because we are now talking about thousands of people who have been involved in that lineage. And that is an essential thing for us to have in mind relative to the past, present and future.

Bert Sharp: Quite happy to be recorded. Just a little point I would like to make in relation to the past, present and future. It seems to me that a very significant practical change has occurred very recently that will affect the future. It began to occur less than fifty or one hundred years ago. If you go back one hundred years, hardly anybody left their village. There was virtually no contact of ordinary people with other parts of the world, with other religious groups, other philosophical groups at all. There was no interchange. Now we are all different, and it is important that we are, and therefore words, expressions, that suite one person don't necessarily register with another. And so we tend to be attracted to different approaches. But now for the first time, people move around the world. Lots of people move around the world, and they therefore, in Europe, come across things like Buddhism, Hinduism, and so on and so forth, whereas before you were either Christian or nothing. Now this is a significant change. Perhaps it does not directly relate to the Gurdjieff Work but it must affect it in some way. This movement of people, movement of information. So perhaps we are all the information society and we are therefore exposed to all the good and all the bad.

Nicolas Tereshchenko: I don't mind this being recorded, right or wrong, and I am sorry to disappoint our Chairman that my voice is heard more often than that of some other people. It seems to me that what is important is to come back to the constitution of the Work as it was when given to us by Mr. Gurdjieff. That is to say, everything that he has left must now be made available to all those who wish to work. I have listened very carefully to what James Moore, our Chairman, has just said about Ashiata Shiemash. But initiates are not born, they are made, and they are self selected, because only the people who come for initiation will be initiated. In exactly the same way, only people who wish to Work will Work if they can, within their capacity. It is true that many people who come to the Work leave it. This is true of all the groups in which I have been. As I mentioned yesterday, I have had the very good fortune to meet quite a lot of the people who worked with Mr. Gurdjieff. And there are quite a lot of advantages of being able to speak many languages. I have also been able to read Beelzebub in the original. Now I think it is a shame that it has not yet come out in its original version, because neither the English, the two English, nor the French versions are really able to express what Mr. Gurdjieff has put into the book in the use of certain words in Russian which have more than one meaning. But leaving that particular thing aside, it seems to me that we have not taken enough notice of what Ouspensky has already written in his book, *In Search of the Miraculous*, which incidentally I am quite sure which instead of being submitted to Mr. Gurdjieff himself for authenticity, if it had been submitted to some of the self selected guardians of the Gurdjieff Work nowadays, would never have been published. And as Mr. Ouspensky has written in his book, the Fourth Way is not a permanent way. It appears, it persists for a length of time, and then it disappears. That is part of the Law of Heptaparaparshinokh, because in the absence of someone like Mr. Gurdjieff, the Heptaparaparshinokh turns back on itself and does precisely the opposite of what it had started to do. And this is what I think is happening to the so-called Gurdjieff groups now. Most of them no longer transmit what Mr. Gurdjieff has given us. In fact many of the people love preciously what they have learnt from him, and they will not share it. I know for a fact that there are writings of Mr. Gurdjieff which have never been revealed as yet. I also know for a fact that very important parts of the Third Series which exist, have not been published. Now this brings us to the question. Are we going to try and change the nature of the Fourth Way in some way or other? Mr. Gurdjieff himself told Ouspensky that what you cannot get under law, you must steal. Are we going to try and get for all those of us here and other people who wish to work, everything that Mr. Gurdjieff has left, or are we going simply to admit that it is a type of Rosicrucian group which by the year 2020 will disappear in the normal course of events by the Law of the Heptaparaparshinokh. I think it is possible perhaps for us to preserve it a little longer, provided the secrecy no longer applies.

There may have been good reason for secrecy in ages past, when people could be severely chastised by organizations, churches, governments, or other organizations. But nowadays there is no real secrecy. So I am an optimist by nature, but about the Work, I am very pessimistic. Unless something very drastic is changed in the way the Foundations and Institutes work, I think the real Gurdjieff Work and teaching will disappear within the next twenty years.

Bill Murphey: The highest a man can attain is to be able to do. I think the Work should focus on learning how to do things, becoming more and more self reliant and more and more an individual. I don't think the change in the economy, the way people live, is going to change people. They are going to be the same, except they are going to evolve more or involve, so to speak. I spent one weekend at Mrs. Staveley's in 1985, and we had a Work weekend. And that weekend we killed a steer and dressed it, and some people worked in the gardens, and some people did this and did that. But there were several of us who dressed the steer that day who could not do it the day before. We learnt how to do it. And I think that is the most important thing. All any of us can do is learn to do, and to do as many things as possible. I think the learning of it, the self reliance, the individuality, is what gives us some objectivity. The guy who can do the most is the highest man, not the guy who knows the most. I think in the future we will all look towards extending our ability to do. In my little group in Phoenix we have a half dozen physicians. We did one little job, learning how to do something. We built a grape fermenter. We had a large vat. Woman there was a cancer doctor working like the rest of us. Another couple of doctors did all the carpentry work. It was a great experience for all of us.

James Moore: John. John Scullion. Come on, say something to us, because you are an authority on an aspect of modern life. Will you not say something in response to this idea of the use of the Internet? I'm sorry, you want to be in.

Warren Alksnis: My name is Warren and you may certainly record this. I would like to tell a story. St. Peter went to God and said, "Heaven is getting very crowded. What can we do?" And God said, "Well you see down there, the fork in the road? Put up two signs. One of those signs to say, this way to Heaven, and the other sign to say, this way to lectures on Heaven, and that will solve your problem."

Second Open Forum - Gurdjieff, the Past, Present and Future Tense of the Work

John Scullion: In relation to what Nicolas Tereshchenko said. You were talking about Mr. Gurdjieff's transmission and that transmission does not only consist of texts and writings and exercises, techniques. There is a personal element. And if you talk about going from the past to the future, anyone can read a book or get hold of an idea and project it into the future. But I don't believe that we possess, own, or understand anything without understanding where it comes from and how it becomes. And one of the difficulties about Gurdjieff Work from the past to the future and this spreading and the adoption of Gurdjieff's ideas by other groups, is that they do not give weight or value to the personal transmission. And I feel that is something that has to be taken into account and given its due weight. If we talk about taking Gurdjieff's transmission into the future, we cannot leave out the personal transmission, and we cannot start from any book or anything. We must be connected to the past in some authentic organic human way by human to human, heart to heart transmission. That is one thing. Another thing which struck me from what Jeff Taylor said and Bert, is that we do live in the information age and there is the possibility of communication across the planet. I understand that many people who see the Internet for the first time say, what a bloody mess it is. It is full of junk, full of rubbish, and you have to comb through it and sift through it. And I think to use the Internet effectively for even a small thing, I sometimes experiment a little. You have to get to know it quite well as a new medium, and not just take the first snapshot and think you know what the movie is like. So I think there is a kind of parallel, a kind of echo here. In Mr. Gurdjieff's day people travelled, not to the extent they do now. People travel much more now. There is much more contact between people, More than there was then, which makes this possible. The Internet is something new. It is still forming. I think it will develop and so many people will become much more able to sift and discriminate and communicate discreetly. And I think that is something that those of us who are familiar with the Internet should maybe try and take some responsibility for. It is not something we should ignore. There are a lot of people who are relatively isolated. I am in that situation, and quite often in my isolation, I will get a report from Richard/ or I will read something on the Internet or will receive an Email from that someone, and it is real. I am really hungry for that and so glad in my flat in Carlisle I am able to receive that, even though it is only words on a flat screen. Somehow we have met and you speak to me after that, I can connect with you, I can receive something. So it is not something to be discarded.

Forrest McIlwain: I don't mind this being recorded. I wanted to say something, not so much in the sense of defence of Nicolas Tereshchenko, but I think that in the past there have been remarks of a similar nature to those he made. It came over as pessimistic and negative, and I am sure that that is not what I heard him say. Judged by the fact that he is here is indicative that as much as I am here and want to work with everyone, I am sure he is here for the same reason. And I think that because we have not made a lot of effort towards trying to understand what Mr. Gurdjieff referred to as sacred laws, there are certain things that become obvious and unfortunately it is lawful and it can be lawful without being negative or without one having a pessimistic view of life or the direction in which things are moving. And I just want to make sure that we don't go away feeling that there was some negativity cast on the proceedings or our coming together to work in a certain way. I certainly have a number of views that in general may be perceived as being pessimistic and I have certainly been called a pessimist on a number of occasions, but that is not how I feel about life and it is certainly not how I feel about people. And I am here because I am very much interested in trying to carry on as long as I can. I just want to thank you for your remarks.

Keith Buzzell: It is important to re-focus on what we mentioned earlier about the entry of the Fourth Way, of a Fourth Way impulse into the overt life of man. This is for a purpose. This it to meet a need. And it is my understanding from what Mr. Gurdjieff says, that it has to do with some very great need. That need is not an individual circumstance or need. If we are not part of meeting that great need, that this Fourth Way effort enters into life for, then we must ask ourselves the question, it seems to me, what is this Work on myself for? If I do not serve, if I do not see somehow and understand for myself and for all the people that I try to share with, if I do not see that we are some how or other tiny little particles of some greater effort that we may have great difficulty putting precise words on, if we don't understand what that great need is. - - We all, especially myself, blah, blah, about some aspects of what that great need may be. But that need is there and is the justification, if you will, in a cosmic sense, for the entry of a Fourth Way effort into life. It is behind the incredible accident that happened in each of our lives that made it possible for us to have a contact with this work. The other end of that stick is, how do we serve that effort. Not how do we serve ourselves or our immediate compatriots.

Bert Sharp: I am happy to be recorded. I am a little apprehensive trying to follow Keith on that one. He did it so well. But while he was talking a memory suddenly came back to me which some of you may think is relevant. It was when I must have been about four years old. There was a vacant lot next door to our house. This was a long time ago of course. Some one must have bought this lot, and a young man, a builders labourer, came along with a shovel and a pick and a piece of string and some pegs, and he proceeded to mark out and dig the footings for the new house that was to be built next door. And having done that he then proceeded to dig a large pit in what was to be the front garden, about as big as this wooden floor in front of us. And he slaked lime and filled the pit with slaked lime. This was the way they used to build houses. I was very inquisitive so I kept questioning him, and he with patience answered. He took sand, lime and water, and made mortar. You see I remember it as a rhyme. He then started putting the footings in, bricks laid with the mortar, for the foundations. And he then started putting up the scaffolding. And all this was preparing the way for the builders who came along afterwards and used the lime that he had produced and the bricks he had unloaded and they put up the brick walls of the house. And then the carpenters came along when it was ready for them, put the floorings in, the roof and so on. And when it was all finished, you see they had all played their part, and the more experienced, the higher paid people, if you like, could not start until the ground had been prepared by the young labourer. He had to fulfil his task first, and the others later. And then eventually the owners came and lived in the new house next door to me. That to my mind is what it is all about. We are all in different positions in regard to that kind of scenario. But that is the scenario. That is the future which we have to prepare for in the present.

Marlena Buzzell: I request that whoever is transcribing, makes it comprehensible. First of all I am reminded of the 14 years that we spent with Mrs. P until her death. And Mrs. P's great wish that she often stated was that we become a bridge for the Work. And her house was always filled with

Second Open Forum - Gurdjieff, the Past, Present and Future Tense of the Work

people from all different lineages. She had worked with Mr. Ouspensky. She has worked with Madam Ouspensky. She had worked with Gurdjieff. She worked with Mr. Nyland. And she was a great lady. That was a very important thing for her that she often said - cross pollinate. And I guess one of the things that I have really appreciated that was just mentioned about this group is that it is a group of people who come together from many different lineages. And in the past three years, speaking for myself, I feel that I have really learned a great deal from each and every person that has been here. There have been many good lessons. I have watched interactions with people from different lineages and have learned tolerance. And so many people say, well this is a very intellectual thing and we are all here and it is too intellectual and so we need to do something different. But I think that when I look around that is not my experience being here. I think working on the Planning Committee has been a wonderful opportunity to really work on myself, both with others and for a higher purpose. It is for the purpose of the Work. Another thing that I really appreciate here in the present is that we have had in the past many experienced speakers, and it has always been an opportunity for those of us to look up to those who are more experienced. And now there is a different kind of thing that is happening. There are some younger people who have come in this time and are also speaking. And I see that as very valuable as well. Because for those people who are more experienced and have longer time in the Work, it is an opportunity to share what has been learnt from those who have gone before in the Work. So I guess my hope is that in the future this continues to grow. It was mentioned, how do we reach other people, how do we reach the masses? And it is my thinking that with us even working with this task we have of being externally considerate to the hotel staff, that this is one of the ways in which we can reach other people, because hopefully people will begin to say, well, but who are these people. And so perhaps we can become a vehicle for transmitting more B influences into their world that needs them so desperately.

Richard Liebow: I am happy for this to be recorded. I would like to say something about the Internet. I really don't feel that the Internet is any more than an extension of the proliferation of communication media that has happened in the last 500 years. I would not be a bit surprised to hear that there are now as many items printed, published, distributed, every year as existed in all the years prior to this year. I have heard that, that the number of printed articles, magazines, books, doubles every year in our time. So, that issue of striving to be a responsible human being, that image has caused to crystallize in my behaviour an image that I call, the burden of selection. And this is true when I walk into the public library. It is true when I walk into Barnes and Noble, where they publish five hundred thousand titles, a typical corner book shop. And it is specially true on the Internet. So the answer for me is to only use the Internet to establish or sustain a connection that is already meaningful to me in a personal way. I am holding this list of information, names, addresses, phone numbers, Email addresses. I feel the need to establish and sustain communication with individuals in this group and with individuals all through the whole scope of my experience, but in a very personal way. I think that if I keep that image of the burden of selection clearly in mind and that image of communicating with the human beings in a responsible, warm, meaningful way, that the Internet, the public library, the Barnes and Noble, the TV, will enhance and enrich my experience and my quest. But if I allow it to become mechanical it will destroy me. That is all I have to say.

All & Everything Conference 1998

Martin Buckley: I am happy to be recorded. I have a question and I wonder if it can be answered. I have heard a lot about lineage, about different lineages being here. I personally don't give a damn about lineage. It does not matter to me. If I detect something that seems to have value, then I will pursue it. But is Gurdjieff's lineage known? Gurdjieff himself, does anyone know who Gurdjieff's teachers were?

James Moore: Well I don't know, but perhaps as someone trying to make the discussion cohere, I would just offer something. It is very difficult really to even pretend to objectivity there. The ideological lineage itself seems to be very eclectic. It is tackled in the final chapter of James Webb's book, The Harmonious Circle. You probably know, the sources of the system. In so far as we look for the lineage in the way that John Scullion has spoken about, definite human to human contact, we can only try to imbue *Meetings With Remarkable Men* with a certain sense of authenticity. In so far as his father was a formative influence on him, that father obviously existed. He is an historical figure. When one turns off and looks for other figures like Prince Lubovedsky and so on, one is on less firm ground I think. I myself am deeply distrustful of any attempt to pigeon hole Gurdjieff as flowing from a Sufi, a Tibetan, or any other dispensation. But I also feel that we can lose so much in an address to the past which does not at the same time encompass a real sense of our acceptance of the challenge here and now. I mean some of us here have been fortunate enough to meet and work with people who knew and worked with Gurdjieff, and that shock of that encounter with those people was in a way something that precipitates work in us without any recourse to a quest to establish lineage in the deep past. It had its immediacy. But may be I don't answer your question in the idiom which is amenable to you. I don't want to pontificate, but that is how I feel it.

Martin Butler: Basically you are saying we don't know the exact lineage of Gurdjieff.

James Moore: Now, suppose we did, what sort of answer would satisfy you?

Martin Butler: I don't want to be satisfied.

James Moore: No, but I am striving to understand what you mean by lineage.

Martin Butler: The reason I asked that question…

James Moore: No. What do you mean by lineage?

Martin Butler: Who were his teachers.

James Moore: Well we have *Meetings With Remarkable Men*, and we know the people he claims to have learnt a great deal from like Father Giovanni and so forth. If you ask me if they are historical figures, I would guess they are composites.

Chris Thompson: Korkaptilian Thought tapes.

Second Open Forum - Gurdjieff, the Past, Present and Future Tense of the Work

Martin Butler. But when we go back to the past, it is fixed and it is safe and it is secure, and so on and so forth. And when we are dealing with the present, the present is insecure, uncertain, and so on and so forth. And it really strikes me that this thing will develop the way it will develop. The notion of doing in this situation is an illusion because the whole thing will move forward of its own spirit, I am sure. It just seems a fallacy that we should try and go this way of that way or whatever. I am sure that in fifty years time people will look back and say, ah well, this is the way it should be because this is the way it went. But right now we don't know.

James Moore: I think you do well to remind us it might be something which because of time we have to consider as a closing chord in this meeting. I don't know. But the idea of what should be is infused with phantasy. We can make a contributive endeavour in terms, not only of doing as Bill Murphey said, but in terms of being. Being is anterior to doing and having. That is such a striking thing for me in the teachers like Madam Salzmann and Madam Lannes, with whom I was lucky enough to work. It was their being. That for me is anterior to and subsumes any question of what we can do. If even in the confusion that we are, the rich confusion that we are, an aggregate of people from disparate backgrounds. We can sometimes come back to the question - - I am sitting here. To what extent am I? To what extent is there some presence there? Then I think you are quite right to say that we can confide cheerfully to the dispensation of fate or higher powers what will ensue. Did you want to add to that?

Unidentified: No, I don't think so. It is good to have that recorded.

James Moore: Then I think it is time to go. Let me off.

End of Session

Joy Without a Cause: Work on the Emotional Centre in Daily Life

Robert Bryce

Robert Bryce was born in Australia and was trained as a Shipwright, Chartered Engineer, and Dispute Mediator. He now lives in the UK. He first came across Gurdjieff's thinking through Gurdjieff's *Meetings With Remarkable Men* at the age of 21. This led him to study the work with a group in Sydney, Australia. This was a group led by Dr. Philip Groves.

Robert Bryce was introduced by Nicolas Tereshchenko. Nicolas mentioned that Robert was a pupil of Dr. Philip Groves. He went on to say that he had the pleasure of meeting Dr. Philip Groves on one of his visits to Sydney. Nicolas commented further to the effect that Dr. Groves is a very learned man who has three Doctorates in three different subjects, one of which is Divinity. He is also an Egyptologist and has also been accepted by one of the Aboriginal tribes as one of their Initiates. Nicolas said that some day, when it is not so late perhaps, he will tell us the story of how he came to know Dr. Groves, but it would not be appropriate to take the time tonight.

As a prelude to the paper Robert then played some of Debussy's "La Mer", which he considered appropriate to set the scene.

Joy Without a Cause

As we try to work and live the Work we are continuously presented with challenges and some of them are so subtle it is easy to fall into their snares.

Gurdjieff was merciless in his treatment of the human foibles of those around him and this should remind us to be equally merciless of our own foibles. The processes of self-remembering and self-observation are of paramount importance. The subtly of where "we" observe our "selves" from needs to be observed as well.

We all find it easiest to observe our intellectual and mechanical centres and those consequences and acts which flow from them. It is much harder to observe and monitor the non verbal or mentation processes of the emotional centre. A difficulty which arises from work on the emotional centre is that we try to reconcile what is going on and to explain it intellectually. Often what we unearth about ourselves from within the emotional centre is very unpleasant. Gurdjieff discusses the "terror or horror of the situation" and how if we were faced with our true nature of ourselves we would instantly slit our own throats. What is interesting to observe is how certain affections flow into the intellectual constructs which give life to those landscapes we provide in our natural internal world.

Joy Without a Cause: Work on the Emotional Centre in Daily Life

We continuously seek to dissect those truths or teachings we receive from the Work. Gurdjieff speaks directly about this in *Meetings With Remarkable Men*. The story centres around the Seekers of Truth meeting with the yogi under the tree. There is a meal and Gurdjieff is still masticating his food when all the others have finished. The yogi admonishes him and then proceeds to explain that it is important for our digestion to swallow the food in decent sized chunks and let our internal organs perform their functions.

This passage is dealing directly with our predilections to disassemble Work teachings by reductionist thinking and wiseacreing. We find it so much easier to approach the Work from the intellectual centre that despite our efforts to work on all the centres, we become bound up in searching for the truth and miss the opportunity to live it.

We live in the illusion that "we" are reforming "ourselves" by "our own efforts". Our efforts and the affections which feed them are setting the scene for the processes of Higher Life to work to good effect internally. We perpetually want to know the Truth about everything. We may get disappointed and demolished by the realisation that we can not know everything and this is an important state to reach. It is important that the devastation of this I or ego state occurs. For it is what lies beyond this state that is really exciting.

Ouspensky makes some very pertinent observations on how we view the world in *Tertium Organum*. He takes us through a progression of the view a being would have whilst living in a one and then two dimensional world. He then moves into the world we view and the possibility of how we should live.

At certain stages of the Work we are like fish. We live in a world in which there is light above and darkness below. We can move freely in this world and fall prey to the currents of life and the predators which also inhabit the environment. We have the abysses which increase the obscurity of our vision and action if we become weighed down by heavy states. The pressure of this environment means that those organisms which survive down there have forms which can not live in the upper reaches of the ocean. The vents of the ocean floor show us that life can be found in very hostile and toxic environments. We can see an analogy of the constraints upon life at this level and rules which govern it if we think of it in terms of the Hydrogens. And we can chose to descend to corresponding states if we so wish.

But in that realm of the ocean where there is sufficient light life is full and rich. It is multi-coloured and it has a relatively stable temperature. It is also an intensely interesting part of the world in which we live. The coral reefs teem with life from microscopic polyps to schools of fish. The oceans are traversed by whales which can descend to great depths to feed upon large squid or dwell in its upper levels and live by consuming large amounts of very small plankton. If we ponder upon the image of the whale we can see that it is possible to construct impressive structures by "feeding on small food". We could further ponder upon this image in relation to the yogi's advice to Gurdjieff and the story of Jonah.

But no matter how interesting this world is, it and the fish which live there are restricted by the surface of the ocean and this restriction can be similar to that which we impose upon ourselves if we only live and work from the intellectual centre.

The aerial world above the surface of the ocean is less dense and has a greater range of temperature. The aerial world is freer and more immediate to the source of life, the sun. It is the warmth of this environment, or its variations, which in large measure sets the oceans in movement. Those currents which sweep around the oceans of the world are difficult to observe by the fish and life which live in, and are carried by them. They are easier to observe from above the ocean and even easier by remote sensing technology from satellites.

The sense of devastation which was mentioned above is in some respects reflected in the intertidal zone. As we move from the world of the ocean we are battered by parts of our being which correspond to ego states or I's which seek to restrain our growth into higher and finer states. At this time we are gradually becoming accustomed to the new state of being or life as we cling like limpets or cungevoi to rocks to prevent ourselves from being swept away by the tides. At a low tide we can escape to the beach and leave behind the ocean and move into the aerial world.

If we view the aerial world in the context of the emotional centre we can immediately see that it has an immense range of opportunities and possibilities. A new mode of living is necessary as we grow. In the aerial world it is possible to construct new things and processes which are totally beyond the possibilities of the ocean world.

With the increased possibilities of the new space or mode of living come increased responsibilities. We realise that there are very powerful forces which can be harnessed for good or evil and it is within our choice to align our affections to the landscape we find most pleasing. The landscapes can range from the frigid polar wastes to grass lands, forests and majestic mountains and are inhabited by diverse plants and animals.

So if we can choose an orientation or a mode of living for an internal landscape it is surprising, or a comment on the general conditions in which we all function, that so many people choose to live in swamps. We must seek to align our affections in the direction of a wholesome, sustaining and inspiring landscape if we are to have a chance of living a half decent existence. We must remember that the Holy Sun Absolute is in the sky above
and is giving us warmth and light to live in new states.

This new mode of living is at once light-hearted but strong. In this state we can view the landscapes and seascapes we must live in with equanimity and not fall prey to all the changes of season of our inner world. It is living in a state of joy without a cause.

In many passages throughout *All and Everything*, Gurdjieff describes how Higher Life is continuously seeking to guide us into finer states of being. Our own growth does not come about solely through our own actions or prudence but can only be nurtured if a trust in the Divine takes root. The peace which the trust provides allows us to live in joy without a cause. The paradox is that there are very definitely end, cause and effect present. The joy is not caused by an external.

Just as the ocean does not govern the aerial world so our external can not dictate to or govern our internals. The conditions within the ocean can have a profound effect on the aerial world's landscapes and so too do our externals upon the internals. But it is all too easy in our arrogance to consider that we ourselves are guiding our own growth. Gurdjieff's *Beelzebub* comes down to the earth to sojourn amongst its arch-absurd inhabitants.

It is essential that we allow those influences of Higher Life to guide us and this can only happen when we have truly seen the terror of our situation and have chosen to trust. We must seek a new language beyond that with which we have grown into adulthood to even start to be able to live in more refined states.

To be graced by a state of joy without a cause is to live in active peace.

© Copyright 1998 - Robert Bryce - All Rights Reserved

The Evolution of Evolution

Bert Sharp

Dr. Sharp took a first degree in Physiology, and an M.Sc., in Metallurgy by private study while working in industry. He later took a Ph.D., in Material Science.

Subsequently he has become involved in the psychological transformation of himself and others, a much more difficult field of endeavour. In this he has been helped by many, including Ronald and Muriel Oldham and Lewis Creed, when he was able to visit the Dicker, John Castanios Flores, who led a large Work group in Mexico and came to Littlehampton to end his days, and Nicolas Tereshchenko and Sy Ginsburg. There have been many others speaking through the written page and in other ways and perhaps most of all, in a very special way, his dear wife and daughter.

Dr. Sharp presented two papers at the '96 Conference -

"The Message of Gurdjieff and where Humanity Stands Today" and "Telepathic Teaching and Transcendent Experiences". He also presented a paper at the 1997 Conference – "Gurdjieff's Neuroanatomy of Man and Modern Science".

Dr. Sharp was introduced by Seymour Ginsburg who opened the session by a reading, the basis of a led meditation on the theme of The Divine Compassion.

The Divine Compassion

Sit in your usual meditation position and relax. Observe your breathing. As you become aware of the thoughts of the day intruding, turn back simply to watching your breathing. Your body is breathing for you. When settled in this way begin the meditation.

Become conscious of the existence of the cells which form your planetary body; become conscious of how they freely consented to differentiate in order to go beyond themselves, their individuality, and become specialist cells, part of a particular organ of your body. Did they do this consciously or mechanically?

Go further and become conscious of how these individual organs have given up their individuality in order to relate to one another and so to form the complex interactive assemble which is your planetary body. Remember that it is only because of such sacrifices on the part of the cells, the tissues formed from the cells and the organs formed from the tissues, that it has been possible for you to inhabit the body which you consider as your own.

Then go further and become conscious of you, the far in you, observing all this, you and your body, your body the result of the sacrifice of all these millions of individual cells. Then begin to realize that you have a responsibility for your body, for its organs, for each of its individual cells. For providing them with all their natural essential requirements. Observe this profound thought. Meditate upon it.

At this point you may experience a Divine Compassion coming with the feeling of responsibility, of compassion for all the living cells which make up your planetary body. Are you also able to sacrifice your individuality in order to become no longer a human being but an infinitely small cell in the totality of Humanity?

Hold for as long as possible this feeling of the Divine Compassion flowing through you. What is it that is aware of it? Real I? Be aware of the very small, the very low, and at the same time of the very large, the very high, and that you, Real I is the intermediate between the two, the whole assembly forming the Eternal Totality.

If you want more then consider the following either or of formatory thinking:

Is it that the "irresponsible" human fears God and so in the ultimate expects help and forgiveness from Him? Or by contrast, does the "responsible" human know that he or she cannot know God who therefore may or may not exist, and as a result has to accept that it is all up to him or her, that he or she is responsible for the future of humanity and so must act in the interests of humanity and not of himself or herself? So to be a "responsible" human brings one face to face with the terror of the situation.

The Evolution of Evolution

Introduction

The following is the third version of this paper. I have been fortunate to have the benefit of much constructive criticism and comments on previous versions by my good friend, Nicolas Tereshchenko. One result of all this is that I have tried vigorously to use the terminology of Gurdjieff whenever possible. P. D. Ouspensky, in his *In Search of the Miraculous*, I am sure did his best to leave us what he understood of Gurdjieff's teaching, but in particular, he does not appear to have correctly understood the Heptaparaparshinokh, relying too much on the musical octave as a model. Gurdjieff tells us, in Chapter 40 of the *Tales*, how much misunderstanding has come in as a result of trying to link the Heptaparaparshinokh with the Chinese and Greek musical scales.

What does the word Heptaparaparshinokh mean? Hepta comes from the Greek for seven; para means next or related or resembling or beyond; arshin is a unit of measurement in old Russian;

okh is the root of the verb okhat, to sigh in Russian, related to making an effort. So the whole word seems to imply "seven similar related contiguous working units".

But what does Gurdjieff tell us about this fundamental law? Referring to *Beelzebub's Tales*, first, at page 750-751 we have:

"'The-line-of-the-flow-of-forces-constantly-deflecting-accordingto-law-and-uniting-again-at-its-ends'."

"This sacred primordial cosmic law has seven deflections or, as it is still otherwise said, seven 'centres of gravity' and the distance between each two of these deflections or 'centres of gravity' is called a 'Stopinder-of-the-sacred-Heptaparaparshinokh"

At page 139, referring to the effect of the Law on the Omnipresent-Okidanokh, we have:

"- - it is correspondingly changed, in respect of what is called the 'Vivifyingness of Vibrations' according to its passage through what are called the 'Stopinders' or 'gravity-centres' of the fundamental 'common-cosmic sacred Heptaparaparshinokh." (the prime-source substance filling the whole Universe, Etherokrilno, the basis for the arising and maintenance of everything existing, includes its active form, the Omnipresent-Okidanokh.)

We must not forget that everything, including in particular - all matter, is at base, vibrational energy.

Then at page 753-754 we have:

"And, namely, with the purpose of providing the 'requisite inherency' for receiving, for its functioning, the automatic affluence of all forces which were near, HE lengthened the Stopinder between its third and fourth deflections."

"This same Stopinder of the sacred Heptaparaparshinokh is just that one, which is still called the 'mechano-coinciding-Mdnel-In"

"And the Stopinder which HE shortened, is between its last deflection and the beginning of a new cycle of its completing process; by this same shortening, for the purpose of facilitating the commencement of a new cycle of its completing process, HE predetermined the functioning of the given Stopinder to be dependent only upon the affluence of forces, obtained from outside through that Stopinder from the results of the action of that cosmic concentration itself in which the completing process of this primordial fundamental sacred law flows."

"And this Stopinder of the sacred Heptaparaparshinokh is just that one, which is still called the 'intentionally-actualized-Mdnel-In'".

"As regards the third Stopinder, then changed in its 'subjective action' and which is fifth in the general successiveness and is called 'Harnel-Aoot,' its disharmony flowed by itself from the change of the two aforementioned Stopinders."

So we can write the Heptaparaparshinokh as follows:

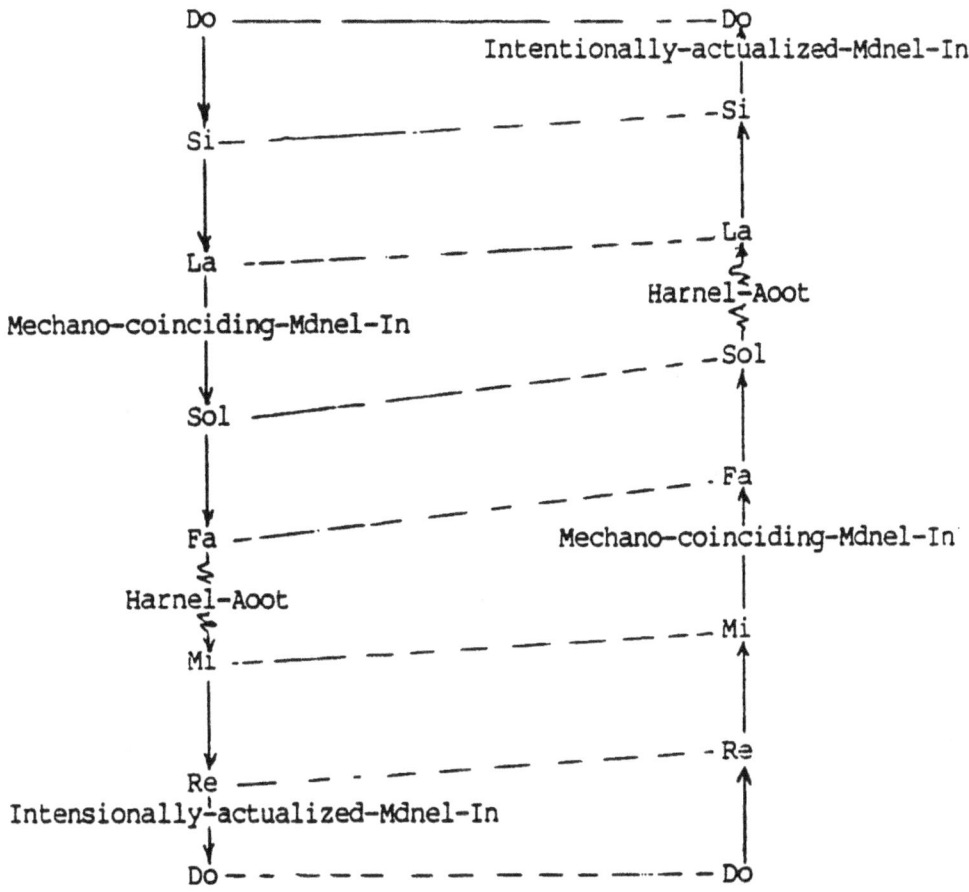

The Evolution of Evolution

Objective Science tells us that there is Eternity and Time. Eternity is the realm of Being, Time the realm of becoming. Time in *Beelzebub's Tales* is referred to as The Merciless Heropass, since its property or intent is, apparently, to destroy whatever is by introducing the element of decay. Unless, however, there is a period in which change can occur, and change inevitably means the decay of that which is so that it can be replaced by the new, there can be no development, no evolution.

All & Everything Conference 1998

Beelzebub's Tales[1] can be said to deal with three principal aspects; what Gurdjieff calls elsewhere, the Ray of Creation or the evolution of the Cosmos[2], the domain of the Descending Involutionary Cosmic Heptaparaparshinokh; the psychological evolution of the human, the domain of the Ascending Evolutionary Being Heptaparaparshinokh; and thirdly, the means of psychological development of the human based on the concept of the Three Brain Being.[3]

Eternity

Eternity is beyond our comprehension. We do not have the mentation equipment to have any real conception of it. Perhaps the nearest we can come to an understanding of it is to postulate that it is the World of Ideas. Ideas and possibilities exist out of time and space eternally. When an idea becomes manifest, it is manifest in time and space. As in the Qabala we have the four worlds; Atziluth, Emanation; Briah, Creation; Yetzirah, Formation; Assiah, Manifestation. These four worlds are the result of the existence of that which is beyond them, the Ain or Void, the Ain Soph, Endlessness, and the Ain Soph Aur, the Limitless Light, sometimes referred to as the "Veils of Negative Existence".[4]

Perhaps we can see that the Ain, Ain Soph and Ain Soph Aur are in effect the three principal attributes of the World of Ideas which is Eternity. Note that it would be incorrect to say that they exist in Eternity, rather they are Eternity.

The First Divine Emanation
The First Phase of Evolution
The First Order Sun

I consider the first phase of the evolution of the Cosmos to be what is now called the Big Bang. At this point, the First Divine Emanation occurs in the form of the manifestation of an enormous burst of cosmic energy together with the laws of the manifest and the dimensions of space and passing time. This occurred some 15,000,000,000 years ago.

This first phase was directly under what Gurdjieff calls His Endlessness, a conscious action taken by "God", by whatever is the Ain, Ain Soph, Ain Soph Aur, the World of Ideas. This action was taken subsequent to the realization by His Endlessness that his abode, the Sun Absolute, was diminishing. To counter this He changed the two fundamental laws, the Law of Seven, the Heptaparaparshinokh, and the Law of Three, the Triamazikamno, so that in future a system based on Reciprocal Maintenance, the Trogoautoegocrat, was in place, instead of the Autoegocrat process.

---

[1] Gurdjieff. *All and Everything*. Routledge & Kegan Paul. 1962.
[2] P. D. Ouspensky. *In Search of the Miraculous*. Routledge & Kegan Paul. 1964. P. 82, 137, 167, 305.
[3] G. Gurdjieff. *All & Everything*. Routledge & Kegan Paul. 1962. P. 146 et al.
[4] Gareth Knight. *A Practical Guide to Qabalistic Symbolism*. Vol 1 & 2. Kahn & Averill. 1975.
  See also - Frater Achad. *The Anatomy of the Body of God*. Bantam Press. (reprint) 1991.

The Evolution of Evolution

"And so my dear boy, our COMMON FATHER CREATOR ALMIGHTY, having then in the beginning changed the functioning of both these primordial sacred laws, directed the action of their forces from within the Most Holy Sun Absolute into the space of the Universe, where upon there was obtained the what is called 'Emanation-of-the-Sun-Absolute' and now called, 'Theomertmalogos' or 'Word-God'."[5]

"This Most Great common-cosmic Trogoautoegocratic-process was actualized by our ENDLESS UNI-BEING, when our Most Great and Most Holy Sun Absolute had already existed, on which our ALL-GRACIOUS ENDLESS CREATOR had and still has the chief place of His existence".[6]

The Second Phase of Evolution

The second phase of evolution then begins in a law conformable way so that the undifferentiated energy evolves to positive and negative energy, to the sub-atomic entities and finally the original Hydrogen and Helium which the Cosmos consists of in its earliest stages. These two elements then, again under the laws of the Cosmos, form centres of gravity which evolve into the various bodies, the principal ones being the stars, which form the galaxies.

We need to be clear that while the first phase, including the emanation of the enormous burst of Cosmic energy, and the changing of the two basic laws, the Law of Seven and the Law of Three, was the action of His Endlessness, all subsequent action and evolution was the result of delegation, the first stage of such delegation being to the Absolute, the First Order Sun, the Protocosmos.

"And, namely, they named the Most Most Holy Prime-Source Sun Absolute itself - 'Protocosmos'."[7]

Any efficient management system is based on the delegation of authority and responsibility. The top manager delegates to the next level the responsibility of all actions below his level of authority. He provides the next level down with all the necessary authority, all the rules or laws, required to carry out the responsibility delegated. He at the same time gives up his authority at all the lower levels, but not the responsibility. In this way he does not interfere with the actions of those below him. In the same way, His Endlessness, having provided by the operation of His Will the enormous burst of energy and the changed two basic laws, from then on plays no part in the subsequent creation of the Cosmos, but is still responsible for it in the ultimate. The next level down is under the authority of the Absolute 1. This is the First Order Sun, World 1, the Protocosmos.

---

[5] G. Gurdjieff. *All and Everything*. Routledge & Kegan Paul. 1962. Page 756.
[6] Ibid. Page 136.
[7] Ibid. Page 760.

The entities evolved in this second phase are of such structures and properties that they reflect the Will of His Endlessness now delegated as the Will of the Absolute so that they will evolve to the next stages in conformity with this Will and the Laws emanating from His Endlessness with the original injection of energy from Eternity.

The second phase of evolution, the phase concerned with the evolution of the sub atomic entities and their combining to form Hydrogen and Helium, comes under the Law of Chance. This is the Principle of Indeterminancy of modern physics. The elements finally making up the structure of the Cosmos are those having a suitably high degree of stability. Those at the lower end of this stability are the radioactive elements. If we consider a radioactive element, we have no way of knowing when a particular atom of that element will disintegrate. It may have an infinite life, or disintegrate in the next moment. If we take a statistically large enough group of such atoms, however, then we can predict the time by which half of them will have disintegrated. This is the functioning of the Law of Chance. The situation is subject to calculation and so predictable in the mass, but not at the individual level. It is this Law of Chance which governs the evolution of the elements from the sub-atomic entities. In the same way the behaviour of a crowd is predictable, but not that of an individual human.

So the second phase of evolution, evolution at the atomic level, at the level of the elements, is under the Law of Chance. So the Law of Chance, together with the laws of the Cosmos itself take us to the level of the evolution of the Suns, the Second order Suns.

The Second Divine Emanation
The Third Phase of Evolution.
The Second Order Suns

From the moment of the Big Bang, we have an expanding Cosmos, expanding at the speed of light, since under the laws of the Cosmos, it cannot expand any faster. Very soon after the beginning, the sub atomic entities have generally combined to form 75% Hydrogen and 25% Helium. The next stage is the accretion of the basic Hydrogen and Helium into the stellar masses we see today. These correspond to the "Centres of gravity" of Gurdjieff.

It is interesting to note that although the Cosmos is an expanding Cosmos, once a centre of gravity has formed, a star, it is no longer subject to this expansion, but in effect forms a centre from which the rest of the Cosmos is expanding. The analogy is of the human who becomes sufficiently conscious to know he or she is an individual, separate from the rest. Then this individual acts as a centre from which the rest is observed. This stage precedes the stage at which one is conscious of this temporary centre and the Universe as well as of that which is observing it. Self-Remembered. Hence the importance to our psychological development of first forming a stable individuality, an observation platform.

Keeping our description as simple as possible, once a star begins to form, it attracts further Hydrogen and Helium to itself from its surroundings, and then progressively increases in density under the force of its own gravity. As this density increase proceeds the temperature of the star increases, until it eventually switches on as a thermonuclear reactor. The energy resulting is from the conversion of Hydrogen into Helium, and in the process all the elements up to those with the density of Iron are produced by nuclear fusion reactions. It would seem that our Sun became switched on as a star together with its evolving planetary system around 5,000,000,000 years ago. The creation of the elements can be considered as the second phase of evolution. In order to produce the heavier elements another mechanism is required. This is the function of a Supernova. A Supernova is produced when a star twenty or more times as massive as our Sun has expended all its nuclear fuel through nuclear fusion reactions. The force of gravity forces the electrons and protons in its inner regions into one another forming a neutron core. As the core forms, it undergoes radical shrinking. The outer layers of the star then have no support and the lower layers fall rapidly towards the neutron core. When they reach this they squeeze it further from all sides in a massive implosion. The neutron core rebounds violently sending a shock wave back through the star. This all happens in less than half a second. The upper masses of the star begin to slow the shock wave down, but at this point a flood of neutrinos produced by the squeezing of the neutron core is ejected into the shock wave, giving it a further boost which results in it blowing the outer layers of the star apart. In this way the elements that have been produced in the star are scattered throughout space. Calculations have now shown that the shock wave alone is not able to blow the Supernova apart. It is also now known that what is called the Weak Interactive Force that determines how strongly neutrinos interact with protons and neutrons has to be just what it is in order for the shock wave to be boosted sufficiently. This is known as an anthropic coincidence. Others include the fact that the Weak Nuclear Force is exactly the strength required to give the ratio of Hydrogen to Helium in the later stage of the Big Bang. If the proportions had been lower, the majority of stars would have burnt out by now and there would have been insufficient time for us as observers to evolve to our present level of consciousness. Such anthropic principles can be taken to be evidence of the Will of His Endlessness delegated to the Absolute and determining the evolution of the Cosmos. A "Habit of Allah"!

"each newly arisen 'Second-order Sun' with all its consequent definite results they called 'Deuterocosmos'."[8]

The Will of His Endlessness is also seen in the structure of the elements which inevitably determines their combining power to form the various possible molecules. As the elements are formed in the star in conformity with the Law of Chance, they also conform to the Law of Seven, the Heptaparaparshinokh. When we arrange the elements into what is called the Periodic Table (Page 19), the basic divisions of the Table are seen to centre on the six inert gas core structures, each of which is responsible for a series of elements. These six series or periods together with Hydrogen make up the seven centres of gravity of the Heptaparaparshinokh. Thus Hydrogen is the first DO of this Law of Seven. Then we have Helium series as Si, the Neon series as La, the Argon series as Sol, the Krypton series as Fa. At this stage in the Descending Heptaparaparshinokh we come to the Mi-Fa discontinuity, the Harnel-Aoot. This is bridged by the Rare Earth series of

---

[8] Ibid. Page 760.

elements, from Lanthanum to Leutecium, which form part of the Xenon series, represented by Mi. Finally there is the Radon series as Re, with the Table rounded off by a lower Do which is the beginning of another Heptaparaparshinokh of which we know nothing.

There are many interesting further relationships. To begin with we see Hydrogen and Helium in a class of their own in which no Heptaparaparshinokh structure is apparent within them. Hydrogen and helium were the first elements formed after the Big Bang and were formed in the expanding cloud of radiant energy. The other elements were formed in the stars as a result of thermo nuclear reactions. The Helium nucleus, however, forms the core for all subsequent atoms and so we can consider it as the upper Do of a series of sub Heptaparaparshinokhs, starting the second period in the table of the elements. So it could be said that the relationship of Hydrogen and Helium to the other elements reflects the similar relationship in the Cosmos where we have the beginning of the Descending Cosmic Heptaparaparshinokh represented by a Do which corresponds to the Protocosmos, the First order Sun, World 1, Absolute 1, Spirit, in effect Emanation of the Qabala; this is followed by an interval filled by the Will of the Absolute 1, and leading to Si, corresponding to the Hagiocosmos, world 3, All Worlds, Soul, or perhaps better, Essence, in effect Creation of the Qabala. Then there is the gap between the first two centres of gravity and the rest. The rest is the Megalocosmos, Our World, Body. The Megalocosmos starts with La, the Macrocosmos, World 6, All Suns, the Milky Way, in effect Formation of the Qabala. Then we have a Mechano-coinciding-Mdnel-In which has to be overcome before we come to Sol, Second-order-Suns, Deuterocosmos. World 12, Our Sun, when we reach the level of manifestation of the Qabala. Then the Descending Cosmic Heptaparaparshinokh proceeds to Fa, Mesocosmos, World 24, All Planets. This brings us to the Harnel-Aoot between Fa and Mi. At Mi we have the Third-order-Suns, the Planets, Tritocosmos, World 48, the Earth as a Living Being, and finally Re, Tessarocosmos, world 96, the Moon.

So we see the overall arrangement of the elements taking the form of a Major Heptaparaparshinokh consisting of Hydrogen and the six inert elements, each of which starts a new period or Sub or Inner Heptaparaparshinokh. The six inert elements are inert because they have a complete outer compliment of electrons. Thus while Helium has 2, the others have in effect 8. All the other elements have less than 8 outer electrons and so can combine with any other elements to complete an outer stable octet, by giving or sharing. Thus the combining power of the elements depends upon their imperfections. The perfect need nothing, but we are able to relate through our imperfections, interacting with one another as the elements do in order to together produce perfection. Thus we see that the intelligence and Will of the Absolute is reflected down the Ray of Creation, occurring in the inner structure of the elements in order to determine their combining power, and so the possibility of the evolution of molecules which in turn enable the evolution of organic life. So we see how the elements are evolved in conformity with the Will of the Absolute so as to be suitable for the next stage of evolution required for the purpose of His Endlessness. Much of the above is summarized in the Table of Relationships (see my Appendix).

The Evolution of Evolution

The Third Divine Emanation
The Fourth Phase of Evolution
The Third Order Suns

The fourth phase of evolution is the creation of organic life from the elements and molecules. As we have said the Helium nucleus forms the core for all the elements other than Hydrogen. Considering it as the upper Do of the Heptaparaparshinokh of the second period, this period can be seen as a Descending Heptaparaparshinokh with Lithium as Si, and Beryllium as Fa. Then we come to the Harnel-Aoot between Fa and Mi where two quantum jumps are necessary instead of the single jumps between the other elements. So this is a place where a shock is required, a resonance in order to bridge the gap. In relation to this Nitrogen is found to exhibit two principal valences of 5 and 3. It can combine with elements or groups of elements that are five electrons short of eight, such as in nitric acid, HNO, or with a group having three electrons surplus, such as in ammonia, $NH03$. So it as it were offers a hand in either direction. The three elements Carbon, Hydrogen and Oxygen were used by the alchemists to represent the three forces in the triads of the Law of Three. Thus Carbon with its four bonds forming the basis of so many compounds, was taken as typifying active force. Oxygen, ready to combine with almost every other element but never the primary element itself, was considered as typifying the passive force. Nitrogen with its ability to look both ways, typifies the third or relating or enabling force.

The way in which with each period, because of the inert gas core structure that makes up its main structure, and the outer electrons in the process of being added as the period unfolds, is a situation which resembles the human as being made up of Essence that one is born with and which determines our essential character or possibilities, and our Personality which we have acquired and which therefore is not really our own, but which can be either used by us appropriately, or which can use us and so lead to the demise of Essence. It is the outer electrons that determine the combining power, and therefore the more obvious behaviour of the elements.

This fourth phase of evolution which starts with the combining of the atoms of the elements to form molecules comes under the Law of Destiny. Once the conditions are suitable, the appropriate elements combine with one another. This situation is also calculable and so predictable. As the evolution of molecules proceeds, they become ever more complex and we see ring structures and long chain structures evolving and eventually self replicating molecules. These are in effect the Prions which we are now beginning to hear about and which can have major destructive effects as evidenced by Bovine Spongiform Encephalitis and other disorders. Such destructive disorders are the result of the invasion of a living cell by a non-living self-replicating molecule.

This brings us to the origin of life itself. Appropriate long chain molecules floating on water, because of electrostatic forces originating from the force fields present in all molecules, will tend to arrange themselves in the form of rafts. If one end of these molecules happens to be water compatible, they will form rafts of upended molecules. Agitation of the supporting water, will cause portions of the rafts to form hollow spheres filled with water. These are in effect proto-cells, but not yet living cells.

It is at this stage that a further major evolutionary step occurs. If extra energy is available, such as by a warming of the medium in which the proto-cells are suspended, in order to accommodate the extra energy, what is called in quantum mechanical terms a Bose-Einstein condensation occurs. The long chain molecules forming the proto-cell wall, instead of all vibrating at the same frequency but independently, suddenly come into resonance and all vibrate together as a unity. The entity then becomes a living cell and emits what are called bio-photons, emits light.[9] This in my terminology is the Third Divine Emanation. So as a result of the Sun of the Solar System involved supplying extra energy to its Planetary level, living cells evolve from non-living cells. The living cells are able to ingest material from their surroundings, to grow and divide. Such living tissue, besides emitting light which is the basis of the auras which some say they can see, is also able to go against the second law of thermodynamics and make energy go uphill from lower to higher energy states.

As organic life began to be established on Earth, the planet began to undergo its most important phase of its evolution, a change from being a planet to the Earth as a Living Being. In this way it began to become what it was intended to be, a Third Order Sun.

" 'Third-order-Suns, ' i.e., those we now call 'planets' , they called 'Tritocosmos'. "[10]

"As regards the second-being-body, namely the body-Kesdjan, this body, being formed of radiations of other concentrations of Tritocosmoses and of the Sun itself of the given solar system."[11]

A whole range of such living cellular structures began to form at this phase of evolution, each particular form maintaining that form and producing enormous rafts of living cells, known as the blue-green algae. This was the first phase of living organisms on Earth. They were known as Prokaryotic Unicells, the Monera, because they do not have any nucleus. This came much later as the beginning of an information storage system for organic life.

This earliest form of organic life on Earth began some 3,000,000,000 years ago and persisted alone for some 2,000,000,000 years. The main effect of its presence was to modify the Earth's atmosphere so as to make it even more suitable for a proliferation of the present diverse forms of organic life. In particular most of the carbon dioxide was replaced by oxygen.

Then some 1,000,000,000 years ago, as some of these proto-cells were still forming on water surfaces, there were sufficient self replicating molecules present so that under the Law of Chance, significant numbers of them became encapsulated in particular proto-cells, so that the resulting

---

[9] H. Frohlich. *Long-Range Coherence & Energy Storage in Biological Systems*. International Journal of Quantum Chemistry. Vol. 2. Pp. 641-9.
[10] G. Gurdjieff. *All and Everything*. Routledge & Kegan Paul. 1962. Page 760.
[11] Ibid. Page 768.

living cell formed from them became a new type of living organism, a living cell with a nucleus. This was the stage of evolution of the Eukaryotic unicells or Protista. So this was the arrival of the information storage and control system represented by the present day spiral helix of DNA. It was also the beginnings of the operation of the Law of Will, a force so far removed from the original Will of the Absolute, as to appear to be independent of it. Such independence, however, is not real, the will of organic life being simply a faint reflection of the Will of the Absolute since it is virtually at the lowest level of the Ray of Creation and so subject to many subsidiary laws, extra laws and restrictions having been acquired as each level is reached. This is why at the level of the human, we are so restricted by a multitude of laws that in effect as Gurdjieff said, "As we are we have no free will and cannot do".

The Purpose of Organic Life

The true situation may be more apparent if we consider the language we use. We today uncritically adopt the concepts of the new generation of geneticists who maintain that the various organisms based on nucleated cells are gene survival and replication machines. This definition is applied to ourselves. If we, however, turn to Aristotle, we realize that the system of ethics which he evolved, he called by a Greek word "organon".[12] This means a tool. He stressed in effect that his system of ethics was a tool to be used and not an end in itself. It is significant that we use this same word root for organic life. This tells us that organic life far from being a gene survival and replication machine, is a tool for use for a higher purpose. This concept brings us directly to the Doctrine of Uses of Emanuel Swedenborg. Simply put this maintains that there is the One, the Absolute, and it gives rise to and sustains a whole series of levels, a stepping down of a whole series of levels or more limited orders of existence. So in this way the One is manifest on all possible levels, revealing its nature through all possible limitations. Thus all levels of existence are symbolic representations of the Absolute. This is why we begin to see recurring patterns of relationships.[13] As far as evolution is concerned, particularly while we have the operation of the Law of Chance and the Law of Destiny, together with the general background laws of the manifest, evolution proceeds in a pattern already established at higher levels, the lower level being a tool for the higher level in order to permit the evolution of the next lower level.

The Fifth Phase of Evolution
Genetics

The fifth phase of evolution is the formation of the whole variety of forms of vegetable and animal organisms. This is the result of the manifestation of a whole range of possible structures having specific uses and the interaction of the resulting organism with their environment. So this phase of evolution is a combination of compliance with the Law of Destiny and the bringing into manifestation of possibilities already existing out of time in the Aeon. The design of the eye already exists as a possibility in accordance with law, and at a suitable stage is made manifest. It is

---

[12] Aristotle. *Ethics*. Penguin Classics. 1963.
[13] J. H. Reyner. *The Universe of Relationships*. Vincent Stuart. 1960.

intended as a tool for a specific use, to further the survival of the organism involved. This in effect is the World of Ideas which is independent of Time and Space, and awaits the appropriate conditions in the world of Form which leads to the manifestation of the Idea, the Design, in passing time and three dimensional space. So here we have two causes at work, causes linked with the Law of Destiny, and causes linked to a higher influence from the Aeon. In the same way the previous three phases of evolution show the influence of a similar pattern, which can be called the "Signature of All Things" or the "Intelligence of the Absolute".

For this phase of evolution to be possible a language is required, a language that will store information and instructions so as to bridge generations. In this way chance changes, if of advantage, can be transmitted to future generations. The same situation exists with the latest development of the human into a Three Brain Being, the last brain to develop, the intellectual brain or mind, having language and so able to store the experience of any lifetime and transfer it to other individuals and future generations. The next generation can then build on the progress already made by those who have gone before.

But do not let us make the mistake of thinking that the genetic material drives evolution. It is the external circumstances which determine which evolutionary changes produced by chance which survive and so succeed, and which do not succeed. Gurdjieff took the view that we are machines driven by external events. In the same way evolution, particularly the fifth phase, is the result of changes occurring in the genes by chance, these changes being either confirmed or aborted by external circumstances. Thus the gene survival machine is not driven by the genes themselves, but by external events. And so while our form, structure and behaviour are determined by the genes, their continuance and survival from one generation to another is determined by external events. This is the survival of the fittest.

And how does this genetic system, this information storage system work in the newly acquired nucleus? As most of us know it is based on the self replicating DNA molecule which has the form of a double helix and is for convenience packaged into chromosomes, 46 in the case of us humans.

How does it change? How are new forms and behaviour patterns introduced? Such changes are the result of changes in the genetic material known as mutations. By far the largest number are simply the result of errors in copying. Other causes of mutations are the effect of radiation and of certain chemicals. Ageing is due to the accumulation of mistakes in copying over our individual life span.

A little information is lost every time a cell divides. Hence the greater likelihood of defects in children born to older parents.

Another important source of evolutionary change is sex. While every human body cell contains 46 chromosomes, in the maturation of the sex cells a reduction division occurs, so that each ovum or sperm contains a relatively random selection of half the genes present in each parent. These recombine on fertilization so that a new combination of genes arise all the time. Each generation produces successful individuals who have been dealt a favourable hand of mutations, while others inherit a less advantageous mixture and fail to pass them on.

In every generation thousands of new mutations appear. Some are harmful, some are not. Sex is a convenient way of bringing together the best and purging the worst.

The difference between women and men is that women have two of what are called the X chromosome, while men have one X and one Y chromosome. The Y chromosome is dominant and so femaleness needs two X chromosomes, one from each parent. Many serious inherited diseases are carried on the X chromosome. In girls an abnormal X is usually masked by a normal X and so the defect does not show. In boys, if the X is defective, it shows. For this reason sex-linked abnormalities are much more common in boys.

Our understanding of genetics has advanced so much in the past few years that the majority of people are now hopelessly out of touch with the real situation, a situation in which we are beginning to realize how little we do know for certain. What we are beginning to realize is that our genes are messages from the past. So we begin to realize that we are controlled, at least in part, by messages from our ancestors, as well as by external events. Our present behaviour is largely determined by forms proved successful by our ancestors. So as the Work says, as we are we have virtually no free will and cannot do of ourselves. But the Work also indicates a means of escaping from this situation. This entails a special form of evolution, the seventh stage, dealt with later.

But what is the scale of the genetic code and what can we learn from it as we begin to grasp the situation? Interpretation of the fossil data is not positive and so only gives us hints about the past. In contrast, everyone of our genes must have an ancestor and so we can use them to piece together a picture of human history. Modern genetics can take us back to the beginning of humanity 100,000 years ago and even to the origin of life based on nucleate cells, 1,000,000,000 years ago. A very good up to date review of what we know about genetics was given by Steve Jones as the 1991 Reith Lectures[14] and is the source of much of what follows.

Genetics is a language, a set of instructions passed from generation to generation. Its vocabulary is the genes themselves, a grammar, the way in which the information is arranged and a literature - the thousands of instructions needed to make a human being. The language is based on the DNA molecule. It has a simple alphabet, not 26 letters, but only four. These are arranged as three letter words. The DNA in each cell of our body, however, has some 3,000,000,000 letters. It is interesting that this is the same as the age of life itself in years. The DNA in each of us is different unless we are identical twins. On average the DNA in any two people differ in about one DNA letter per 1,000. So there are around 3,000,000 places which differ in the code.

In addition to the DNA comprising the genes, there is also mitochondrial DNA. Male sperm contains little of this form and so it is passed through the female line and thus contains the history of the world's women. The African Pigmies give us an example of how we can use genetics to

---

[14] Dr. Steve Jones. The 1991 Reith Lectures. *The Language of the Genes.*

establish ancient history. In the African Pigmies, mitochondrial types are rarely found more than around 20 km apart. The genes carried by both sexes cover a much wider range. Communities 500 km apart are not very different in genes which pass through males as well as females. This may be a message from the distant past about the role of men and women in society. Men have ranged widely through hunting and warfare, while women tended to stay at home.

The fossil evidence indicates that our ancestors appeared in Africa some 100,000 years ago. There is now evidence that there may have been even earlier separate beginnings both in the Gobi and Australasia. African chimps are also close to us. We share 98% of our genetic material with chimps. Only as recently as 1906, an African Pigmy - Ota Benga - was exhibited in the same cage as a chimpanzee at the Bronx Zoo. It caused an outcry simply because it promoted the idea that apes and humans are related. We also have a lot in common with mice in whom scores of human genetic diseases are found. "The best laid plans of Mice and Men can gang awry".

People from the far North have shorter arms and legs and more compact bodies; an adaptation to the cold. So as we migrated from Africa this change in shape began to appear. Neanderthals living in an even colder climate were even better adapted. Fewer than 10 genes are responsible for the difference between the blackest and whitest human skin, so ideas about major differences between so called "races" are all nonsense. This applies to the idea that the various animals and races form a kind of ladder of evolutionary development with the different kinds of humanity being at different stages. This is just not true. Custom and culture is of greater impact in relation to behaviour. Down's syndrome is known to be due to a chromosome error. It has become known in the West as Mongolism. In the East, certainly in Japan, it is known as Englishism.

The dark skin of people living near the equator is not to protect them from the heat of the Sun. It is to prevent the destruction of vitamins in the blood by sunlight, particularly the destruction of folic acid needed for growth and pregnancy. As migration proceeds further North with less sunlight, there is a problem with the production of vitamin D since black skin needs much more exposure to ultra violet light than white skin. Thus natural selection favoured those with genes for relatively light skins as humanity began its long walk North and South from the tropics.

In the world today there are around 750,000,000 fertilizations a year. There are also around 600,000,000 natural abortions and 600,000,000 induced abortions, leaving 90,000,000 actual births. Each of these is a source of mutations among the 3,000,000,000 DNA bases. Much of the DNA as far as we know at present is unproductive, being the corpses of abandoned genes. About a third of the 3,000,000,000 consists of tens of thousands of repeats of the same short message, often just C + A repeated thousands of times. There are about 50,000 groups of DNA bases which are active, many in groups making related products. In the brain more than half are producing something - what we do not usually know. In other tissues far fewer are active.

The migration of peoples is an important factor in genetics, serving as a special selection mechanism. It is difficult to appreciate how small but significant such early migrations were.

The Evolution of Evolution

By 10,000 years ago humans had filled the world, but there were in total only about the same number of people as in London today. Based on gene distribution it would now seem that there was not a mass migration from Africa around 100,000 years ago. There was a bottleneck to this migration as to all other major migrations. It would seem that the number of those who did leave Africa and spread out over other parts of the world giving rise eventually to the majority of its population was only around 100 people or perhaps less. In the case of the migration across the Bering Straits into Alaska and on into America, this was only some ten individuals if that. In other words it was a small band of a size that seems to be the size that humans can work in together as a group. So the small number of founders, and the brief period since they arrived has ensured that all founder Americans from Alaska to Cape Horn are more alike than peoples separated by only a few miles in other parts of the world. America is truly a young country.

Patterns of disease depend upon the numbers of people available. The longer a disease has a hold on to somebody, and the more efficiently it is transmitted, the smaller the population needed to allow it to persist. Measles does not last long and is not particularly infectious. It needs a community of at least half a million to keep it going. We have lived in groups as large as this for only about 2,000 years, so measles must be a fairly new disease. 10,000 years ago humans lived in small bands and infectious diseases may scarcely have existed. People starved, froze, or were eaten by other animals, died in accidents and were plagued by lice, tape worms and other parasites. When settled agriculture arrived and populations shot up new diseases appeared, additional to the defects produced by incorrect copying of DNA. But in mitigation, mutations often proved to be a means of defence against infectious diseases and this is now an important factor in evolution.

The lesson from all this is that the information storage and application technique evolved in organic life, in particular humans is most complex so that our understanding of it is at present very limited. There is much, however, that we can learn from it. In particular we need to realize that it is not the genes which drive evolution and society, but rather that the genes are driven by social and economic changes. The gene survival machine, as Gurdjieff said, is driven by external events.

And how do the genes actually work and what is the pattern involved? The DNA is considered so important that it is never allowed to leave the nucleus of the cell. Instead it makes a copy, RNA. This contains the same four coding bases but has a slightly different backbone and is a single strand helix. So in the nucleus we have the beginning of a new Heptaparaparshinokh, a Do - DNA - followed by Si - RNA. Then outside the nucleus of the cell itself, we have Messenger RNA represented by La. This has to bridge the Mechano-coinciding-Mdnel-In, reaching Sol as another variant, Transfer RNA, which in turn co-operates with Ribosomal RNA at Fa. The Harnel-Aoot is then reached at which resonance is needed in order to attract the required molecular species to the Ribosomal RNA scaffolding and the Transfer RNA template. The result is the production of the required proteins and enzymes at Mi. These are the material of construction of new cells which differentiate into organs at Re. At this point the Intentionally-actualized-Mdnel-In is reached, after which a new Do is sounded and a new body is the result. So we see again in our Table of Relationships the now familiar pattern of the two higher and the five lower.

All & Everything Conference 1998

The Sixth Phase of Evolution
Technical Evolution

It is during the sixth phase of evolution that higher level functions begin to emerge with a resulting degree of awareness. It includes the development of a three brain information processing and control mechanism. The emphasis by Gurdjieff on the concept of the three brained being is extremely interesting. Paul D. MacLean has much of interest to say in the introduction to his mammoth book, The Triune Brain in Evolution.[15] He reminds us of the concepts promulgated by Kant,[16] that time and space do not exist per se, but are derivatives of the subjective brain, being purely information that is of itself neither matter nor energy. He also develops the concepts of the three brained being, the human equipped with the "Triune Brain".

And how does the basic structure of the Three Brain Being develop as a result of the interaction of genetics and the environment? The First Brain to evolve was the Moving brain and this was characteristic of the age of reptiles. It is a fully automatic nervous system triggered by external events in order to ensure the physical survival of the animal. It is represented in humans by the spinal cord and base of the head brain. It was originally based on a molecular system of information transfer and this still operates at the nerve-muscle synapses. As the animals became larger, however, the pathways became too long for rapid responses based only on a molecular system and so an electrical component developed.

The next phase of development was of the Paleomammalian Brain formation, the Second Brain, characteristic of mammals who developed maternal care and nursing of the young, audio-vocal communication for maintaining maternal offspring contact, and play as a means of learning. This stage occurred with the dominance of the dinosaurs. In humans this corresponds with the limbic system and the hormonal system of the ductless glands. Since it relies primarily on molecular messengers, the electrical component is available for other uses. It is suggested that this enables a higher level system to operate which gives the beginnings of awareness. Thus the organism begins to become aware of the operation of the internal control and regulation systems operating as well as their responses to external events, both threatening and desirable. This awareness it comes to recognize as "feeling afraid", "feeling hungry" and so on. So this is the stage of evolution to the Two Brain Being. The First Brain would seem to have been established around 450,000,000 years ago with the Second Brain arriving around 250,000,000 years ago. It was not until some 100,000 years ago that the Third Brain became established, although its beginnings may have been some 40,000,000 years ago.

One of the important distinctions between the Paleomammalian, Second Brain, and the Neomamnlian, Third Brain, is that the former involves direct awareness without language or symbols intervening. A special features of the Third Brain which enables it to more efficiently communicate with others and also to bridge generations, is the use of symbols and language. This

---

[15] D. MacLean. *The Triune Brain in Evolution: Role in Paleocerebral Functions*. Plenum Press. 1990.
[16] E. Kant. *Transcendental Aesthetic*. 1899.

brings with it a disadvantage, however, in as much as instead of knowing, one only knows about. Perhaps an important aspect which we need to grasp is that the Instinctive Mind serves as the control and regulation mechanism for the physical body, and in the same way the Intellectual Mind, the relatively new Third Brain, should serve as a tool for the use of the Feeling Mind, as does the First Brain and the Instinctive Mind.

Instead of this proper use of the tools, the Third Brain, the new Intellectual Mind, tends to be used of itself with little regard to the other Minds. Hence we have the intellectually dominated Western civilization of today with the emphasis on quantity and the neglect of quality and the feelings of ordinary people.

It is the application of the Third Brain that has led to what I call Technical Evolution by means of which we have organized the further evolution of plants and domesticated animals for our own use. While the production of specialized plants, more disease resistant, maturing earlier and able to be grown further and further North and South of the Equator, has been of advantage to us humans and the domesticated animals, the forced evolution of such domesticated animals would seem to me to be an affront and encouragement for ordinary people to go against the chain of feeding laid out in the "Table of Everything Living".[17]

The Fourth Divine Emanation
The Seventh Phase of Evolution
The Third Order Inner Sun

Based on the Doctrine of Uses the three brains should be considered as three tools for the use of something higher. Instead, generally they act from themselves independently and individuals already well developed in one particular brain tend to be used by it ignoring the other two, and so the most developed function tends to become ever more dominant.

This is the stage of the new individual who while born with the possibility of further development, of further evolution, often never realizes what is possible for it and so stays incomplete. Thus it is said that the human is born incomplete but with the possibilities of completion. It is this possibility of completion which is the seventh phase of evolution and which has to be undertaken by the individual in life. This personal evolution is the province of the Work. The first stage is to increase awareness by practicing self observation as often as one can remember. This strengthens what is called "Observing I". This "Observing I" gradually begins to be aware of the functioning of the three brains or aspect of mind, Moving, Feeling and Intellect and begins to use them when appropriate instead of them operating automatically and outside the conscious awareness of the individual. It is the beginnings of this individual psychological evolution which marks the start of "The Way of Return", of the end of the Descending Cosmic Heptaparaparshinokh and the start of the Ascending Being Heptaparaparshinokh. A new Do is sounded as the human begins his or her completion and awakening.

---

[17] . D. Ouspensky. *In Search of the Miraculous*. Routledge & Kegan Paul. 1964. P. 322-323.

All & Everything Conference 1998

An early stage of this individual evolution is the conscious use of the appropriate brain even though they may only be used separately. Later they begin to be used additively and later still interactively. Once interactive conscious functioning occurs this gives rise to a higher level function which is of a holistic character. The exact demarcation of the additive and interactive use of the three brains is a point on which I need further clarification. In my view at present, however, I would suggest that it is at the interactive stage that the Fourth Divine Emanation occurs. This is characterized by the coming of a special kind of light or illumination, this light appearing to be both within and without, because one's individual consciousness has transcended the bounds of the individual and so there is no longer a distinction between the within and the without. It is at this stage that the use of words to describe the situation breaks down. In the Gurdjieff terminology this phase is known as Man No. 4, Balanced Man. It is a state which is not necessarily permanent, but may be reached in special moments. Much later it may become permanent. A similar state may be reached in suitable meditations and this is known as photism, since a light comes which is said to be an indication that the meditation is proceeding correctly. It is in my opinion also the subject of Maurice Bucke's Cosmic Consciousness.[18]

This evolution-of the individual in life is not under the Law of Chance or the Law of Destiny, but under the Law of Will. As Gurdjieff said, "As we are we have no free will and cannot do". This is meant to shock and is not strictly true or all effort would be a waste of time. As we are we can only do little things. But by making the effort to do what we can, to practice self observation, gradually our will is strengthened and once by our own effort of will we for the first time reach our goal of being at this higher level of brain function, the experience of it will never leave us and our will is permanently strengthened so that at least at special moments we are given help from a higher level and in those moments have will and can do. This help, this higher energy, in my view comes from Higher Emotional and Higher Intellectual Mind already fully functioning but out of space and passing time. Perhaps this area is what is sometimes called the Collective Unconscious. When one's consciousness moves to this level, there is no time, the timeless moment.

The Fifth Divine Emanation
The Eighth Phase of Evolution
The Second Order Inner Sun

But there is a further phase of evolution which a small number of humans would appear to have made. This entails a permanent change of consciousness so that both the lower balanced functioning of the Three Brain Being which has been achieved by Balanced Man is enhanced by the consciousness of Higher Emotional and Higher Intellectual Mind. This is the arrival of the Fully Realized human. Since there is a union of the lower and the higher, this stage is known as the God-Man. It is dealt with in the Epic of Gilgamesh,[19] Jacob wrestling with the Angel,[20] and other sources. In the Christian teachings it is known as the Transfiguration. While when the

---

[18] Richard Maurice Bucke. *Cosmic Consciousness*. E. P. Dutton. 1969.
[19] *The Epic of Gilgamesh*. Penguin Books. 1972.
[20] Genesis. Chapter 33. Verses 24 to 30.

previous stage is reached the light comes which appears to be both within and without, this light is not apparent to others. In this next phase of evolution the light also comes and is such that it is apparently visible to others. Hence the halos depicted in the images of the Christian Saints and mentioned in the Christian Gospels and other sources.

Such fully realized individuals, humans who have completed the second phase of their possible evolution in an individual life itself, would appear to have been the founders of the early civilizations, the teachers of us ordinary humans, the Messengers from Above, bringing essential knowledge to us which exists out of time, eternally, in the Aeon and so unaffected by the Merciless Heropass. It is at this stage that such individuals can say, "Not my Will, but Thy Will".

The Sixth Divine Emanation
The Ninth Phase of Evolution
The First Order Inner Sun

But there is a final phase of evolution, also under the Law of Will, and this is when the fully realized human, the Messenger from Above, returns from whence it came. This phase is referred to by Meister Eckhart who said, "Man's last and highest leave-taking is leaving God for God". Similarly Ramakrishna said, "At the break of day He disappears into the secret chamber of His House". The Sixth Divine Emanation which is present at this final phase of evolution cannot be seen by any of us at this level of manifestation, since it occurs as the fully realized individual re-enters the Aeon.

The Creation of Inner Space

It may have been noticed that the headings for the later sections have included reference to the Inner Suns. We have only referred to Six Divine Emanations so far. Some of us think there should be nine. It is perhaps of some significance that there is the Wall of Nine Dragons of the Imperial palace at Peking; the Orthodox liturgy is constructed on the basis of nine fixed points, between which occur the variable elements according to the seasons, days, celebration of feasts, veneration of saints; the ceremonies of the Elusis Mysteries lasted nine days; the Apollon of Musagete presided over nine Muses; in particular the cathedral of St. Basil the Well Blessed erected at the Kremlin in 1555-1560 by Ivan the Terrible, the redoubtable, in commemoration of his victories at Kazan, represents a complex of nine churches, the one beside the other, crowned by nine bulbous domes, symbolic of the fully developed pineal gland, the "Third Eye".

The three orders of Suns of the Cosmos, would seem to exist in what to us is external space. Once we reach the stage of beginning the return journey and experience, initially only in special moments, the Fourth Divine Emanation, we have in effect begun a psychological evolution which proceeds through the two higher order Suns. This in effect entails the creation of an inner space. This inner space is referred to by Jung in his Seventh Sermon of his Seven Sermons to the Dead:

"… Man is a gateway, through which from the outer world of gods, daemons, and souls ye pass into the inner world; out of the greater into the smaller world. Small and transitory is man. Already is he behind you, and once again ye find yourselves in endless space, in the smaller or innermost infinity. At immeasurable distance standeth one single Star in the zenith…"[21]

So perhaps here we have a clue to the total situation. The Descending Cosmic Heptaparaparshinokh is characterized by three levels, each presided over by a Sun, The First Order Sun, the Abode of His Endlessness, the Second Order Sun, including our Sun, the centre of our Solar System, and the Third order Sun, the Earth as a Living Being, of which we are a part. Similarly the Ascending Being Heptaparaparshinokh is characterized by three levels, each presided over by an Inner Sun, the Third Order Inner Sun, Man Awake, the Second Order Inner Sun, the God-Man, and the First Order Inner Sun, the human who has realized all that is possible for him or her and makes its final leave taking.

But then there may well be three other Suns which link in some way the outer and inner Suns we have some knowledge of. Is it that the pattern is sustained, with the Descending Cosmic Heptaparaparshinokh and the Ascending Being Heptaparaparshinokh together forming a double helix of Heptaparaparshinokhs similar to the DNA? The third set of Suns might then be the result of resonance between the other two sets, between the outer and inner Suns, each a Do of one of the ascending or descending sequences of Heptaparaparshinokhs.

Perhaps we should conclude with a few lines from the written some 1,500 years ago:

Perhaps we see here the operation of the modified Law of Three, modified from sequential to interactive operation. As far as I am aware, Gurdjieff did not tell us about the details of this change in the law. Maybe he hoped we would try and work it out for ourselves and others. After all no one can do the Work for us, we have to do it for ourselves. You cannot taste it for me. You cannot digest it for me. And all the preceding intellectual descriptions and explanations are but the use of words to try and make some sense, to enable us to say or think that we know about it all. We have to in some way, perhaps by opening ourselves to the immensity and wonder of it all, to switch off the third brain and, conscious in second brain, just to know.

"Reason will guide thee, but only to the door. While reasons digs for the Truth, thou hast already reached thy goal on the plane of love."

Perhaps we should try and interpret what is in the last chapter but one of the *Tales*, Chapter 47. At page 1176 we have Beelzebub ceremoniously being restored to his true level of being and in the description nine levels of being are noted. The first and second are not named; the third is Degindad; the fourth is the sacred Ternoonald; the fifth is the sacred Podkoolad; the sixth, the level now reached by Beelzebub, is the sacred Anklad. This level is the third in degree from the

---

[21] C. G. Jung. *VII Sermones ad Mortuos*. Stuart & Watkins. 1967.

The Evolution of Evolution

Absolute Reason of His Endlessness. So there are un-named seventh, eighth and ninth levels of being, the ninth being that of His Endlessness Himself.

Perhaps we should conclude with a few lines from the Rig Veda, written some 1,500 years ago:

"Who knows the secret? Who can unfold it?
Whence indeed this Manifold Whole arose?
The Divine Individuals were subsequent to its arising. Who then, can tell whence the great Creative sprang?
Whether beyond it there is a Will or whether there is none.
Only He who is the Consciousness of all that Exists
Only He knows - and even He may not know!"

© Copyright 1998 - H. J. Sharp - All Rights Reserved

Appendix - The Evolution of Evolution

Table of Phases of Evolution

1st Phase of Evolution.
The Big Bang. First Order Sun.

2nd Phase of Evolution.
Creation of Hydrogen and Helium.

3rd Phase of Evolution.
Switching on of the Second Order Suns. Creation of the Elements.

4th Phase of Evolution.
Creation of molecules and eventually Living Cells.

5th Phase of Evolution.
DNA and Variety of Form. The Earth as a Third Order Sun.

6th Phase of Evolution.
"Technical" Evolution.

7th Phase of Evolution.
Arrival of the Third Order Inner Sun.
Man No. 4. The Single One.

8th Phase of Evolution.
Arrival of the Second Order Inner Sun.
The God-Man.

9th Phase of Evolution.
Arrival of the First Order Inner Sun.
Leaving God for God.

Appendix - The Evolution of Evolution

The Table of Relationships

Protocosmos: Proto from the Greek meaning first.
"And, namely, they named the Most Most Holy prime-Source Sun Absolute itself - *Beelzebub's Tales*, page 760.

Hagiocosmos: Ayne - first born. Ayne-Aghio-Hagio-Holy.
"The Most Most Holy Theomertmalogos began to manifest itself in the quality of the third holy force of the sacred Triamazikamno" B.T. Page 757. The primordial cosmic energy becomes subject to the Law of Three and so becomes the sub-atomic entities on which the whole of the Megalocosmos is based.

Megalocosmos: The Great Cosmos.
"And all those cosmoses, which together compose our present World, began to be called the 'Megalocosmos'," B. T. page 760.

Deuterocosmos: Deutero from the Greek meaning second.
"Each newly arisen 'Second-,order-Sun' with all its consequent definite results they called 'Deuterocosmos'." B. T. page 760.

Mesocosmos: Meso from the Greek meaning middle.
See *In Search of the Miraculous*, P. D. Ouspensky, page 205.

Tritosmos: Tri from the Greek meaning third.
"'Third-order-Suns, i.e. those we now call 'planets', they called 'Tritocosmos'." A planet does not become a Third-order-Sun until it has become clothed with organic life, which is the source of its radiation, the Third Divine Emanation.

Tessarocosmos: Tessara from the Greek meaning fourth.
See Boris Mouravieff, *Gnosis*, Volume 1, page 110 & Table 42.

		Sub-atomic structure and the Periodic Table of the Elements																	Centres or Minds	Ductless Glands	In Jungian terms	Chacras	
		Orbitals :	1s	2s	2p	3s	3p	3d	4s	4p	4d	4f	5s	5p	5d	5f	6s	6p	The Androgyne				
Do	Hydrogen		1																Do Higher Intellectual	Do Pineal	Do Collective Unconscious	Do Crown	
Si Do	Helium		2																↑ Intensionally-actualized-Mdnel-In Si Higher Emotional	Si Pituitary	Si Animus/Anima	Si Head	
La Si	Neon Lithium		2 2	2 1	6														La Intellectual ↕ Barnel-Aoot ↕	La Thyroid	La Personal Unconscious	La Throat	
Sol La	Argon Beryllium		2 2	2 2	6	2	6												Sol Feeling	Sol Thymus	Sol Individuality	Sol Heart	
Fa Sol	Krypton Boron		2 2	2 2	6 1	2	6	10	2	6									Fa Moving	Fa Adrenals	Real "I" Fa Observing "I"	Fa Navel	
																			Mechano-coinciding-Mdnel-In				
Mi Fa	Xenon Carbon		2 2	2 2	5 2	2	6	10	2	6	10		2	6					Mi Instinctive	Mi Gonads	Small "I's" Mi Personality	Mi Genital	
Re Mi	Radon Nitrogen		2 2	2 2	6 3	2	6	10	2	6	10	14	2	6	10		2	6	Re Molecular	Re Living Cells	Re "I" of the Body	Re Root	
Do Re	Oxygen		2	2	4														Do Elements	Do Protocells	Do External	Do External	

The Table of Relationships

Appendix - The Evolution of Evolution

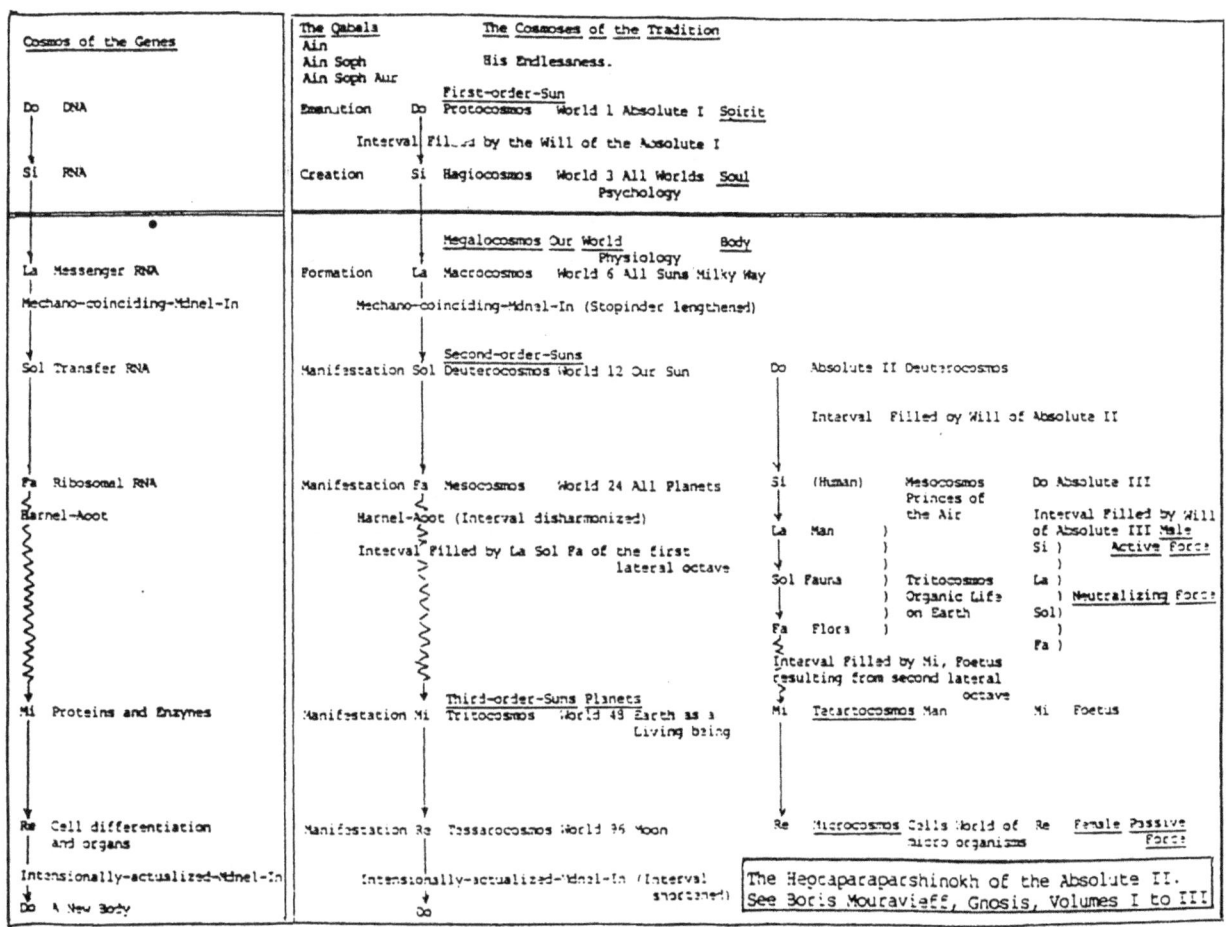

The Table of Relationships

All & Everything Conference 1998

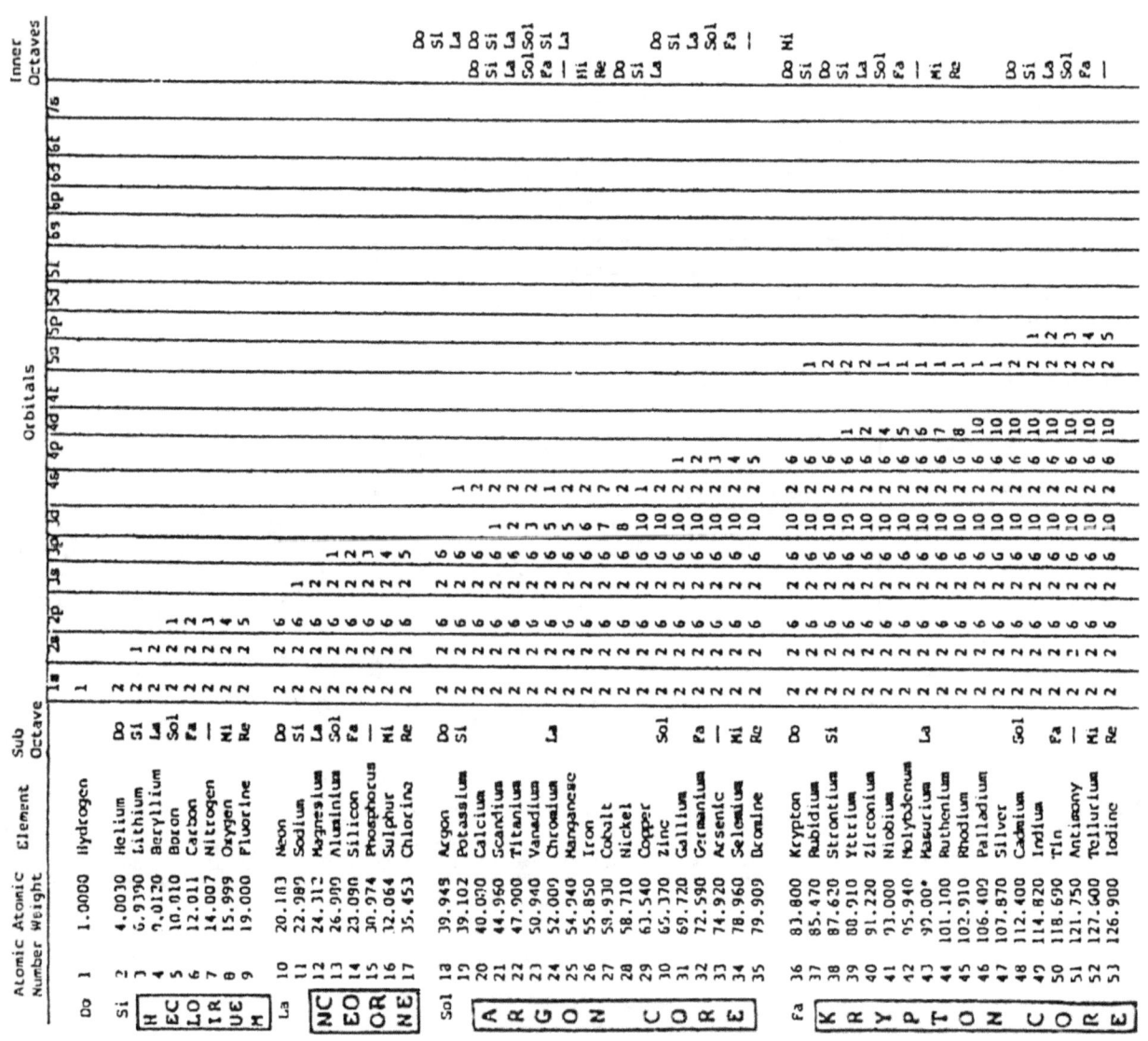

Subatomic Structure of the Octave

Appendix - The Evolution of Evolution

Subatomic Structure of the Octave

The Evolution of Evolution - Questions & Answers

Jim Gomez: How do you get these numbers, one thousand million years and so on?

Bert Sharp: They are approximations. There are various ways in which we can arrive at such approximations.

Jim Gomez: But it is staggering. One thousand million years, that is inconceivable.

Bert Sharp: Correct. And you see the message to me is that it took two thousand million years, of that order of time, for the beginning of organic life to prepare the Earth's atmosphere for multi-cellular organisms. If you have a single cell floating on water, the diffusion path for oxygen to its centre is very, very small, so it can exist in a very low oxygen atmosphere. But if you get a mass of cells, like you and me, even assisted by lungs, by a pump, there is still a need for a higher oxygen level for sufficient diffusion to get the oxygen into the deeper cells, and this needs a higher oxygen atmosphere, which has been produced, and which we, in the last 50 to 100 years, have begun to degrade. It is as simple as that.

Forrest McIlwain: First I have an observation. I want to thank Frank and Noel for the efforts they have been making. I am sure that all of the presenters are very much appreciative of what you have done. I have been on the other side and I know that it takes a lot of work. And to Dr. Sharp, I just want to say that I really appreciated your paper. There were a number of things that I heard. One of the things I heard was the observation of the interconnectedness of everything, and that is a very special subject for me and I very much wanted to say that it is just very special. I would like very much if you would speak a bit more to the relationship between emanation and radiation and how this is connected to the evolution of evolution.

Bert Sharp: Yes. The connectedness of everything. This is Jacob Boehme who talked of "The Signature of All Things". As your awareness increases and you look around you and you see this Signature everywhere. It is like that. Now the other part of your question, I did not quite follow. Radiation and Emanation.

Forrest McIlwain: Yes, related to the way Mr. Gurdjieff spoke, the difference between emanation and radiation, and its mention in your paper. At one point you speak about the different Divine Emanations.

Bert Sharp: Emanation from the Absolute and so on. I don't know. It is just that the word Emanation seems right. A giving out, to emanate, to give out, whereas radiation is more specific. A hot metal body radiates in the infra red region. A star radiates its energy as light. You are throwing me and making me think. Thank you.

The Evolution of Evolution - Questions & Answers

Ken Pledge: I think the difference is that in emanation the source remains in contact while in radiation it does not.

Sy Ginsburg: Some of us have observed, or believe we have verified that not all people, in fact most people, are not open to ideas of this kind. How do you relate that to what you said about genes, and that everything is carried forward by the genes.

Bert Sharp: Yes. Some people are more open to these sort of ideas than others. One has to be careful with this. Some people are content. Perhaps they are asleep, a little more asleep than we are, and so these questions don't arise. I have had quite a lot of people who have come to me and said "I never think about things like that". No point. They eat, they sleep, they go to work and that is it. They are not looking for meaning and purpose. But it is as if one comes to a certain stage at which one is looking for meaning and purpose, you begin to ask these questions which cannot really be answered in language, in words. Now how do you relate this back to the genes. Well the genetic material is not really interested in this. This is something I have been thinking about for some months. You can see how, probably most of us can accept -- OK, the genetic material can organize a body structure, enable people to be mobile, to walk, to eat, and to digest their food and all the rest of it. Can organize us so that one functions in that sort of way, and that one behaves in certain ways, the cerebral functions. Depending upon the genetic material one has certain behavioural patterns, and if they fit the external conditions, they will survive and those people will reproduce and thereby that genetic material survives and is passed on. But what happens when a person psychologically evolves in life. That has nothing to do with reproduction. It has nothing to do with being passed on by the genetic material. The possibility of such psychological evolution may be passed on, but not the evolution itself. This is why it is so vitally important that a sufficient number of people do undergo psychological evolution in life, because that is the only time in which it can occur. And it cannot be passed on, only through culture, whatever that is. Does this answer the question? I have not got the answer really, but those are my thoughts on it.

Sy Ginsburg: Partially. The idea, the non scientific idea of "Old Souls". When young people come in with a feeling if you like, for esoteric teaching, would that be in the genes?

Bert Sharp: I don't know, This is something I have been thinking about, and I have recently come across, as I mentioned the other day I think, Theodore Flournoy's work and others. You begin to start to have the temerity to ask the question - - It makes sense to you at certain stages of your psychological evolution, that there is Higher Mind. And that you have to align yourself so you can be used, the information comes to you. So where is Higher Mind? Is it in the genetic material? And you somehow by aligning your mentation equipment, your neurological equipment, do you then gain access to these secret files in the DNA? Or is there access to what I call the World of Ideas which is not in time and space? Is this Higher Mind? You see Flournoy (1) in the late 1800's did a lot of work with a particular medium, and he came to the conclusion that the majority of the material which she produced she had actually experienced, but forgotten. But he noted that some higher part of her mentation equipment used that material, those memories, re-arranged them into scenarios which were in effect parables, teaching scenarios, which she then channelled, as we would say today. These were messages, and as he wrote all this and published it, he did not actually say there is nothing beyond us, there are no messages from the dead, which was a very popular belief at that time. He said this is all within the person, but some Higher Entity within us, some higher neurological function can process it and send it back in order to be creative through that individual. That was what he actually said, but he was misread as saying all the medium business is a waste of time, all rubbish, the dead do not survive and so on. So his book was literally swept under the carpet for some 20 years, and everybody forgot it. It has recently been re-published in America with a quite interesting introduction. Nearly a 100 years later!

I don't know these answers, but there are areas where we can do real work to try to extend our knowledge and thereby to extend our Being by the processing of that knowledge. There is more in Heaven and Earth. What else can one say. But the important thing as I see it is, we must guard against wishful thinking. Psychologically I think there are three basic stages in the human development. The first stage is covered largely by Freudian psychology, sexuality, children growing up, eating, sleeping, feelings, etc., and eventually it leads to puberty, marriage and reproduction. The second phase is covered largely by Adler, compensating psychology, in which having got yourself organized as a married man or woman, the man in particular has aspirations and he is smitten by the will to power and to become the boss, to make money. But there are a lot of people having done all that, having raised a family, having made a lot of money, a few of them come to the third stage, what's it all about Alphie? And that is when Jung comes in and can be helpful in finding meaning and purpose, what is it all about. And this is an ongoing thing you see, and I think Keith Buzzell will probably agree with me on this. He again yesterday lauded MacLean for his work on the Triune Brain (2), which has led to other people publishing things like Evolutionary Psychiatry (3), published only last year. This shows how the possibility, or the necessity for our survival, needs to take all this into account and for us to go from the Agonic mode to the Hedonic mode. At the moment the whole of society, the whole of the culture of humanity is essentially based on the Agonic mode. The big gorilla. He is physically big so he can defend his group against all the other groups around and he is intelligent so he leads them in the right way to the right food sources, etc.,. In return for this he expects respect and praise and all the best young gorillaresses and the best food. Now that is the whole structure of humanity at the moment. It still is. But there are little pockets, occasional things that happen, in which we do make the next step which is the hedonic mode, in which there is mutual help and co-operation, giving up oneself to relate to others. But as soon as you do that, unless you do it with great intelligence and under the right circumstances, you immediately get thumped by the big gorilla. So it is going to be very difficult if not impossible for us to make this next major step, which is all to do with, perhaps, going from what is quite right at the early stages for humans, in which most of us have a feeling of individuality and feel to some degree that we are in control of our environment and people around us, to go from that to being humanity, an organism, not the ant hill. The ant hill and the beehive are perhaps changes like that that went wrong, went so far and then got stuck. Now one of the reasons why they got stuck was in relation to the fact that bees and ants don't have lungs. It comes back to the oxygen level in the atmosphere you see. They have diffusion channels. That is why in the insect world, which never developed lungs, they have always remained small in size, for that practical reason. As it is said, breath is life! But what this Work is all about, as I see it, is what I was trying to put into the introductory meditation. One has to transcend oneself and actually be part of humanity. Am I making any sense? But this is a very big thing and no individual can do this without help from above.

Adam Petts: I would just like to add a comment if it is relevant, if it is useful. It is something I have heard. This word human, humanity, I heard described as being a composite of manus from the Sanskrit, meaning mind, and hu, referring to a spirit, and that in fact in reference to the concept of a Higher Mind or a Higher Consciousness, that we can label as Mind, that the true human is the Spirit Mind or the Spirit Manus, or is that being or Consciousness that has achieved the possible evolution. So in giving ourselves the title humans, we are really three brained bipeds with the possibilities of reaching the level of true humanity.

Bert Sharp: Born in the image of God. And again you see, what comes to me again emphasizing the end. What to me seems wonderful is the way in which organic life took some two thousand million years, roughly, to start, to put the foundation in for an information storage and processing system, the DNA, which has taken over one thousand million years to reach its present level of information storage and processing. And relatively recently of course, we have the Third Brain, the Intellectual Mind, which as distinct from the First and Second Brain, has developed language as a means of communication of information storage and processing. But the trouble is, of course, that it is so new, so inexperienced, that we tend to end up with the language determining our actions, and every new impression that comes in is modified by all the previous impressions stored in words in us. That is something we have to watch. It comes back to learning to use language constructively, to use the First and Second brains, instead of them using us. And this is so simple. I don't know the origin of all these things, but to me it is so simple. It is in the Fairy Tales. It is Aladdin's Lamp. It is the Genii in the Bottle that was found on the sea shore. Now of course, the sea is the most powerful symbol of the unconscious, and thrown up from the sea, from the unconscious, is the bottle. And the poor fellow there, he takes the bottle, takes out the cork, and the Genii comes out and overpowers him. You have got to learn and to know how to make contact with the Genii in the bottle, to let it out to do your will, not for it to use you and to inveigle you into making stupid wishes. Something like that. And knowing when to put the Genii back into the bottle. This is all the basis of psychiatric practise, now helped by an armoury of neuroleptics to directly influence the physiology. You help the person to gain access in a reasonably controlled way to their unconscious mind, to what they have repressed. But it can only be tapped and allowed out of the bottle when the individual is sufficiently strong as an individual and-or suitably supported. This is working in a group, is it not? We support one another. But it is a very dangerous field.

Stefanos Elmazis: You said about the organism. The ancient Greek word for human is anthropos, which means "look up and beg for help". It is a very ancient word.

Bert Sharp: Can you give me that again. Are you saying that the very ancient Greek word for "human" means "Look up and beg for help"?

All & Everything Conference 1998

Stefanos Elmazis: Yes, exactly.

Bert Sharp: Most interesting. Thank you very much.

Details of the three publications referred to in the text are as follows:

1. Theodore Flournoy. *From India to the Planet Mars*. (Originally published 1899, first English translation 1901) Princeton University Press. 1994.

2. Paul D. Mclean. *The Triune Brain in Evolution: Role in Paleocerebral Functions*. Plenum Press. New York & London. 1990.

3. Anthony Stevens & John Price. *Evolutionary Psychiatry: A New Beginning*. Routledge. 1996.

Approaching the Neologisms of the First Series

Harry J. Bennett

Harry Bennett tells us simply that he is a carpenter living and working in Portland, Maine.

Harry Bennett was introduced by Nicolas Tereshchenko who opened the session for him by reading from *Meetings With Remarkable Men*, starting with the last paragraph on page 150, Chapter 7, Prince Lubovedsky:

"The second time our eyes were uncovered was when we were about to pass a caravan. Evidently not wishing the peculiar cowls over our eyes to attract attention or excite suspicion, our guides considered it advisable to remove them for this encounter. We did so just as we were going by a monument typical of Turkestan, standing right at the top of a mountain pass. In Turkestan there are many of these monuments, which are very cleverly placed; without them, we travellers would have no possibility of orienting ourselves in this chaotic, roadless region. They are usually erected on some elevated spot so that, if one knows the general plan of their placement, they can be seen a long way off, sometimes even from a score of miles. They are nothing more than single high blocks of stone or simply long poles driven into the ground.

Among the mountain folk there exists various beliefs concerning these monuments, such as the following: that at this spot some saint was either buried or was taken up alive to heaven, that he killed the 'seven-headed dragon' there, or that something else extraordinary happened to him at that place. Usually the saint in whose name the monument was erected is considered the protector of the entire surrounding countryside, and when a traveller has successfully overcome any difficulty natural to the region - that is, has escaped an attack by brigands or wild beasts, or has safely crossed a mountain or river, or surmounted any other danger - it is all attributed to the protection of this saint. And so any merchant, pilgrim or other traveller who has passed through these dangers brings to the monument some kind of offering in gratitude.

It became an established custom to bring as an offering something which, as is believed there, would mechanically remind the saint of the prayers of the person who brought the offering. Accordingly, they bring gifts such as a piece of cloth, the tail of an animal or something else of the kind, so that, with one end tied or fastened to the monument, the other end can flutter freely in the wind.

These things, moving in the wind, make the spot where the monument is placed visible to us travellers from a great distance. Whoever knows approximately the arrangement of these monuments can locate one of them from some elevated spot and make his way in its direction, and from it to the next, and so on. Without knowing the general pattern of their arrangement it is almost impossible to travel through these regions. There are no well defined roads or footpaths and, if some paths do form of themselves, then, owing to the sudden changes of weather and the ensuing storms, they quickly change or are totally effaced. So if these landmarks were not there, a traveller trying to find suitable paths would become so confused that even the most delicate compass would be of no help to him. It is possible to pass through these regions only by establishing the direction from monument to monument."

Approaching the Neologisms of the First Series

In speaking to everyone, I have come to see that the way I had formatted my paper and what I had planned to say, is much more difficult than I thought it would be because of the extraordinary differences between everyone who is here. People who have spent decades studying the First Series and people who have yet to even read it. And so between these two extremes there is this huge space within which to bore everyone. So I am going to try to move away somewhat from what I prepared. I would like to speak a little bit about three things. One, my subjective experience with the First Series of Mr. Gurdjieff's written legominisms. I would also like to speak a little bit about language in general, and then much less than I had originally intended about the neologisms that are in the First Series.

I have placed an enneagram behind me simply to give some of you an opportunity to place some of what I say on there as I'm speaking. These three themes are tied together for me and I can not separate them; the neologisms, language and my subjective experience. So I would like to start with my subjective experience at 3 and end at 3 again.

When I first read the First Series it was prior to any time that I had worked with groups or even met anyone older in work. It was, as I am sure it is for many people, completely inexplicable. Because of my type perhaps, my assumption was that the problem was in me and not in the book or in the writer. Subsequently, as I have come through different experiences in work with different group leaders I have been exposed to different approaches to the First Series and different attitudes and opinions about it. I would like to speak out some of those.

It has been said to me that young people coming to work should not be exposed to the First Series because it's too complex and too convoluted, at times intentionally misleading, and that younger people should be exposed first to literature such as *In Search of the Miraculous* or Nicoll's, *Commentaries*. I have worked in groups where it was understood that the reading of the First Series was an obligation for people who are in work. The recommendation was that it should be read literally, sequentially, as Gurdjieff put forward in his friendly advice and that when it was read in groups it should be read aloud with no discussion. I've had it said to me that Gurdjieff

Approaching the Neologisms of the First Series

buried the dog too deeply, and consequently made his thoughts inaccessible, and that everything else written in work is fragmentary.

Later in my life I came to an influence that was quite different from all of those and I will try and paraphrase that by saying that the *First Series* of Gurdjieff's writings is as significant a container of his teaching as any other of his Legominisms, and it deserves to be gone after with every resource that we have available to us to get to the gist of what it has to say about where we come from, why we stay where we are and where we need to be headed.

All of those influences, as a younger person in work I, by the nature of the circumstance must take on because , I am in relationship with older people and it is not mine to teach but to learn. But what I found for myself is that I would never have come to the place of taking this Legominism seriously had I not been put in an environment, come into an atmosphere continually, week after week, where notions as to its inaccessibility and impenetrability were considered to be false, and was enjoined to take it on and given food and indications for how it was possible to do that. That eventually sparked something in me over time, and I began to take it seriously and to take it as an individual effort to understand it. When that happened it blended with the effort of the group from which, for me, that effort or influence first came, and that intensifies yet again its possible accessibility. A question that comes out of that experience for me is that there may be types of people who are capable of coming across the *First Series* or can be told to take it on for themselves, and will have capacities to do that, but I was not that type of person. So the question that comes is to what degree do older people in work stifle possibilities for where it could be taken and how much sooner, how much sooner could something have been come to with it.

Studying the *First Series* led me to the question of language, and what I'll say about language is completely from my readings in the *First Series*, *Views from the Real World*, and *In Search of the Miraculous*. I am not a linguist of any kind, I simply took it as a theme to have the word 'language' in my mind as I went through these pieces of literature, which are for me the core literature of the work. It is a difficult thing to encompass in this period of time, but I would insist, particularly in this environment and given what I have been taking in as impressions, that the question of language in work is primary. If you take that question and go to the literature with that in mind you will see that it is primary. It is one of the first questions that must be dealt with.

When Ouspensky records his initial meetings with Gurdjieff in the first chapter of *In Search*, it is one of the immediate tasks that Gurdjieff puts on Ouspensky. "In order to speak with us you must learn a new language" and the purpose of this is that in the ordinary language in which people speak they cannot understand one another, period. Well, that's my period. This initial question is in the first two presentations in *Views from the Real World.* After you pass through *Glimpses of Truth*, the first two lectures in the series take up in some manner, or address the question of language. Language is addressed in the *First Series* at the beginning and at the end in the *Arousing of Thought*, and in *From the Author*. It also takes up a significant portion of the introduction to *Meetings With Remarkable Men*. From my reading, what Gurdjieff continually insists upon is that our words and our grammar and the way that we ordinarily use language is an insufficient means with which to transmit his teaching. So, if the aim of the *First Series* is to destroy mercilessly, with no compromises whatsoever, in the feelings and mentation of the reader the beliefs and views rooted by centuries in them about everything existing, then we have to look at how we use language and at the oceans of books and papers we are producing that are written in this language, and what Gurdjieff had to say about language, and ask whether we can understand any of that and if it can have any value in our personal and group work or work for the work.

If you follow the sequence of language through *In Search of the Miraculous* you will come eventually to chapter fourteen, which from my current perspective is the culmination of his presentation of language through *In Search*. It is the chapter in which he presents the enneagram, and it is the chapter in which he refers to the enneagram as the fundamental hieroglyph of a common universal language. So the conclusion that I come to, through taking language as a theme is that the language Gurdjieff is referring to is not a language of words, it is a language of laws and lawful relationships; of the laws of three and seven and their perfect synthesis in the enneagram.

There is a place in *In Search* where he is speaking to people and says that there is much that is incomprehensible to you because you do not take into account the meanings of some of the most simple words, such as 'serious.' What does it mean to be serious? What can be serious for one who is in prison but to escape? It is not that we have a serious attitude, it is that that which is the recipient of that attitude is objectively serious. A question that comes for me is are we serious about this Legominism of the *First Series*, which has been written, according to Gurdjieff's understanding, in a certain language that is not just the words. If we were serious what attitude would we have towards it? How would we approach that? Would we approach it in isolation? Would we sit in our prisons with our fellow cell mates and not want to know how they perceived it so that we might get the hell out of our prisons a little sooner, or try and get a sense of whether we are misunderstanding it? If you were standing outside of a prison and you were looking at prisoners who had a book entitled '*How You Got Into Prison, Why You Stay In Prison*, and *What You Need To Know To Get Out*' and it were written by a master escape artist, and you saw people sitting in that prison reading it for an hour once a week would you consider that serious?

It was my research of what I am referring to as the neologisms in the *First Series* that first brought me to a more serious study of language through the work literature. It is a difficult thing because something in me wants to understand these neologisms or special words which, if you have yet to read the *First Series*, are one of the aspects that give people, in the atmosphere that they put around this book, tremendous difficulty. So I wanted to take it as a task to put some time aside to research these words; the impulse for this coming from a number of places. As I went through that process and considered attempting to translate these words from the Armenian, Greek, and Russian, which is this small dictionary effort that is on the table over here, one of the questions that came up was; what difference would it make to me if I knew that a particular word or root of a word came from an Armenian, Greek or Russian word? More importantly, if I were to do this and it would in any way end up in circulation how could that be of benefit to anyone? We can remember the reading from yesterday (First Series, pg., 901-902) about the difference between 'mental-knowledge' and 'knowledge-of-being' and it does impress me as being quite absurd that one could translate, which would inevitably be an interpretation, any of these special words in the *First Series*, and put that on a piece of paper and have someone read that and believe that they understood anything. At the same time there is this difficult place because we take certain attitudes towards these special words and these attitudes are not rectified.

I start from the assumption that these words were created with intention, to convey meaning and to be of help. It does make the reading difficult but that difficulty is not the point. In reading it we come to the word and it's strange and we hop to the other side and keep going, or we sit in a group and listen to how others pronounce it because they have heard how other people pronounce it, and we put the pronunciation into our brain so that we can say it smoothly, so that when we come up to it we can go by it before we have gotten to it. But who or what is it in our environment that is insisting that these words have meaning? So I do not intend to say anything about what a particular word does or does not mean in a particular language, because what I came to conclude is that there is that which we can do for ourselves and that which we cannot. I am attempting, and I am not claiming that I have found the middle in that, but I am seeking a middle ground, where that which we cannot do as individuals could be one collectively by a competent group of people, provided that the aim was maintained not to interpret but to give the most objective accounting of all possibilities in each word. I arrived at that because being completely ignorant of languages, knowing nothing of Greek, Armenia or Russian or the other languages that I attempted to look through to find correspondences for these special words, I simply was not in a position to assume that I understood anything or could identify within a word anything that belonged to a particular language. So I was required through that ignorance to take each word out of its context, which is a danger, and break each word into every possible combination of letters, transliterate those letters based upon what could possibly be a quite wrong phonetic pronunciation, into the characters of the Greek, Armenian and Russian languages and look through the dictionaries for any correspondences I would find. In the majority of cases what came out of that was a wealth of possibilities many of which, when the word was placed back in context, seemed completely absurd and had no correspondence at all in me. But the question that I had to ask myself was, well, who is me to say that me understands what Gurdjieff was attempting to convey? I would say the same to any group of competent linguists or individuals with years of experience in work going through the same process. If, and this is of course my opinion, such a group of people were to offer their interpretation by selecting from all the possibilities their best guess and put that into the flow then that establishes a foundation in interpretation, and that is not necessary because given the data we can do it for ourselves. If we are sufficiently motivated to try to come to understand what the words mean; if we have the data (and I am speaking of course at the coarsest level of what they mean in terms of word correspondences) if we have the data and all the possibilities of a given word then it does not matter which ones are more or less appropriate. We are then given the task of deciding that for ourselves through our own understanding of the context. I think it would be very valuable, though I am open to hearing contrary opinions, for that work to be done, and what I have tried to attempt is a rough draft of how that might be gone about. So the point is not to interpret but to help one another, to give one another a substrate from which to explore for ourselves. It seems to me that that is attempting to find the middle ground by insisting that we do make the effort on our own, but not completely without some measure of assistance.

All & Everything Conference 1998

Most importantly the meanings of the words must be derived from their contexts. But there must be someone present insisting of us that we understand that and that the task is worth taking on. In a sense, having a linguistic correspondence can do nothing but verify for an individual what they have come to already through their own efforts in context. On the other hand what it could do is spur them to think from a different place as to what else might be possible.

More importantly than attempting to find what 'partkdolg' means in Russian or Armenian is the introductory reading. For me the *First Series* is reminiscent of this image, which is for me a story with multiple levels, applications and ways it could be understood. The *First Series* is a very complex, difficult terrain we must travel through to come to the place that Gurdjieff wished for us with all his being to come to through reading this. But for someone whose attitudes towards words and language and particularly our use of it was so denying of ordinary language, to produce this ocean of words and then take this and put it into the flow of ordinary life, which is where it was placed, such that it would be fair game for anyone with forty five or fifty dollars in their pocket; to do that without giving us some indication of how we might find our way through that terrain would be an incredibly bad joke to play on anyone. The possibility I would present is that we could see these neologisms or special words as markers on this landscape that we could use, if seriously studying it, to make connections and find our way from one point to another and have questions we would otherwise never have in studying, so that we can find our way to some inaccessible place inside of it.

I would like to give just a couple of examples of how that's done.

Probably about the only value I see, besides getting all the possibilities in a given word, in looking at the words out of context is that you begin to see that these words have forms and are symbols much more dense and rich than words and the language of words. When you see that there is Oskiano, Hanziano, Tirzikiano and Chirniano you can see that there is this recurring pattern at the end of the words. The same is true of Antkooano, Teskooano, Boolmarshano and Hertoonano. Those symbols are placed at the ends of these words and they are similar. So what of the notion that Gurdjieff would have cooked these up impromptu on the spot just to make things difficult? We have to look at those correspondences and see those similarities and ask what these words may have in common and if we have that question then we can begin to look at these different words in their different contexts which can be very, very different in different places in the *First Series* and perhaps we will tie together in our search for the meaning of an 'ano' or 'iano' something that we would never have connected together before. In that context what 'ano' or 'iano' may mean in another language is much, much less important. For myself in that process, in looking at this ending 'ano' on these words, that was eventually connected together for me with the word 'Mechano' and I invite anyone interested to pursue that and see if you find any corresponding meaning that ties these themes together.

The last thing I would like to speak about is more of a technical thing that has to do with the number of language versions of the *First Series* that are now available including the revised 1992 translation and the French which are the only ones I have, spent any time looking at. I am sure

Approaching the Neologisms of the First Series

there are many others: the German, Dutch, Greek and perhaps Japanese. This is a technical concern for someone who attempted to do what I did. When I compare these different words in the different versions; those three the original English, the French and the revised, I found a number of instances where changes and alterations had been made in all three and places where all three did not correspond with one another. As an example of this there is a word in the *"Arousing of Thought"*, in the story of Karapet of Tiflis, where Karapet loses his taste for something called 'Makhokh', and when I looked for that in the French it was not there. When I looked for that word what I found, not speaking French, was something that looked very much like onion soup. The revised translation kept 'Makhokh' from the original but dropped an 'h' spelling it 'Makokh'. If you are a linguist and you are trying to transliterate that word the dropping of the `h' in front of the 'k' is extremely significant because many of the languages have completely different letters to indicate what is transliterated in English as a 'k' or 'kh'. There is no way to know how that all came about and which one is more accurate, so you are left having to include more possibilities, which I guess we could see as the richness of the whole thing. But it would be helpful to have a version that paid specific attention to the renderings of these words.

'Makhokh' turns up again in the first chapter of the sixth descent, only it is added to and referred to as 'Makhokhitchne'. We have an opportunity to connect together through the form of the words places in the *First Series* which are five hundred pages apart and offer very different viewings of how that word is used, and what does that mean and what do they have to say about one another? In the French, 'Makhokhitchne' is also not present and the word was what in English is gelatinous. I do not know if I were a French speaking person whether I would connect through five hundred pages gelatinous with onion soup. Maybe there is something about being French that you cannot see the word gelatinous without thinking of onion soup. I don't know that but I suspect it would be much easier if the 'Makhokh' were there in both places. I certainly did not miss it.[1]

I should quickly finish.

This symbol (the enneagram) is so important for language because of the way we use language with one another. Every word that we use; thinking, being, understanding, you cannot speak to someone and say the emphasis of our work is on being; being, what being? Where on this symbol is being? How many levels of being? How are we to understand what the word being means? Simple words that we use with one another all the time we do not understand them. We need to use this symbol to help us to see there is a place for thinking at every one of theses points and a place for being and understanding. All these words that we use continually are not specific enough. Our understanding of them is too general and we put to much into them in our sleep.

We all come from so many different places with so many different experiences and this book is like a point or core in the middle of a circle. We can come to if we wish to speak a common

---

[1] Subsequent conversation with Nicolas Tereshchenko revealed that what I thought was 'onion soup' in French referred in fact to the word 'Hachi'. The connection referred to therefore is erroneous while the fact that these two words are not in the French version remains.

language with one another; come to a place of a common value and move from that. For me the Gurdjieff work is unique in and of itself. To the degree to which I can understand anything in my own past, Christianity or science, I have to move from here, from the work, to that. I don't come from the outside of the circle with my understanding of what is out here and bring that to this. Which does not mean that that does not have a value. But these Legominisms of Gurdjieff are the center of it and these will, for me, become in the future, a defining characteristic of the uniqueness of a tradition that has these and will become indicators for people on the circle of what is an authentic form of work. And they will all be present in those groups who are carrying that on seriously.

© Copyright 1998 - Harry J. Bennett - All Rights Reserved

Approaching the Neologisms of the First Series - Questions & Answers

Chris Thompson: I would like to express my appreciation to you Harry for opening what I think is a very, very important subject, which really is the ostensible theme of this gathering which is how to study this book. And I especially warm to the fact that you spoke without notes, extremely coherently and touchingly which is, in a way I feel, that all our meetings should be conducted, where what is said is crafted in real time from our thought and effort. I would just like to say that I hope it will be a lively conversation, almost a forum about your talk, but if the organizing committee would wish it and if you are interested I do have a small document which was produced in response to another effort to make an etymology, not written by me, but it might be interesting to read simply as a kind of additional context. It is entirely a matter of our choice.

The other thing I would like to say is that you have raised truly searching and worrying questions about the translations. I don't mind confessing that I am very heavily involved in this question and that there will one day, probably in the next millennium, be the kind of version that you are referring to where the effort at transliteration and the effort at making the translation of certain words coherent through the book and various things like that will have been done with very great care. I happen to know that Nik was involved in the early stages of the editing to the Russian text which will eventually be published, and will allow the verifications of certain issues. But the individual language versions have diverged even in the time of Mr. Gurdjieff and they each have their own identity to some extent. But you do really raise in a very touching manner, some very serious questions for all of us.

Harry Bennett: I would very much like to have that read at some point.

Chris Thompson: Maybe at the end we could have it read off the record just to share.

Nicolas Tereshchenko: Yes, I agree with more than ninety nine percent of what Harry has told us. The only small point that I would disagree with is about the availability of the book to even beginners in the work. I feel it is not for nothing that Mr. Gurdjieff has advised people to read it three times. The first time, purely mechanically, with out trying to understand really without paying attention so to speak to what they are doing; as a discipline just as you would do your morning exercises or something like that. The second time was to be read as if you were reading to somebody. I took it and I believe some other people did that It meant you had to read it aloud to yourself, which is what I did. The third time and obviously subsequent one was to read it with attention and try to understand what it is that's being said in every sentence, passage or chapter.

Now in order to understand something you have to have two factors, knowledge and being. Now knowledge, this is exactly what I think is the purpose of work such as Harry has undertaken, that is to say to take strange words that Mr. Gurdjieff uses, and if I may say so I feel that we should call them Hapax Legomena rather than neologisms, because nobody else used them before him and I don't think anybody will ever use them except when commenting on his own work, but be that as it may, so knowledge of where do these words come from and what do they have in common, just like Harry exactly brought some examples to us, and what do those different parts mean either in known human languages such as Russian, Greek or whatever or perhaps Mr. Gurdjieff, as a messenger from above, has used languages which are not those languages into which he has therefore initiated some of us.

Now the second thing is being and where does that come in these words, the Hapax Legomena? I feel that unfortunately we no longer have Mr. Gurdjieff, we no longer have his presence, we no longer have his personal Baraka to use a Sufi term. We do have his great work and I think that is Mr. Gurdjieff for us and wherever this book is there is his presence also and these words have been designed by him, I am quite sure, with a special usage in view. Some of you may have read perhaps texts of magic and whatever and may have read criticisms of the barbarous names of invocations, well the reasons for all those names in traditional magic is that those names produce a certain vibration in the air. I am quite sure that the words of Mr. Gurdjieff are also meant to produce a particular vibration which will have an effect on our being and it is the combined attempts to know what are the roots of these words and the effect of this vibration on us that will give understanding of what Mr. Gurdjieff wishes to tell us.

I am glad to have confirmation from Chris that the publication of the Russian text has not been abandoned. I finished reading the last proofs which were entrusted to me in 1995 so I am somewhat surprised that it has not come out yet but I do hope it will come soon because without the correct spelling of the original Russian I don't think any modern transliteration can be feasible. There is one small problem and that is that some of the pages that have survived, or at least that I have seen, are carbon copies of such thin paper that many of the letters are just black blobs. That was one of the jobs I was asked to do was to try and work out what the words should be and some of the transliterations of words in all the three translations known to me; the two English and the French one ultimately when compared to the various surviving manuscripts are not at all what apparently is on the manuscripts. So what is going to happen when the Russian comes out is that some of the words will look very different. In particular one word that has struck me is the one in chapter seventeen when it talks about the remorse of conscience; "Aieioiuoa". Well, in one of the more legible Russian manuscripts it came out as "Anemomus" which is completely different from what has been translated. Well, that is all I have to say, that is enough for me.

Paul Taylor: I appreciate that very much too, it is an interesting problem. By the way Nicolas, 'Hapax Legomena' is a single occurrence in a finite and nonextendable corpus so you're right 'neologisms' can't be otherwise. But along other lines, how many of you here have heard Gurdjieff speak? There are recordings. I know there are recordings because (garbled tape) have those recording been heard? All right, the reason I say that is because, and I'll address this to Keith, from my own memory the syntactical limits in Gurdjieff's oral speech which he tried from 1927 to incorporate into the written was the reason he wanted to revise, in 1927, the whole of All and Everything was to get his voice into what he had already seen as a translation which somehow obscured that voice. But it seemed to me in my own experience and maybe you can help me here, that the syntactical frame of his utterances was a breath. And in all of his speech, now I can't go back to the Ouspensky days on this, but in his late days it was a breath.

But there is another problem which bothered me terribly which is the interchangeability of languages in one speak. Now recently It has been claimed by linguists, cognitive scientists actually, perhaps this is psycholinguistics, but a recent study on language acquisition claims that if you learn more than one language in those early years of language acquisition two different parts of the brain records or frames each language. A perfectly bilingual person will have a different part of the brain for each language. When you have gone past the time of language acquisition and learn a new language it laminates, it occupies the same area as your fist acquired language. It didn't work that way with Gurdjieff. In other words, you never had an idea that there was any shifting within one area of the brain or in the lamination from one language to another and thus was in cognition as well as in the production of speech. I had never seen Gurdjieff struggle to understand what someone was saying when it would be French, Russian, English. I mean its remarkable. I don't command many languages but sometimes I can listen to three full sentences of a language I know very well and not know which language I'm listening to. But never with Gurdjieff. When he shifted languages or actually lamitions, syntactical, grammatical as well as phonological. This to me; I just can not understand but I think its amazing and I think it is something he tried to bring into the text and I think its something you're working towards unravelling to some extent too.

Keith Buzzell: Just to add some of the recent neurophysiological studies in children and ages of language acquisition which are maximized. Between four and seven the multiplicity of language formation has been investigated by some folks working specifically in the areas of speech development and one very, very interesting study done by a woman in Baltimore working with a group of inner city children who were cross ethnic, mixed groups essentially from relatively low income and found that it was possible for all these children. I mention the low income and lack of special privilege to underscore that there was nothing special in the backgrounds of the children coming into the study. At the end of a year she had these twelve children, by bringing in people from native countries, from Estonia, from Paraguay, from wherever, talking with these children, interacting with them and at the end of a year all these children were simultaneously able to move flexibly between twelve languages. Just in a moment, moving, moving and never get mixed up. There is an echo of this capacity in what Paul is saying. So it is there in us, but unfortunately due to our Itoklanoz that door almost closes. It is extraordinarily difficult for any of us at our age to take on a new language, we can do it but boy its hard going and as Paul points out its laminated and we must cross translate while we are in motion. We never really fluidly flow into the new language where, by every evidence these children were able to flow from one to the other. It is an interesting confirmation of a capacity that is there and that Gurdjieff had either retained throughout his life or developed and opened again.

Michael Smyth: I would just like to underline something that I agree very much with. That book is our common language. Regardless of the Russian, German or French. I am convinced it will be the thing that bonds this teaching in the future, down the line. I am sure there will be arguments over syntax and all this stuff and we will get into all these scholarly things where we break up words and things. I think its good to keep it as pure as we can and as close as we can but there is a spirit, as Nik said, that's in that book and if people work together, regardless of the differences that we have this is the thing that will keep us together. This is what he left us, that was his teaching, he knew he couldn't give it all to one person, two people or five people and he spent nearly half a lifetime putting that book together putting his teaching in that. So I really underline what you said; that's our common language, that's our bond.

Keith Buzzell: Beautifully imaged in Harry's placing the book in the center of the circle.

Robert Curran: I think there is a section in Beelzebub that is very relevant to this. After Beelzebub has used the word 'Hasnamuss' for the third time Hassein interrupts and says, and I'm paraphrasing, "Grandfather, can you please tell me the precise significance of this word because so far I have only been able to gather from the intonation of your voice and the consonance of the word itself that by this word you mean to refer to a being deserving of objective contempt". Since we don't have the benefit of these intonations and sometimes even the right accent and weight of the consonance is hard to come by vocally, I would just think that that might put, not a pause on this kind of inquiry, but a restraint of a certain kind of intelligence on just how much we could expect from that.

Nicolas Tereshchenko: I just want to add one thing which I feel is important. The Russian text, as written by Mr. Gurdjieff, contains quite a number of words which are now no longer used, at least not used since the Soviet revolution. It is unfortunate also that many people who do know Russian now are not aware really of the true meanings of these words because many of the old Russian words have double meanings; the common meaning and the inner meaning. Now, one of people who had to deal with reviewing the text and correcting it proposed quite a number of changes which were completely unwarranted, in my opinion. In spite of the fact that she was a professional interpreter of Russian she obviously did not know what the inner meanings were of the words she wanted to change. I do hope the delay in publication between 1995 to now does not mean that her advise prevailed and that a certain number of words have been changed for common Soviet words which have not the inner meanings Mr. Gurdjieff obviously attributed to it. This is in reference to what Paul Taylor has told us that he had a perfect control of which word, which sentence and how to use it. I am quite sure because some of the passages quite surprised me. It was fortunate that my father was a philologist as well as some other things and that he had a number of books actually printed in the old Slavonic so I had to read as a child the old Slavonic and to look up in the dictionaries a lot of words that I didn't know with their etymology in the philological books he had. I very fortunately have been able to know which of these words have, in my opinion, to be kept absolutely in tact otherwise some of the inner meaning is lost. And that is of course one of the difficult circumstances of translation. Translating from one language to another how to get the inner meaning as well.

Approaching the Neologisms of the First Series - Questions & Answers

Sy Ginsburg: The idea has been mentioned here that the vibratory sound of the word is very important. In fact some years ago I saw a kind of hand written dictionary or lexicon that attempted to give symbols for how words should be pronounced. I no longer have a copy of that but maybe somebody here could address whether there has been any work done to produce that sort of thing so that whatever language, if the vibration has an effect when spoken on the person hearing or speaking it, such that it could be properly received.

Andrew Rawlinson: I'm not sure if I'm answering your question but the notion that there exists a language which directly corresponds to the meaning of the object and states to which it is directed exists in all the great traditions. It applies to Hebrew, Sanskrit and Greek. Its hardly news to many people here. The only one I know from my own work is Sanskrit. Its the myth of this language that holds that at a certain state of awareness or consciousness this language arises of itself. You don't have to learn it and if you think about it you wouldn't if it does have a direct connection to the objects to which it applies and this is the language which is spoken between the yogis. And its the only language that makes sense.

Jim Gomez: I would like to talk something about that as well. There have been some studies done by the Rudolf Steiner people where they take vowel sounds; Hans Jennings has done some work on this, where they project it into different mediums and it begins to make geometric forms. Its a fascinating study.

I also thank you very much for that talk. I think that this is important. The book is obviously the center as you're saying but also the enneagram like you're talking about that as well and I think the enneagram is more difficult in a way to talk about because there is not as much really. We don't know as much about the enneagram in a way and I think they are connected. They are definitely related together. It would be real difficult to see how we can move into that but I think its important cause the enneagram is a symbol and it doesn't necessarily have any language associated with it. Its a form language and yet it can be a very powerful thing as well. I know you're interested in geometry as well. Do you have any sort of statements about your interest in that aspect of things.

Harry Bennett: If you take language as a theme in work I think you will find that mythology is a language and all symbolism is a language, mathematics, music. These are more external things that fill the space between us for communicating with one another but there is a whole teaching about a corresponding inner language. I am focused on the relationship between people and groups and on words specifically but there is a whole teaching regarding work on oneself that is the inner language of centers and connections between centers and this comes out of a thorough study of the coquettish secretary in the formatory office and the horse-carriage-driver. I think Gurdjieff is pointing us towards these higher forms of language through the symbols and diagrams that have been recorded in In Search. That does not mean it is easy to learn or gain capacity to begin to utilize them but in my experience one doesn't get that by waiting for it to happen. You start by investing yourself in it by exploring with what happens if I try this and I try that with the symbol.

All & Everything Conference 1998

I would like to mention one more thing. This image that I keep hearing of this teaching that was brought and was something whole and complete and perfect and now as time proceeds it expands and the quantity of people increases and the quality of the work decreases and the inevitable law of Heptaparaparshinokh with its deflecting Stopinders is going to eventually see the disappearance of the Fourth Way. I have heard this image spoken out by people in many different ways. If we go at the laws, and if there is reciprocal maintaining and feeding, and there is the collection of that which is dispersed, upward, then the potential exists to consider that Gurdjieff was smarter than that, and that he was not going to make the mistake of all the other previous Sacred Messengers from above, not that I perceive him in that role, but as he puts the story in the *Tales* a certain thing happens to all these teachings. My hope against pessimism is that there is this counter balance and that these Legominisms have been left to get this reciprocal maintaining and feeding going so that it will not inevitably follow the path of involution.

Marlena Buzzell: I guess I just wanted to underscore something that Chris said and that is to thank you, for clearly something came in through your Mechano-coinciding since you came here and you came prepared to give a talk but because of your value for the book and your sincerity you demonstrated a Work on yourself and shared it with others for the book and that's a great teaching in itself.

Edgar Clarke: I found *All & Everything* when I first read it to be incomprehensible. There was a thread running through the book which I could pick up in a meaningful manner at a general level but immediately got in the book work on octaves and work on energies and the terms he used were completely incomprehensible to me. I had to leave this. And my way of getting over this was to make the best sense I could of them in the context in which they were. Secondly, I was able by asking people, who either were in contact with Mr. Gurdjieff and knew intimately or with those who were in contact with these people, how these words were used and I was able when really stumped to ask them the meanings of these words as near as possible. I think its possible to do a great deal, not only by reading *All & Everything* but by reading the works of people who were with him like Mr. Bennett and Mr. Nicoll. You can pick up a great deal of data in the commentaries and the book explaining the terms and references to *All & Everything*. I found that as a non academic way of getting to grips with these terms and it seems to me one of the ways if one wants to get a pure, as for as one can, understanding of these terms would be while the opportunity is still here to ask people who were used to hearing these terms as Mr. Bennett used them that they should make the best use of those people who are available. I'm speaking in terms of going back in family history. If one goes back to a place and starts rooting around one can learn a great deal about them and even more one can learn from the people who were present at the time and who can overcome with evidences the encumbrances of time.

Tracking Oskiano In Beelzebub's Tales

Robert Curran

Robert Curran was born April 8, 1943, participated in Lord Pentland's Work in San Francisco from 1966 to 1987, and now continues the Work in Washington, DC. (March 13, 1998).

Robert Curran was introduced by Jeff Taylor and the session was opened at the request of Robert by Jeff Taylor reading a short passage from *Beelzebub's Tales To His Grandson*, starting at the lower part of page 24, Chapter 1, The Arousing of Thought. This passage was read twice with a short pause between each reading:

"…I shall expound my thoughts intentionally in such sequence and with such "logical confrontation," that the essence of certain real notions may of themselves automatically, so to say, go from this "waking consciousness" - which most people in their ignorance mistake for the real consciousness, but which I affirm and experimentally prove is the fictitious one - into what you call the subconscious, which ought to be in my opinion the real human consciousness, and there by themselves mechanically bring about that transformation which should in general proceed in the entirety of a man and give him, from his own conscious mentation, the results he ought to have…"

Tracking Oskiano In Beelzebub's Tales

INTRODUCTION

Some narrative artifice and the *Tales* are underway: Beelzebub returns from his long exile to the planet Karatas, sees his grandson Hassein for the first time and undertakes his education (55). Beelzebub is the author's mouthpiece, telling tales in flight on the ship *Karnak*. Hassein maintains his active mentation. Ahoon plays along. The stage is set--a plausible stage from which the author freely assaults our sensibility with his objectively impartial criticism. We can appreciate that, and returning the author's favor, make our own efforts to advance a line of inquiry the text truly welcomes: How does Beelzebub execute his self-imposed responsibility as Hassein's educator?
Beelzebub is a voice from another cosmos, not of our world. He uses a strange vocabulary--words we've never seen in print and can hardly pronounce. One of these words, Oskiano, is a not-too-close approximation for what we call "education." Education on earth perpetuates, and proceeds as a consequence of, the properties of the organ kundabuffer; it perpetuates, and inextricably combines with, the abnormal conditions of ordinary existence and the peculiar strangeness of our reason. We have no interest here in "education." We are tracking Oskiano--Beelzebub's guidance for Hassein in his preparatory age.

All & Everything Conference 1998

Tracking Oskiano is an uphill climb on a shifting slope. It is a thread intersecting other threads, tapestried into a greater whole, weaving its way in one direction, stretching in another, but always on the move, impeccably intent on completing its action through Hassein's maturing life. Beelzebub's Oskiano--though never called "sacred"--is something not possible in our world.

However we experience *Beelzebub's Tales* and construe its intent, we can always appreciate three factors. One, it is a sacred text. Two, it excels commendably in putting categorical strains on the potency of the reader's re-educability. Three (excusing for the moment a mulla-nassr-eddinism), its entertainment values are exceeded only by those we find in the county morgue.

We will try to explore how Beelzebub's Oskiano for Hassein conveys guidance, engenders responsibility, reflects the significance of the teacher, and engages repetition in transmitting knowledge.

This paper is most of all a form of literary criticism, a self-enclosed textual analysis, making no reference to outside commentary nor to the author's other work, but thriving on one admittedly unresolved question: In seeing how Beelzebub effects his Oskiano for Hassein, can we further advance the possibility of cooperating with the author's designs on our mentation? With this in mind, let us put our fingers on the pulse of Oskiano's emphatically drumming persistence, let us see how Beelzebub commands his self-imposed responsibility, and, while coming up short as we inevitably must, let us nevertheless revel
in the challenge.

REPETITION

All repetition conveys emphasis, makes the narrative flow, the text cohere, the ideas circulate. Beelzebub uses repetition to convey insistence, heighten Hassein's receptivity, and texture layers of thematic nuance with increasing significance.

Laws of World Creation and World Maintenance

Seven times in Book One Beelzebub repeats the need to fully expound the laws of world-creation and world-maintenance in detail (86, 123, 124, 127, 136, 148, 279). He calibrates these anticipatory repetitions to increasingly expand Hassein's receptivity until its dimensions are proportioned to the significance of the material to be conveyed. In Chapter 17, "The Arch Absurd," Beelzebub says:

> Although I have promised to explain to you, only later, all the fundamental laws of World-creation and World-maintenance in detail, yet the necessity has here arisen, to touch upon, if only briefly, the questions concerning these cosmic laws, without waiting for that special talk I promised. And this is necessary, in order that you may be able better to take in all that we are now talking about, and also in order that what I have already told you may be transubstantiated in you in the right way. (136)

"[W]hat I have already told you..."?! Hassein needs a working knowledge of the laws so what has been and will be told to him can be made his own. The repetition tempered in Beelzebub's Oskiano reflects in part learning how to re-learn, or learning that re-vivifies the cognitive import of what is already "known."

It is only in relation to the subject of these laws that we see anticipatory repetition. Beelzebub begins to elaborate the long-anticipated laws of world-creation and world-maintenance in Chapter 39, "The Holy Planet Purgatory": "Now, my boy, listen further very attentively. . ." (752). A few pages later: "I repeat, my boy: Try very hard to understand everything that will relate to both these fundamental cosmic sacred laws" (755). And at the end of the chapter, Beelzebub, nowhere more insistently, adds: "because I have already said much to you about this first fundamental sacred law of Heptaparaparshinokh, I would therefore be very distressed if for some reason or other you should not succeed in understanding clearly the particulars of this law" (870).

Messengers

Beelzebub, with his forever compelling allegiance to history, tells of the Messengers intentionally actualized from Above to the planet earth. In Chapter 12, he passingly mentions "Jesus Christ, a messenger from Our Endlessness" (99). The idea resurfaces more fully in Chapter 21: Saint Buddha, a Messenger sent by certain nearest helpers of our Common Father with a task laid upon him from Above to aid the three-brained beings of the planet earth in destroying the crystallized consequences of the properties of the organ kundabuffer (233). It resounds with greater depth in Chapter 25: Ashiata Shiemash, a definitized conception of a sacred Individual intentionally actualized from Above with the same preassigned mission. The idea of a Messenger is fully embraced throughout Chapter 38, "Religion."

In this graduated unfolding of meaning and importance by repetition to full embodiment, Beelzebub's Oskiano paints the picture of the Messengers on the canvas of Hassein's psyche with increasingly heavy brush strokes. Thereafter, whenever he mentions a Messenger, he knows Hassein has the appropriately grounded egoplastikoori to fully cognize this idea.

Nothing Changes

Nothing changes on earth--an idea we can follow in its thematic repetition to see the brilliance and subtlety in Beelzebub's Oskiano, and how seemingly inconsequential elements are intentionally building the detailed structure of an idea.
Maralpleicie was eventually populated by hunters from Atlantis who killed pirmarals to powder their horns because someone invented the notion that this powdered horn was effective against diseases (208). In Chapter 34, in contemporary Russia 334 pages later, Beelzebub relates the story of the pharmacist composing Dover's powder--a totally ersatz product, not even made as it is prescribed, which people believe improves their health only because they have heard others say so (545). By connecting these powders, the ancient pirmaral and the contemporary Dover's, Hassein derives the conclusion: Nothing changes, or as the old phrase goes, "the more things change, the

more they stay the same." The narrative is structured and timed to challenge Hassein's active retention because the information could be derived no other way.

Paralleling this in narrative structure, we are told that Pearl-land was also eventually populated by beings from Atlantis, also hunters, who pursued pearl-bearing creatures for profit because beings of "former as well as contemporary" times liked to adorn their exteriors with pearls, turquoise, and other such precious trinkets. In this simple "former as well as contemporary" (227) the fact--nothing changes--is handed out readymade with no effort necessary on Hassein's part.
The information from the powders is the same from the pearls, only the derivation differs. Through Beelzebub's exactingly uncanny Oskiano, Hassein subjectively senses the information earned by active retention through the powders is more alive and meaningfully charged than the same information readily handed out through the pearls. (For the reader, the idea--nothing changes--also vibrates with more depth of significance through the powders because the duration of reading time over 334 pages comparably approximates a subjective representation of historical time from Maralpleicie to contemporary Russia.)

The idea becomes fully embodied in Chapter 37, when Beelzebub, alone at the time in a French bistro, has his second Sarpitimnian-experiencing--his sad and distressing reflections:

> During these long centuries many sacred Individuals have been sent down to them here from Above... yet nevertheless nothing has changed here and the whole process of ordinary being-existence has remained as before. During this time, no difference whatsoever has arisen between those three-brained beings of this planet, who existed nearly a hundred of their centuries ago, and the contemporary ones. (674)

Beelzebub later asks Hassein if he recollects the information on the settlers of Pearl-land and then relates how the contemporary Europeans move to Pearl-land (now India) under the abnormally compelling necessity to engage in reciprocal destruction. Between intervals in this reciprocal destruction, they manufacture "beads, earrings, bracelets and various other such gewgaws" for profit and trade with those in their home country--exactly like the original settlers of Pearl-land from Atlantis with their identical weakness for pearls and precious trinkets (718). Nothing changes.

We can look even further. The idea--nothing changes--is reflected in how the contemporary American prohibition on alcohol retells the story of the beings in Maralpleicie compulsively chewing poppy seeds (926). Again, how the contemporary League of Nations, formed to end man's reciprocal destruction, retells the same futile story of the society "God is where man's blood is not shed," established in the country Tikliamish for the same purpose (1062). Nothing changes.

Static Repetitions

The above three examples--the laws, the Messengers, nothing changes--illustrate dynamic repetition. With each appearance new factors add to a sense of achieving fullness and re-sound ideas with expanding emphasis. Other repetitions are static. The consequences of the properties of the organ kundabuffer, the abnormal conditions of ordinary existence, the strangeness of our reason monotonously pound on with a straightlining flatness, have no story line, give in themselves no sense of heading for or contributing to anything. Even the changing intervals between their appearance don't alleviate a sense of being weighed upon. In short--they are exquisitely perfect. The entire narrative repeats kundabuffer 69 times, abnormal conditions 71 times, strange reason 72 times. On the average, these static repetitions appear once every five pages. This repetition, its ineluctably demanding now-ness and one dimensional factuality, is teleologically appropriate as a movement towards complete saturation. These static repetitions, by saturating the narrative flow, saturate Hassein's cognition and effect an enforced participation in the extent to which they have commensurately saturated the life of beings on earth. Kundabuffer, abnormal conditions, strange reason--saturate earth history in gross misorientations, muddle the present, darken the future.

All repetition conveys emphasis, and the force added by repeated ideas may even be magnified here as dynamic and static repetitions mutually contrast and complement one another. We are also left to ponder the mantra-like, relentless, static repetitions as supporting continuity in Hassein's work on sustaining active mentation.

Retention and Immediacy

Beelzebub perseveringly compels Hassein's retentive presence, as we see, taking examples only from Book One: Four times he says, "I have already told you..." (81, 168, 268, 361). Three times he says, "do you remember. .." (177, 179, 302). Twice he says, "as I have already told you. .." (143, 317). Once each he says, "I may remind you. . . " (110). "As I have already said. .." (112). "You remember I told you. . ." (282). "I have already more than once told you. .." (347).

The repetitive insistence on retention carries throughout the text as Beelzebub recalls for Hassein information previously presented, sometimes just for the re-collecting itself, other times as a preface for introducing new material on subjects already raised.   It: moves   Hassein   to actively hold what transpires in a readily accessible presence-of-mind, being poised to know how what has been said may bear upon what is to be said. It heightens the readiness that accompanies and preconditions the possibility for assimilation of the whole as it unfolds.

This repeated insistence on retention is further compressed by Beelzebub's insistent immediacy. Again, just from Book One: "Now listen" (90). "You must know and remember this also. .."(142). "Here it must without fail be noticed. .." (235). "In any case you must know and bear in mind. . . " (274). "It is imperatively necessary to inform you. . . " (292). "[T]ry to transubstantiate in the corresponding parts of your common presence the information concerning . . . " (293). "Now listen very attentively to the information concerning. . ." (347).

These unwavering repetitions in Beelzebub's force and manner persist throughout the text and create the inexorably pressing sense of development--something is at large, possibilities are pending, Oskiano is on the move.

All & Everything Conference 1998

GUIDANCE

The guidance afforded Hassein through Beelzebub's Oskiano takes many forms. The following two illustrations reflect guidance for interpreting his own experience and guidance for living in a way that fulfils the reason for his existence.

Interpretive Guidance

In Chapter 7, "Becoming Aware of Genuine Being-Duty," the Captain relates the history and development of space ships. Hassein experiences remorse. The previous labor of beings devoted to the welfare of their unknown descendants by advancing space ship design and function never occurred to him. In Chapter 17 we are told Remorse takes place in the atmosphere of certain planets when, owing to the sacred process Aieioiuoa, Djartklom proceeds in the Omnipresent-Okidanokh. This cosmic law, the sacred Aieioiuoa, is called Remorse, a process whereby those parts that arise from any one Holy Source of the Sacred Triamazikamno revolt and criticize the former unbecoming perceptions and manifestations of another part of its whole. This occurs on certain planets when in direct touch with the emanations of the Most Holy Sun Absolute or any other sun. It also happens in beings from their conscious labor and intentional suffering (141).

Are we seeing Beelzebub's Oskiano relate the as-above-so-below lawful parallel between cosmic and individual phenomena? This perspective is encouraged by the distinctly human language representing the action of this law--revolt, criticism, perception. Beelzebub does not expressly articulate this connection. He leaves Hassein to establish it for himself, thereby letting us know that Oskiano proceeds as much in what is said as it proceeds in what is said without having to say it. This interpretive guidance will allow Hassein to establish the cosmic lawfulness at the source of his experience.

Teleological Guidance

After Hassein's remorse, Beelzebub provides direct guidance and the reason for following it:

> Every day at sunrise bring about a contact between your consciousness and the various unconscious parts of your own presence... convince the unconscious parts that if they hinder your general functioning, in your responsible age you will not be able to be a good servant for Our Common Endless Creator and by that will not even be able to be worthy to pay for your arising and existence. (78)

Beelzebub gives Hassein direct guidance: Consciousness should be increasingly self-concentrated and stabilized to guide the manifestations of his unconscious parts, a precondition for being able to be a good servant, which is in turn a precondition for being able to pay for his arising and existence--the completing action of which will return to Hassein in the form of consciousness even more self-concentrated and stabilized. (We see this in Beelzebub's response to the Archangel

Looisos mentioned below.) The guidance is teleological--discerning the innate purpose for the existence of three-brained beings.

This guidance is also reflected from its source in Chapter 39, "The Holy Planet Purgatory," when our Endlessness discerns the Tetartocosmoses automatically moving about on the surface of planets, giving Him the "Divine Idea of making use of them as a help for Himself in the administration of the enlarging world" (782).

Beelzebub re-awakens the sense and significance of "a good servant" when the Archangel Looisos explains to him how sacrificial offerings by beings on the planet Earth jeopardize the common-cosmic harmonious movement of the Solar System Ors. He urges Beelzebub to rectify this situation on the spot and thereby render a great service to our Endlessness. Hassein notes the instantaneous affirmation in Beelzebub's response, "to carry out the said task at all costs," and his reason for it: that by this explicit aid to our Unique-Burden-Bearing Endlessness he may be worthy of becoming a particle of everything existing in the Great Universe (183). This episode recalls Beelzebub's guidance: "bring about a contact between your consciousness and the various unconscious parts of your general presence... to be able to be a good servant of our Common Endless Creator" (78). Beelzebub's readiness to act on the guidance he has given further crystallizes its significance for Hassein.

At the end of Chapter 41, Beelzebub calls Hassein his heir, to whom everything will be transmitted by inheritance, and adds, "of course only insofar as you yourself will deserve it by your own conscientious being-existence and honorable service to the All-Common Father Maintainer, our Endlessness" (1051).

This orientation is quietly brought to life again in Chapter 39 as Beelzebub relates the reason for the state of persisting anguish in the higher-being bodies on the Holy Planet Purgatory: after "inexpressible, consciously suffering labors" they reach the threshold of perfection but "are still unable to help Him in the fulfilment of His most sacred tasks for the good of our whole Megalocosmos" (805).

RESPONSIBILITY

Beelzebub's Oskiano infuses Hassein's preparatory age with data for being able to be responsible, being able to respond to the sense and aim of his existence.

The Fate of Hassein's "Fancy"

Oskiano is an all-providing ground for Hassein's growing responsibility and begins early in the *Tales*. Hassein wants to know if there are three-brained beings where his grandfather was exiled and whether higher-being-bodies are coated in them. Beelzebub says earth-beings have a very strange and exceedingly peculiar reason--no hoofs, horns or tails--but once got fixated on the idea of perpetual motion. In this way Beelzebub sows seeds of wondering in the field of Hassein's interest. Later, when the ship *Karnak* is delayed, Beelzebub tells Hassein he will talk about whatever he would like, but knows what he will ask because he has already paved the path of Hassein's inquiry for him: "Tell me more about those. ...slugs." It is a light-hearted, inquisitive, fanciful inquiry--what we , would expect from a 12 year old. And so it begins, Beelzebub's recurring phrases--"your favorites," and "the three-brained beings on the planet earth who have taken your fancy"--each time cuing Hassein to follow the changing course and character of his initial inquiry and his own development in relation to it. Beelzebub never relinquishes this reminding factor. We see the progression of Hassein's initial "fancy" reaching completion at the end of Chapter 43, when he says, "from this present moment, the aim of my existence shall be to understand clearly why the souls arising in these terrestrial three-brained beings are in such an unprecedented, terrifying situation" (1117). Hassein shoulders the increased weight of responsibility that develops from his fanciful inquiry. We sense his being actually becoming responsible.

Beelzebub's farsighted Oskiano brings this about. When the ship Karnak is delayed and he informs Hassein he will tell him whatever he wants to hear, he says, "Tell me anything you wish" (79). But Beelzebub insists, "No, you yourself ask what interests you most." This seals a sense of responsibility in Hassein from the beginning for what follows.

Hassein, Beelzebub's Heir

At the end of Chapter 41 Beelzebub unequivocally refers to Hassein as his heir, to whom has already been transmitted and will be transmitted by inheritance, everything acquired by him during his long existence (1051). He refers to him later as "the heir to whom will devolve the fulfilment of the obligations which his predecessor took upon himself, and which for some reason or other were left unfulfilled" (1051), and also as "my future substitute" (1119), "my direct substitute" (1129). Beelzebub awakens in Hassein a beginning sense of pending responsibilities, which will in turn further awaken the need to prepare for what is required. Beelzebub's Oskiano, while transmitting information, anticipates the time needed to gain strength for responsibly relating to it.

Ancestral Lineages

Hassein's sense of responsibility matures naturally from the suppositions at large in his world. It is simply understood that beings try to fulfil the reason for which they exist and, in doing so, they become more responsible for further doing so. This is illustrated in the many ways Beelzebub speaks of ancestral lineages.

Beelzebub's sons both leave the solar system Ors to fulfil obligations commensurate with their place on the scale of Objective Reason (1121). Hassein's uncle, one of the assistants to the director of the etherogram station on the Holy Planet Purgatory, later becomes the chief director. Hassein's father, Zirlikner in a part of Karatas, later becomes the Chief Zirlikner for the whole planet. It is simply understood in Hassein's world that beings assume posts of responsibility as a service to our Common Father to the extent their higher-being-bodies are perfected.

Beelzebub conveys this again by example through some of Hassein's more meritorious favorites. The twin brothers Choon-Kil-Tez and Choon-Tro-Pel - who rediscover the sacred Heptaparaparshinok as a result of their conscious labor and intentional suffering - are great grandsons of King Konuzion, later a saint, from whom they derive their sense of being-duty to others and acquire an interest in experiments with opium. King Konuzion is the grandson of the great grandson of the unnamed Astrosovor from the Society of Akhaldans on Atlantis, from whom the brothers derive knowledge of the Nirioonossian World Sound, or the absolute vibrations of the note "do."

The significance of the ancestral line is underscored most clearly with Gornahoor Harharkh, Beelzebub's essence-friend on the planet Saturn, and his son Gornahoor Rakhoorkh. Gornahoor Harharkh's son, who is also Beelzebub's godson (166), devotes his life to the study of the Omnipresent-Okidanokh and is considered one of the higher degree common-cosmic learned three-brained-beings, whose attainment so completely supersedes his father's that the latter destroys all his inventions, finds data from his prior convictions totally decrystallized, and concludes his long occupation with this study is an absolutely unredeemable sin (1153). He comes to this in light of his son's far greater attainment in the same field. What we see here for Hassein's Oskiano, like a logicnestarian-implantation, is the accelerated evolution of hereditary endowments.

"The Effects of Every Cause..."

Hassein gathers further data from the above situation for a real lesson on the idea of responsibility. After Beelzebub's pardon, the planetary ruler of Mars, the Toof-Nef-Tef, asks him if he could find out why the potency for self-perfecting is diminishing among his subjects. Beelzebub then leaves Mars for Saturn and meets his essence-friend Gornahoor Harharkh and his son Gornahoor Rakhoorkh. The latter profoundly thanks Beelzebub for being his god-father, as he "assuredly fulfilled with the feeling of full and thorough cognizance the divine obligation taken upon himself" (1154). Gornahoor Rakhoorkh, having received Beelzebub's great goodness in this regard, returns something of this to him when--unknowingly!-- he provides the data necessary for him to answer the question from the Toof-Nef-Tef. This illustrates a truth from Makary Kronbernkzion's' Boolmarshano: The effects of every cause always re-enter the cause (1138). Beelzebub's godfatherhood as a cause sets up effects in Gornahoor Rakhoorkh, the goodness of which return to Beelzebub as an answer to the question given him. The lesson in these lawful sequences will help Hassein know how to be self-responsibly active, in what direction and why.

Are we left with wide open minds on how Beelzebub's self-assumed responsibility, as cause of Hassein's Oskiano, (issuing from his love for Hassein) must also be moving from within to set up certain effects that will, in some form unknown to us, return to him? The overwhelming repetition of retentive, anticipatory, and immediate insistence already noted, gives a sense of great importance. The returning effects of his Oskiano for Hassein are more far reaching than the *Tales* have time to tell.

All & Everything Conference 1998

MULLAH NASSR EDDIN

The sayings of Mullah Nassr Eddin run throughout the text to encapsulate, condense and complement what has just been said. These succinct, oblique perspectives always distil the gist of the subject, as though with a gracious air, gifting the reader's pleasure with the last and only word.

They often translate vaguely obscure situations into a form that is more readily intelligible or, to the contrary, into a form that is even more vaguely obscure, half begging for the reader's future comprehension.

Beelzebub's "objectively impartial criticism" often addresses conditions that are hopelessly pathetic, lamentably unredeemable, instigated, it would seem, to foment the reader's mal-disposition. But the Mullah's sayings--with the force of raw earthiness, rudimentary craft and summarily stinging precision--often follow to neutralize negatively congested concerns, encourage the good sense of inner resignation, and so rattle in words the naked bones of reality that they lighten the load without changing its weight.

Because the inherent absurdity, pathos, and nonsense of some situations are so far beyond the pale of language, the Mullah delights in scrambling consonants to replicate, for example, the apparent sound of someone throwing up, gears grinding, or some such combinations.

These sayings often effect a mind-twisting pirouette, defy expectations, and dissociate the reader from conditioned ways of thought--yet always seem aptly placed and right at home in the flow of the narrative. Fused with gallows humor, even at their dullest, these sardonic, conclusively self-contained perspectives have a way of rounding off a greater detachment. They provide textual syncopation, a change in the timbre of the narrative voice, lend the material a more fully bodied substance and stir subcurrents of an oskiano within the Oskiano.

These psycho-anaglyphic sayings provide an insight-bearing lens for seeing from a uniquely cultivated point of view. Mullah Nassr Eddin: our caustic, folksy, unflappable teacher--the genius with a self-honed edge.

THE TEACHER

The Oskiano relating Beelzebub and Hassein has already been established before the narrative begins (55). In Chapter 39, Beelzebub makes this relation explicitly clear by telling Hassein, "among many other tasks I have set myself in respect of you, as regards your Oskiano...is an exhaustive knowledge and understanding of this holy planet (744). In Chapter 46, he tells Hassein that he voluntarily took upon himself "the responsible guidance of his finishing Oskiano for the Being of a responsible being" (1164). From the following examples we will see how Beelzebub aligns diversely sourced elements on the significance of a teacher so Hassein will more intensely value and follow the guidance needed for becoming responsible.

Tracking Oskiano in Beelzebub's Tales

Beelzebub's Teacher

Beelzebub creates in Hassein the perfectly measured egoplastikoori--concentrated psychic imaging--to represent the sense and significance of a teacher. After his pardon, Beelzebub wishes to see his teacher, the Great Saroonoorishan, to receive his creator-benediction. This wish is stronger than his wish to first return home to Karatas. In Chapter 35, Beelzebub decides to stop on the planet Deskaldino, where he can again visit his teacher, the fundamental cause of all the spiritualized parts of his genuine common presence, since the being-impulse of gratitude towards him is still inextinguishably maintained (658). In this way Beelzebub quietly previews for Hassein the real meaning of what is coming to life between them.

The Oskianotsner

Beelzebub relates the commonly held perception of beings on most planets regarding the significance of a teacher: "Our Common-Father-Endlessness is only the Maker of a three-centered being. The genuine creator, however, of his essence during the period of his preparatory existence is his Oskianotsner, namely, he whom your favorites call tutor or teacher" (818).

Oskiano for Tooloof and Tooilan

Beelzebub's sons received their Oskiano from the remarkably learned Pooloodjistius, also exiled on the planet Mars. He created outer and inner conditions so they should take in impressions to crystallize in themselves being-data required for responsible existence and for the cognizance and sensing of true information about cosmic concentrations and their functions. Both sons were inseparably attached to their teacher, who enlightened their reason and afforded them practical explanations (1122).

Practical Explanations

Beelzebub relates the tale of his experience in Gornahoor Harharkh's Hrhaharhtzaha, an apparatus for demonstrating the particularities of the Omnipresent-Okidanokh. He remembers the promise given him by the All-Quarters-Maintainer, the Most Great Archcherub Peshtvogner, to have transported from Mars to Karatas, the apparatus Gornahoor Harharkh made for him, adding to Hassein, "you will be able to see it all with your own eyes, and I shall be able to explain everything in detail practically" (176).

Beelzebub gives Hassein the "sequence of the historical course of development" regarding the constatation and cognizance of the sacred Heptaparaparshinokh in Chapter 40 and tells him about the experimental apparatus Alla-attapan created by Choon-Kil-Tez and Choon-Tro-Pel. Beelzebub brought home from his exile an instrument with sound engendering strings that can be arranged to duplicate the middle section of the Allaattapan. Because of this instrument, Beelzebub adds, "I shall be able to explain to you by demonstration what is called the 'successiveness-of-the-process-of-the-mutual-blending-of-vibrations.' Thanks to these practical explanations of mine you will more easily be able to represent to yourself and approximately cognize just how and in what successiveness in our great Megalocosmos the process of the Most Great Trogoautoegocrat proceeds and in what way the large and small cosmic concentrations arise" (847). This instrument is called a piano.

These practical demonstrations will amplify for Hassein the explanations Beelzebub provides in words, and will enlighten the words with the force of reality from his own experience not otherwise possible.

Appreciation by Contrast

The *Tales* overflow with opportunities for Hassein to appreciate his grandfather's Oskiano by contrasting his good fortune with the sorry plight of his favorites on earth One example stands out most poignantly when Beelzebub says:

> ...my essence again enjoins the whole of my common presence to express my sincere condolence on the fate of all contemporary terrestrial three brained beings who thanks to their persevering being-Partkdolg-duty peculiar to them finally attain to the state of that degree of Reason when it becomes inevitable for them to have in their presences also the data of the genuine information relating to the law of vibrations.
>
> About this, I by association at the present moment remember with the impulse of regret, because at the period of my last sojourn among them I happened more than once to meet those three-brained beings there who according to their state of, so to say, 'psychic perfection' ought of necessity to absorb and transmute in themselves just the true information concerning the law of vibrations and at the same time I clearly understand that they could not extract such information from anywhere. (859)

Ahoon's Place in the Oskiano Progression

Hassein's deepest impression on the importance of the teacher follows the Most Great Universal Solemnity in Chapter 47. Ahoon's participation in bringing this about is best understood by first seeing how he appears in the course of the narrative.

1.) When Hassein becomes joyous over the delay in the falling of the ship Karnak, Ahoon refers to him as a "growing egoist." Hassein asserts himself to the contrary, and Beelzebub confirms Ahoon's error (59).
2.) Beelzebub says the increasing elevation of the Tibetan mountain range could precipitate a catastrophe on a general cosmic scale. Ahoon interrupts to "rattle off" a conversation he had with Archangel Viloyer regarding these same mountains and says the Archangel Looisos is already on his way to investigate the matter (264). There is a subtle impression that Ahoon passively enjoys an enhanced sense of himself by personal contact with those in high places.

3.) Ahoon's frustration in trying to find a doctor to accommodate an obstetric emergency leaves his whole sensibility involuntarily deranged by association whenever hearing this word "doctor," which makes him grumble like his friend, Dame Bess (554). This parallels the comparable plight of the headmistress and governesses at the private school where, during a walk with her classmates in the countryside, Elizabeth yells to Mary, "Look, there goes a bull!" (1037). The word "bull" deranges the headmistress more than "doctor" deranges Ahoon, but the message sticks: slavery to word-related reactions.

4.) For diminishing sacrificial offerings in Maralpleicie, Beelzebub circulates the notion that the Holy Prana Saint Buddha mentioned is also present in one and two-brain beings, for which reason they should not be destroyed, should even be acknowledged every kind of respect. Ahoon enjoys reminding his Right Reverence how he became a player in this comedy of his own making: "Do you remember how many times in that same city Gob we ourselves had to flop down in the streets during the cries of beings of different forms?" Beelzebub recalls these episodes and two pages later says, "You noticed, my dear Hassein, with what venomous satisfaction our old man reminded me, after so many centuries, of that comical situation of mine" (223).

5.) Beelzebub asks Ahoon to mention any factor about Hassein's favorites that may have taken his interest. Ahoon, with "a timid look and in a hesitant tone," mentions contemporary art, following which he takes the tip of his tail to wipe off the drops of sweat on his forehead (449). Ahoon later asks Beelzebub if he could give Hassein "a good piece of practical advice." Ahoon proceeds "without waiting for the requested permission," and, "as if confused," advises Hassein that if he ever has to live among his favorites and has to have dealings with contemporary artists, to always titillate the consequences of the properties of the organ kundabuffer unfailingly crystallized in them (511). Having said that, Ahoon rearranges the folds of his tail "with the affectation of a Moscow suburban matchmaker," or "like the proprietress of a Parisian fashion workshop" (516). We see, 559 pages later, Ahoon's advice does not compare with Beelzebub's more widely applicable directions for Hassein to stay on good terms with his favorites: "Act upon them through this specific peculiarity--the psycho-organic need of theirs to teach others sense and to put them on the right road, and therefore, always pretend that you wish to learn something from them" (1075). Ahoon's advice, phrasing and manner ironically issue from the very "psycho-organ need" Beelzebub disparages in beings on earth, since Ahoon was giving Hassein advice, as in, setting him straight, putting him on the right path, teaching him sense. Despite certain ambiguities, this conclusion is valid because Beelzebub did not explicitly give Ahoon permission to give Hassein "a good piece of friendly advice."

In short, there is a disconcerted, tentative, and distinctly passive element in the composition of Ahoon's character, clearly supported by reference to Dame Bess, the matchmaker, the proprietress, the headmistress. With this in mind, we will better understand his place in Chapter 47.

All & Everything Conference 1998

After the Most Great Universal Solemnity when Beelzebub's place on the Scale of Objective Reason is known to all as the sacred Podkoolad, Ahoon falls at Beelzebub's feet and says in a sincerely entreating voice:

> Sacred Podkoolad of our Great Universe! Have mercy upon me and pardon me... for my past disrespectful manifestations... towards Your Sacred Essence. Have mercy and pardon me, just this three-centered-being, who, though he has existed a long time, yet to his misfortune--only because in his preparatory age nobody aided the crystallization in him of the data for the ability of intensively actualizing being-Partkdolg-duty--had until now been so shortsighted. (1179)

Hassein now more deeply appreciates the importance of a teacher by seeing Ahoon's irremediable plight in never having had one during his preparatory age. Torrents of profound gratitude flow in him from his good fortune in having as his teacher the sacred Podkoolad, his very own grandfather. This is the doing of Beelzebub's Oskiano. Remember Ahoon's "venomous satisfaction"? Beelzebub providentially instigates the variables to allow Hassein this all-penetrating impression for crystallizing egoplastikoori on the meaning of a teacher and the significance of the preparatory age as the time Great Nature provides to assimilate data for a future responsible existence.

Hassein's Most Vivifying Impression

In Chapter 47, "The Result of Impartial Mentation," Beelzebub, the sacred Podkoolad, through his conscious labor and intentional suffering, has reached that place on the Scale of Objective Reason only one away from the sacred Anklad, the highest possible attainment for any being ever. The responsible being of a sacred Podkoolad is reflected in Ahsiata Shiemash, "one of our seven Most Very Saintly Omnicosmic Individuals, without whose participation even our Uni-Being Common Father does not allow himself to actualize anything" (405). The language forming the significance of this event--so direct, soft, simple, modestly blissful, emotionally charged yet subliminally contained--almost understates the dimensions of the event it relates, unleashing an awesome brilliance, a truly radiant splendor, a profoundly moving happiness for all, in short--a Most Great Universal Solemnity.

At the end of Chapter 43, on reciprocal destruction, Hassein despairs: "How will it all end? Is there really no way out at all?" Beelzebub heaves a deep sigh and responds:

> Certainly there is something not quite right here.... But if nothing could be done for the beings of that planet by that Being who now already has the Reason of the sacred Podkoolad and is one of the first assistants of our Endlessness in the government of the World, namely, the Very Saintly Ashiata Shiemash--if he could do nothing, what then can we expect, we, beings with the Reason of almost ordinary beings? (308)

"[W]e, beings with the reason of almost ordinary beings..."?! Beelzebub gives the impression he does not know he is a sacred Podkoolad. He knows, and lets us know. In Chapter 35, talking with the Captain about going to visit the Great Saroonoorishan, Beelzebub says, "since just now, returning from my perhaps last conference, the entire satisfactoriness of the present functioning of all the separate spiritualized parts of my common presence was revealed not only to me myself, but also to most of the individuals I met" (658). He already knows his place on the Scale of Objective Reason, yet, in response to Hassein's despair, says they both have "the reason of almost ordinary beings." Beelzebub intentionally preserves Hassein's unquestioning assumption that his grandfather is just that--his grandfather--to all the more increase the inner collision pending between his unquestioned assumption and the five-forked horns of truth he will witness.

For the Most Great Universal Solemnity, Beelzebub's Oskiano has readied all the factors in the outer and inner circumstance for Hassein to take in a powerfully vivid impression of the being of the sacred Podkoolad which will, in proportion to its vividness, accelerate the holy affirmative will to perfect himself, or, as the venerable archangel puts it, be a revivifying shock for his ability to struggle against his own denying source (1178).

The force of this event--the very forks on his horns seen multiplying--will intensify the active mentation for his remaining Oskiano and will always be for Hassein an inextinguishable replenishment, ineluctably fused in his being.

CONCLUSION

We have seen how the narrative performs as the action of an influence, how Beelzebub executes his self-imposed responsibility with foresight and measured repetitions, providing guidance, conveying responsibility, creating the true sense of and gratitude for the teacher. Strength, knowledge and newly harmonizing tempos arise in Hassein. And in the reader?

Know the book by its effects, as we know the tree by the fruit. But how to know the fruit? By how it comes across in relation to other impressions of like-kind fruit already experienced, thereby distorting what we learn with recombinations of associations already acquired. If these associations were not derived so much by our strange reason from the abnormal conditions of ordinary existence, instead of distorting, they might be complementing the assimilation of new impressions. Subjectively peculiar distortions insinuated into our disproportionately reactivating brains with their suspect connections, especially from influences during the preparatory age, leave us, unlike Hassein, wrongly crystallized for the author's purposes. The author tells us this immediately in Chapter One and explicitly persists in elaborating variations on this idea 14 more times (see Addendum) throughout the text:

> In my opinion, the trouble with you, in the present instance, is perhaps chiefly due to the fact that while still in childhood, there was implanted in you and has now become ideally well harmonized with your general psyche, an excellently working automatism for perceiving all kinds of new impressions, thanks to which 'blessing,' you have now, during your responsible life, no need of making any individual effort whatsoever. (6)

All & Everything Conference 1998

Know the book by its effects, for example, with the static repetitions--kundabuffer, abnormal conditions, strange reason. These repetitions persistently tunnel their way more deeply within, become stronger, less ephemeral, begin displacing accidentally acquired and thoroughly habituated forms of related thought, presumption and logicnestarian trivia. They can tap through the formatory little know-it-all in the self-calming domain of our fictitious consciousness, or possibly by-pass it altogether, and help the reader be more serious about the truth.

For cooperating with the author's designs on our mentation--the admittedly unresolved question from the beginning--we might initiate an inquiry (and end this paper) with the indications he gives from Chapter One:

> I shall expound my thoughts intentionally in such sequence and with such 'logical confrontation' that the essence of certain real notions may of themselves automatically, so to say, go from this 'waking consciousness'. .. into what you call the subconsciousness, which ought to be in my opinion the real human consciousness, and there by themselves mechanically bring about that transformation which should in general proceed in the entirety of a man and give him, from his own conscious mentation, the results he ought to have. (24)

© Copyright 1998 - Robert Curran - All Rights Reserved

Addendum - Tracking Oskiano in Beelzebub's Tales

Note: All quotes from Gurdjieff, G. I., *Beelzebub's Tales to His Grandson*. New York: E. P. Dutton, 1950.

It was only during later periods that the three-brained beings of the planet Earth began to have this particularity in their psyche, and just this particularity arose in them only because their predominant part, which was formed in them as in all three-brained beings, gradually allowed other parts of their total presences to perceive every new impression without what is called 'being-Partkdolg-duty,' but just merely as, in general, such impressions are perceived by the separate independent localizations existing under the name of being-centers present in the three-brained beings, or, as I should say in their language, they believe everything anybody says, and not solely that which they themselves have been able to recognize by their own sane deliberation. (Chapter 13, p.103)

Here it must without fail be noticed that by that time there had already been crystallized in the presence of Saint Buddha, as the same detailed researches of mine had made clear, a very clear understanding that in the process of its abnormal formation, the Reason of the three-centered beings of the planet Earth results in a Reason called "instincto-terebelnian," that is, a Reason which functions only from corresponding shocks from without; yet in spite of this, Saint Buddha decided to carry out his task by means of this peculiar Reason of theirs, that is, this Reason peculiar to the three-centered beings there; and therefore, he first of all began informing their peculiar Reason with objective truths of every kind. (Chapter 21, p. 235)

The mentioned duality of their general psyche proceeded because on the one hand various what are called 'individual-initiatives' began to issue from that localization arising in their presences, which is always predominant during their waking existence, and which localization is nothing else but only the result of the accidental perceptions of impressions coming from without, and engendered by their abnormal environment, which perceptions in totality are called by them their 'consciousness'; and on the other hand, similar individual-initiatives also began to issue in them, as it is proper to them, from that normal localization existing in the presences of every kind of being and which they called their subconsciousness. (Chapter 27, p.377)

You must know that in the presences of the three-brained beings of the present time, as well as in the presences of every kind of three-brained being in general, every new impression is accumulated in all their three separate 'brains' in the order of what is called 'kindredness,' and afterwards they take part with the impressions already previously registered in the associations evoked in all these three separate brains by every new perception in accordance with and in dependence upon what are called the 'gravity-center-impulses,' present at the given moment in their whole presence. (Chapter 30, p. 486)

All & Everything Conference 1998

As regards the question why it became the custom among them to assemble, often in considerable groups, in these theatres of theirs, it was in my opinion because these contemporary theatres of theirs and all that goes on in them happen to correspond very well to the abnormally formed common presences of most of these contemporary three brained beings, in whom there had been already finally lost the need, proper to three brained beings, to actualize their own initiative in everything, and who exist only according to chance shocks from outside or to the promptings of the consequences crystallized in them of one or other of the properties of the organ Kundabuffer. (Chapter 30, p.500)

After the need to actualize being-Partkdolg-duty in themselves had entirely disappeared from the presences of most of them, and every kind of association of unavoidably perceived shocks began to proceed in the process of their waking state only from several already automatized what are called 'series-of-former-imprints' consisting of endlessly repeated what are called 'Impressions-experienced-long-ago,' there then began to disappear in them and still continues to disappear even the instinctive need to perceive every kind of new shock vital for three-brained beings, and which issue either from their inner separate spiritualized being-parts or from corresponding perceptions coming from without for conscious associations, for just those being-associations upon which depends the intensity in the presences of beings of the transformation of every kind of 'being-energy.'

During the latter three centuries the process itself of their existence has become such that in the presences of most of them during their daily existence those 'being-confrontative-associations' almost no longer arise, which usually proceed in three-brained beings thanks to every kind of new perception, and from which alone can data be crystallized in the common presences of three-brained beings for their own individuality. (Chapter 30, p. 506)

As a result of all this, that mentioned peculiarity of their general psyche just obtains which is derived from the following: firstly, the general functioning, present in their whole being, of the sum of almost all their functions for active being-manifestations, little by little adapts itself to respond only to the sum of these false and fantastic ideas; and, secondly, the whole presence of each one of them gradually accustoms itself to perceive all subsequent new external impressions without any participation at all of those being-factors which in general are put in the beings for new perceptions, that is to say, to perceive them also only according to these previously introduced false and fantastic ideas present in them.
In their new perceptions, the contemporary three-brained beings there ultimately lose the need itself for embracing as a whole everything newly seen or newly heard, and the newly seen and newly heard only serve them as shocks, so that in them associations proceed of the information previously installed in them and corresponding to this newly seen and newly heard.

This is why, when these contemporary favorites of yours already become responsible beings, everything newly seen and newly heard is perceived by them of its own accord automatically without the participation of any effort whatsoever on the part of the essence-functions, and without

Addendum - Tracking Oskiano in Beelzebub's Tales

at all evoking in them, as I have already said, the being need itself of sensing and understanding everything proceeding within them as well as without. (Chapter 37, p. 686)

As regards the third kind of being-Reason, this is nothing else but only the action of the automatic functioning which proceeds in the common presences of all beings in general and also in the presences of all surplanetary definite formations, thanks to repeated shocks coming from outside, which evoke habitual reactions from the data crystallized in them corresponding to previous accidentally perceived impressions. (Chapter 39, p. 770)

And in consequence, in this way all possibilities for the free formation of all that which is required for the engendering of objective being-Reason is gradually atrophied and finally disappears in these unfortunate, so to say, 'still-innocent-in-everything' newly arising beings during the period of their what is called 'preparatory age,' and as a result, when these newly arising beings later became responsible beings, they, in their, so to say, 'essence-center-of-gravity,' become the possessors, not of that Objective-Reason which they ought to have, but of that strange totality of automatically perceived artificial even deceptive impressions which, having nothing in common with the localization of their spiritualized being-parts, nevertheless acquires a connection with the separate functionings of their common presence. In consequence of this, not only the whole process of their existence flows automatically, but also almost the whole process of the functioning of their planetary body becomes dependent only on chance, automatically perceived, external impressions. (Chapter 40, p. 816)

At the present time any one of them can become animated and manifest himself outwardly, only when there are accidentally pressed the corresponding what are called 'buttons' of those impressions already present in him, which he mechanically perceived during the whole of his preparatory age.
But unless these buttons are pressed, the beings there are in themselves only, as again our highly esteemed Mullah Nassr Eddin says, 'pieces of pressed meat.' (Chapter 42, p. 1029)

And since it is impossible for all the three-brained beings of the Universe and therefore also for all the beings of your planet to exist without the process of mentation, and since at the same time your favorites wish to have the possibility of indulging very freely in their inner 'evil god self-calming,' they then gradually and very efficiently accustom themselves that a sort of thinking should proceed in them purely automatically, entirely without the participation of any being-effort of their own.

One must give them their due; in this they have attained perfection, and at the present time their thoughts flow in all directions without any intentional exertion of any part whatsoever of their presence. (Chapter 43, p. 1059)

During their responsible existence these intelligentsia beings there always act or manifest only when they receive corresponding shocks from outside, and it is these same shocks proceeding from outside which give them the possibility of becoming correspondingly animated and of experiencing, only through the unrolling of the series of former corresponding automatic perceptions already present in them and not depending at all on their own wish or will; and these external shocks of theirs for the said kind of experiencing are usually in the first place, animate or inanimate things accidently coming within the sphere of their organs of perception of visibility; secondly, the various beings they meet; thirdly, the sounds or words reverberating where they happen to be; fourthly, scents accidentally perceived by their sense of smell; and finally, unaccustomed sensations that proceed from time to time during the functioning of their planetary body, or as they say, their 'organism' and so on. (Chapter 43, p. 1081)

And as for that Reason which for most of your contemporary favorites has become habitual and which I called the Reason-of-knowing, every kind of new impression perceived through this Reason, and likewise every kind of intentionally or simply automatically obtained result from formerly perceived impressions is only a temporary part of the being, and might result in them exclusively only in certain surrounding circumstances, and on the definite condition that the information which constitutes all his foundation and entirety should without fail be from time to time so to say 'freshened' or 'repeated'; otherwise these formerly perceived impressions change of themselves, or even entirely, so to say, 'evaporate' out of the common presence of the three-brained being.
(Chapter 46, p. 1166)

The whole psychic inner life of the average man is nothing but an "automatized contact" of two or three series of associations previously perceived by him of impressions fixed under the action of some impulse then arisen in him in all the three heterogeneous localizations or "brains" contained in him. When the associations begin to act anew, that is to say, when the repetition of corresponding impressions appears, they begin to constate, under the influence of some inner or outer accidental shock, that in another localization, the homogeneous impressions evoked by them begin to be repeated.
(Chapter 48, p. 1216)

Tracking Oskiano In Beelzebub's Tales - Questions & Answers

Paul Taylor: Just a comment. The name Eddin, Mullah's name, means both man and God in purely Semitic languages, that is, it's Adonai and Adam, so that gives you the nice reach. It's also a lot of other things: the Don, the Neper, the Danube, the Dane, the Tidings and this is a transmission of a holy name through Indo-European nations, but the Mullah is both simultaneously man and God.

Sy Ginsburg: On the Oskiano--I appreciate the things you brought up because it's shown me many things in tracking Oskiano that I had never seen. In the education of Hassein I have the feeling or idea from the *Tales* that this should be, as applied to human beings, the education of relatively young people. This is my subjective view, and yet, in *In Search of the Miraculous* he speaks about good householders and a kind of requirement for a certain experience and responsibility developed in life and is that theme--I haven't seen that in the *Tales*. Can you comment on that?

Robert Curran: What theme are you talking about?

Sy Ginsburg: In the *Tales* versus *In Search* I get a different impression about the period of time for the education of a responsible human being, that is, in the *Tales* it appears to me that the period of time is earlier in one's life, in *In Search* it seems to require more time.

Robert Curran: I don't recollect from *In Search* anything relating to the time period for a right education being able to take within properly, but from the *Tales* I very much get the impression it's all decided in the preparatory age. It's been wound up and it just unwinds-that it's so decisive and irreversible--what happens then, insofar as the consequences that arise from there for the continuing responsible age. I don't know that there's anything mentioned about that in, *In Search*.

Nicolas Tereshchenko: I think, Sy, you may be slightly mistaken about this. In the sense of the word "obyvatel" as used in *In Search* this is applied to the type of person who is capable of doing the Work as opposed to a lunatic or a tramp or a hasnamuss who is not capable of really being in the Work. "Obyvatel" is a Russian word for which the ordinary meaning is the ordinary man in the street who works for his living, who's got a job, family, children, etc. so he can work if he wants to, is capable of doing so. But there is a different meaning because "obyvatel" also has the roots of someone capable of having being.

Sy Ginsburg: Isn't it said somewhere they can support twenty people?

Nicolas Tereshchenko: Yes, exactly, the "obyvatel" who has a job, a profession, by which he can feed people, his family. He was talking more of family than a number of people. That's why the Oskiano applies to the people who are yet underage for earning their own living but who have to be prepared.

Keith Buzzell: There are so many points of differentiation that were made very well. If I remember correctly, you emphasized that the Oskiano Hassein receives is not applicable to the three-brained beings of earth. This is a point of some essentiality. What Beelzebub-Gurdjieff--is speaking out here he speaks out of Itoklanoz. This is the process that, over time, three-brained beings of the planet earth sadly come under, the same principle as one and two-brained beings, and because of the unbecoming behavior, etc., etc., we now, our upbringing, including our education, comes under the seven principles of the octave of Itoklanoz. So the whole Oskiano of Hassein applies to a one-natured being. This differentiation is made so clearly early on. We are one-natured, as Beelzebub speaking to Hassein. They are two-natured. Both are Keschapmartnian, but we are one-natured, they are two-natured, and there may be a connection between the Oskiano and Itoklanoz relative to our natures as well.

Robert Curran: With respect to what's possible and what's not possible?

Keith Buzzell: Exactly, because Hassein speaks at the very end, coming out of the Djameechoonatra, opening "Form and Sequence," there is that which is impossible for man and that is much of what brings him to his sadness.

Bert Sharp: I was going to comment on - it sort of struck me - that in regard to the education, it relates very much to the form and sequence of the obligolnian strivings. You have to satisfy the first two and then you begin to start on the third which would be the second phase of education.

Robert Curran: Just one thing in closing, with the fourteen items that are referenced as an addendum, extracts from the text, a form of repetition saying essentially the same thing pertaining to the strangeness of our reason, you get an idea of what magnitude is coming across on that subject.

Beyond the Life-Death Antagonism: Prayer and Compassion in the Gurdjieff Hymns

Wim Van Dullemen, W.J.J.M.

In 1968 I met John Bennett, which was to have a decisive influence in my life, and became a member of the French 'Foundation'. I played the piano for the 'movements' classes of Solange Claustres for 13 years. In 1970 my membership ended. Although I have been independent since, I am still in regular contact with Mme Claustres and have organized seminars - open to all - for her in '95 and '96 in Amsterdam.

Wim Van Dullemen made important contributions to the 1997 Conference under the titles:

Gurdjieff's Law of Octaves and Harry Mulisch's Canon.
Examples of the Law of Three and Seven in the Music of Gurdjieff/de Hartmann.

Wim Van Dullemen was introduced by Michael Smyth.

Beyond the Life-Death Antagonism: Prayer and Compassion in the Gurdjieff Hymns

I first thank the organisers for the opportunity to play here the music of Gurdjieff and de Hartmann for, as they say, kindred souls. It is always special when you can share this music in Work-context.

For this presentation I have two aims:

The first is to give a brief of the little that is actually known about this music. I will try to recapitulate the basic facts.

Second I am going to give my personal interpretation. So there will be a mix consisting of facts on one hand and subjective interpretation on the other, 'facts and fantasies' if you like.

The title of my presentation means to say that this music comes from a source that is not dependent upon the life-death antagonism. Life and death completely annihilate one another and in this duality there can be no meaning. Somewhere in this music there is a reverberation that is not caught in this deadly trap.

Before I will play the first example I would like you to prepare yourselves by realising two small things:

All & Everything Conference 1998

Thing one. In the western musical tradition something has gone wrong. Due to the 'wiseacreing' of the late romantics such as Paganini and the like, people have got the idea that the performer or composer is active and the listener passive. The listeners are the grey, anonymous, mass that fills up concert halls and consumes CD 's, while only the performers or composer are `special'.

That's crap. Any serious composer composes for listeners. The listener provides a necessary link in the creative chain of the musical impulse by completing the composition with the sharing of the composer's vision by the listener. So I would like you to relax, but at the same time to contain yourself and to be *face to face* with the music. Face the music as a responsible person. Don't think in yourself: 'I have no musical education so I cannot understand music'. Again that's crap. You are a human being. That is enough to understand music to the very bone.

Thing two: Depict to yourself the inner attitude out of which the musical impulse flows. In the area of the world where I was born we had a saying:

'A man (meaning in my mother-language both man and woman) that sings is a good man'. I could give a long intellectual talk about the creation of music, but this saying formulates the basic process. Every human being that makes music starts from the most simple and honest point where he or she is in harmony with life and wants to express it's flow.

This is a point of harmony that a rational or mechanical man will never be able to understand. All true composers and the whole 'cast' - if I may say so- of musicians know that this is true. A man alone that sings is a good man. It is a natural but important thing for him, and maybe for the world also. A woman singing for herself and her children in the kitchen while preparing the food; that's a good woman and an important event.

So I don't care if Gurdjieff is an impostor or a second coming of Christ. His music has the true and simple sound that characterises a valuable and above all - like the saying defined - good man. That's as simple as it is!

Please realise in yourselves those two simple things while I am going to play a hymn for you. A very peculiar piece. Almost no one plays it and those that recorded it did not understand it very well. For many of you it will be the first time to hear it.

(A 4 minute musical example…)

The most interesting question for me is: where does this music come from?

What state of mind and what state of feeling created it? From where did it originate? In my presentation last year I had two pieces that were clear in the sense that a mental representation of their possible meaning could be given, but this hymn is much more difficult to understand. I can't say much more about it than that it sounds as if coming from a long distance, almost as if the

Beyond the Life-Death Antagonism: Prayer and Compassion in the Gurdjieff Hymns

composer is looking down at us from beyond our atmosphere but despite this distance we feel there is an enormous concern.

Coming back to the basic facts of this music; this piece is typical first of all because it is written for the piano; the whole oeuvre of about 300 compositions was composed for this instrument. Perhaps some scores for orchestra were made, but to my knowledge these have not survived. The length is also characteristic. Most pieces are 3 minutes at most. This musical legacy could be called a collection of valuable *miniatures*.

By the way whatever you say about this music, whatever characteristics you give, will never even approach the compelling impression that it creates on a sensitive listener. As an analogy; you can describe and put together all the details of a face one by one, but that will never create a human face.

Some people have told me that it brings to mind the works of Erik Satie, the well known French composer, but to me that similarity is only superficial. The only composer I know of that has anything to do with this music is Bela Bartok. Bartok, probably this centuries greatest classical composer, uses the same harmonic solutions in his conversion from Oriental material to the Western key. Some of his compositions therefore are remarkably close to Gurdjieff's.

Most of you will know how this music used to be composed: Gurdjieff called for De Hartmann, whenever he was ready to compose something, and played the basic melody with one finger on the piano, or just hummed it. Then he gave the rhythm, the harmonics and De Hartmann, being a trained and talented composer, wrote it down on the spot.

Basically the Gurdjieff/De Hartmann works can be divided into several main groups. First of all the material that is clearly related to folk origin. That means songs he heard in his youth or during his travels.

Now I imagine that this musical material was simply remembered. Let us take a simple piece like this:

(2 minutes of music…)

This is the main theme, very simple, very beautiful, it is called ' Kurd melody from Isfahan'.

(music continued....)

Perhaps a particular night during his travels in Persia came up in his mind, when this song was sung... and he remembered the melody…..it sounds like an echo from a distant place and time…..

(music continued....)

So this melody, sung in the orient during the last century was remembered and he instructed De Hartmann to write it down. We don't know exactly where the authentic folk music ends and 'Gurdjieff' begins in these folk-type compositions, but basically they stem from folk-origin.

The vogue in ethnomusicology these days is to pick up a portable tape or DAT-recorder and record some unknown tribe. The clue is that here there was no tape-recorder. The melodies were taken in by a *human consciousness* and remembered out of that.

Have you noted that in a group of people when somebody relates an event that he himself witnessed, this makes a much stronger impression than if others, who only saw it on television or read about it, talk about it ? The same mechanism makes this section of Gurdjieff's music so impressive. It is a very important part of his oeuvre, a treasure house of over fifty melodies that probably all vanished in the locations where they were once heard.

The second part of the musical works come already from inside the walls of religious communities or brotherhoods; the 'sayyid chants' and dervish dances and songs. The build-up of many of these follows a pattern that still exists in certain Oriental traditions; a long recitative, one melody without a harmonic accompaniment, going on a fairly long time followed by a short, conclusive, rhythmic statement. The 'sayyid' cycle consists of pure master-pieces for the piano, one could say that here the experiment of presenting Oriental material in a transcription for the piano, that most Western of all instruments, is phenomenal; the nostalgia, the loneliness, the emotional impact is very strong in the recitative...

(musical example...)

after this recitative it seems as if the community answers; for one part they confirm the emotion, from the other hand they introduce a rhythmic element to create a different perspective, they really help that way, a beautiful combination of question and answer....

(music continued....)

The third group of compositions is the 'hymns' and then as the fourth component the music composed as accompaniment to the 'movements'; with this last segment we will deal tomorrow.
The hymns sound in general simple and quite familiar, but they have a particular 'taste' that makes them strikingly original. It is like a familiar landscape, but here and there are strange sounds that keep you alert and seem to lead you, step by step. A good example of this procedure is the hymn called 'Hadji-Asvatz-Troov' that is entirely based on only three chords, the basic three songs of every simple or popular song, or even the blues; tonic, sub-tonic and dominant...

(music continued....)

Here is the initial statement of these basic chords...
but the piece goes on a long time and sounds new and important all the time....

Beyond the Life-Death Antagonism: Prayer and Compassion in the Gurdjieff Hymns

(music continued....)

that is because these three basic chords are played in such a way, with very slight but effective modifications, that the attention is constantly mobilised. Despite it's simplicity the composition creates a whole spectrum of peace and tolerance as well as awareness.
Now I show you another interesting example of a hymn…..

(music continued....)

Did you hear that in the beginning a vibration was created, like a strong quest?

For me this is the vibration of a conscience, the same sort of conscience that we have but only much stronger, much more, as they say, trans-substantiated and therefore able to *Respond*...

This brings me to the title of my presentation because I think that precisely through this 'reverberation of conscience' this music, as a 'third force' if you wish, not only escapes the antagonism between life and death but creates a balanced spectrum of forces.

A couple of days ago I saw on the streets of a big city a man dying. Actually it was a nightmare to see a human being - it was a beggar - dying out on the street in total lack of dignity, of human dignity. It could be you or me, this dying man.

A strong spasm , the forebode of death, passed over his face that, white as parchment, radiated pureness, perhaps caused by a suffering beyond our comprehension. In a strange but very real conversion it suddenly seemed as if he was the only living human being in a street filled with shadows and automats, I being one of those. I prayed.

'The first shall be the last, and the last the first'.

This experience made me feel ashamed that I had chosen the life and death antagonism as a title . When you see death in the face philosophy is impossible. A life and death situation is very acute.

Andrè Breton, the great French surrealist, wrote about death:

'Has man been given a place under the sun only to suffocate there in the skin of an animal?'

Gurdjieff has been reported to answer a question about death by saying that 'no one who has not actually died himself can know anything about it'. After a silence he added: But there is another way of dying, *in life.*'

This last addition represents to me an important clue to understand his music.

But first I will tell you how I tried to study the 'life and death'-relation in music in general. The first type of music that comes to mind is the Requiem-format. But in a requiem it are the living ones giving their grief for the dying ones. In much music, not usually associated with this theme, the problem is expressed much deeper, for instance in Mozart's piano Concerto's. All Bruckner's Symphonies sound like the struggle of life and death. Bruckner was a small man, vilified by his contemporaries as an idiot. But in his symphonies you feel the enormous forces of this permanent struggle for man.

Now for me there is third way, after those of the requia and the music dealing with the struggle between life and death, in which music can be relevant to our theme. I can only describe this to you in the form of the following analogy.

An example, perhaps for you not expected, of this third way is the playing of a negro blues-pianist from Chicago, who died in 1951, called Jimmy Yancey. His playing, that I heard on the radio when I was young, was the most decisive musical influence that I have ever had. Not only was his touch on the keyboard putting into life an unheard strong vibration but the slow, deep quietness sounded as if it was not coming from the earth at all, but from much father away.

Yancey had in his repertoire a 'death'-theme-piece, probably his most compelling composition. This was in B-flat...

(music continued....)

But later in his life he used the exact same music in a more philosophical way and then he called it: 'At the window'. This title tells me that he was no longer directly involved in life, but rather looked at it, as if from a distance.

This is an important lead; to realise that there might exist a form of music, for instance some hymns from Gurdjieff, but also in religious and other music, that has been made by a composer that describes life as seen from another view-point. From, as they say, *the other side*.

(musical examples of several hymns are now played with comments on specific chords and compositional procedures…)

I have now come to the end of my presentation and I can, after the above speculations, only repeat that, as regards formal facts, we hardly know anything. To give you another example, the first hymn I played for you has no time indication, so we don't know in what time it should be performed. We don't even know the title. It is sometimes said that 'those who know, know' but from a historical point of view this is of no help.

A last interesting, point is related to the discussion we had last year about the hymns that were meant as accompaniment to the reading of Beelzebub. At that time I knew only a limited number of examples; for instance, Hadji-Asvatz-Troov, The Resurrection of Jesus Christ and the 'I Am -

Beyond the Life-Death Antagonism: Prayer and Compassion in the Gurdjieff Hymns

Father Son-Day Night-Yesterday Tomorrow' that was played with the 'Ashiata Sheimash'-chapter. Recently I read a copy of an old article, published in the New Republic in June 1929. It is difficult to read, written by Mr. Zigrosser.

Paul Beekman Taylor: I can get you a fresh copy. (Copy included in Appendix 1)

Wim van Dullemen: Actually this is one of the best articles about the music that I have read so far. Interestingly it states that the hymns were definitely planned as a accompaniment to Beelzebub, an emotional version of the intellectual version in the book, making the two complimentary to each other.

This is historical evidence, based on talks with Gurdjieff and Orage at that time and I have never come across this so clearly and concisely. It might be that this was a plan, but has never been worked out in detail.

Gurdjieff obviously never planned the music to be published during his lifetime or after his death. For the movements, performed in Carnegy Hall, he had a different approach. But I have sometimes the impression that the music was more intimate, although with a defined purpose, to be played for those that formed, so to say, the family.

Anyhow I thank you for your attention.

© Copyright 1998 - Wim van Dullemen - All Rights Reserved

Third Opern Forum - What is Authentic Form of the Work

Facilitator: Dr. Andrew Rawlinson

Dr. Andrew Rawlinson has been Lecturer in Buddhism at the University of Lancaster, England, and visiting professor at the University of California at Santa Barbara. Now retired from teaching and living in France, he remains an active researcher and writer with a long standing interest in the Gurdjieffian field. His lengthy study *The book of Enlightened Masters: Western Teachers in Eastern Traditions* (Open Court Publishing Company, 1997) contains a significant module on The Work.

***

Andrew Rawlinson: We are all wilting, I feel. Third day. I'm impressed by your determination.

As I understand it, and I'm speaking as an ex-scholar, now retired, I'm here to throw out a few ideas that may spark a few of yours. And that's it.

So why have I chosen this topic? What, even, is my contact with the Work that I should ask this question? There is a history behind it, which I will give, because I think it might provide a context for my interest.

I went to Cambridge to read English Literature but I quickly changed to Philosophy - because you don't have to go to lectures, you can just make it all up. So I studied British empiricism (Locke, Berkeley, Hume); philosophy of logic (Russell, Hibbert, Gödel, Wittgenstein), that sort of thing. And while I was there, I came across my own teacher, Maharaj Charan Singh, who came from north India, and I was initiated by him. I've followed that path ever since - that's thirty-plus years. Some hiccups. But basically I've been doing the practice from that day to this.

My interest, therefore, was the nature of the human condition - the only thing that *is* of any interest. And I was lucky enough to go on a Ph.D. programme at a British university, which enabled me to study Buddhism - specifically, early Indian Buddhism. I learnt Sanskrit and did some quite technical investigations into manuscripts: their forms, why they change, the relationship between them, how reliable they are. That kind of thing. And I do believe - I've always believed - that scholarly work does have to have a certain irreducible core of technical expertise.

But it wasn't just genitive plurals in Buddhist Hybrid Sanskrit, interesting though I find that. It was: What are these texts conveying? What is their meaning? What is their significance? These are magnificent works - like the *Lotus Sutra*. And when I started to teach, I had to get over these ideas so that people could access them. So I got interested in the tradition. And the dimensions of a tradition are very large, very rich and quite amazing.

How to you **enter** a tradition? Lots of different answers, depending on the tradition you're talking about.

What **way of life** does that tradition inculcate and expect?

What qualities are required in order to follow it and participate in it? Qualities like chastity, investigation, calmness, courage. There's a long list.

What is the **teaching**? I mean, the word 'teaching', you could write a 400-page book on it without any difficulty whatever. Subdivisions of the term 'teaching' **ontology**, **cosmology**, **anthropology** (the nature of man), **soteriology** (the nature of salvation, liberation, realisation - you interpret it how you like). There are several 400-page books in each one of these.

What is **transmission**? How does the tradition transmit itself?

What **spiritual practice** - or just ordinary practice if you want to miss out the word 'spiritual' - exists within a tradition?

What **states of awareness** - oh ghastly phrase! but I can't think- of another without making it so specific that it's misleading - are significant, aimed for, and so forth?

And what is the **state of realisation**? What's the point? What's the aim? What's the attainment?

That's just the notion of a tradition and its form.

Then there's the question of how traditions change, which of course they do. And there's the question of what changes does a tradition accept? And what does it reject? And what does it resist kicking and screaming but ends up accepting anyway? How does this occur?

Now all of this can be applied just to Buddhism in India. The next move is: Buddhism goes to China. A magnificent tradition enters another culture - an extraordinary story. And huge changes occur because of what the Chinese expect and what they see when Buddhism appears, and what Buddhists see when they come from India. And they're not seeing each other very clearly, as you might imagine. It took at least four centuries for Buddhism to get into gear in China.

Then you have Japan and Tibet. You can see the gears just keep winding up.

Then there is Buddhism back in India and how it is affected by other traditions there, including Hinduism.

And I'm doing all of this - with varying degrees of expertise. I don't know Chinese. If I were here amongst a group of Chinese scholars, I'd be out of my depth in three sentences. Yet I wanted to investigate these things in order to understand the context of what I do know and which I can read in the original, and which I can investigate with some degree of ability.

And then, of course, these traditions come to the West: Buddhism, Hinduism, Sufism - from Thailand, Burma, Tibet, Japan, Persia, North Africa. And what happens when they come here? They meet what is already here: a form of Western esotericism, going back to the Greeks, or to the Renaissance, or to Theosophy and Steiner, depending on how you look at it.

And in amongst all this, which is an extremely broad canvas, we have the Work, which I would certainly consider a tradition. So all the questions I raised earlier would apply to it: What are its dimensions? How does it change? What influences have come to bear upon it? How do people assimilate what it teaches?

There are some questions that can be applied to traditions *per se*, which can, in my view, be applied to the Work. What is essential to a tradition and what is not? Can these essentials be found elsewhere in other traditions and teachings? I would like to suggest that all traditions have to ask these questions. I would also like to suggest that traditions don't ask these questions unless they have to. I'm not trying to put pressure on anybody to ask them. I'm just saying that they are natural questions and will arise by themselves when someone in a tradition comes across something that hits them in some way. And I would like to suggest that in order to answer those questions you have to go beyond the limits of the vocabulary of your own tradition, because if you don't, you are effectively dragging in the other tradition, the thing that's hit you, and sieving it through what you've already got. I'm not saying that it can't be done. I'm not even saying that it shouldn't be done. But if that is *all* one does, then it's a kind of damage limitation exercise. When one studies how traditions develop and change, one always finds that when someone says, 'Hello, this makes sense but I don't quite understand it, I don't quite know where it's coming from', then you have to extend your vocabulary in order to absorb what's been brought to your attention.

So that's my starting point. Now we come to the Work, and I want to ask three questions. Actually, I want to ask four questions but the first one is slightly different from the other three. And it's this - it's a rhetorical question: 'Is there anyone here who believes that he or she is not involved in an authentic form of the work?' And there is a sub-question connected with that one: 'Do people here think that everybody else who asserts that they are involved in the Work *is* involved in an authentic form of it?'

These are obvious questions to ask. And I must say right now: this is not Eight for content, seven for style (*Cries of 'Boring!'*). I'm not saying that you shouldn't do that. But I really do not want to set groups within the ramshackle edifice that is the Work ticking each other off in terms of excellence and authenticity. I'm just saying that these are natural questions to ask.

Then there are the three other questions. The first is: 'What is transmission in the Work?' The second is: 'Is there such a thing as Work or Gurdjieffian orthodoxy?' And the third is: 'What elements from outside the Work, from wherever they may come, are acceptable in it?'

I would like at this point to hand out the sheet, 'Associations with Gurdjieff'. Now this is so incomplete that I'm embarrassed. But in a sense it doesn't matter because the question I'm asking is about transmission. From whom does transmission in the Work proceed and to whom has it gone? And what is the significance of that process? Now I'm absolutely not trying to impose a particular model of how transmission within the Work operates. I know that the example I've got on this piece of paper - the sort of lemma which applies to the kings and queens of England, where the oldest son becomes king and then the eldest daughter becomes queen, and so on - is too hard edged for the way transmission operates within the Work. So I'm actually not asking the question, 'Have I got these people in the right place?' Rather, I'm asking, 'Could a model of transmission in the work be represented in principle in any way at all - in any way that you might choose to do it?' You can have a piece of paper the size of Iceland. It can be three-dimensional. You can have on it every single individual who has ever been involved in the Work and put them in any relationship you like. I'm not restricting how it could be done. I'm just asking, 'Could how the Work has been transmitted be represented in such a way that it would satisfy you?' ('You' being anybody here.)

The reason I'm asking this question is to clarify what happens when the Work is made available. And it doesn't have to be made available in the same way by everybody, whether they are on this piece of paper or could be in a version that you would yourself come up with. It doesn't have to be that the way Gurdjieff made it available is the same as someone else - let's take somebody who's dead - Ouspensky - made it available. I think most people would say that they didn't make it available in the same way. So I'm not prejudging that at all. I'm simply saying that transmission does occur and asking, 'How?'

Because that leads to the next question as to whether there is such a thing as orthodoxy. And I'm including orthopraxy, right practice, in orthodoxy (which means 'right view' or 'right doctrine'). So the question as to what is orthodox would include: Should there be movements? Have there got to be movements? What is essential to the Work in order that one could say that it was transmitted at all? Would it have to include the *Tales*? Would it have to include the music or group work?

I'm not even proposing answers to these questions. I'm simply trying to pose larger order questions. That is: Are there necessary elements in the Work, or a set of necessary elements, such that some of them would have to be present, otherwise what we would be talking about would be the transmission of something other than the Work, however excellent?

All & Everything Conference 1998

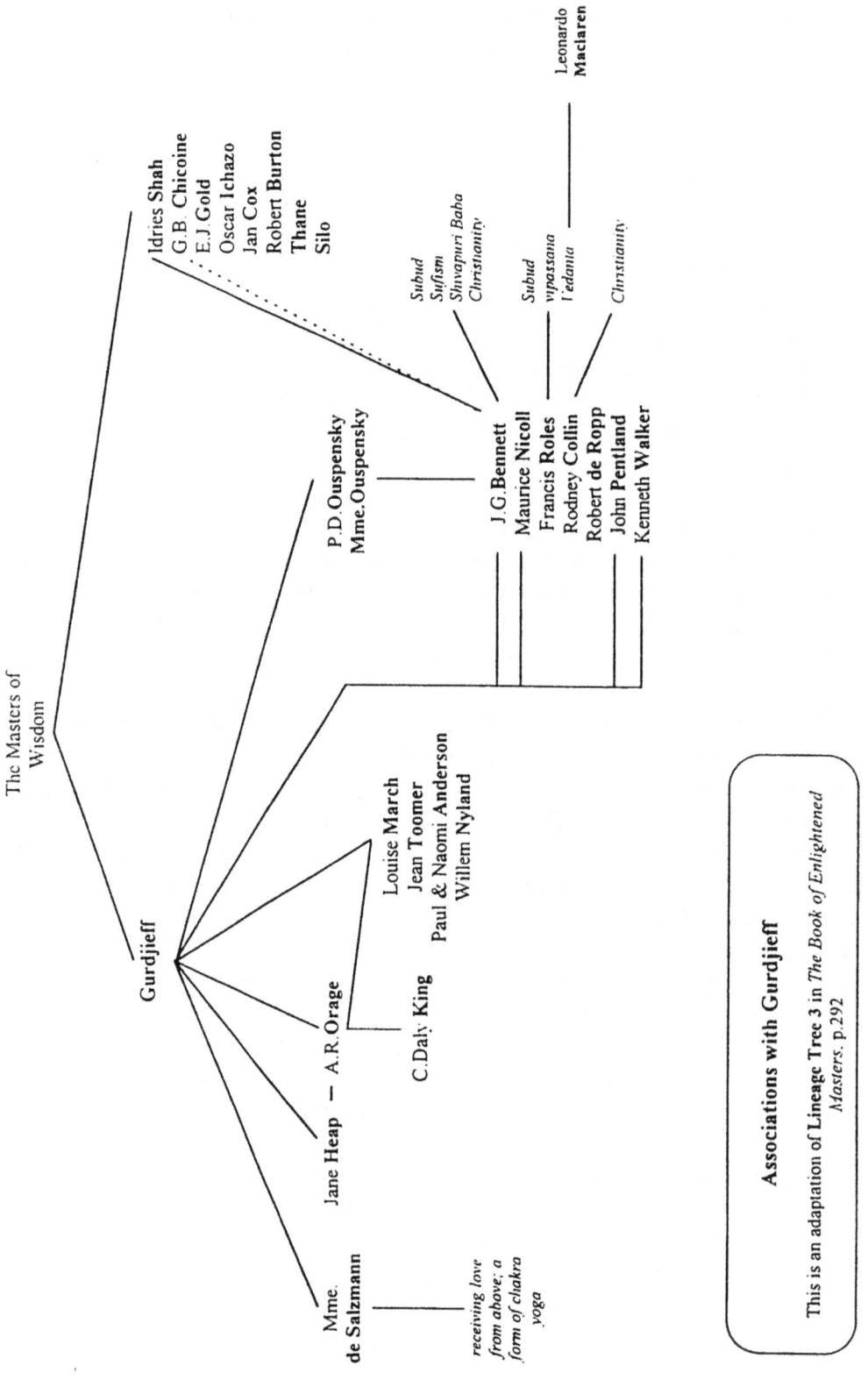

Third Open Forum - What is Authentic Form of the Work

Now transmission is a complex matter and there are lots and lots of ways in which it's done. But I'd like to make a distinction because it might help later discussion: between formal transmission and authenticity. For example, someone becomes a doctor by a certain formal process. Either that person has gone through that process and is an MD or he or she hasn't and isn't. Now if a person is an MD and can quite properly use those letters, they may not behave and act in a way that is acceptable. There are doctors who are proper doctors but who do their doctoring in such a way that that are struck off. They are not competent.

You may or may not know that the opposite also happens. Every year in Britain - and I'm sure it happens in America, which is much more esoteric - there are a few people, usually surgeons, who do operations in accepted hospitals but who have no qualifications whatever. They are simply conmen. (I don't think there are any women who do this but there might be.) And the interesting thing is that those who are working with them, who *are* qualified surgeons and MDs, don't know that these people are not qualified. Because what they do is OK. And then one day there's a phone call: 'That Dr. Smith - he's a welder. Or he was the last time he had a job. He's just filling in.' And this guy is never paid. He just turns up, says hello to the doorman, puts on the white coat and does the operation. But he's not legitimate. Yet if you look at what he does, he's alright. And then next to him, theoretically, you can have a real MD who's drunk. Hardly authentic. Struck off. Goodbye, Charlie.

So there are four possibilities. There are people who are **legitimate** - that is, they have been formally acknowledged to have the right to do something - and they are also **authentic** - they fulfil the criteria that people should behave in a certain way. Then there are those who have been formally transmitted in some way **(legitimate)** but are not **authentic** - the drunken surgeon. There are people who are not **legitimate** but are **authentic**: they can actually do it but they haven't received formal transmission. And then there is the unfortunate fourth group who are neither **legitimate** nor **authentic**: the welders who actually look like welders when they're doing the operation. So they don't last very long.

It's interesting that different traditions have different ways of assessing these. Some traditions insist on very, very strict formal transmission. Others say that all that is required is that the person produces authentic results. If someone is producing something authentic, it doesn't matter what their pedigree is.

Now, I'm not going to mention any names because I don't want to. But there are people within the Work who could be said to make the claim that they are authentic but don't claim any pedigree or lineage or formal transmission whatever. There are others who have been given permission to teach - whatever that means, and I know it's contentious - who are later judged or evaluated to have gone off on a tangent that is no longer acceptable, and who are thus in a sense judged to be inauthentic (whatever that may mean).

All & Everything Conference 1998

I think there are quite a lot of people here who could give examples that would fulfil the criteria that I've just given. I'm not asking these questions in order to start a bun fight. I'm saying that you *have* to ask these questions to know where you are yourself.

So we come to the last question, which concerns what is acceptable from outside the tradition. On this sheet there are a number of influences written in italic which are connected with certain individuals. If I've made mistakes, by all means correct me; I accept that this could have been done differently. What I'm trying to get over is this immense range of influences which certain people who could be said to be within the Work have accepted as being authentic or of use to them.

We have the one connected to Madame de Salzmann. People here knew her and worked with her and will know more than I do. From J. G. Bennett, a very unusual man, we have four different influences. He wasn't the only one who was interested in Subud or went into Sufism. He was the only one who made the connection with Shivapuri Baba - at least in the sense that everyone else in the Work came to that teacher through Bennett, as far as I know. And he wasn't the only one to be attracted by a certain form of Christianity.

We have *vipassana*, insight meditation, which is self-remembering - *smriti* or *sati* in Indian languages - which influenced Francis Roles. We have a version of Vedanta at the School of Economic Science under Leonardo MacLaren. There must be someone here who knows this story - though it doesn't matter if you don't.

All I would say in conclusion is that I've studied a lot of groups - I'm not trying to pull rank by saying that I know more than any of you just because I've done that, but I have done it and over a long period of time; it was my profession and I have some training in it - and no group has this range of influences from outside itself which have been considered in the way that people in the Work have. It's very, very unusual. So I finish by asking myself this question: Is this great range because people in the Work are more open, more generous? Is it because the Work really is different, even unique? Or is it, as has been mooted by people in the Work itself, because it is incomplete?

* * *

James Moore: In a small booklet by Henri Tracol, he posed the question, 'What is unique or specific to the Gurdjieff Work?' And having posed the question, answered by saying that it was Gurdjieff himself. And certainly there seems to be there a kind of fulcrum or epicentre: that all authenticity within this very broad range has as its concomitant some living and fruitful attempt to find a relationship with that man, to his being and to the dispensation that he offered. And it is certainly clear that radiating from that there are many segments. But I feel that if that kind of dimension can be kept in mind, then the schematic that you propose and the questions that you raise, albeit perfectly legitimate on a certain level, are in a way eclipsed by a kind of inner criterion or critique: that this question of authenticity is cast back to us as individuals. Not whether

Third Open Forum - What is Authentic Form of the Work

we adhere to a particular lineage or posit our endeavours in a particular set of groups, but in the minute by minute effort to find some authenticity in us, in our relationship to Gurdjieff and to his legominisms, his book, *Beelzebub*, that extraordinary vehicle, the movements. It's there that the question of authenticity fluctuates amongst us all, of whatever tribe. Moment by moment, one of us will be in an authentic relationship with that epicentre; in another moment, we will betray it. Any kind of classification is null and void, in my opinion.

Nicholas Tereshchenko: I must first correct a word which is completely incorrect and in my opinion, very important. I was in a group presided over my Madame de Salzmann for 9 years and I have never heard her use the word 'love'. She has always insisted that there is a force coming from above but she never called it love. It is capable of entering us only when we have the proper relationship between what she sometimes called 'brain', sometimes ' mental', sometimes 'intellect', and the body. And she insisted that this relationship could only be done if one had the proper inner and outer attitude - attitude of the body, attitude of the mind. And only when this force entered, it brought with it an emotion that is otherwise not available to us. `Love' is a stupid word anyway because it means so many things to many people. So I do feel that that should be corrected. She never spoke of love at all - always of a higher force or a force coming from above.

Robert Bryce: Surely the criterion for being authentic must be the results in our practice of the Work, in achieving what the Work is supposed to be about, which is to wake ourselves up.

John Scullion: As I understand it, and I may be wrong, it may not be entirely the truth, the reason one comes to the Work and the reason the Work exists and is available, is to awaken conscience in man. That, I think, is what matters. To refer to the case where someone, spuriously and from outside a tradition, with no lineage - the welder who performs surgery - if that person is authentic then he will seek to reconcile himself with the transmission that does exist. I think the essential factor is the awakening of conscience in individuals and in mankind.

Andrew Rawlinson: I am of course aware of the points that have been made. But first of all, the people who are judges to be outside will themselves claim that they're not outside. And they will also say that what they are doing is to wake themselves up and to wake up those who are around them. Take the Christians as an example. All groups who call themselves Christian use the term for a reason. The Mormons and the Christian Scientists think that they are following the teachings of Christ. The terminology is used by all of them. The question is, do they mean the same by it and how did they come to use it the way that they do? To simply say that the test of whether someone is an authentic Christian is that they are committed to Christ or that they accept Christ as saviour, or any other terms that you want to use - it doesn't advance the matter. Because people can use exactly the same phrase but not mean the same by it.

John Scullion: The essential thing is to return to Mr. Gurdjieff and to understand what that dispensation consists in. And it would be a matter of whether the person or the group or the school will recognise that necessity.

All & Everything Conference 1998

Keith Buzzell: It struck me, especially in the last reference you made, that perhaps a significant aspect that would be useful to keep in mind is conviction, and the different forms of conviction. Because we all stand, in one relationship or another, convinced that we-are legitimate or connected, that this is authentic, and so forth. And perhaps what is as important is the question of the basis of that conviction. We could spend the next 5 days talking about that without seeing that each of us has come to a certain conviction within ourselves that is infused with that distinctive emotional quality that cannot speak and yet gives the force to it. So that whatever we have taken in sensorially or whatever we have placed in a logical sequence, once infused with that feeling, we are, without impartiality, stuck with it.

Sy Ginsburg: Even though I've been in groups for 10 years connected with Madame de Salzmann, the Work was transmitted to me, as I've mentioned here before, by Madhava Ashish, whose name doesn't appear on this sheet at all. And yet there have been an unusual number of well-known Gurdjieffians, from Olga de Hartmann to Dr. Courtney-Myers, who seem to have made their way up there. I don't know what this is really all about but maybe there's only one real religious tradition, which is what I feel from the *Tales* Gurdjieff speaks about, and he's transmitting that tradition in the 20th Century.

Bert Sharp: This is very difficult. I'm convinced that I was given the Work before I came across it. Very briefly, by the time I was about three, I could just climb the stairs. At the top of the stairs, near the top, there was a picture of three dead 1914-18 war soldiers, leaning against a tank, and an enormous Angel enveloping the whole scene. And I began to notice that at times the Angel left the picture and would follow me around. And I always had this impression that there was an Angel near my shoulder. I later realized that this was a projection, but as I grew up there was one when I was doing physical work, running, I became a cross country runner. This was the Moving Angel. And when I was upset, afraid, there was another one, the Feeling Angel. And there was another one when I was doing my sums, Intellect. And then when I was about 38 or so, I began to really look for real meaning and purpose. And I tried all sorts of things, looked at all sorts of ideas. And I developed for myself a series of exercises which I used to indulge in before going to bed, trained myself to fall asleep without losing consciousness. And I was doing this one particular night and as usual I entered the dream, awake, so it was like a lucid dream. And the three Angels assembled and appeared to be relating to one another. And then there was a voice in the dream that said "Ah! We were wondering when you were going to appear". And a fourth Angel appeared which seemed to envelop the three. And then there was nothing but light, light within and light without. And the all pervading voice said "He has come to the end of his life which will now begin". So these if you like, were the Centres, Moving, Feeling and Intellect. And when they all came together as a group there was something higher. And it was as if I knew everything but could understand little of it. The feeling of this lasted two or three days. And then about three months later, a friend gave me the little book, "The Psychology of Man's Possible Evolution", and there it all was, the same basic structure. And I have since found this structure elsewhere. Now maybe I am lying and maybe I am remembering it wrongly, but that is what is for me, and I have been convinced ever since that it is all to do with the way we are constructed and realizing our possibilities, putting ourselves in order. And that is the Work. Thank you.

Third Open Forum - What is Authentic Form of the Work

Toddy Smythe: My feeling is that Mr. Gurdjieff threw his seed out, so to speak, as Robert Ennis said, and I think genuinely through any vehicle, whether *Beelzebub* or the movements, that he entrusted the teaching to whomever came across it. The way that I can verify that is that all of these different lines have popped up. Somebody in a group a year ago gave a lovely image of a mountain and we're all at the base of the mountain. All these different lines are around the very broad, broad base. But as each of us is committed to whatever line, by accident or miracle or design, we ended up in, we ascend. And as we ascend, we get closer and closer. And it seems to me that whatever Mr. Gurdjieff's conviction - not in the ordinary sense of our conviction ... that this teaching was needed at the time, whomever it touched. The people who were touched have a certain trueness to whatever seed they got, and through that, as we go deeper, it seems to me we get closer - and not just in the Gurdjieff teaching but in all teachings.

Andrew Rawlinson: I did actually want to say, and I hope you don't mind me saying it - as a university lecturer, I've got into certain habits and I used to do this all the time, though I can see that it may not be appropriate in this particular context - but there hasn't been anything that's been said, and I've been to all the talks, which I haven't heard elsewhere. That's my job, my interest, to go elsewhere. Apart from specifics, like the terminology that comes from Gurdjieff - but that's true of all groups, that they have something specific: there's something specific to the Pali canon; to Shankara, to the *Mathnawi*, and so forth - but apart from that, everything that I've heard, I've heard elsewhere. Now you might say, `Well, obviously.' But I actually don't know whether it is obvious to you.

Adam Petts: I'd just like to say something that a teacher said to me. And this was at a stage when, as people have expressed, in the enthusiasm or the search or the quest, one begins to look for meaning and purpose, explore various avenues and schools, be they Eastern or Western. And I remember attending a certain training of meditation. During the course of meditation a discourse was given: put yourself wholly in this practice, of mindfulness, of awareness, and give this technique your fullness, to experiment with it. If you find that the teaching, these ideas are for you, be compassioned for all beings, for all three brains in other beings, but beware of digging shallow holes in search of water. But when you find a teaching that resonates, then dig deep and work with that to realise within your own consciousness, your own being, the fruits of that. Which reminds me of the quote from the Bible: `By their fruits ye shall know them'. And in this sense, true expression of the values of the potential within any human being - these values of compassion, awareness, of a fullness of life, to be fully and truly present to all the richness of our existence, the miracle of our existence in this moment, and to strive, the obligolnian strivings, in whatever context ... I think that's the link we have, whatever title, school or lineage. We stand as human beings, and as Mr. Gurdjieff said, if we could have that one thing crystallised in us constantly - to be constantly consciously aware that I myself am subject to death and that everyone that I lay my eyes upon is subject to death - that would wipe out this insanity of reciprocal destruction. But I feel a great shared sense, whatever contradictions we share, of the Work, and the fact that we are gathered here in this circle tonight.

All & Everything Conference 1998

Harry Bennett: Could you qualify what you said before? Because I didn't understand what you meant when you said that it's your job to travel round ...

Andrew Rawlinson: You mean what did I mean by 'It's my job'?

Harry Bennett: No, when you said that you've been all these different places and you haven't heard anything different than you've heard here. I don't have enough context to understand.

Marlena Buzzell: Didn't you say that 'Everything I've heard here, I've heard elsewhere. I don't know if it's obvious to you'?

Andrew Rawlinson: The context is that I was someone who taught and researched in Indian traditions and in these traditions as they have appeared in the West, over a very long period of time. That research took me to - there's a long list of names - Swami Nityananda, Muktananda ...

Harry Bennett: OK. So you're speaking in terms of the other traditions that you've investigated. And you haven't heard anything in the Gurdjieff tradition that you haven't heard somewhere else.

Andrew Rawlinson: That's right.

Harry Bennett: Just here today or in your whole experience with the Gurdjieff Work?

Andrew Rawlinson: Generally speaking. What I mean by that is that I can see a form of words - and not just words for the sake of words - that someone within the Work and someone in another tradition, both of whom had goodwill towards the other and towards the excellence of the other tradition, could use in order to describe what both of them are trying to do. Is that OK? Is it clear?

Marlena Buzzell: So do you mean that the methodology may be different but the aims and purposes are the same?

Andrew Rawlinson: Let me give an example. Terms like 'being', 'accepting responsibility', 'struggle', 'courage', honesty', which are floating around in various subdiscourses, have a particular significance in one tradition or another. And I have been with people from different traditions who have been happy to use such terms to describe what each of them does and to acknowledge that the other one does the same. Not in every detail. There's a story that when Hazrat Inayat Khan, who was an Indian Sufi, first went to California, he met a Japanese Zen teacher who was living there, Nyogen Senzaki. They were introduced by an American called Samuel Lewis - recognised as teachers, masters in their separate traditions, Sufi and Zen, not normally regarded as talking the same language. There was an inner connection between them, and Lewis said that they went into Samadhi. So you have a Sufi teacher and a Zen teacher, and a Hindu term being used to explain the fact that they came together.

Third Open Forum - What is Authentic Form of the Work

That's an example of what I would call the authentic meeting of two true people. And it's simply a matter of what would be the way one would express that meeting of minds. You see, we've already got to qualify the word 'mind'. Do you understand what I'm trying to do here? It's really quite simple. It's just saying that there are no new moves - they've all been made. Speaking as someone who has practised in my own tradition, I could now give a talk using the vocabulary of Surat Shabd Yoga. I know that vocabulary because I've been in it for 30 years. I can also translate out of that vocabulary into a higher-order one - not `higher' in the sense of `superior' but higher because it's trying to cover a larger terrain - in which people can meet. So now to backtrack to what I said before. Because I've spent a lot of time with people who follow teachings, saying, `What do you do? What's the essence? Give it to me in one sentence' - and they give it, and then of course they have to flesh it out, so `Give it to me in five sentences, in twenty' - that I've learned from this process that ... like there are only five jokes. If I told you a good one now, you'd all laugh. But there are only five moves. That's it.

Ken Shear: I was wondering if in this sharing we have been engaged in, people are asked the question in their own vocabulary, if that could include the experience that Mr. Gurdjieff called his morning exercise. Picking up on your point about nothing being particularly unique, that is something that might represent some uniqueness. In the sharing of these exercises obviously if you are working in different traditions you will have meditations and exercises of each tradition. This could represent some uniqueness. I wonder if you are familiar with the morning exercises.

Andrew Rawlinson: There's a lot in there. The short answer is that I don't know the morning exercises. But the larger answer is that I don't know lots of different kinds of meditation - and actually I don't think you can do that. I don't think you can say, I'll be a Sufi for a weekend or for 6 months.' There is a question then as to how you can compare things if you don't know them from the inside. It's a natural question to ask and there are a lot of answers that could be given.

Ken Shear: I was just thinking that the exercises that were handed down would represent something different from the vocabulary.

Andrew Rawlinson: Yes. I'm going into lecturer mode now. The analogy that I tend to give in these circumstances is with natural history. An elephant, a mouse, a dolphin and a giraffe are all mammals. There's a way of understanding why that's so. When you tell children they just don't believe it. But you can show that the basic form is the same. That doesn't alter the fact that the elephant is the only mammal that feeds itself with its snout. It's unique. But of course it's not because it's a mammal.

John Perrott: I have a question. Actually it is a view but it is implicit in the present topic. If it were collectively seen to be true that somewhere close to the essence of the Work is a transformation somewhere that is seen to be true also with other forms of tradition, but I personally am actually sure of the transformation that occurs as one applies the Work. Why, other than for virtue of a psychological survey, would one put to the group of people involved in transformation and could therefore only know the answer to the question if that transformation were completed, as to what they considered to be an authentic form of the Work? Why would one do that?

Andrew Rawlinson: Why would I do it?

John Perrott: No. I can think of several good reasons why you'd do it because of your background. What can we see as an objective purpose in asking people who might not yet have met the essence of the Work, but who are on their way, as to their opinion of what is an authentic form of the Work? How would they know?

Andrew Rawlinson: Well, all I can answer to that is: I've lived in France for 5 years. I'm English - quite English - and I didn't understand a lot about England until I lived abroad. Now obviously in a sense I know more about England than people who are not English. But equally there's lots of stuff about England that I don't understand because I am English. Therefore, you have to know what it is to be English; you have to know where you are. And one of the ways you can find out where you are is by seeing that you could be elsewhere - and by seeing excellence elsewhere. Because when you see excellence elsewhere, it reflects back on what you consider to be excellence. That's the way I've actually done it in my life. And that's the basis of the questions I'm asking. Because I see excellence in the Work and I see excellence in other traditions. And my natural instinct is to say, `How do they work?'

Robert Ennis: You've asked a number of questions but to me the most important could be expressed in the following way: Is the Fourth Way going to be inclusive or exclusive? That is, is it only going to consider what might be called blood relations as authentic or will it also consider converts and adopted children? And I would say that the Fourth Way is particularly rich in that kind of diversity and so it has to be decided whether that is an obstacle. That is people who claim to be in the tradition who do not appear to be blood relations, or whether that is an obstacle.

Nicholas Tereshchenko: `What is an authentic form of *the* Work?' That obviously implies that we are only talking about Gurdjieff's Work; *the* work is Gurdjieff's Work, not the Work in any other tradition. Now the word `authentic' has two meanings. First of all, the meaning that you mentioned yourself: a lineage. If that is the case, there is only one lineage. Mr Gurdjieff chose Madam de Salzmann as his successor, and when Madame de Salzmann a couple of years before her death, was asked was she going to name a successor, she said, "Obviously my son". So from that literal point of view, the only authentic Work is the one which is decided by and personally approved of, Michel de Salzmann. But authentic has also got another meaning. Now I heard from a friend of mine, a psychiatrist, the following story. A family brought to him one of their members who was a cretin. Cretin in the medical sense is one born without a thyroid, and that was at the time when we did not yet recognise that, and did not have any way of treating it. And he insisted that he wanted to become a monk. And they wanted to persuade him that that was not a suitable life for him. And so they brought him to a psychiatrist to find out if there was any way they could get it into his head that he would not be fit to be a monk. And the psychiatrist asked him one question. "For whose sake do you want to be a monk? And after five minutes he answered "For

Third Open Forum - What is Authentic Form of the Work

God's sake". So the psychiatrist said, "He is authentically a religious man". Now in the same way `authentic', the word in the British tradition, must start with what Gurdjieff himself says is the first thing one must have. One must have an aim. Without an aim there is no Work. And once one has an aim, then one can find out what you need to achieve your aim, and is therefore good for you, and what prevents you from achieving your aim, and which is therefore evil and not good.

End of Session

The Organ Kundabuffer

Stuart Goodnick

Stuart Goodnick holds degrees in Physics from the California Institute of Technology and the University of California at Santa Cruz. He is a member of the teaching staff at Tayu Centre, a Fourth Way school in Sebastopol, CA, where he lectures, writes, and leads group work. He also works as the manager of the Power Products Engineering Group at Parker Compumotor, an electronics manufacturing firm.

Stuart Goodnick's paper was presented on his behalf by Martin Butler.

Martin Butler was introduced by Robert Ennis with the following comments:

Stuart Goodnick has been associated with Tayu for about 11 years, and he is now a study group leader with us. When I first read this article I was very impressed because to me at least it demonstrated a practical understanding of the material covered, not just a theoretical understanding. He had made his own ideas that he was presenting, not just some intellectual framework or conception. That to me is a very important consideration in papers dealing with important subjects like this. A person presenting such material, even if it sounds good, if they have not verified it for themselves, then in a sense it is not fitting.

So we were very happy when we learned about this conference to offer it as a presentation, and Martin who is a student of ours who lives in England, was very gracious to offer to present it for us. Martin is also in the process of forming a study group here in England and anyone who might be interested is welcome to contact him. His name is on the mailing list. I will keep these introductory remarks short so that there is more time for questions later.

The Organ Kundabuffer

Part I

One of the pivotal ideas in Gurdjieff's masterpiece, *All and Everything: Beelzebub's Tales to His Grandson*, is the concept of the organ Kundabuffer and the dire consequences its crystallized properties in the psyches of humans have had on the evolution of our species. In the course of his tales, Beelzebub describes the great cosmic catastrophe that occurred when the comet, Kondoor, collided with the still forming planet Earth. This collision blasted away two major fragments, the Moon and the lesser known and smaller Anulios.

The Organ Kundabuffer

In order that these fragments remain in stable orbit about the Earth and not cause further discord in the Universe, a Most High Commission of Sacred Individuals, with the sanction of Our Endless Endlessness, guided the evolution of life on our infant planet. Their aim was that Earth "should constantly send to its detached fragments, for their maintenance, the sacred vibrations askokin." Thus was the normal course of planetary evolution facilitated, ultimately resulting in the arising of certain bipedal, three-brained beings, endowed with the possibilities for perfecting the functions for the acquisition of Objective Being-Reason.

A second Most High Commission later descended to Earth to assess the progress of the measures that the first Commission had taken. Unfortunately for the future of humankind, this second Commission decided that there was a danger that humanity might attain to Object Reason prematurely and rebel at the discovery of the real cause of its arising and existence, that is, that humanity existed to maintain the detached fragments of the planet Earth. They feared that should this early discovery take place, humans might reject this imposed slavery to circumstances not of their making and would "on principle destroy themselves."

To forestall this possibility, this second Most High Commission decided to implant into the common presences of humans, at the base of the spinal column, a special organ called Kundabuffer. The organ Kundabuffer had the property of causing humans to "perceive reality topsy-turvy" and to create the effect that "every repeated impression from outside should crystallize in them data which would engender factors for evoking in them sensations of pleasure and enjoyment." Having caused this organ to grow in the presences of humankind and having demonstrated that it was indeed functioning properly, this Most High Commission returned to the cosmic center.

Much later, after human evolution had had a chance to proceed under the influence of this organ, a third Most High Commission descended to Earth to determine the status of the situation. This Most High Commission concluded that the maintenance of the existence of those two detached fragments of Earth no longer required that the organ Kundabuffer continue to function. At this time, then, the Most High Commission caused this organ to be eliminated from the presences of humans.

Unfortunately, after much time had passed, it became clear that although all the properties of the said organ Kundabuffer had been removed from the presences of humans, "a certain lawfully flowing cosmic result existing under the name of predisposition, and arising in every more or less independent cosmic presence owing to the repeated action in it of any function, had not been foreseen and destroyed in their presences." Thus did the consequences of the various properties of the organ Kundabuffer begin to pass by inheritance to succeeding generations and to be gradually crystallized into our presences.

These crystallized consequences of the properties of the organ Kundabuffer to which Beelzebub refers include egoism, self-love, vanity, pride, self-conceit, credulity, suggestibility, and many more, all of which are unbecoming to the essence of a normal three-brained being. On a mass level these properties give rise to that uniquely human reciprocal process of the destruction of each other's existence, that is, war. It is through these properties that we indeed see the world as topsy-turvy.

In pondering the meaning of this accounting by Gurdjieff for the peculiarities of the human psyche, we can come to understand some very important principles for our practice. The original purpose of the organ Kundabuffer was to forestall an existential crisis in mankind. The Most High Sacred Cosmic Individuals felt that if mankind achieved Objective Reason prematurely, it might perceive its place in the cosmos as serving a strictly mechanical function with no hope of any higher purpose. They felt that the ensuing pain of such a discovery would drive mankind to self-destruction.

To avoid such a catastrophe, these Most High Sacred Individuals chose to inoculate humanity against reaching such a conclusion. To prevent us from perceiving ourselves as small and the Universe as big, they implanted an organ that impelled us to see ourselves as big and the Universe as small. To further protect us from the pain arising out of identification with the idea of our own insignificance, they implanted an organ that would impel us to seek pleasure and enjoyment from outside ourselves, in external habits, and to avoid anything challenging or uncomfortable (especially introspection).

Of course, the ability to see one's relationship to the Universe objectively, and the willingness to endure conscious suffering are two prerequisites for the perfecting of oneself to Objective Reason. However, the Most High Sacred Commission determined that a temporary retarding of humanity's spiritual evolution was justified on the grounds of cosmic necessity.

Because of the plasticity of the human mind, however, the imprint of the effect of this organ Kundabuffer remained in humanity's psyche long after its physical properties had been removed. Consequently we have all inherited, both through the conditioning our society provides and to some extent though our physical organisms themselves, the tendencies to see ourselves as big and everything else as small and to seek pleasure in things outside of ourselves, things we perceive only through the filter of our distorted self-image.

One way in which we can understand the crystallized consequences of the properties of the organ Kundabuffer is as the foundation of desire. Desire arises in our organism in response to data crystallized within us which engender those factors for evoking the sensations of pleasure and enjoyment. And these data become crystallized within us through repeated impressions outside of ourselves. In other words, certain experiences we have can cause a response of pleasure, which in and of itself is not a problem. But when we learn that certain experiences repeatedly produce pleasure, we tend to internalize the idea of those experiences and henceforth seek them out regardless of their objective effects on us. That is, they become habits or even addictions.

If one has a chocolate bonbon and finds that it creates a very pleasurable response, one gets the idea that a chocolate bonbon will always create this pleasurable response. One may then want to have this bonbon instead of other food more appropriate for sustenance, which would satisfy the real needs of our body. This obsession can reach such a pitch that one can experience suffering (unnecessary suffering) if one does not get that bonbon. Further, after overindulging in bonbons for a while, getting or eating yet another bonbon produces no real satisfaction, either. In fact, it can cause genuine discomfort or harm to our bodies. But fulfilling such a desire can nevertheless engender an even more urgent need to get yet another bonbon, because the desire is born of the idea of pleasure rather than from actual pleasure itself.

A clue to a subtler aspect of the formation of desires in our psyches can be found in Beelzebub's emphasis that repeated impressions from the outside crystallize the data that lead to the evocation of the sensations of pleasure and enjoyment. In this sense, repeated impressions create the sense of pleasure called comfort. This comfort is a psychic rather than a physical comfort. It is the comfort born of familiarity. This sort of comfort forms the basis of our conditioned response to life. In our formative years we have repeated experiences which create for us our sense of what is normal and what is our relationship to life. Later in life, we tend to strive to maintain that sense of normalcy, that comfortable sense of psychic familiarity.

If we are raised with repeated impressions that we are loved by our family and that the world is a positive place, we will expect from life that this is what we should experience and will attract to ourselves just those situations which confirm this disposition. If we are raised with repeated impressions that we are insignificant or defective in some way and therefore deserve neglect or abuse, then we will likewise endeavor to create experiences for ourselves that confirm this disposition. Our sense of safety and security therefore depends on the re-creation and maintenance of past impressions, however pointless, unpleasant, or even harmful.

During our formative years we receive impressions and shocks which induce us to crystallize our foundational ideas about ourselves. We may receive affirmation that causes us to think well of ourselves, and we may be subject to psychic wounding that causes us to crystallize protective and compensating ideas. After years of layering ideas upon ideas of ourselves, we tend to end up as a curious collection of contradictions. At a deeper psychic level we will inexorably act to return to the familiar, but at a superficial personality level we will almost invariably deny responsibility for doing this.

We will blame outside forces for conspiring to arrange circumstances such that we are led again and again to that inner feeling that is so familiar. Yet in reality, we are merely responding to that core desire originally induced by the organ Kundabuffer, that is, the desire for the preservation of our self-image. But as in the example of the bonbon above, fulfilling this desire is not satisfying to our essence, it only produces the empty urge to continue in this vein. There can be no ultimate satisfaction in this desire to return to a familiar conditioned state because this desire has no connection to the true needs of our essence.

Part II

Beelzebub offers additional clues about the nature of the organ Kundabuffer. In one of his tales about German "ingenuity," Beelzebub relates that the substance cocaine "has an effect on the psyche of the contemporary beings of the planet Earth surprisingly similar to that which the famous organ Kundabuffer had on the psyche of their ancestors." Among the subjective effects created by cocaine in the human psyche is an exhilaration and an intensification of one's ideas of self. It has the very effect described earlier of making one's self big and the rest of the Universe small.

In addition, the more cocaine one ingests, the greater the need for more. One begins to compulsively orient one's life around the recreation of the sensations associated with the drug. Experiments in which chimpanzees are given the choice between normal food and cocaine demonstrate that the chimps will invariably choose cocaine and starvation. We can see in this analogy how the introduction of the organ Kundabuffer into humanity could lead to the compulsive intensification of the experience of one's ideas of oneself at the expense of experiences that provide the food for normal essence growth.

In the cocaine-induced state, the whole Universe revolves around oneself. One effectively numbs thereby the essence pain of remorse which is intended to guide us away from a life of total selfishness. This pain is a necessary concomitant of learning to be a genuine and mature individual. While this pain is perceived to arise from within us, as a result of the crystallized consequences of the properties of the organ Kundabuffer the source of our pleasure (as with cocaine) is seen to be outside ourselves. Thus, as our mental centers begin to coalesce symbols by which we can comprehend the world, we inevitably coalesce an idea of self that has as part of its foundation a sense of separation.

We therefore come to identify with the idea that there is something not right about us because of this sense of a part of us having been "cast out." Depending on the conditions of our various upbringings, this sense may be intensified or compensated for by further impressions. But as we layer more elaborate ideas about our self over this basic early conception, we tend to seek ideational strategies that compensate for this nagging sense of inner emptiness. These strategies typically take the form of an exaggerated concept of self and a self-centered mode of relating to the world.

One's ideas of reality take on far greater gravity than any direct experiences one might have to the contrary, simply because the ideas sound good to one or stimulate one's exaggerated sense of self. The action of the organ Kundabuffer also lead to an intensification of self-ideation. Vital, creative energy in our organism, potentially available for the crystallization of the data necessary to engender the impulses toward Objective Being Reason, was instead shunted into the crystallization of data that gives rise to impulses of vanity, self-importance, etc.

Such data arise in reaction to our earliest experiences of the world around us. Through the residual influence of the organ Kundabuffer one is impelled to preserve and confirm the perspective engendered by these early impressions. One takes one's ideas about reality to be the same as reality, and one substitutes subjective response to these ideas for objective mentation. One experiences oneself as cut off from the rest of the creation. One becomes a dog chasing its own tail.

Though the organ Kundabuffer was long ago physically removed from the human organism, Beelzebub explains that its effects continue to live on. This is principally due to the distorted conditions of being-existence that humanity created for itself while subject to the action of the organ. Vanity is a good example of this process. Vanity can be considered to have arisen in the human psyche as a consequence of the exaggerated focus on self-image that followed from the action of the organ Kundabuffer. But a lifestyle arising out of vanity by itself provides all the impressions necessary to sustain its existence in subsequent generations.

When people in the habit of indulging in vanity raise children, they cannot help but provide some seriously distorted impressions. The stronger the action of vanity in the parents, the greater the degree to which they will treat their children as reflections on themselves. The quality of attention that such parents give their children will therefore ultimately feel inadequate to the child. The child will naturally and inevitably feel that something is missing when the attention lavished upon the child is not truly directed at the child's essence, but instead at an image that the parents have of the child. The child will not at this point be able to conceptualize this sense of something missing, but this void in genuine attention forms in part the data for a later conceptualization of self doubt and lack of self worth.

The term Vanity describes a psychic condition in which one is obsessively concerned with one's self-image and how one appears to others. One indulging in vanity will tend to see all happenings in one's life as some kind of reflection on oneself. But vanity is only a symptom of a more basic self identification. It indicates that one has accepted at a deep level that in some fundamental way one is not acceptable as one is.

Vanity causes people to compensate for their deep seated, unconscious sense of lack of self-worth by seeking self-value in external artefacts and symbols. These may be jobs, clothing, sports cars, etc. So vain parents, even mildly vain parents, will tend to affirm their children for what they do and have rather than for who they are. The impression that these children will pick up is that their self-worth is conditional. They will come to believe that their validity as a person depends upon something outside of themselves.

When this message gets reinforced later in a child's development by his/her interactions with peers and society as a whole, the child has all the data necessary for the engendering of vanity in his/her psychic life, and few if any countervailing impressions. Because the adults who have chief influence on the child's development can demonstrate no other way of being, the child learns to recapitulate the patterns of vanity of its elders. Even if on a superficial level the child later rebels at the ways of the previous generation, the underlying pattern of vanity will continue unaltered, even if expressed in somewhat different ways.

All & Everything Conference 1998

Further, the habit of vanity can never genuinely address the deeper sense of being imperfect and unacceptable to which it is a reaction. The conceptualization of self doubt which arises from the earliest impressions of the essential child is in no way diminished by the expedient of seeking for self worth in things external to the Self. Rather, as described above, the action of vanity preserves the integrity of that earliest self identification.

Vanity effectively buffers the individual against having this early idea of self challenged by real experience (hence the term Kundabuffer). In this way, the primary and subtly acting desire for comfort (i.e. the security of the familiar) continues to operate through the medium of vanity. Vanity hides from one the suffering caused by the deeper self identification of self-doubt by redirecting one's attention away from the Self and onto things external to it.

If one were truly to accept one's own perfection as a Being, even with one's various limitations and with the knowledge of the possibility of continued growth, if one were to truly accept who one is in the moment, then vanity would have no ground on which to exist. You can test this claim in your own meditation. Consider how you would feel if you truly could accept yourself as you are now. Imagine how you would feel if you could simply love yourself unconditionally. What would happen to your vanity?

Part III

Part of the beauty of Gurdjieff's master work is that not only does he describe the problem we all face as inheritors of the crystallized consequences of the properties of the organ Kundabuffer, but he provides hints and keys about how we can ultimately dissolve these crystallizations. One such key to eliminating these from one's presence appears in the story about the labors of the Very Saintly Ashiata Shiemash.

Ashiata Shiemash was a messenger from Our Endless Endlessness sent to Earth to assist the three brained beings here to free themselves from the effects of this organ. He grew up and lived in the region of ancient Babylon. Ashiata Shiemash determined in his observations of the contemporary humans that the way to assist humanity in freeing itself was to create conditions in which the sacred being impulse of Objective Conscience could pass from the subconscious mind into the conscious mind. In short, he realized that when properly trained, people could use their conscience as a guide to lead them beyond the limitations of their own egoism.

From the point of view of our work with essence, conscience is that "small still voice" within us that speaks without words. It is a voice of silence. Ashiata Shiemash's conclusion was that if one consistently lived one's life in accordance to the direction of one's conscience, one would gradually dissolve those crystallized consequences of the properties of the organ Kundabuffer. To become aware of one's conscience, one must learn to distinguish its subtle "sound" from the din of one's thoughts and emotions, many of which are expressly designed to drown out this objective voice.

The Organ Kundabuffer

Our conscience is a gift from the Absolute. It is our direct connection with Our Endless Endlessness. The goal of our practice as well as that of the many true spiritual traditions is to enable one to reach the state of Being in which one lives one's life in continuous accordance with one's conscience. In such a state one knows exactly what to do from moment to moment because that knowing arises in one's presence as naturally as one takes a breath. One does not have to think about what to do, one simply does what presents itself to be done. One lives in the awareness of continuous connection with the Absolute. Although this goal is lofty, the first step on this path begins with Self-Observation.

Self-Observation is a practice in which one learns to observe the activities of each of the three brain systems (the mental, emotive, and moving/instinctive centers) from a point of view of silent awareness. One does not attempt to engage the thoughts, emotions, and sensations that one observes, one simply sees them as they are: events in one's field of awareness.

One of the purposes of Self-Observation is to enable one to get a good look at the crystallized consequences of the properties of the organ Kundabuffer operating in one's own organism. One can learn to see the thoughts about oneself and the emotions that these thoughts stir up as something separate from one's essential self. The Tayu practice of Co-Meditation (two-person Self-Observation) further extends this perspective. In Co-Meditation, one has the opportunity to see the activities of the properties of the organ Kundabuffer as they arise in conjunction with other beings. Together these practices can begin to open one's awareness to the nature of one's essence, which extends well beyond the isolated, conditioned, and reactive personality that most people take to be the sum total of who they are.

As one begins to see clearly through Self-Observation the automatic processes of one's conditioned android, and one's contact with essence deepens, one eventually reaches a point where one can begin to make efforts of will to move beyond one's assemblage of mechanical habits. These efforts can take a variety of forms, from physical exertions to the letting down of one's emotional defenses to refusing to express an emotion that automatically arises in connection with a thought. One might let go of an identification one has had with a particular self-image, or one might even make dramatic changes in what one does in one's everyday life. Whatever the form it may take in an individual instance, the practice is the same: one is making efforts to act from essence rather than through the android, and one is making efforts to allow one's essence to experience life directly. One is engaging in what Gurdjieff calls Being-Partkdolg-Duty.

Gurdjieff's story of the origins of the organ Kundabuffer can be read as the literal truth or as a spiritual allegory. What is important is that it gives us a mirror in which we can begin to comprehend that our various thoughts and emotions and our ego-centered living habits keep us in a continual state of separation from our true Self. In particular, Gurdjieff points us to a path by which we can begin to move beyond this state of separation and to regain our sense of connection with the Universe.

© Copyright 1998 - Stuart Goodnick - All Rights Reserved

The Organ Kundabuffer - Questions & Answers

Wim Van Dullemen: Thank you for this presentation. I could not understand everything, but what I could follow was very concise and very interesting. My question is simple. How would you personally understand and explain the fact that all the information is totally clear for every child. Nevertheless, the force is such that even people grappling with this material for almost all their lives, sometimes have the feeling that they are still in the grips of the same basic habits. We are the monkey grabbing for the cocaine. So how would you deal specifically with the situation, for instance, for people like us that are trying to find our way. Is my question clear?

Martin Butler: Yes, your question is clear. I know Robert will want to say something on this, but I would like to share my experience with you. What I have acquired through Robert's school is a practice of self observation which allows me to embrace the things which go on within me. What I mean by this is, for example, I am frightened of flying. I don't like flying in aeroplanes. previous to this I tried all sorts of things. I tried taking tablets, I tried a variety of things. But what I have found is that through Self Observation in the way I have learnt it, I can embrace the fear of flying. It does not mean that I am not frightened of flying any more, but it means that I can feed off that emotional situation as it occurs. I certainly don't try to change it. And I have found that this sort of psychological Judo, if you like, is what I have been looking for to enable me to experience the sense of separateness from the things that go on within me. And that has been very important to me.

Sy Ginsburg: I have a question. In the Third Series, Gurdjieff gives us an exercise or a hint about how his Endlessness dealt with a particular problem by excluding one of his nearest and dearest. And gives us an analogy that in order to be aware of ourselves we need to exclude something from ourselves, our identification. Is that what you are talking about or is it actually something else?

Robert Ennis: When you think about it, our most precious possession is our Ego. I sometimes call it our first born child, because the Ego is really our own creation. And by Ego, I am referring to the pattern of thought by which we consider ourselves. Everything we think about ourselves and think about is very precious to us. Most people find it inconceivable to exist without a constant pattern of thought maintaining our sense of self. But it is exactly this protective thought web that we must be willing to give up if we hope to get in touch with Essence. It is exactly this pattern of thought which buffers us against the true nature of our existence. And so this is the great sacrifice that we are called upon to make if we wish to awaken.

Sy Ginsburg: I only experienced your meditation exercise twice and you said there were many more exercises. But I am making an assumption that this is an exercise that you practice in a group at certain periodic times of the day or week. If our aim is Self Awareness, more or less continual in duration, frequency, and penetration, how do you bring that experience, let us say of your meditation, into to a kind of ongoing Work during the course of the day for this purpose.

The Organ Kundabuffer - Questions & Answers

Robert Ennis: Well basically the co-meditation practice is just that practice. It is intended to teach us how to relate to consider other people, to consider other people externally in a totally different way. One in which the experience of others is virtually as important as the experience of self. Egoism means to put yourself before everything else in the Universe. And that begins to change our egoism, because we now need to satisfy the essential needs of others as well as ourselves.

Nicolas Tereshchenko: Well it seems to me that there must be something wrong with what you are saying, because I am quite sure that Mr. Gurdjieff has been reported as saying that only something that you have experienced yourself is of any value and is the only thing that can be taken as the truth for you. That nobody else's experience can do anything at all for you. So it seems to me to contradict what you have just said.

Robert Ennis: I am not saying that one is experiencing other peoples experience, but one's experience of others can become much richer or deeper.

Nicolas Tereshchenko: Oh. I misunderstood.

Bert Sharp; A saying I heard about 70 years ago has come back to me, I don't know why. It simply said: Sticks and stones may break my bones, but words will never hurt me.

Richard Liebow: On hearing an assumption that there is a difference between co-meditation that leads to external considering and external considering, what I am saying is that I am proceeding, have been, and may continue to proceed with this assumption that external considering will of itself change my relationship with others. You seem to be suggesting that it must be combined with co-meditation.

Robert Ennis; No. Co-meditation is just a means to an end. It is not the end.

Richard Liebow: The other question that I have relates to a feeling I have that there is some way to quantum leap ones self from Ego to Egolessness. Is that possible, or is it an A, B, C, D, E, G?

Robert Ennis: The Eastern tradition talks about it as being a sudden process. But I think that is partially the result of the nature of cultural restraints there, which is a long story. I think here in the West the process of awakening is likely to be a gradual process with lots of milestones on the way.

Keith Buzzell: Two points. First it seems essential to go back to the early part of the paper if I remember it correctly. There was a connection between Kundabuffer and war. And I think it would be important to emphasize that in a sense it seems to me that Gurdjieff does not make it so simple. The whole purpose of the Sixth Descent, the longest and the most penetrating descent of all, follows on the failure of Ashiata Shiemash's efforts. There is something beyond Kundabuffer, beyond that thing that is immensely more powerful. That is our real dilemma. It is important to me to always keep that out front, because we can mislead ourselves into thinking that something is happening when it really is not, because there is this that is beyond that, that issue of Kundabuffer that is going to pull the plug.

Robert Ennis: We are not under the impression that the Fourth Way is likely to end war. That it is possible for you to end war for yourself.

Keith Buzzell: That is my point. Through Kundabuffer alone within ourselves, because we can. There is a way of seeing the whole of the *Tales* as being each of us, that it is taking place inside of us. So my point is still the same. Individually or collectively, unless we reach and penetrate into the Sixth Descent, beyond all that kundabuffer can bring us in our understanding, and work on that and so forth, until we go beyond that, we are still caught.

Robert Ennis; Do you agree that it is possible? OK.

Sebouh Der Bedrossian: Robert, I want to ask you about hearing a subtle voice and quietening down the "I". Would you tell me your method, maybe?

Robert Ennis: Well we have found that the simple practice of self-observation done consistently will begin to quiet the internal dialogue. As the light of attention is brought to bear on some habitual thought pattern and so on, and we realize their silliness, they tend to disappear. After that though it is necessary to put attention on persistent thought patterns. And we have a number of techniques or processes by which one puts attention, does not identify with, and then acknowledges various regions of thought. And when one has - we liken thoughts as basically communications that we have never received. And like an answering machine, they keep playing until we finally receive them and acknowledge them. Once we have received and acknowledged the message, then it does not need to keep playing anymore. And most of us have an enormous back-log of verbal data that we have never looked at. In some cases there are mental patterns that we have pushed away so powerfully that they come back with renewed energy and so become obsessions. But it is possible through self-observation and this later process I was talking about, to begin to basically digest or re-absorb all of the energy that is involved in maintaining this constant roof-brain activity, this formatory activity, with the result that one can hope gradually to have ever increasing periods of silence. And in that silence then it is possible to hear conscience. When we are not convincing ourselves of what we believe and what we need to do, we can then receive guidance. And so it is a very organic process and it is a very fulfilling process as one gets more and more in touch with conscience.

Edgar Clarke: What I have is not so much a question as a notion that I will just mention, because it is in some respects real to me. It seems to me that the planetary effects of the properties of Kundabuffer have resulted in the authority of the institutions of power. It seems to have such a grasp on the planet's condition that I can't see how it is going to ease. I just hope that the next entry Commission is not very far away and it is going to be more effective than the last one.
Nicolas Tereshchenko: I have a comment. Back to the question of Ego and Egolessness. We have been told by a very great Messenger from Above that you must render unto Caesar what is

Caesar's and to God what is God's. Now if you are Egoless you cannot render anything to Caesar because you have not got anything to do it with. So I think that there is some sort of error that has crept in. I must not destroy the Ego. One must learn how to use it in such a way that it is not eliminated. So it is not a question of jumping from, one - yes, I have an Ego - no I have no Ego. It is a question of - I have an Ego, but whatever it is, obeys these rules and not its own. That is my First comment. The other one is not a question relating to Kundabuffer as such, but an entirely new thing. You mentioned this experiment of which I have also read, of chimpanzees choosing cocaine over food. Now I have never read the original or spoken to anyone who knows directly about it, but it seems bizarre to me that without knowing what cocaine is, it seems to me that the only way that will get the result that apparently has been obtained, is first to make the chimpanzees addicts. Then, of course, they will go for the cocaine, but then that means nothing. I am quite sure that a very hungry chimpanzee which has got banana on one side and a sachet of cocaine on the other, wont even look at the sachet of cocaine. It will go for the banana. Unless it has already been conditioned.

Robert Ennis: Yes. When we reach responsible age we are already conditioned. If the chimpanzees are already conditioned it does not really matter.

Nicolas Tereshchenko; Well, they are already addicts.

Robert Ennis. But that is the analogy. They are already addicts. We are already addicts. With regard to your first question or comment, we do not see the Ego as an enemy or something to be destroyed or cast out. And so our aim is to re-absorb it, rather than have it as a separate creation. And so that access to all of the knowledge and data that it has and we have use of its functions whenever necessary. The Ego is False Personality.

Keith Buzzell; Would you call it Ego when I Say "I"?

Robert Ennis: I would call it a collection of "I's". It is not a unitary "I". It is a collection of "I's". Every thought we have is an "I".

Keith Buzzell: But the "thinking about". This is my point I think is just to try to focus on that "I", even the sense of "I" that the Third Brain brings is not something that we can think about. We cannot have thoughts about that. That is in the Second Brain in sense of self. Now when we have a construction that we can begin to become aware of, that we can begin to see, that we have formulated over time that is a sense of self that is not "I". For me that is an extremely important differentiation, because much of the emphasis of the approach that you have, seems to me to be focused very strongly in the emotional part, in the Second brain, and that is a very important work. I am not in any way trying to speak other than to try to make clear that there is an enormous difference, a very important difference, between that which structures the sense of self and our necessary work in regard to that, and that is what concerns "I".
Robert Ennis: I don't think we actually have a dispute. We have not had time to talk about it.

All & Everything Conference 1998

Bert Sharp: If I might just go back to what you were saying a few moments ago about how in the meditation mode, the way in which one quietens, clears the decks as it were, rather like when the sun comes out the stars disappear, but they are still there. So when the sun goes down, when in the meditation you turn away from the thoughts of the day, then one begins to see the stars are there. In my terminology that is when you make the way clear for the inner teacher, the Teacher Within. I would like to read a little poem that describes this, which I had difficulty in finding:

I am the great sun, but you do not see me
I am your husband but you turn away
I am the captive out you do not free me
I am the captain you will not obey.

I am the truth, but you will believe me
I am the city where you will not stay
I am your wife, your child, but you will leave me
I am that God to whom you will not pray.

I am your counsel, but you do not hear me
I am the Lover whom you will betray
I am the victor but you do not cheer me
I am the Holy Dove whom you will slay.

I am your life, but you will not name me
Seal up your soul with tears and never blame me.

Robert Ennis: Thank you. I think that is good place to end.

The Origins, Meaning and Purpose of the Movements

Wim Van Dullemen

There was a delay in starting this session due to a problem with setting up the video projection equipment. The problem was finally solved and Wim Van Dullemen opened the session by asking those present how many had direct experience and realistic training in the Movements, in a direct transmission, for say more than five or ten years. There were very few who were able to answer this in the affirmative, only two or three.

Wim then began his presentation as reported below.

* * *

You see, talking about the Movements, that is impossible. You either do them or you don't. To do them you have to have instruction. This is the difference between knowing and knowing about. In Movements you have to have instruction from someone who knows. If not you don't know and stay at the stage of only knowing about them. It is as simple as that.

I would propose the following procedure for this session. We will first of all have an impression of the Movements by a few video tapes. You can all see them, and at least have an impression of them. You will take in your own impressions. The first video that we be shown is a small part of a BBC video which was a program about Sherbourne House and John Bennett. The BBC program was billed as "Through One Pair of Eyes", and it gives a very interesting and historical view. It shows John Bennett himself in front of his class trying to instruct them and so on. It shows a few good Movements, performed by a fine class. it is one of the best classes I have seen and I have seen many. The part of that video which we will show takes about five minutes. The next video is a little longer and is the result of transferring to video a series of badly deteriorated films made at Sherbourne House. It includes various views of Sherbourne House together with an interview with John Bennett. And then the children start doing their own Movements. That is real fun to see, because they imitate the Movements of those who know, but they imitate them in a very nice way. Ken has told me and I am permitted to tell you that this material is authentic, because Ken was there. You were in the class, Ken? (Ken answers yes). I apologize because the picture quality is very bad, but at least it will give you an impression.

After the videos, I will talk to you about my own opinions and impressions relating to the Movements and also pass on to you some information I have from Solange Claustres which she has shared with me.

All & Everything Conference 1998

I have recently been involved in conducting an interview with Solange Claustres about the Movements. The resulting article which I produced based on this interview was published last November by the Dutch Press. I will try and find time to translate this into English and if I can get the copyright position cleared we will be able to make the English version available to all of you who are interested. I doubt I will be able to achieve this in time for its inclusion in our Proceedings.

I will then invite questions from you which I will be pleased to try and answer. Finally I will conclude by playing, as I promised yesterday, the Essene Hymn of Gurdjieff. This will take about five minutes and will conclude my presentation. Is this all acceptable to you?

The audience were in complete agreement with these proposals, and so the exerts from the two videos were shown and then Wim Van Dullemen began his talk on the meaning and purpose of the Movements as follows:

The Movements for me and for anybody involved with them are a very powerful medium. My personal position in the field of Movements is not easy, but I am regularly involved in a Movements class in Amsterdam now, that is doing very, very well. I have got a waiting list, but the class as it is now is performing very, very well. So that gives me a lot of true satisfaction. If I am allowed to say it, for me the Movements are breaks through of a higher level into our own level.

We should remember that Solange Claustres met Gurdjieff while still a young woman and so when she talks about Gurdjieff's teaching and the Movements, she is talking from direct experience. And the original impressions she had have since been worked and reworked through over many years. During all of this time she has been directly involved in Movements classes.

Her first encounter with Gurdjieff's teaching and the Movements was when she was in one of Gurdjieff's study groups. This was of twelve people, although she remembers that in fact there were fourteen, since there were three who were sisters and Gurdjieff did not want to count them other than as one person. So the three sisters were one.

Each week the study group Solange was in met up with other groups as a Movements class. This was in the 'Salle Playel' in Paris. This went on for her for some seven years. During this time Gurdjieff would usually bring a new Movement to the class each week.

Solange remembers that whenever Gurdjieff brought a new Movement to the class, he never explained much. In Solange's view, Gurdjieff's presence was so strong that it filled the entire Movements hall into the smallest corners. Because of this "Presence", it was as if you could absorb the new Movement or dance in a direct way rather than with the intervention of intellect.

It was also forbidden to make notations of the Movements after a class and Solange has continued with this prohibition in her own classes. Her view on this is that the first complete impression can

The Origins, Meaning and Purpose of the Movements

be afterwards distorted by intellectual consideration. This does not mean that one should not recapitulate a Movement outside of the Movements class. Solange recalls that whenever she had to wait somewhere, such as on the Paris Metro, she would recapitulate one Movement after another in their full details as a visualization. This she found more valuable than any choreographic notation.

While many of the Gurdjieff movements and dances come from the Middle East and the Far East where Gurdjieff was able to study them with special people or religious communities, many of them come from Gurdjieff himself.

After Gurdjieff's death, Jean de Saltzman arranged for all the Movements Gurdjieff gave us to be re-enacted and filmed on twelve films. These films are now with the Institute Gurdjieff in Paris. Solange tells me that these reconstructions are reliable, but that not all of Gurdjieff's dances have been kept in this way.

That Solange Claustres should be considered an authority on the Gurdjieff Movements and dances with direct personal practical experience is supported by the fact that when Gurdjieff went to America he asked Solange to take over his Movements classes. As can be realized appropriate piano music is an essential factor in a successful Movements class. At the time Solange took over the classes there was still little music for the Movements. She was instructed by Gurdjieff to improvise the music. This experience showed her that the music is not simply an accompaniment, but is a living integral part of the inner Work that takes place in the class. Solange during my talks with her made, among many points, one extremely relevant comment which I think describes well the meaning and purpose of the Movements.

What she said was; IN THESE MOVEMENTS AND DANCES IS LYING THE LAW OF THE EVOLUTION OF THE HUMAN CONSCIOUSNESS. THEY EXPRESS HOW AND IN WHICH DIRECTION THAT PROGRESSION HAS TO GO AND AS SUCH THEY ARE A SCHOOL IN THE REAL SENSE OF THE WORD.

But when Solange uses the word law she feels that to differentiate between Gurdjieff's psychological and cosmological law is too limited. The word psychological is much too narrow and the word cosmological much too vague.

But what does a person experience through the Movements? I would suggest that they have nothing to do with ecstasy or enlightenment. Rather they demand total precision and are a discipline and in this way are very similar to authentic Eastern Martial Arts. The posture of the body should be exact. Even the slightest deviation, a slightly bent head, a not precise arm posture, does not only change the effect of what you see. It changes something much more important. It changes the feeling one has inside oneself.
Solange recalls how at one time she was talking personally with Gurdjieff and told him how again and again she had been deeply touched by his Movements. Gurdjieff simply said to her, "Yes, they are medicine".

All & Everything Conference 1998

But what does one experience when doing the Movements? To use Solange's own words it can be described as follows:

The body itself understands the Movements in its own way. We have to develop a new attention not to be brought into confusion by all these complex and asymmetrical patterns. We have to use our own thoughts consciously to visualize the chronology of the dance or to pronounce the words that belong to the dance. If we do all this we will be touched by a total new vision. The music and the group as a whole is new for us. In this vision we realize that we are but part of an objective construction that we cannot fathom, but that is of immense beauty. We have become part of an objective form of art which practically means that we are then in the conditions where we can experience the laws of consciousness, because she emphasized it is about laws. For one moment we are free of our so-called habits, we are free of the heavy chain of our so-called civilization and our social conditioning. A pure perception is possible. This process is what she called consciousness.

Solange said that Gurdjieff's teaching has nothing to do with an organization, with a religion, or with a philosophy, but is a methodology of becoming conscious, of being face to face with oneself.

From my discussions with Solange Claustres, it is very apparent that she takes the view that today there is a pressing need for greater unity among the many different kinds of Gurdjieff groups scattered around the world. There is also a need to differentiate between groups which more or less work according to Gurdjieff's own teaching and other groups which try to incorporate Gurdjieff's teaching with their own teaching. She is also concerned at the exposure of many people to new movements teachers, many of whom have a very distorted idea of Gurdjieff's methods and who thus teach without complete knowledge. She considers the difference between complete and incomplete knowledge is similar to the difference between white and black magic.

She uses the analogy of the lost dog. Imagine yourself as a dog lost on the streets of an immense big city, in the labyrinth of streets and little alleys. he trots without aim, there and then there, sniffs something, sniffs there, goes on without aim. Suddenly he waits. He pricks up his ears. Was that the voice of his master he heard in the distance? Listen again. No. Without courage he starts to trot through the labyrinth. That dog is our body.

There is a feeling about that as many people as possible should make contact with the Movements. Solange makes the point that it is important to understand the esoteric principle. Nothing is hidden but people themselves shut up themselves because of lack of courage. She emphasises that you have to be humble. Very few people are. But only quality can bring something. The radius of one small but precise and conscious activity will reach over the world. In her view you should not be disturbed by the mutual hostility of so called spiritual organizations, because as she says, these organizations are composed of people. And if you want to know what humans are, just pick up a Newspaper and see what they do all the time. The danger to feel oneself 'on the Way' is always present. You can be part of an organization, but you have to be above the place that you actually

The Origins, Meaning and Purpose of the Movements

have in the organization. You can only take a place if inside yourself you are already above that place. Gurdjieff himself did not want any explanation of the Movements because the content is clear for those who know. The content of the Movements talks to the being, not to the mental.

That is the reality of the esoteric principle. As well as the personal, as well as the collective, existence is for her an alchemical process. It is a transformation of substance. No intellectual effort whatsoever can define it. What kind of substance are these and how they get into involvement. It is only the wish to Be and the wish to understand. Only then can the impressions of the outside world and those that come up from out of yourself, feed something. What said the Christ, she asked. The Christ said, Wake up, but everybody forgets all the time. She recalls that Gurdjieff told her that through this Work everybody can understand his own religion much better. In himself he has touched the common roots. She remembers as a small child she really understood that there can only be one God. She saw many different spiritual things and religions. In her view they come about because the times change and especially the places where these religions are active change.

I asked her to put it into One, Two, Three, because that is what she always asked me. You had an idea and then you had to come up with one, two, three, and then you had to come up with your own idea. I said, yes you have talked a long time, now take three - She said, I don't need three. Two is enough. Be simple!

© Copyright 1998 - Wim van Dullemen - All Rights Reserved

The Origins, Meaning and Purpose of the Movements - Questions & Answers

Nicolas Tereshchenko; What language was it in?

Wim Van Dullemen: French.

Nicolas Tereshchenko; You have a recording in French?

Wim Van Dullemen: No. Actually the interview is made up of two days of a long chain of experiences. So I tried to compromise.

Seymour Ginsburg: It is in Dutch in that book?

Wim Van Dullemen; Yes. I will try if I have time to make a translation. Did it get across more or less what was useful to you?

General answer from those present of Yes.

Wim Van Dullemen: I just felt that she had to tell what she had to tell. If you have any questions I will be delighted to try and answer them. if not I go and play the Essene hymn.

Nicolas Tereshchenko: Did I understand you correctly to say that the music originally was not written for the Movements?

Wim Van Dullemen: Oh yes it was. But at that time it speaks about several Movements, especially the Movements that Gurdjieff was working on at that time, what we call the 39 series. Some Movements were without music. It is a bit distorted.

Nicolas Tereshchenko: So it is Mr. Gurdjieff's music, not Solange's music?

Wim Van Dullemen: Oh no. It is Gurdjieff's music. That is maybe a bit awkward in the interview. It is an established fact that of about 100 musical pieces that exist for the Movements, probably 85 are definitely composed by Gurdjieff and the 15 remaining are questionable, so that the vast majority of the compositions are Gurdjieff's.

Nicolas Tereshchenko: Thank you.

Wim Van Dullemen: No more questions? Great. So I promised to play the Essene hymn. It is the only piece from Gurdjieff, the only one out of the 300 that has three definite components. Component one, component two, component three, and in the third component of the Essene

The Origins, Meaning and Purpose of the Movements

hymn, also called Hymn of the Great Temple, No. 12. In the last, it goes to a sort of Amen. Open chord, I will say, final chord. Is that OK with you? So again I repeat that this is for me as a musician, very important that there is no misunderstanding at all. Normally Gurdjieff's pieces are of one theme alone. This is not. This is three different things.

Theme one: plays.
Theme two: plays.
Theme three: plays
Last statement: Plays.

Applause.

Fourth Open Forum - Where Do We Go From Here?

Facilitator: Professor Paul Beekman Taylor

Seymour Ginsburg: This is the final session of "All and Everything 1998." It is the fourth forum of this conference, "Where do We Go From Here'?" Professor Paul Beekman is the Chair.

Paul Taylor: In this unenviable position moderating, or mediating, such an important issue for this, our third Bognor Conference, I recall that about every three years Gurdjieff would challenge his pupils with such a reflection. July 1924 was one such moment, November 1927 another. 1930 was portentous for re-organization of his groups, and in 1933 the Prieure closed, and two and one-half years later in 1935 the locus of teaching changed. Gurdjieff engaged all of his pupils in these turns, but few could suggest the necessary changes, so Gurdjieff found himself deciding "where we go from here." What remains important, however, is the idea of change, adaption, transformation, renewal. As one who spent time on the road with Gurdjieff. I know how impatient he was with holding aimlessly to a single direction.

I will open this forum by reading a note given to me in response to the question by one who has been influential in guiding our efforts here to change:

"I would like to express my sincere thanks to Dr. Sharp and to Frank Brzeski for all the practical work in connection 6th with the Conference. I wonder if we all appreciate the amount of practical work entailed. I wish future conferences well, however connected to any realistic proposals for their evolution. Conferences afford generous people endless speculative thought along the lines of knowledge. but I cannot perceive what work there is in the line of our Being which can proceed fruitfully. When we, a) are all linked with the mainstream of Gurdjieffian material and endeavour, or b) able to salute here and there among ourselves the quality of Being, then I would be far more hopeful. Frankly, I do not feel that the pattern of attendances at presentations entitle me to a voice in our deliberations, Good luck with your decision.

Chris Thompson: Mr. Moore.

Paul Taylor: I asked myself when I received this note: How should I proceed with it? I can play advocate's devil and take either side of the question, but Gurdjieff always said that one should not succumb to an identification; be an entity, not an identity, He might say here, "on which side is your ego attachment?"

Chris Thompson: Vested interest.

Fourth Open Forum - Where Do We Go From Here?

Paul Taylor: Yes, and that raises the problem of how to separate oneself from what a vested interest might be. After three years sensing what James Moore once called a "complicity in sincerity," I feel we can proceed in any number of directions. We can cam forward any amount of material to sustain a momentum of uninvested interest. So, the floor is now open for discussion.

Richard Liebow: I'd like to Suggest March 17, 1999, a Wednesday, to open our next meeting , and that there should be another gathering at this hotel, and the formal conference to begin on Thursday and conclude at 2:00 pm on Sunday when we can carry on this autopsy. There are a number of contingencies. One is for Bert and Frank to see if the hotel manager can give us the same deal as we have this year. The other is the date of Easter.

Paul Taylor: Easter 1999 is on Sunday. April 4.

Richard Liebow: That would normally when we foreigners would get the same deal with the airlines as we get now. Air fares jump dramatically on April 3.

Bert Sharp: I would respectfully suggest to Richard that you can only carry out an autopsy on a dead body.

Paul Taylor: This is now a question of chronology and continuation, only two of a number of considerations. Let's get to others.

Dorothy Usiskin: Speaking as one new to the work, having been involved for just under two years, it is my hope that you will continue the presentations at as high a level as you can. I feel it is very acceptable if I can only understand 5% or 10% of what is said. That's OK, but don't bring them down and make them too simple.

Paul Taylor: Along these lines I have asked Chris one fundamental question: How can this organization serve the Gurdjieff work in the broadest sense? How can we help to disseminate Gurdjieff's ideas in a positive way?

Adam Petts: I am concerned with the music. In talking with Wim yesterday. I heard that there are 300 incredible pieces left to us by Gurdjieff and de Hartmann. They haven't been recorded, so it is not possible to study this music. Is it not possible among various groups of people to get some funds together to have the music recorded and made available? Wim has said that there is a very profound body of knowledge in this music. We can go to a shop and find Mozart, Beethoven and all the others, but not this special music. I would be willing to invest time and energy to bring this music forward. And, as Wim said, there is a lot of politics and other aspects involved, but I feel this is the way to go.

Paul Taylor: I propose a way to make 1999 a celebratory conference. and that is to assemble personal records of people who knew Gurdjieff in the last year of his life, and recite them here.

All & Everything Conference 1998

There are Gurdjieff's own children as well as some among his last group of young pupils who might be persuaded to give us their recollections.

Sy Ginsburg: Marlena Buzzell spoke about the Planning Committee arriving at a consensus. Perhaps that is what we are trying to do here, and there are preliminary questions to be answered. If we do have another conference, we ought to consider the following questions:

Do we have another conference? Do we have it next year? Do we do something related to the 50th anniversary of Mr. Gurdjieff's death? This could be a year and a half from now. I just want to throw these in because I hope in some way we can come to a consensus of where we are going before this meeting is over.

Michael Smyth: Seeing that we have had three of these conferences, and I'll look at this sequence in a very literal way as a Do, Re, Mi, So we are at a Mi-Fa interval coming up in the fourth one. I look to Keith as I see him as an authority for me about the Laws. What is lawful? Maybe we can relate it to us and our situation.

Keith Buzzell: The MI-Fa of hopefully an ascending octave is where something from the outside must enter that represents, that is both food and also that which can be the source of feeding the entire octave. So, depending upon how we see the upper Do of that octave, that Do which Michael referred to as the lower Do, Re, Mi, that perhaps we can take to represent the last three years. What comes in from the outside for me is the question that I tried to address previously relative to how we understand this great task that is to be addressed by the entirety of a fourth way effort into the common life of man. For me this is of extraordinary central importance in my own life to try and understand, because I feel astonishingly, remarkably, impossibly, blessed by the accident that I was able to make contact with this Work and to be a part, potentially, of the fullness of that Work which involves service, not to me and beyond our work together. It means that this great task has something to do with where this world is now. I am not so naïve as to think that that is a suitable question of something we can suitably put together and answer to. The needs are nearly infinite. The difficulties in our world that represent enormously significant hazards on this plunging road to chaos and savagery that we are on. That's how I understand this entry. It has very much to do with effecting sufficient change through the introduction of new B influences. This is one of the main tasks of this effort, to introduce and give form to B influences that can be a saving and harmonizing influence on the world. That service seems to me related to the question: "How will this serve?" We cannot serve ourselves. We cannot serve each other. It seems to me and however sensitive we are wholly in the Work. So, there has to be some way of trying to get a grasp of that significance for our children and our grandchildren and the future of this world. That what I think is coming in the door, that comes in at that Mi-Fa interval, out difficulties, and all those difficulties. How can we begin collectively not to come to a final solution or anything, because I think that is going to become our food if we are going to be a whole that can go and do anything in the future and reach, hopefully, higher parts of that Oneness. It has to have something specific to do with feeding that great arena of needs, thousands and thousands of needs.

Fourth Open Forum - Where Do We Go From Here?

Paul Taylor: As moderator, I can see a consensus here that we have another meeting. Whether Bognor is its site or someplace else, the Bognor conferences have defined themselves here for better or worse, and I invite such forums for introspection. But, there is a material question involved, and that is planning and organization. For the latter, Bert Sharp cannot year after year continue to do what he has done.

Bert Sharp: That's not a problem for me.

Paul Taylor: I have another consideration in mind. I am not a member of a Gurdjieff group and have not been since the early 1950s. I do not feel that we should bond ourselves into a sort of group here. A rogue group would hardly serve a purpose for the Gurdjieff work at large. We should, as Dorothy suggested, disseminate Gurdjieffian idea in presentations of the highest standard possible. We must aim high. I think it absolutely essential, otherwise we will fail the most modest of our aspirations. If we take seriously what James Moore has said. we must try to work on and coordinate the quality of our ideas and our growth of Being.

Nicholas Tereshchenko: I think I am reasonably pragmatic and as far as I am aware, the cheapest month for air fares is March, April, especially with Easter, is going to be expensive, so I was wondering whether it would not be better for us to keep to March and to meet in Bognor because we want Bert to be with us.

Now, the other thing is, if I understand Paul correctly, he, as I do, feels that the Gurdjieff Work should be much more widely known. Perhaps one of the ways is a meeting of what I will loosely call "patrons," and I hope you are going to consider it. What about two "patrons?" One could be Bill Gates, who apparently wishes to distribute a lot of his money to deserving causes, and another would be the Prince of Wales who is apparently interested in the Work. In that wav, not we, but the Work will become well known. Moreover, if we do get any of Bill Gates' money that would take much of the weight off Bert's shoulders, because then we would have enough money to employ many people and have any type of apparatus we wish, and in that case perhaps the question of the cost of travel will not arise. I am just throwing this in for people to tell me whether they think it is ridiculous or if it is having this type of gathering of people who genuinely and authentically wish to work within the parameters of Mr. Gurdjieff's Fourth Way.

Bert Sharp: If I might follow that with one or two comments. The first is that the interest of the Prince of Wales is, from my information, limited to an order for Beryl Pogson's book, In the East My Pleasures Lie. That may not be significant. Don't let us run too quickly. The other thought that came to me now may be totally ridiculous. Because my memory is so full. I am not sure of the title, but Gurdjieff in the early days advertised the ballet "Struggle of the Magicians" If we meet again next year, is it sensible and practical to put aside one day, perhaps Saturday, for a public gathering at which we demonstrate various things, having hired a theatre or a hall, in a similar way, and so we could reach out and offer opportunity?

All & Everything Conference 1998

Bonnie Phillips: It seems very good to look at proposals in a practical way as this being an interval, and my idea to put forth for that interval, or external influence that is needed here is that we might bring our children or our grandchildren or a guest to next year's Conference in order to have that experience and influence reach out to someone quite directly.

Paul Taylor: Having children attend is certainly in the spirit of Gurdjieff. I remember Gurdjieff's fondness for children and the special care he seemed so readily to take with them. One example will suffice. One day Lida bounced about in front of Gurdjieff at tea while she played with a little Mickey Mouse play watch that someone had given her. It was her love for the day. Gurdjieff watched for a while, and then grabbed the watch and crushed under his foot. Lida ran to her father Dimitri in tears. Dimitri was one of the few people who dared redress his brother, but he ignored his daughter's tears and said nothing. The next day Gurdjieff invited Lida to him and he gave her a real watch.

Sy Ginsburg: Just a piece of information. I am quite certain that May will not be a least expensive month to travel. It is not in the off-season period. It would cost considerably more than before Easter or in the autumn or winter. The second thing is that we talked of consensus before, and I think it important as a preliminary step. I have heard two conflicting things. One, earlier today, that there is a certain bonding going on. I was told that there were 17 people who had been to all three conferences, and that sounds like a group in some way. On the other hand, I heard it expressed that "I don't want to be part of a group here, I don't want Bognor to be a group." I do not see Bognor as a Gurdjieff group, but I am willing to listen to a consensus among us. The other thing I would like to mention is that I am reluctant, having been here three years in a row, to have us do the same thing exactly for the fourth year. This would be a bit stale. Maybe, as Keith suggested, we need something from outside to cover the interval from Mi to Fa. Next year is the 50th anniversary of Gurdjieff's death, but I have been told that any activity at that time would conflict with the marking of that anniversary by other groups. We could possibly have something before or after that date.

Nicholas Tereshchenko: They say mass at the Russian Cathedral at 8 in the morning, then people go to Mr. Gurdjieff's tomb at Fountainbleau-Avon. Those who have known Mr. Gurdjieff meet at 6, rue des Colonels Renard. That is open only to those who have personally known him. So what is going to happen in a few years' time, I do not know.

John Perrot: I haven't anything particular to say, and I am aware of this. I would make a contribution here. I have some observations as is frequently the case for me: but, it is dependent upon there actually being a process, as Michael suggested. I am not saying this as an idea, but if it were, then perhaps we are looking at Do-Re-Mi. Therefore, it seems to me that there are questions that are quite easy for me to answer. I just put them into their context. If there is a process going on, it may or may not be working on an event-by-event basis. It may be all Do. I cannot perceive what the event is. If it is an event, then it is Law Conformable. Then at some point, yes, we hit the Mi-Fa interval. That may be now, and Keith has said enough about it. On the other hand, it could be that it is not Law Conformable, or it is each person within himself, but there is not a process going on which we see as Do-Re-Mi. If it were, it would become stale next year and we would all probably decide not to come again. The trick is to discover whether it is a process or not. It has not grown stale for me yet. For some strange reason every time I come here, something really astonishing happens to me. I am fully convinced of that and no one here is causing it. I mean "astonishing" to the point where those who here last year will remember that I hardly articulated a single word, because I was so full of feelings. Astonished synchronicity if nothing else. I also noticed that among other people who are very interesting to me, the little solar patterns, planets moving from one to the other and so on, are all moving a lot more this year than they ever did at the first. To my perception or misperception, there are rough corners, aggressive bits rubbing off, so maybe there is a process, or maybe it is just erosion. Against that background, more of which I am sure you will agree is worth pursuing in the discussion here. And in my view, if there is a Conference next year. I'm likely to come to it if I'm in England. It seems to still have a life for me, though I, for one, cannot yet see what that is.

Keith Buzzell: There is one way of viewing an evolutionary octave. The Mi of that octave can be looked at as a triad of Law and the way in which we are familiar of working with that is that it is a Law of Interaction. It is not a Law of Relationships. To me it is important to differentiate that interaction as a profitable and useful mixing because it is a process of sorts. Relationships cannot emerge by Law until you get all the way to the La of that octave. So to me it is just important to see that. It is trying to recognize that there is that which is outside that really is the food, but also that which is to be served, and in some way it will become stale if we stay inside and do not attempt to recognize the source of what can really contribute to its continuing to grow and to be something. At this stage the interaction which is really necessary has to be differentiated from relationship.

Richard Liebow: Relative to staleness. I came here with my wife in 1996, and she had no real interest in the ideas of this Work. So she goes out and plays. I attended every session in 1996. 1997 was different because I persuaded my dear friend Sebouh to come along, and that made a very different Conference for me, to have another one of our guys involved, and we also involved Dikran Takvorian into that 1997 event. We went to the Prieuré, went to the graveside. Pulled the grass off Mr. Gurdjieff's grave. We went to 6, rue des Colonels Renard. We tried to find the café on Rue Acacia where we could have a sandwich. We went to the Russian church on rue Daru where the memorial service is held, and it was with the knowledge of the technological manager of Eurostar that made the cost of flying to Paris not much more. I am speaking of how we have done it. This time there are four of us, and two spouses, and we might fly to Paris and repeat the pilgrimage. Now, I'm not suggesting that this could be part of the Conference, but it is a possibility that something like this could really be done by us all. The world is smaller and there are ways to make a difference, and I personally have created a task for myself to try to get one of our women who work for us in San Francisco to be here in 1999.

Paul Taylor: It is also a very special experience to visit the Cimetière de Plainpalais on the Rue des Rois in Geneva where Madame de Salzmann is buried. It is a cemetery for those who have contributed to the history of Geneva, and not far from where Mme de Salzmann is buried lies Luis

All & Everything Conference 1998

Borges whose tomb has an inscription "Na forhtedon" --"they no longer fear" (in Old English), a look back at the world of the living that seems pertinent to Gurdjieff's and Mme de Salzmann's continued presence. Between those tombs one feels a pulse of energy.

Sy Ginsburg: If we have a consensus to do something next year. I suggest that we consider it as the 50th anniversary of Mr. Gurdjieff's passing, and perhaps, for those could arrange it, we could meet at his grave and then come here. This would make something a little different instead of a simple repetition.

Kenneth Shear: I would just like to say that there is a certain part of me that is not comfortable with actions that, from my perspective, put unnecessary value onto the past. That has a certain devotional flavour. It seems for me that more should be directed to the future. I know that it is very easy to imagine practical possibilities, but it does not seem practical that a meeting should take place once a year in which people come internationally from everywhere with different group activities going on throughout the course of the year, and to come for one weekend and behave in any manner whatsoever that could be considered like anything I have participated in as group Work. I am not denying that there is a value to the meeting, whether it should not have an aim or that it could not serve a purpose, but we need a view on what that purpose is. Because of our contacts it seems that everyone has a feeling of service and as a theme that makes sense. Perhaps an aim for the Conference could be that all those with different perspectives could meet with the aim of sharing their perspectives. That could be a focus for the Conference. A collage different disconnected presentations and some kind of dialogue could bring to people a greater depth of understanding of the service they could enter into in their own group, where they spend 99.9% of their life during the year.

John Scullion: I have been listening to what different people are saying--what Bonnie said, what Keith said about the octave. I have an idea to think about, but one which could change what we are doing when we come to this hotel, where the food is put before us, the hot water flows, and so on. Maybe we could rent somewhere--I have done this before, and it worked--and look after ourselves, serve ourselves, and then we could interact together as a small community. That might be a possibility. I am not suggesting we form a group, but it would change the way we do things here, because we sit all day here, sluggish, and the tone sinks. I am very tired, even though I have not done very much.

Jeff Taylor: First of all, I agree with John that it might be useful to introduce a change of tempo. My body is sluggish despite the fact that I've been out for walks. One way we might change things is to further what we do in the forums to increase the intensity. I have been interested in what happens in the forums; each time at the point when were starting to get interesting and people have been able to say what they wished, then there has been a possibility to bring things forward, to introduce something new into the situation through interaction. We have not arrived at that stage in the forums yet. There are ways of bringing it forward, like keeping the group smaller. Having smaller groups would allow working together intensely on certain issues, and this would effect a change of tempo as well. To follow what Harry said about the past and instability, I want to focus on the word "devotion," because I think devotion is an important element of our involvement. It has to do with a respect for Mr. Gurdjieff and the motives that has brought us all here. It is to recognize a living tradition and its transmission. This is not something that Mr. Gurdjieff stopped giving us fifty years ago. The tradition did not stop and here we are still working on the old material. If there is something here, then it is still alive and is still being transmitted through books, the Movements and people who knew Mr. Gurdjieff and through people who are connected to his transmission. All that is alive, and to do something which involves recognizing that, and an act of respect may be shown by going to his grave. I don't know. It might be something more modest than that, but an important issue has been brought up, one connected to the past and the future at once. I acknowledge what you said about energies petering out, and that is right as well. We should recognize the past and be open to the new before us. This cannot be pre-figured. This is one of the points where a shock enters, but we can't say what kind of shock we need, and when it comes there will be a tendency to divide ourselves into factions because we all have different reactions and responses to what the shock is. It might pull us apart or bring us together. We need to recognize these possibilities.

Keith Buzzell: One of the important dimensions of the Mi-Fa, of that Mechano-Coinciding interval, because of the motion from that point, is looking at the Fa to note when we come to a coalescence of identity, and we may come to many different coalescences. I just want to add one thing to what Jeff mentioned about the carrying further of presentations. Perhaps because of my own background, being trained in the biological sciences and as a physician, I attend a lot of scientific gatherings, but also because of the number of years I had with Mrs. Irma Popoff when she modelled this for us, we were never permitted to say any-thing without being prepared to be subject to reason. "i don't understand it," she would say, "it doesn't appear to be reasonable. Justify in Law what you have said." etc. We have done very little of that. We have been very kind and very polite and very acceptant of each other, and I think this is one of the changes that we might entertain: part of the Mi-Fa. We begin to entertain friction because we are approaching the real friction of any gathering together: to challenge each other, not to challenge in the sense of wanting to get the better or prove one is right or wrong, but simply if something is unclear or appears to have been presented in such a way that it does not fellow reason, because one of our ultimate aims is to help each other, and to challenge each other's reason and so help each other to grow. That would make a big difference in the presentations. We could extend and perhaps spend a whole day on one presentation, because who knows what is going to happen if we really open up an issue and then come back the next day and see what we did learn. What did all us learn by coming into what may appear to be verbal conflict, disagreement or searching and exploring and so forth, and then try to put all of that into the digestive process. By the next day we may all have a better understanding. I delight in the challenge of ideas and am a bit disappointed when a presentation is finished, followed by a few polite questions and no barks. In such situations we should grow.

Paul Taylor: Chris, may I ask you as an outside observer to address a question that means a great deal to me: How can an assembly of this kind, forums of this kind, serve the larger work of Gurdjieff groups?

All & Everything Conference 1998

Chris Thompson: I am willing to comment, but it won't help you. Sitting here with any, powerful backward glances at what we are doing predicting the future. I honestly don't know how this forum can help and serve, but I will give it as much attention as I possibly can, because there is life here, there are relationships building. I have always reported this back to my friends, that you must not belittle the fact that here people come with great sincerity and there is live exchange. This has a meaning, but what meaning I cannot say, and what course you should be pursuing I simply do not know. But to me this unknowing is the real key to the route back to the Fourth Way. Unless I can live unknowing constructively, be part of it here and now, then it is not genuine. It is a projection or other. So if you don't mind, I cannot answer, but I can be supportive in the desire to find a direction. Finding that is the constant search.

Paul Taylor: I recall that James Moore, in his first presentation here two years ago addressed what he labelled a complicity of sincerity. I like that statement because none of us should, or need to, define a "material" direction, but we have to consider the material needs of a conference of this size. This is only a minor aspect, however, of the consensus that we make an effort to do something particular to celebrate the 50th anniversary of Gurdjieff's departure, and not necessarily by looking "backward," but in order to better see forward.

Richard Liebow: I would like to give my impression of the last three conferences. The first year we all walked into the hotel. The second year, at least 50% of the people who attended had not been here before. That is freshness: and, this year at least 50% of the people here had not attended before. This freshness has brought new blood.

Bert Sharp: A good turnover.

Sy Ginsburg: As a practical matter, because there is so much diversity here. I wonder if this is something that a Planning Committee--and it could be an entirely different one for '99--could somehow get together, and in today's world, I wonder if that can be done on Email, not at the conference. but for whatever committee there is to consider these things in detail and come to a productive consensus.

Bert Sharp: I mentioned earlier that this seems to me from a practical point of view--bearing mind what happened in the run-up to this Conference--one of the things we ought to think seriously about, that the new Planning Committee ought to think about, is getting a consensus about the format of the next Conference, and to publicize this as soon as possible in a newsletter to the whole list of participants by August or September, hoping to receive some further feedback to firm up the general invitation which should go out before Christmas, and organize things so that we get paper proposals early and construct a programme that can be sent out with a reminder, a month before the Conference. Something like that, from a practical point of view, is necessary. We need to learn from past experiences.

Fourth Open Forum - Where Do We Go From Here?

Marlena Buzzell: I think also from a practical point of view, considering the respect we have developed for each other, that people should be more willing to get their papers in on time, and I think that for those of us who are not speakers we should act as participants. I would suggest that people think of the things we have discussed today and think about service, think over the months to come how it could be different, and pass suggestions on to the Planning Committee.

Bert Sharp: That would be the basis of the Newsletter.

Paul Taylor: In academic circles there is a system that works very well, and that is to have the papers assembled before the conference, so that the participants can read them before they are presented, so that the presentation would be a summary to provoke discussion.

Bert Sharp: I agree that this is the way it has worked in academic circles, but to be blunt and honest, for this Conference I heard from something like 50% of people who would attend, and half did not send in their coupons, most did not send in their money. It finally filtered in. It is all sorted out now, but this is to my mind a lack of responsibility and dilatoriness.

Chris Thompson: So this Conference is at a lower level than ordinary life.

Bert Sharp: I feel that in a way perhaps it has merit because there is an assumption to the effect "Oh. Of course I am coming. You did not expect that I would not come." Still, a lot of people did not make it clear that they were coming, and we had to commit ourselves to the hotel, and so on.

Nicholas Tereshchenko: Well, it seems to me that we should elect a Committee now, and a Committee that will be able to work together by E-mail or otherwise, and I think we have everybody here who is likely to be on the Committee. I feel personally that I have been an unnecessary member. I have not done any work except to write to people. Apart from that I have done nothing, so I should be replaced by someone who will be more active, and now that Dr. Andrew Rawlinson now lives in France, he could represent the French and the Europeans on the Committee.

Dr. Andrew Rawlinson: I feel an outsider in the strict sense since I am not a member of the Work in any real sense.

Paul Taylor: A Planning Committee and an Advisory Board are two separate functions. For an Advisory Board it is wise to have representatives with a variety of interests and maybe geographic. That matters nothing to me. A Planning Committee has to be the committee that supports Bert. My own feeling is that it must be local, and work on the spot. I can do little from Geneva, but on the Advisory Board I can do much from Geneva. We must distinguish these two bodies and their functions. You are right that, Andrew. The Planning Committee is what is often called elsewhere the Local Arrangements Committee, one that does the entire donkey work that Bert and Frank have done for us. The Advisory Board can be given the task of supporting that Committee by screening paper proposals and making contacts.

All & Everything Conference 1998

Nicholas Tereshchenko: So the Committee should be composed of people who live locally?

Marlena Buzzell: I don't think it is necessary for everyone to be local, because we do have E-Mail, and I put myself at Bert's disposition. He can use me as he likes. Earlier I said that I would put the Proceedings together, but we now agree that we will wait until next year. It seems a bit late to decide on another Planning Committee, so we should stay as we are.

Paul Taylor: At any rate, we are not here to elect a Planning Committee. Anyone can express his feelings on the subject elsewhere. I am also willing to serve Bert in anyway possible. In a sense, I regret that I haven't served enough to date. I am one of those that are open to accusation of being silent.

Nicholas Tereshchenko: I did that last year and the year before.

Keith Buzzell: I get the feeling that there may be a degree of consensus relative to the question we went past rather quickly, but this is perhaps one of the most essential steps in getting what I believe a number of us see as more discipline in the form and sequence of the programme itself: that we should have a date limit on all papers proposed for submission, and we should make use of the Advisory Board for this purpose.

Bert Sharp: We did have a date limit of 31 January for the submission of papers, which very few met.

Chris Thompson: Then why did we accept late entries?

Bert Sharp: Because without them we would not have had a programme.

Chris Thompson: This is a great mistake. You should have had a much better programme with more time for exchanges- You did not need so many papers. If you were afraid the Conference would not work if there were not enough papers, there is something wrong. You need a few quality starting points for an exchange of ideas, really serious data from which we can work, lots of opportunities for exchange so that we could really deepen and face the problems and that sort of thing. I think packing a programme is like ordinary life. It is cheap and unprofitable.

Keith Buzzell: We need time. There has to be time and has been the Advisory Board with respect for authority because we ask them to advise and evaluate. Now we hope they have suggestions for improvement, re-submission and so forth. I have been through this when I was anxious to deliver a paper at a Conference; you send it in six months ahead and get it back a month later saying this is unclear, too long, etc., and that you'd better rewrite the whole thing.

Bert Sharp: We had a date of 31 January on the call for papers, and by that date we had less than one paper proposed per programme day.

Fourth Open Forum - Where Do We Go From Here?

Paul Taylor: I think the Board should have been called upon to collaborate better with you along these lines.

Nicholas Tereshchenko: I still think we should go ahead and appoint the Committee to arrange next years meeting, if there is going to be one. At this moment there is no Committee as far as I can see. We don't know who will arrange things. Will you stay on, Marlena? Sy? Frank?

All: Yes.

Nicholas Tereshchenko: Then, there are the addresses. We need somebody practical for the main areas. We have two residents of England here, Bert and Frank, and a third who might serve, Robert Bryce.

Paul Taylor: How many do we need on the Committee? Six?

Nicholas Tereshchenko: Six or seven.

Paul Taylor: All right. We have Sy, Bert, Frank, Dimitri, Marlena and myself. We would be glad to include another.

Nicholas Tereshchenko: Just a few minutes ago we were talking about the local men who could help Bert, now you are mentioning one in Greece, another, Marlena, in the United States, you in Switzerland. Which leaves only Frank?

Jeff Taylor: I would be prepared to serve on the Planning Committee. I am not so concerned about the locality, because what I see as the main work that is coming out of this meeting at present is putting together a programme that is more on the line of what various people have said in terms of going into more depth, which does not need people necessarily to get together, because most of us have E-mail facilities. I think we can go from there and really start off working up the structure. I think we have learned a lot this year, particularly about the structure.

Marlena Buzzell: Then, we have Michael Smith on the Planning Committee as well.

Paul Taylor: For conferences of this sort, normally one has a local planning group, and Bert and Frank fit that bill very well. You can have any number of people from outside to help organization, so I have no reservations about continuing to serve on the Planning Committee, as long as I can be useful. There must be a distinction, however, between the Planning Committee and the Advisory Board. There has been some confusion of distinction this year, but the Planning Committee can continue to function as it has. Are you willing, Frank?

All & Everything Conference 1998

Frank Brzeski: Oh yes, I think so and I think perhaps if Jeff is prepared to undertake some of the work that Bert has done in the past, then the burden will shift from Bert, and the change in roles might be useful, an organic development in that context as well.

Paul Taylor: The members of the Planning Committee from each general area--North America, England and Continental Europe--can be responsible for filtering communications through to the local planning group. I am willing to do that for Mainland Europe, just as Sy does that for North America. That way, many problems need not come directly to Bert and Frank.

Keith Buzzell: The Planning Committee does not have to be involved in the papers. I hope that is clear. What I mean is that there could be an announcement that anyone who has an interest in submitting a paper can do so directly to a member of the Advisory Board, so the Planning Committee need not get caught up into thinking it is their responsibility for that.

Paul Taylor: Exactly. The announcements that go out should not direct all papers to Bert, but by geographical zone. This will give appropriate responsibility to regional members of the Advisory Board.

Bonnie Phillips: But with respect, I propose that the details we are talking about are really up to the Planning Committee, up to the people who have done this before and who have the knowledge to carry it on. I would hate to see the endeavour we have been through just dribble away. I would like to see an intentional goal, and with that we can begin. This Forum is "Where do we go from here.?" and I think that on a practical note we don't need to determine all these details. We have lost half our audience already.

Chris Thompson: Just more indiscipline, you see. The hallmark of this Conference is the name of whatever has been. People don't attend the meetings on time; the conveners do not ask the meetings to start on time. There is an attitude of indiscipline which is terribly characteristic and completely inappropriate, and it marks everything. You know you are just drawing attention to it. It shows that people talk but are not serious.

Paul Taylor: Yes, that is why I began by saying that when Gurdjieff brought things to an end over and over again, he'd look to his pupils as if to ask. "Ladies and gentlemen, how are you going to continue?" He reminded others that one cannot keep going without a pause. He said again and again. "Let's stop here."
And, perhaps we should stop here as well. The consensus is that we should plan a meeting next year, and we agree to place the organization in the hands of the Planning Committee to receive and transmit suggestions.

Keith Buzzell: One more thing before you leave and that is that everyone should feel a sense of responsibility for communicating perceptions and impressions, whatever you feel may be helpful. Put it on paper and send to somebody, anybody . And do it soon, perhaps by the end of April, before the first of May. Have your own ideas in the hands of people who can generate what we want.

End of Session

Appendix 1 - Gurdjieff by Carl Zigrosser

(This essay was first published in The New Republic, New York: Vol. LIX (757), June 5, 1929, pp. 66-69.)

One of the most interesting developments of modern times in the realm of philosophic ideas is the system expounded by M. Gurdjieff with which many Americans have become familiar through the work of Mr. A. R. Orage. The following article by Mr. Zigrosser makes no attempt to explain the Gurdjieff philosophy, but gives a vivid picture of a visit to the Gurdjieff Institute, at Fontainebleau, and a personal sketch of its head.

When I visited the Gurdjieff Institute at Fontainebleau for the first time, one gray and showery June Sunday morning, I was taken out into the garden to meet Mr. Gurdjieff, who was strolling there with an old Russian friend. As they approached me, Mr. Gurdjieff was walking with a slow, firm step, his hands behind his back: I saw a man of medium height but powerful build, swarthy complexion and piercing black eyes. He was dressed in almost shabby clothes, a rusty black overcoat, and a slouch hat, all of which he wore with indifference to ordinary standards of fashion. He thus presented a deceptively undistinguished appearance. In contrast, I remember how impressive he looked in oriental clothes, in an old painting by Mr. Salzmann which I saw later. I also have another, and still more vivid impression of Mr. Gurdjieff sitting cross-legged in his Turkish bath and wrapped in an enormous white towel, which set off the swarthiness of his face.

When we came near, he opened the conversation by saying, "I smell American." I had been prepared for this sort of greeting by the reports of previous visitors, so I was not as startled as I might have been. He went on to explain in his curious English: "You no take bath here last night; I smell American smell." After some conversation he asked if I could drink. When I replied that I hoped I could, he invited me to sit beside him at dinner - a place which I learned later was reserved for those who drank. He laughed and added that he liked three kinds of people; those who could drink, those who could tell stories - and the third he would tell me about some other time. A few minutes later, he left us and went to his room.

While waiting for dinner I explored the grounds with Mr. de Hartmann, a brilliant musician who has been associated with Mr. Gurdjieff for many years. The Chateau and the grounds had the lovely, quiet charm of old French country places. This one had been left practically unchanged since the seventeenth century, when Madame Maintenon, among others, is supposed to have lived in it, and when it was remodelled with royal funds. The house consisted of a central building with a wing on either side, and a rambling addition containing the kitchen, stable, and former servants' quarters. The main building - called "the Ritz" by those at the Institute - faced a sloping lawn, laid out with gravel paths and a fountain, and said to have been designed by Le Notre.

Mr. de Hartmann and I came back in time for dinner, which was served to about six or seven older members of the community in the main dining room. The meal was much like those that I later discovered were served on feast-days or other special occasions, beginning with platters of hors d'oeuvres, potato and other mixed salads, smoked fish, onion tops and other herbs, eaten by hand, such as mint, fennel, parsley, tarragon, and exotic plants that have no English names.

These herbs were always on the table at the Institute. The soup was followed by Russian meat cakes, and a rhubarb compote. At other times, kasha or the Armenian madzoon was served as dessert. Occasionally a whole sheep's head was cooked as a delicacy, and served by Mr. Gurdjieff to his guests with smiling reflections on the foolishness of a civilization which allowed him to buy such a morsel for a couple of francs. Some kind of spirits, either Vieux Marc or Armagnac, was usually passed around. There was a ritual for the drinking of this brandy: seven rounds were served, each with a toast, to which everyone was expected to drain his glass. The toasts seldom varied from the following order: (1) To the health of all idiots; (2) To the ordinary idiot; (3) To the candidate for idiocy; (4) To the superidiot; (5) To the archidiot; (6) To the hopeless idiot; (7) To the compassionate idiot.

I once asked him why he always toasted idiots, why he did not invoke a benevolent power in his toasts, such as Beelzebub, for instance. He answered that he sometimes did, but that he never could venture - and here his tone assumed the greatest reverence - to drink to Beelzebub himself. "To the tip of his tail, yes, or his hoofs, or his horns, maybe - but never to the great being himself." And he showed me the chair that Beelzebub always sat in when he visited him, pointing out that there was room for him to curl up his tail comfortably, and so on.

As we rose from the table, Mr. Gurdjieff asked me whether I was full "like American man or like donkey." When I answered, "Like donkey," he replied: "Much better to be full like donkey than like American man. Americans have weak stomachs. European man ruined by his head, American man ruined by his stomach." Then we went up to his room for coffee and a liqueur.

Toward evening I was invited to go to Paris with Mr. Gurdjieff. He, Mr. de Hartmann, Mr. Salzmann, and I, got into his car and we were off, Mr. Gurdjieff at the wheel. He took a special route to show me the beauties of the forest of Fontainebleau, and talked of the many lovely sights in France that the tourist in the railroad train can never see.

On reaching Paris we stopped off at the Cafe de la Paix for brandy and coffee, while Mr. Gurdjieff worked on the manuscript of his book, *Beelzebub's Tales to His Grandson*, on which he has been busy for the past four years. He did much of his writing, or revising, in some crowded cafe, "his office" as he called it. And certainly the Cafe de le Paix, with the stream of passers-by on the Boulevard, should be crowded enough for anyone. Mr. Gurdjieff once remarked that he preferred

Appendix 1 - Gurdjieff by Carl Zigrosser

to work thus, because the pageant of idiots under his eyes gave him a more detached view of the human race, and so put him more in the frame of mind of a visitor, like Beelzebub, from another planet.

We sat at the Cafe de la Paix for some time, until Mr. Gurdjieff suggested that we go to his apartment. He had at first intended to visit a restaurant where he sometimes went to eat crayfish imported live from Russia, of which he was very fond. But he decided that he did not deserve to go there that night: he had not done enough work during the day and did not feel that he could indulge himself. So, at about ten o'clock, we went to his own place, an ordinary furnished apartment in the seventeenth arrondissement. When Mr. Gurdjieff was comfortably stretched out on the bed, we had our evening meal, oriental and simple. There were slices of cold meat and smoked fish, chunks of bread, handfuls of green herbs and onion tops, all eaten with the fingers without plates, and the whole washed down with brandy and coffee. I shall never forget the picture of Mr. Gurdjieff reclining on the bed, as only an easterner can, a glimpse of his hairy chest showing through his open shirt, his frame shaking with laughter at some story told by Mr. Salzmann. It struck me then what a Rabelaisian gusto for life (among many other things) the man had - a gusto for life in its essence, undiluted by the affectations of culture. At the table, his quick movements and gleaming smile expressed a huge relish for plain food. He had an oriental love of story-telling, the racier the stories the better. Even his English speech had an oriental simplicity that gave a deceptive impression of naïveté. Then, like the forest philosophers of India, he had little use for books and the external aids for learning. It is interesting to notice that even in revising his own book, he often had someone read it aloud to him, for his grasp of it was better through his ears than through his eyes. With us in the West, the eye has become almost our only means of absorbing ideas.

Looking back on my meetings with Gurdjieff, I feel that it is important to distinguish between Gurdjieff the man, with a certain life history, and Gurdjieff the exponent of a certain philosophy of life. If one places too much emphasis on Gurdjieff the man, responding, pleasantly or otherwise, to his rich, incalculable personality, but making no attempt to divine his ideas, one misses practically everything of value in the contact. Primarily Gurdjieff is a man, with a childhood and maturity behind him, crowded with associations and impressions, which, according to his own deterministic philosophy, are shaping his present behavior; he too has his prejudices and mistakes. But he is also expounding certain ideas, obtained from God knows where, a certain standard of values, certain attitudes to life, and a certain technique for meeting it, which I, among others, have found extremely interesting and, as far as I have been able to try them out, sound. These abstract conceptions are expressed in terms that are provided by his past experiences, and are more or less unintelligible to a person of my past. In his company I always had to make an effort to assimilate his language - both his speech and his actions - extract the pure ideas from it, and translate them into terms of my own experience. If I merely reacted to his personality, I would be missing a unique opportunity, and he would laugh at me and put me down as one of the "idiots." In such matters he is quite ruthless. He makes use of people when he needs them, but always under conditions that will allow them to derive a benefit for themselves if they make the effort. It is only the opportunity that he offers them; if they do not choose to grasp it, he laughs at them and uses them anyway. But if he is convinced of the seriousness of their efforts, he can be untiring, patient, and most ingenious in providing opportunities.

From what I saw of him, Mr. Gurdjieff's personal conduct can best be understood if one thinks of him as an artist in life. As an artist, he works not only through words, and music, and dances, but directly on human beliefs. His energies at that time were concentrated largely on writing and music, and he was apparently gay, or depressed, or tired, largely according as his day's task had gone well or ill. In matters of food, and shelter, and a sense of responsibility for the well-being of dependents, he is much like a patriarch of old; and he is treated as such by these dependents. But he is not explicitly a teacher, nor a prophet. He has none of the airs of saintliness, which so often make for hypocrisy in teachers and confusion in their pupils. Realizing that it is impossible to impart experience, he does not teach his philosophy. He believes, with the self-made man, that there is no royal road to understanding; what he himself acquired and could only acquire by effort, others must also acquire by effort. If they do not make the effort, so much the worse for them. He aims merely to induce this effort in others, to spur them on to further self-exertions.

It is natural, therefore, that he sets a high value on purposiveness: the quantity and direction of conscious human effort. I remember once hearing a saying of his, which ran something like this: "The difference between an ordinary man and a conscious man is in the persistence of their aims. There are some people who maintain an aim for a week, or a month, or a year. They are relatively ephemeral, like insects. There are some whose major purpose animates them during their lifetime: they have attained human stature. Then there are the rare few whose aim is so intense and all-embracing as to endure beyond the human span. These are immortal."

Mr. Gurdjieff often undertakes the role of a destroying angel, and this is, I think, an important part of his work. His destructive force is aimed chiefly at breaking down old associations, verbal and otherwise - the tyranny of our unconscious impressions. He plays the part of an irritant or friction producer, to shock and challenge those about him into consciousness. In doing this, he plays many roles, parts which in the eyes of most of us may often seem not only capricious but foolish.

Besides a number of week-ends at the Chateau, I spent several days during the week working at the Institute. The atmosphere at the place was quite different then from that of Saturday and Sunday. The relaxation of the feast day was over, and work was the order of the day. Many of the older members, such as the Salzmanns and the de Hartmanns, were engaged in special tasks, and were not seen by the manual workers, whom I joined. The work, besides that in the house and the kitchen garden, consisted mainly of making roads, clearing the forest, and breaking up stone for road metal. The work was arduous and the hours long, but whatever one did was purely voluntary. It was this knowledge that I did not have to do a stroke of work unless I wanted to that made what I did so valuable to me. When my muscles ached and my body asked, "Why are you doing this?" I could answer with peculiar poignancy, "I am doing this for consciousness." The manual work lasted from eight until twelve, from one until four, and from four-thirty until seven. The meals were served either out-of-doors or in a dingy room in the former servants' quarters. The menu was about as follows: for breakfast, coffee and toast without butter; for lunch a huge bowl of vegetable soup with meat in it, plenty of greens, and sometimes a cooked vegetable or macaroni, with large chunks of bread; for tea, bread and tea; for supper, much the same as for lunch. But cooking was not a fine art at the Institute. Food was given its proportionate place in the scheme of things by being served in simple courses in quantities sufficient to sustain existence. Elaborate meals were reserved for special occasions.

One of the most interesting experiences at the Institute was the bath every Saturday night. The bathhouse was built into a hillside, to retain its heat. All through the afternoon, Mr. Gurdjieff's brother, Dmitri Ivanovitch, was busy stoking up the fires, to make sure of plenty of hot water and steam. The bath-house consisted of three rooms: a cooling chamber with couches and benches to rest on; a large circular room, moderately hot, with benches and showers to soap oneself and wash; and then a small room for extremely hot temperatures. In the cooling chamber were frescoes by Salzmann, some of them faded by the steam. Saturday night was always a special occasion at the Institute. The women took their bath at five o'clock. When they had finished, and everybody had eaten a light supper, all adjourned to the study-house for coffee, some time between eight and nine o'clock. There everyone sat about while a chapter from Mr. Gurdjieff's book was read aloud or - as happened the first time I was there - Mr. de Hartmann played the organ. Then, when Mr. Gurdjieff gave the signal, men and boys went to the bathhouse. The bath was the regular Russian steam bath, accompanied with much joking and storytelling; but sometimes Mr. Gurdjieff's most valuable remarks came out in the course of this apparently casual conversation. He used to call upon each newcomer to tell two or three stories as a payment for his bath.

The study-house, on the lawn, was a wide, irregularly shaped octagon - or rather a pentagon with three of its corners blunted to make additional sides - with a slightly arched roof. The ceiling was lined with a canopy, painted in bright colours, many of which, alas! had faded in that damp climate. The electric lights were hooded with shades of oriental design. The windows, running in an unbroken line along six sides, were painted with Persian and Hindu designs. On the balcony above the entrance was a collection of exotic musical instruments. On the canopy were painted, amongst the designs, a number of proverbs and sayings, of which the following is characteristic: "Happy is he who has no soul; happy is he who has a soul; terrible is it for him who has a soul germinating in him."

Still another side of Mr. Gurdjieff is revealed in his music, a music whose quality is so different from what one would associate with his outward appearance, that it was hard at first to believe that it had come from him. For, from this extraordinary man with the Rabelaisian exterior issues music that is spiritual in the fullest sense of that much abused word. For me, this music was an important clue in estimating the range of his character, for it reveals depths of tenderness and sensitiveness that were seldom visible during my brief stay with him. This music seems to fall into two chief groups: pieces that are strongly oriental in tone, and others that are similar to early church music, and which, I was told, Mr. Gurdjieff had composed for the prayers and invocations in his book, under the general title of Temple Music. It is said that he plans to compose a body of music which will express the same meaning, in the world of emotions, that he is expressing for the mind in his book, making the two complementary to each other. Few of the pieces take more than five minutes to play. I have been told that these short pieces are studies for subsequent choral and orchestral compositions. During my visit, they were played by Mr. de Hartmann, sometimes on the piano, and sometimes on the harmonium—a small house organ. Occasionally Mr. Gurdjieff played a tiny organ, specially designed to be held on the lap, while Mr. de Hartmann accompanied him on the piano. On this instrument one plays the keyboard with one hand and manipulates the bellows with the other.

The pieces themselves have definite musical form, both in the development of the theme and in the harmonic structure. The harmonies are simple but inevitable; some pieces are polyphonic.[1] The rhythms are often subtle and complex, and contribute greatly to the total effect of the music. As Mr. Gurdjieff composes a piece, he plays it over and over to Mr. de Hartmann, emphasizing now the melody, and now the rhythm or harmonic structure, until Mr. de Hartmann has it firmly fixed in his memory and can transcribe it to paper at his leisure.

The most unusual thing about this music, however, was its effect on me when I heard it, different from that of almost any other music I had ever listened to. I can only explain this by describing the effect of both upon myself. Usually music prompts me to day-dreams and lovely fancies; it carries me outside myself into an unreal world of images and undischarged muscular stimulations, with an indirect stirring of the emotions. But this music did not carry me out of myself at all: it centred its effect upon my very essence, it appealed directly to my emotions. It sang as if it had a message for me alone in the world - yet others have told me since that they had had precisely the same feeling. It aroused in me at will the feelings of joy, pity, sorrow, fear, struggle, and above all an exquisite yet terrible yearning. What I heard during those few hours made almost all other music seem tame and haphazard.

---

[1] I have since heard a number of pieces in which the harmony was complex and in which dissonance was used in an extraordinarily effective way.

Appendix 2 - List of Attendees

Warren Alksnis, USA.
Sebouh V. Der Bedrossian, USA.
Harry J. Bennett, USA.
Mrs. Bennett, USA.
David Bramwell, England.
Robert Bryce, England.
Frank Brzeski, England.
Martin Butler, England.
Keith Buzzell, USA.
Marlena Buzzell, USA.
Edgar D. Clarke, England.
Bob Curran, USA.
Wim Van Dullemen, Holland.
Robert Ennis, USA.
Stefanos Elmazis, Greece.
V. Fitch, England.
Seymour B. Ginsburg, USA.
Noel Glendon, England.
Jim Gomez, England.
Richard Liebow, USA.
Forrest McIlwain, USA.
J. McKinley, England.
James Moore, England.
William Y. Murphey, USA.
John Perrott, England.
Adam Petts, England.
Bonnie Phillips, USA.
Ken Pledge, England.
Dr. Andrew Rawlinson, France.
D. Robinson, England.
John Scullion, England.
H J Sharp, England.
Kenneth E. Shear, England.
Michael Smyth, USA.
Barbara Smyth, USA.
Prof. Paúl Beekman Taylor, Switzerland.
Jeff Taylor, England.
Dikran Takvorian, USA.
Nicolas Tereshchenko, France.
Chris Thompson, England.
Dorothy Usiskin, USA.
Sophia Wellbeloved, England.
Penni Wood, England.

Appendix 3 - Planning Committee for 1998-1999

USA

Seymour Ginsburg
Marlena Buzzell

Europe

Professor Paul Beekman Taylor
Dimitri Peretzi

UK

Frank Brzeski
Jeff Taylor
Bert Sharp

Advisory Panel Coordinator

James Moore

Index

A

Absolute, 83, 89, 152, 158, 181, 182, 234, 235, 237, 238, 241, 242, 252, 255, 261, 336
active, 15, 17, 19, 26, 49, 53, 180, 208, 227, 230, 239, 245, 280, 283, 285, 290, 296, 300, 307, 314, 349, 362
Aeon, 242, 250
affirm, 280, 335
affirmation, 287, 333
affirming, 121, 148
Africa, 212, 244, 245, 316
Ahoon, 47, 280, 293, 294, 295
Aieioiuoa, 274, 286
Aim, 30, 32, 33, 36, 51, 64, 69, 117, 152, 213, 268, 269, 288, 315, 328, 330, 340, 342, 348, 355, 358, 369
Ain Soph, 233
air, 34, 35, 36, 43, 45, 46, 72, 88, 197, 274, 290, 353, 355
Akhaldan, 54
Alchemy, 32, 44, 88, 116, 128, 129, 131, 137, 184, 209
alcohol, 284
Salzmann, de, Jean; Michel, 18, 170, 223, 321, 322, 323, 328, 358, 366, 367, 368, 370
Alla-attapan, 292
allegorical, 78, 81, 82
allegory, 77, 81, 337
Amarhoodan, 125
America, 14, 23, 56, 67, 71, 76, 81, 91, 108, 168, 169, 171, 172, 245, 262, 284, 320, 326, 347, 364, 366, 367
Anderson, Margaret, 14
Angel, 73, 74, 121, 129, 250, 323, 369
Anklad, 252, 295
Anthropic, 236

Antkooano, 271
Anulios, 44, 65, 330
Aquarius, 46
Archangel, 287, 293, 296
archetype, 199
Aristotle, 241
armagnac, 367
Armenia, 269
Armenian, 99, 269, 270, 367
ascend, 169, 324
ascending, 45, 125, 127, 152, 178, 233, 249, 251, 354
Ashiata Shiemash, 55, 68, 69, 82, 86, 215, 217, 282, 296, 336, 341
Ashish, Sri Madhava, 17, 23, 67, 98, 99, 103, 323
astral, 117, 128, 131, 136
Astrology, 45, 185
Astrolonomy, 94, 143, 145
Atlantis, 44, 70, 77, 82, 283, 284, 289
Atom, 111, 143, 235, 237, 239
Atomic, 143, 144, 182, 212, 234, 235, 236, 255
Attention, 21, 24, 26, 51, 86, 87, 89, 90, 95, 99, 103, 109, 112, 116, 155, 177, 207, 208, 211, 212, 265, 271, 273, 310, 313, 316, 335, 336, 341, 348, 360, 365
Atziluth, 233
Autoegocrat, 234
awareness, 20, 22, 40, 81, 85, 86, 87, 94, 103, 116, 142, 154, 157, 171, 214, 215, 246, 247, 248, 260, 277, 310, 315, 325, 337, 340
axis, 177, 178

B

Babylon, 69, 212, 336
Bailey, Alice, 75, 76, 91, 93, 102

Bakhtiar, Laleh, 168, 169, 170, 171, 173, 175, 182, 183, 184, 185, 194, 196, 198, 200, 201, 202, 203, 205
Baraka, 274
Beekman Taylor, Paul, 13, 15, 16, 26, 106, 108, 312, 352, 373, 374
Beelzebub, 14, 18, 19, 28, 30, 31, 33, 38, 41, 43, 44, 45, 46, 47, 49, 50, 51, 53, 54, 55, 56, 62, 67, 68, 70, 71, 73, 77, 80, 81, 82, 84, 88, 89, 93, 95, 109, 111, 114, 118, 121, 125, 126, 127, 131, 137, 139, 141, 142, 145, 146, 148, 156, 157, 163, 164, 174, 206, 209, 212, 214, 217, 227, 230, 232, 252, 255, 276, 280, 281, 282, 283, 284, 285, 286, 287, 288, 289, 290, 291, 292, 293, 294, 295, 296, 297, 299, 304, 305, 312, 322, 324, 329, 331, 332, 333, 334, 367, 368
Beelzebub's Tales
  The Tales, 27, 30, 32, 33, 43, 47, 51, 52, 53, 54, 56, 59, 61, 77, 102, 104, 115, 136, 137, 215, 230, 252, 278, 280, 288, 290, 293, 304, 318, 323, 341
Being, 19, 21, 33, 34, 41, 50, 51, 52, 54, 55, 56, 58, 59, 60, 62, 63, 66, 67, 68, 69, 70, 72, 74, 76, 77, 78, 79, 80, 82, 84, 93, 94, 96, 103, 107, 108, 109, 110, 112, 113, 114, 116, 117, 118, 122, 125, 126, 127, 128, 129, 131, 137, 138, 143, 149, 154, 155, 157, 164, 169, 171, 177, 180, 183, 187, 195, 202, 203, 204, 206, 207, 211, 212, 216, 219, 221, 223, 225, 226, 227, 229, 232, 233, 234, 238, 239, 240, 241, 242, 244, 245, 246, 247, 249, 250, 251, 252, 261, 262, 263, 269, 270, 272, 274, 276, 284, 285, 286, 287, 288, 289, 290, 291, 292, 293, 295, 296, 299, 300, 301, 302, 304, 305, 307, 308, 311, 317, 321, 322, 325, 326, 327, 330, 331, 334, 335, 336, 337, 341, 348, 349, 352, 355, 356, 357, 359, 360, 363, 367, 369, 370
being-bodies, 240, 288, 289
being-effort, 302

Belcultassi, 54
Bennett, John G., 14, 16, 17, 31, 41, 47, 81, 93, 137, 165, 170, 265, 272, 273, 278, 279, 306, 321, 325, 326, 345, 373
Bhagavad Gita, 158
Big Bang, 143, 233, 236, 237, 254
biochemical, 57, 63
Blavatsky, Helena P., 67, 70, 71, 73, 74, 90, 91, 94, 102, 103, 104
Bliss, 45, 134
Bodhisattva, 99
Boehme, Jacob, 260
bone, 93, 126, 307
Bose-Einstein, 240
Brahma, 121
Brahman, 90
Brain, 31, 51, 56, 57, 58, 59, 60, 61, 62, 63, 64, 65, 126, 142, 144, 145, 152, 153, 154, 156, 175, 183, 193, 233, 242, 245, 246, 247, 248, 249, 250, 252, 262, 263, 264, 269, 275, 294, 297, 300, 303, 322, 325, 337, 342, 343
breath, 134, 140, 263, 275, 337
breathing, 137, 155, 208, 228
Briah, 233
Brook, Peter, 18
brother, 38, 55, 289, 356, 370
Brotherhood-Olbogmek, 69, 70
Bucke, Maurice, 249
Buddha, 44, 282, 294, 299
Buddhism, 15, 19, 216, 314, 315, 316
Buddhist, 315
Buzzell, Keith, 13, 16, 41, 49, 50, 62, 63, 64, 65, 66, 108, 110, 112, 116, 177, 179, 216, 219, 220, 262, 275, 276, 278, 305, 323, 325, 326, 341, 343, 354, 357, 359, 361, 362, 363, 364, 365, 373, 374

C

Calvados, 47
carbon, 95, 102, 239, 241, 274
carriage, 52, 278
Castanios-Flores, John, 19, 228

Index

Causal, 117, 128, 131, 136
Celestial, 126
center, 15, 17, 20, 25, 49, 58, 61, 64, 67, 68, 71, 82, 93, 114, 122, 128, 129, 138, 166, 176, 177, 179, 180, 182, 183, 184, 186, 203, 224, 225, 226, 236, 237, 251, 260, 272, 276, 277, 300, 301, 329, 330
Cerebellum, 125
chastity, 126, 315
cherubim, 126, 129, 134
Chi, 122
child, 35, 53, 107, 112, 142, 277, 335, 339, 343, 349
children, 16, 29, 35, 44, 65, 106, 121, 165, 211, 243, 262, 275, 304, 307, 327, 328, 334, 335, 345, 354, 355, 356
China, 126, 174, 315
Chinese, 230, 315, 316
Choon-Kil-Tez, 289, 292
Choon-Tro-Pel, 289, 292
Christ, 46, 56, 103, 104, 112, 122, 128, 133, 282, 307, 312, 322, 349
Christian, 174, 179, 216, 250, 322
Christianity, 89, 131, 272, 321
Cingulate, 65
Cingulate Gyrus, 65
coat, 320
  coated, 288
  coating, 125
coccyx, 127
comet, 43, 118, 329
Commission, 118, 330, 331, 342
Communion, 35
compassion, 72, 228, 229, 306, 325
concentrate, 125, 137, 157, 209, 231
concentration, 125, 137, 157, 209, 231
Conscience, 20, 55, 72, 95, 107, 195, 213, 274, 310, 322, 336, 342
conscious, 63, 82, 83, 86, 88, 89, 108, 117, 119, 125, 136, 138, 141, 154, 205, 228, 229, 233, 236, 248, 249, 252, 280, 286, 289, 295, 298, 300, 331, 336, 348, 349, 369
Conscious Labor, 82, 86, 89, 138, 286, 289, 295
consciousness, 41, 44, 79, 83, 85, 86, 87, 88, 89, 98, 106, 107, 115, 117, 133, 147, 154, 172, 195, 237, 249, 250, 252, 263, 277, 280, 286, 287, 297, 299, 309, 324, 325, 348, 370
constate, 303
  constatation, 292
  constatations, 54
contemplate, 141
  contemplation, 171
  contemplative, 155
Coombe Springs, 170
cosmic, 24, 50, 56, 62, 65, 68, 69, 75, 78, 81, 90, 96, 146, 147, 148, 149, 150, 151, 157, 170, 171, 181, 220, 230, 231, 232, 233, 234, 237, 249, 251, 255, 282, 286, 287, 289, 292, 293, 329, 330, 331
Cosmic Consciousness, 249
cosmology, 95, 139, 141, 147, 148, 149, 150, 152, 154, 157, 163, 178, 199, 315
Creation, 22, 38, 43, 44, 58, 75, 88, 116, 121, 128, 152, 180, 197, 207, 215, 233, 235, 236, 238, 250, 251, 254, 281, 282, 307, 333, 334, 339, 343
creative, 35, 43, 45, 121, 125, 127, 252, 262, 307, 334
Creator, 33, 68, 128, 138, 175, 207, 286, 287, 291, 292
Creed, Lewis, 19, 115, 228
crystallize, 83, 118, 125, 129, 221, 292, 330, 332, 333
  crystallization, 82, 86, 89, 127, 128, 295, 334
  crystallized, 53, 54, 55, 56, 62, 68, 84, 118, 211, 282, 294, 297, 299, 300, 301, 325, 329, 331, 332, 334, 336, 337

D

Daghestani, Shaykh, 170
Dalai Lama, 133
Dante Alighieri, 129, 158

daughter, 19, 228, 317, 356
death, 14, 15, 18, 35, 36, 37, 39, 40, 43, 44, 45, 47, 74, 77, 81, 94, 102, 106, 113, 118, 126, 131, 133, 134, 139, 142, 156, 157, 212, 220, 306, 307, 310, 311, 312, 313, 325, 328, 347, 354, 356
deflections, 148, 230, 231
Denying, 121, 148, 270, 296, 358
Dervish, 46, 109, 110, 139, 309
descend, 55, 225, 226
descending, 45, 121, 125, 151, 152, 178, 232, 237, 239, 249, 251
descent, 54, 55, 77, 125, 170, 271, 341
Descent, 54, 55, 341
Deskaldino, 291
Deuterocosmos, 237, 238, 255
devil, 129, 352
Dicker, The, 19, 228
die, 28, 29, 35, 47, 122, 133, 139, 142, 158
digest, 62, 252, 261, 342
digestion, 214, 225
dimension, 59, 96, 97, 122, 136, 137, 173, 211, 322
dissonance, 371
Djartklom, 286
DNA, 241, 242, 244, 245, 246, 252, 254, 262, 263
    chromosome, 243, 245
    genes, 114, 241, 242, 243, 244, 245, 246, 261
dog, 57, 81, 93, 94, 267, 334, 348
Dramatic Universe, 170
dream, 37, 39, 47, 65, 86, 97, 98, 99, 136, 212, 324, 372
Dullemen, Wim van, 14, 17, 25, 306, 312, 313, 339, 345, 346, 349, 350, 351, 373
dying, 35, 311

E

Earth, 33, 34, 35, 37, 38, 39, 43, 44, 45, 46, 53, 54, 55, 56, 67, 68, 69, 70, 77, 81, 82, 84, 94, 96, 110, 118, 125, 133, 140, 141, 144, 145, 146, 151, 155, 156, 164, 197, 212, 227, 237, 238, 240, 251, 254, 260, 262, 281, 282, 283, 285, 287, 288, 293, 294, 299, 305, 312, 330, 333, 336
Eckhart, Meister, 250
Ego, 107, 183, 186, 225, 226, 338, 339, 340, 342, 343, 352
    egoism, 59, 60, 331, 336, 340
    egoistic, 62
Egypt, 174, 209, 212
Egyptian, 45, 97
Einstein, 154, 164
electricity, 46
electron, 236, 238, 239
electrostatic, 239
element, 40, 43, 44, 45, 46, 47, 71, 91, 95, 102, 126, 133, 197, 215, 218, 232, 234, 235, 236, 237, 238, 239, 251, 254, 283, 291, 295, 310, 317, 318, 359
emanation, 180, 197, 233, 234, 235, 237, 238, 240, 248, 249, 250, 251, 255, 260, 261, 286
emotion, 44, 47, 51, 57, 58, 65, 310, 322, 336, 337, 338, 371, 372
emotional, 25, 34, 50, 51, 52, 58, 59, 60, 61, 63, 64, 65, 83, 122, 224, 226, 249, 250, 309, 312, 323, 337, 339, 343
Endlessness, 46, 53, 67, 68, 163, 233, 234, 235, 237, 238, 251, 252, 282, 287, 292, 296, 330, 336, 339
England, 15, 19, 76, 91, 99, 103, 104, 116, 157, 170, 314, 317, 327, 329, 357, 364, 373
Enneagram, 111, 148, 149, 150, 152, 163, 165, 167, 169, 204
epilepsy, 65
esoteric, 16, 19, 35, 74, 75, 80, 84, 88, 89, 93, 102, 103, 108, 117, 121, 131, 135, 171, 172, 261, 320, 349
Essence, 33, 36, 52, 53, 83, 126, 128, 214, 238, 239, 280, 289, 290, 292, 293, 295, 297, 301, 326, 327, 331, 333, 335, 336, 337, 339, 368, 372
Essene, 346, 350, 351

Index

Essentuki, 137
Eternity, 158, 232, 233, 235
Etheric, 136
Etherokrilno, 211, 230
Eukaryotic, 241
Evil, 29, 30, 84, 119, 122, 126, 134, 226, 302, 328
Evolution, 70, 78, 82, 83, 88, 89, 90, 131, 228, 229, 232, 233, 234, 235, 236, 238, 239, 240, 241, 242, 243, 246, 247, 248, 249, 250, 251, 254, 260, 261, 262, 263, 264, 290, 329, 330, 331, 352
   evolutionary, 83, 88, 90, 233, 240, 242, 243, 244, 262, 264, 357
Evolve, 218, 234, 235, 237, 240, 247
Exercise, 64, 94, 136, 137, 154, 156, 170, 214, 218, 273, 316, 323, 326, 327, 339, 340
Exioehary, 122, 125, 126, 128, 129
exoteric, 88, 172
External Considering, 17, 20, 208, 209, 340

F

Faith, 117, 166
Faivre, Antoine, 16
father, 46, 80, 103, 106, 121, 122, 222, 277, 282, 287, 289, 290, 292, 295, 312, 356
feeding, 226, 248, 278, 354
Feeling, 20, 37, 50, 51, 57, 58, 61, 64, 80, 108, 111, 137, 142, 155, 166, 215, 219, 229, 247, 248, 261, 263, 290, 304, 308, 323, 324, 333, 339, 340, 348, 349, 358, 362, 363, 372
Fire, 35, 36, 43, 44, 45, 75, 104, 126, 127, 129, 135, 136, 197
flood, 236
Food, 29, 32, 34, 35, 36, 38, 40, 88, 89, 119, 122, 125, 128, 146, 153, 225, 226, 261, 263, 267, 307, 332, 333, 342, 354, 357, 359, 368, 369, 370
force, 25, 53, 58, 60, 61, 127, 129, 138, 147, 148, 150, 151, 170, 236, 239, 241, 255, 285, 291, 293, 296, 322, 323, 339, 369

Formatory, 229, 278, 297, 342
Foundation, 14, 18, 23, 67, 206, 306
Fourth Way, 15, 17, 20, 91, 217, 219, 278, 328, 329, 341, 355, 360
France, 15, 17, 19, 32, 95, 144, 314, 327, 362, 368, 373
Freud, 135
friction, 76, 83, 84, 86, 129, 360, 369

G

genital, 45, 126
Geometry, 17, 165, 168, 172, 175, 177, 180, 181, 185, 203, 278
Gilgamesh, 250
Ginsburg, Seymour, 13, 17, 19, 23, 26, 27, 67, 71, 97, 99, 102, 103, 104, 105, 110, 211, 214, 215, 228, 261, 277, 304, 305, 323, 339, 340, 350, 352, 354, 356, 358, 361, 373, 374
gland, 247, 251
   Ovaries, 125
   Pineal, 251
   Testicle, 125
   Thyroid, 328
Gnosis, 19, 103, 117, 181, 255
Gnostic, 19, 38, 39, 116, 117, 121, 136, 138
Gob, 54, 294
Gobi, 244
God, 28, 29, 30, 40, 54, 70, 97, 119, 121, 122, 123, 125, 126, 128, 131, 133, 134, 135, 140, 157, 168, 169, 170, 171, 173, 182, 183, 184, 186, 193, 194, 195, 196, 197, 198, 199, 200, 201, 202, 203, 204, 205, 212, 218, 229, 233, 250, 251, 254, 263, 284, 290, 302, 304, 328, 342, 343, 349, 369
Gödel, Kurt, 314
Goethe, Johann Wolfgang von, 106, 113
Good, 23, 116, 352
Gornahoor Harharkh, 54, 77, 289, 290, 292
Gornahoor Rakhoorkh, 289, 290
Gospel, 133, 134

gravity, 58, 61, 138, 148, 230, 234, 236, 237, 238, 300, 301, 334
Great Nature, 33, 34, 295
Greece, 103, 364, 373
Greek, 45, 230, 241, 255, 264, 269, 271, 274, 277
Groves, Dr. Philip, 16, 25, 224
Gurdjieff, G. I., 14, 15, 16, 17, 18, 19, 23, 24, 25, 26, 28, 30, 31, 32, 33, 34, 36, 37, 38, 39, 40, 41, 43, 47, 48, 50, 51, 53, 54, 56, 57, 59, 61, 62, 63, 64, 65, 66, 67, 70, 71, 72, 73, 76, 77, 78, 79, 80, 81, 82, 83, 84, 85, 86, 87, 88, 89, 90, 91, 92, 93, 94, 95, 96, 97, 98, 99, 100, 102, 103, 105, 106, 108, 110, 111, 112, 116, 117, 118, 122, 125, 127, 128, 137, 138, 139, 141, 145, 146, 147, 148, 149, 150, 151, 152, 153, 154, 156, 157, 163, 164, 165, 167, 168, 169, 170, 171, 172, 174, 175, 177, 178, 179, 181, 182, 186, 206, 208, 209, 211, 212, 213, 214, 215, 216, 217, 218, 219, 220, 221, 222, 224, 225, 226, 227, 228, 229, 230, 232, 233, 234, 236, 240, 241, 242, 246, 249, 252, 260, 266, 267, 268, 270, 271, 272, 273, 274, 275, 276, 278, 279, 299, 305, 306, 307, 308, 309, 311, 312, 313, 317, 321, 323, 324, 325, 326, 328, 329, 331, 336, 337, 339, 340, 341, 346, 347, 348, 349, 350, 351, 352, 353, 354, 355, 356, 357, 358, 359, 360, 361, 365, 366, 367, 368, 369, 370, 371
 Mr. G., 137, 138
Guru, 71, 98, 99

H

Hadji-Asvatz-Troov, 109, 110, 112, 310, 312
Hagiocosmos, 238, 255
Hamolinadir, 55
harmonic, 63, 145, 149, 178, 308, 309, 371
harmonium, 371
Harnel-Aoot, 231, 237, 238, 239, 246
Harnelmiatznel, 148

Hartmann, Thomas and Olga de, 14, 17, 18, 306, 308, 309, 323, 353, 366, 367, 370, 371
Hasnamuss, 276, 304
Head-Brain, 247
Heap, Jane, 14, 18
heart, 44, 46, 122, 127, 140, 142, 155, 169, 170, 182, 183, 193, 203, 205, 218
heaven, 15, 16, 56, 106, 133, 135, 218, 262
Heaven, 106, 108, 128, 139, 202, 265
Hebrew, 121, 125, 277
Heechtvori, 55
Hell, 36, 54, 268
Heptaparaparshinokh, 96, 147, 148, 149, 163, 217, 230, 231, 232, 234, 237, 238, 239, 246, 249, 251, 278, 282, 292
Heptaparaparshinokhs, 237, 252
Heropass, 163, 164, 232, 250
hexagon, 176
hexagonal, 177, 181
hierarchical, 73
hierarchy, 70, 95, 97, 98
Hindu, 17, 18, 125, 134, 173, 206, 326, 371
Hoffman, Maude, 71, 91, 92
holistic, 249
Holy Reconciling, 58
Hope, 24, 38, 40, 54, 64, 86, 102, 116, 179, 213, 214, 215, 221, 273, 274, 277, 278, 324, 331, 339, 342, 353, 354, 355, 363, 365
hormone, 57
Howarth, Jessmin, 18
Hulme, Kathryn, 14
hydrogen, 95, 102, 125, 128, 225, 234, 235, 236, 237, 238, 254
Hypnosis, 66
 hypnotised, 127
 hypnotism, 49, 55
 hypnotist, 45

I

I Am, 312
Ichazo, Oscar, 78, 163

Ida, 125
Identification, 26, 86, 87, 89, 118, 144, 331, 335, 336, 337, 339, 352
Idiot, 311, 367, 368, 369
Illumination, 85, 86, 249
imagination, 34
impartial, 53, 54, 66, 80, 207, 280, 290, 295
impressions, 35, 50, 54, 55, 88, 154, 155, 263, 267, 292, 297, 299, 300, 301, 302, 332, 333, 334, 335, 345, 346, 349, 365, 369
In Search of the Miraculous, 14, 65, 76, 79, 82, 83, 84, 85, 87, 88, 89, 95, 117, 129, 147, 154, 178, 181, 182, 217, 230, 232, 248, 255, 266, 267, 268, 278, 304
Fragments, 76, 79, 147, 154
incarnation, 77, 83, 89
India, 65, 90, 98, 104, 116, 131, 264, 284, 314, 315, 316, 368
Individual, 45, 64, 68, 87, 96, 98, 106, 107, 112, 114, 129, 195, 211, 218, 219, 229, 235, 236, 243, 248, 249, 250, 262, 263, 264, 267, 270, 273, 286, 297, 299, 317, 334, 335, 337
initiation, 45, 74, 91, 93, 107, 117, 127, 131, 217
insight, 65, 154, 156, 291, 321
Instinctive, 39, 125, 129, 247, 300, 337
Institute, 17, 18, 19, 23, 47, 49, 51, 67, 78, 79, 80, 91, 116, 117, 138, 165, 329, 347, 366, 367, 370
Institute for the Harmonious Development of Man, 79
Intellectual, 34, 50, 63, 96, 108, 112, 122, 136, 156, 221, 224, 225, 226, 242, 248, 249, 250, 252, 263, 307, 313, 329, 347, 349
intention, 21, 80, 269
interconnected, 30
Internal Considering, 208
Introvigne, Massimo, 15, 25
intuition, 70
Involution, 70, 88, 278

involutionary, 88, 232
Involve, 218
Islam, 204
Itoklanoz, 52, 59, 61, 276, 305

J

Jericho, 36, 37
Jesus, 56, 106, 128, 134, 135, 170, 282, 312
Jew, 32, 33, 47
Jewish, 32, 33, 47
Judas, 46, 56, 106
Jung, Carl G., 15, 66, 91, 103, 107, 108, 251, 262
Justice, 45, 121, 175, 183, 195

K

Kabala, 118, 120, 127, 179
Kant, Immanuel, 247
Karatas, 93, 164, 280, 289, 291, 292
Karnak, 38, 49, 81, 280, 288, 293
Keschapmartnian, 305
Kesdjan, 240
Koan, 214
Kondoor, 43, 118, 329
Konuzion, 54, 289
Krishnamurti, 75, 76
Kundabuffer, 44, 49, 55, 59, 60, 68, 110, 212, 281, 282, 284, 294, 297, 300, 329, 330, 331, 332, 333, 334, 335, 336, 337, 339, 341, 342

L

labyrinth, 348
ladder, 129, 244
Lannes, Henriette, 15, 18, 223
laugh, 139, 326, 369
laughter, 368
Law, 14, 62, 88, 89, 96, 117, 136, 147, 149, 151, 156, 163, 172, 186, 207, 219, 233, 234, 235, 236, 241, 268, 278, 281, 282, 284, 348, 354
Law of Seven, 46, 163, 233, 234, 237

Law of Three, 88, 147, 150, 163, 234, 239, 252, 255, 306
Law-conformable, 234
lawful, 50, 219, 268, 286, 290, 354
Legominism, 69, 70, 267, 268
Lentrohamsanin, 45, 55
Liebow, Richard, 18, 206, 210, 221, 340, 353, 358, 361, 373
light, 19, 32, 39, 44, 71, 72, 73, 91, 96, 104, 107, 112, 116, 117, 121, 129, 133, 136, 137, 138, 141, 154, 157, 169, 203, 225, 226, 227, 233, 236, 240, 245, 249, 250, 261, 288, 289, 324, 341, 370
Limbic, 51, 57, 58, 247
Littlehampton, 19, 99, 228
Logos, 121
Looisos, 54, 287, 294
Love, 18, 47, 135, 139, 140, 170, 211, 213, 217, 252, 290, 322, 331, 336, 356, 368
Lubovedsky, 222, 265
Lucifer, 129

M

machine, 82, 208, 241, 242, 246, 341
MacLean, Paul D., 51, 246, 247, 262
Macrocosmos, 238
magic, 45, 274, 348
magnet
    magnetic, 114
maintenance, 88, 154, 207, 230, 234, 281, 282, 330, 333
Mansfield, Catherine, 18
Maralpleicie, 283, 284, 294
Mars, 43, 45, 65, 77, 81, 82, 264, 290, 292
material, 14, 55, 61, 76, 80, 104, 115, 117, 171, 174, 176, 203, 212, 214, 240, 242, 243, 244, 246, 261, 262, 282, 285, 291, 308, 309, 329, 339, 345, 352, 353, 355, 359, 360
Mathnawi, 324
matter, 30, 43, 44, 46, 50, 63, 83, 84, 88, 89, 93, 105, 114, 136, 137, 143, 147, 150, 151, 153, 156, 170, 208, 221, 226, 230, 247, 270, 273, 294, 317, 320, 321, 323, 326, 342, 361
Mdnel-In, 231, 246
mechanical, 34, 57, 59, 61, 62, 63, 129, 144, 154, 155, 221, 224, 240, 307, 331, 337
Mechano-coinciding-Mdnel-In, 231, 238, 246
meditate, 20
Meditate, 229
meditation, 17, 20, 21, 22, 88, 134, 228, 249, 263, 321, 325, 327, 336, 337, 340, 343
Meetings with Remarkable Men, 16, 18, 47, 48, 78, 80, 206, 209, 222, 224, 225, 265, 268
Megalocosmos, 119, 211, 238, 255, 287, 293
mentation, 31, 38, 49, 53, 141, 156, 224, 233, 262, 268, 280, 281, 285, 296, 297, 298, 302, 334
Mesocosmos, 238, 255
Mexico, 19, 116, 131, 228
migrations, 245
Milk, 35, 46
mind, 20, 51, 63, 65, 79, 93, 97, 108, 117, 147, 151, 157, 166, 171, 177, 178, 201, 207, 212, 216, 219, 220, 221, 242, 247, 248, 249, 250, 262, 263, 267, 273, 281, 285, 291, 295, 308, 309, 311, 322, 323, 324, 326, 331, 336, 355, 360, 361, 362, 368, 371
mindfulness, 325
Mohammed, 168
monastery, 21
monk, 17, 328
Moon, 44, 45, 118, 136, 238, 330
Moore, James, 14, 15, 18, 26, 67, 71, 91, 103, 173, 174, 175, 211, 214, 215, 216, 217, 218, 222, 223, 321, 352, 353, 355, 360, 373, 374
Moral, 109, 193, 204, 205
Moscow, 76, 78, 294
Moses, 127, 128, 135
mother, 15, 30, 33, 34, 35, 38, 44, 47, 121, 307

Mouravieff, Boris, 174, 181, 255
Movements, 14, 25, 64, 345, 346, 347, 348, 349, 350, 359
Moving, 61, 113, 142, 152, 165, 177, 182, 184, 209, 212, 219, 247, 248, 266, 276, 287, 290, 296, 323, 337, 357
Mozart, 311, 353
Mulisch, Harry, 306
Mullah Nassr Eddin, 290, 291, 302
music, 17, 27, 31, 46, 94, 139, 145, 178, 179, 208, 278, 306, 307, 308, 309, 310, 311, 312, 313, 318, 347, 348, 350, 353, 369, 371
mysticism, 15, 47
myth, 33, 35, 118, 174, 277
mythology, 174, 278

N

Naqshbandi, 168, 169, 170
Nature, 32, 33, 35, 36, 37, 47, 49, 50, 51, 52, 55, 56, 63, 64, 74, 80, 83, 94, 96, 112, 128, 129, 134, 136, 137, 144, 153, 154, 175, 194, 205, 214, 217, 219, 225, 241, 267, 314, 315, 333, 337, 339, 341
Needleman, Jacob, 16
Negative emotion, 87, 208
Neocortex, 65
Neologism, 265, 266, 269, 270, 273, 274, 275
nerve, 247
nervous system, 247
Neugebauer, O., 145
neural, 57, 58, 59
Neutral
  Neutralize, 291
  Neutralizing, 58, 60, 89, 148
neutrinos, 236
neutron, 236
New Age, 46, 170
Nicoll, Maurice, 15, 91, 92, 103, 117, 127, 172, 266, 279
nine, 169, 170, 175, 185, 202, 209, 251, 252, 273, 370

Ninefoldness, 180
ninth, 45, 121, 127, 250, 252
Nirioonossian, 289
Nisargadatta, 103
nitrogen, 95, 102, 239
nothing, 37, 52, 55, 65, 69, 79, 92, 97, 98, 107, 111, 117, 127, 128, 133, 140, 141, 142, 156, 170, 183, 186, 212, 215, 216, 237, 238, 261, 262, 265, 269, 270, 273, 275, 283, 284, 296, 299, 301, 302, 324, 327, 342, 348, 349, 356, 357, 362
Nott, Stanley and Rosemary, 18, 41, 48
Nyland, W, 14, 18, 206, 220

O

Objective, 63, 85, 87, 88, 146, 147, 148, 155, 232, 269, 276, 289, 295, 296, 299, 301, 327, 330, 331, 332, 334, 336, 348
Obligolnian, 207, 305, 325
Obyvatel, 304, 305
octagon, 371
octave, 52, 54, 71, 89, 95, 121, 128, 149, 151, 178, 179, 180, 230, 258, 259, 279, 305, 306, 354, 357, 359
Okidanokh, 230, 286, 289, 292
Oldham, Ronald and Muriel, 19, 228
Omnipresent, 230, 286, 289, 292
one-brained, 57, 59
ontology, 315
Opium, 289
Orage, Alfred, 18, 39, 41, 48, 76, 313, 366
oral teaching, 75, 79, 82, 88
organic, 118, 218, 238, 240, 241, 246, 255, 260, 263, 294, 342, 364
organon, 241
Ors, 67, 287, 289
Orthodox, 72, 251
Oskiano, 271, 280, 281, 282, 283, 285, 286, 288, 289, 290, 291, 292, 293, 295, 296, 299, 304, 305
Oskianotsner, 292
Ouspensky, P. D., 15, 18, 48, 76, 78, 79, 82, 84, 88, 92, 95, 102, 117, 127, 147, 150,

154, 158, 164, 171, 172, 206, 209, 217, 220, 225, 229, 232, 248, 255, 267, 275, 317
oxygen, 95, 102, 239, 241, 260, 263

P

Paleomammalian, 247
Parable, 113, 262
paradise, 32, 35, 37, 39, 54, 158
Paris, 14, 15, 16, 41, 72, 78, 79, 80, 95, 106, 144, 171, 346, 347, 358, 367, 368
Partkdolg-duty, 138, 270, 293, 295, 299, 300, 337
passive, 61, 166, 180, 239, 295, 307
patience, 166, 220
pearl, 44, 107, 283, 284
Pearl-land, 283, 284
Pentland, John, 16, 18, 206, 280
Peretzi, Dimitri, 13, 374
periodic table, 95, 237
Persian, 55, 204, 371
personality, 65, 76, 157, 208, 239, 333, 337, 343, 368
Philadelphia, 16, 49
Philokalia, 155
photism, 249
photon, 240
physical, 50, 58, 59, 61, 65, 83, 84, 86, 107, 119, 121, 122, 136, 157, 183, 247, 248, 323, 332, 337
physics, 17, 112, 154, 175, 235, 329
Pingala, 125
planet, 35, 44, 45, 46, 47, 55, 67, 68, 69, 70, 77, 81, 82, 93, 109, 110, 118, 144, 145, 146, 156, 164, 185, 197, 199, 211, 212, 215, 218, 240, 255, 280, 282, 284, 286, 287, 288, 289, 291, 292, 296, 299, 302, 305, 330, 333, 342, 357, 368
planetary, 46, 52, 56, 57, 68, 69, 88, 89, 99, 122, 125, 171, 207, 228, 229, 236, 290, 301, 302, 330, 342
Plato, 112, 175, 178
Podkoolad, 53, 252, 295, 296

Pogson, Beryl, 91, 356
politics, 173, 354
ponder, 164, 208, 226, 285
pondering, 141, 331
Popoff, Irmis, 360
Poundolero, 55
Prana, 122, 294
Pray, 343
Prayer, 131, 155, 169, 209, 306
Prem, Sri Krishna, 98, 99
presence, 29, 49, 50, 51, 52, 53, 54, 55, 57, 64, 68, 72, 84, 118, 122, 125, 147, 157, 169, 170, 184, 186, 193, 195, 197, 199, 201, 202, 203, 204, 205, 212, 223, 240, 274, 285, 286, 287, 291, 293, 296, 299, 300, 301, 302, 331, 336, 337, 347, 358
Prieure, 14, 15, 73, 79, 92, 93, 352, 358
Prime Source, 211
Prions, 239
Prokaryotic, 240
Protein, 246
Protocosmos, 234, 235, 237, 255
proton, 236
psyche, 44, 55, 70, 106, 144, 145, 283, 297, 299, 300, 331, 333, 334
psychological, 19, 25, 75, 78, 109, 116, 127, 129, 147, 168, 180, 193, 228, 233, 236, 248, 251, 261, 262, 327, 339, 347
psychologist, 44
psychology, 15, 19, 106, 117, 128, 138, 175, 194, 196, 262
Psychology of Man's Possible Evolution, 324
Purgatory, 46, 56, 62, 88, 125, 138, 164, 206, 282, 287, 289
Pythagoras, 165, 166, 174, 175, 178
Pythagorean, 174, 175, 178, 179

Q

Qabala, 233, 238
Qabalistic, 233
Quantum, 63, 211, 239, 240, 340
quintessence, 209

R

Rabelais, 368, 371
radiation, 143, 151, 153, 240, 243, 255, 260, 261
Ramakrishna, 206, 250
Ray of Creation, 119, 151, 152, 153, 232, 238, 241
Real, 229
Reason, 25, 50, 55, 61, 65, 87, 93, 108, 110, 119, 127, 135, 136, 137, 138, 147, 157, 163, 171, 173, 193, 195, 217, 219, 222, 243, 252, 263, 275, 281, 282, 284, 286, 287, 288, 289, 292, 293, 294, 295, 296, 297, 299, 301, 302, 305, 317, 322, 330, 331, 334, 357, 360
Reason-of-knowing, 302
Reciprocal, 59, 154, 234, 278, 284, 296, 325, 331
Reconcile, 158, 164, 224, 322
　Reconciling, 121, 148
Relativity, 44, 147, 154, 164, 211
religion, 15, 45, 46, 173, 215, 283, 348, 349
Remember, 19, 21, 26, 32, 41, 58, 72, 99, 109, 113, 116, 135, 145, 149, 153, 216, 220, 227, 229, 248, 269, 285, 293, 294, 295, 305, 325, 341, 346, 356, 357, 366, 369
　Remembering, 146, 157, 324
Remorse, 274, 286, 333
repetition, 281, 282, 283, 284, 285, 290, 303, 305, 358
Reptilian, 63
resonance, 64, 96, 239, 240, 246, 252
resonate, 64
Resurrection, 35, 133, 312
riddle, 113
Rig Veda, 252
RNA, 246
Ropp, Robert de, 17, 20
Rosicrucian, 107, 217

Russia, 72, 76, 94, 99, 163, 169, 217, 230, 269, 270, 273, 274, 275, 276, 283, 304, 357, 358, 366, 367, 368, 370

S

Sacred, 17, 53, 62, 68, 69, 74, 94, 97, 108, 111, 115, 118, 121, 125, 126, 131, 133, 135, 139, 147, 148, 149, 150, 151, 165, 168, 171, 175, 177, 178, 185, 219, 230, 231, 234, 252, 255, 278, 281, 282, 284, 286, 287, 289, 292, 295, 296, 330, 331, 336
Sacred Individual, 68, 282, 284, 330, 331
sacrifice, 44, 137, 229, 339
　sacrificial, 54, 61, 287, 294
sati, 321
Saturn, 46, 107, 185, 186, 202, 289, 290
School of Economic Science, 15, 321
Science, 19, 56, 63, 74, 75, 88, 94, 108, 109, 110, 147, 148, 156, 168, 171, 177, 178, 212, 228, 232, 272
Scientific, 46, 108, 174, 261, 360
seeing, 26, 36, 45, 108, 112, 163, 195, 281, 286, 291, 293, 295, 316, 323, 328, 341, 354
Self, 17, 20, 21, 57, 58, 59, 61, 64, 169, 186, 214, 215, 236, 335, 336, 337, 338, 339, 340
Self Observation, 17, 20, 21, 128, 224, 248, 249, 337, 339, 341
Self Remembering, 41, 128, 224, 321
Self-consciousness, 86, 87, 88
sensation, 50, 51, 86, 87, 145, 146, 147, 154, 155, 156
senses, 37, 57, 58, 62, 63, 116, 155, 283
Sensing, 145, 156, 226, 292, 301, 353
Sensory, 57, 61, 64, 155, 207
serpent, 28, 29, 111, 119, 122, 123, 125, 127, 128, 131, 135, 174
seven, 31, 52, 56, 59, 61, 68, 82, 83, 84, 148, 149, 175, 185, 202, 203, 208, 230, 237, 265, 268, 275, 295, 305, 317, 346, 364, 367, 370

seventh, 83, 181, 243, 248, 252
Sex, 33, 35, 39, 43, 45, 125, 126, 127, 134, 137, 206, 243
   sexual, 32, 33, 34, 36, 39, 46, 121, 122, 125, 126, 128, 129, 131, 134, 135, 136, 137, 138
   sexuality, 45, 46, 133, 262
Shah, Idries, 174
Shakti, 128
Sharp, H. J. (Bert), 24, 26, 28, 63, 65, 103, 104, 105, 106, 113, 114, 115, 182, 216, 220, 228, 260, 261, 262, 263, 264, 305, 323, 340, 343, 353, 355, 356, 361, 362, 363, 374
Shiva, 121, 128, 134
shock, 121, 128, 222, 236, 239, 249, 296, 299, 300, 301, 302, 303, 333, 359, 370
sin, 107, 125, 169, 289
sing, 126, 307
singing, 307
sister, 346
Sitting, 20, 21, 24, 34, 116, 184, 208, 223, 268, 360, 366
Sleep, 85, 88, 125, 261, 272
Smith, Russell A., 24, 181
Solano, Solita, 14
solar plexus, 122
son, 98, 106, 121, 122, 128, 133, 134, 135, 140, 289, 290, 292, 312, 317, 328
Sophia, 19, 24, 28, 40, 41, 48, 50, 63, 102, 105, 373
Soul, 37, 41, 83, 116, 125, 128, 137, 170, 204, 238, 344, 371
sound, 46, 122, 149, 178, 277, 284, 289, 291, 292, 307, 310, 311, 334, 336, 369
sounding, 178
sperm, 126, 243, 244
spinal column, 118, 126, 127, 330
   vertebral column, 126
spine, 125, 127
Spirit, 32, 38, 41, 43, 44, 45, 72, 88, 94, 113, 121, 122, 128, 135, 140, 213, 214, 223, 237, 263, 276, 356

spiritual, 17, 20, 45, 65, 70, 90, 95, 96, 97, 116, 169, 171, 182, 183, 184, 199, 203, 204, 205, 315, 331, 336, 337, 349, 371
spirituality, 16, 96
St. Petersburg (also Petersburg), 78
Staveley, A.L., 17, 24, 165, 218
Steiner, Rudolf, 277, 316
Stopinder, 148, 230, 231, 278
Struggle of the Magicians, 356
subconscious, 58, 280, 336
subconsciousness, 50, 297, 299
subjective, 50, 55, 56, 57, 58, 61, 146, 231, 247, 266, 283, 304, 306, 333, 334
substance, 36, 58, 137, 143, 150, 211, 230, 291, 333, 349
Subud, 321
Suffer, 33, 37
   Intentional Suffering, 82, 86, 89, 138, 286, 289, 295
   suffered, 33, 84
   suffering, 36, 37, 40, 46, 56, 61, 84, 109, 131, 137, 287, 311, 331, 332, 335
   Unnecessary Suffering, 332
Sufis, 131, 169, 174, 177, 181, 182, 183, 184, 185, 186
Sufism, 184, 316, 321
suggestibility, 44, 331
Sun, 35, 44, 68, 93, 140, 144, 151, 163, 164, 226, 227, 233, 234, 235, 236, 237, 240, 245, 248, 250, 251, 254, 255, 286, 311, 343
Sun Absolute, 44, 68, 163, 227, 233, 234, 286
Supernova, 236
Swedenborg, 241
Symbol, 126, 148, 149, 167, 168, 171, 172, 175, 177, 178, 179, 182, 185, 186, 193, 202, 203, 264, 272, 278
   symbolic, 35, 98, 107, 127, 172, 181, 201, 241, 251
   symbolism, 165, 167, 168, 175, 177, 201, 233, 278
Synchronicity, 115, 357

Index

T

Tail, 118, 265, 294, 334, 367
Tarot, 118, 127
telepathic, 97
Tereshchenko, Nicolas, 13, 19, 24, 25, 96, 97, 102, 111, 114, 136, 163, 164, 216, 218, 219, 224, 228, 229, 265, 272, 273, 276, 304, 305, 322, 328, 340, 342, 350, 355, 357, 362, 363, 364, 373
Tessarocosmos, 238, 255
Tetartocosmos, 152, 287
tetrad, 175
Theomertmalogos, 211, 234, 255
Theosophical, 17, 23, 67, 71, 73, 74, 75, 76, 77, 78, 83, 90, 91, 92, 95, 98, 102, 104, 214
Theosophist, 23, 67, 71, 73, 75, 76, 90, 91, 95
Theosophy, 23, 67, 71, 73, 74, 76, 95, 97, 316
third being-food, 125
Third Force, 147, 310
Thompson, Chris, 28, 109, 110, 177, 222, 273, 352, 353, 360, 362, 363, 365, 373
three-brained, 50, 54, 55, 56, 57, 58, 59, 62, 67, 68, 69, 70, 82, 84, 109, 110, 112, 118, 122, 125, 211, 246, 263, 282, 284, 287, 288, 289, 293, 299, 300, 301, 302, 305, 330, 331, 336
Tibet, 90, 131, 133, 316
Tiflis, 54, 271
Tikliamish, 284
Timaeus, 178
time, 18, 21, 24, 26, 27, 30, 32, 38, 40, 44, 46, 49, 50, 51, 53, 54, 58, 63, 64, 67, 69, 70, 76, 77, 81, 82, 85, 86, 87, 88, 90, 91, 92, 93, 96, 97, 98, 102, 103, 104, 109, 111, 112, 113, 114, 116, 118, 121, 128, 139, 140, 141, 142, 143, 144, 145, 146, 147, 149, 154, 155, 156, 157, 158, 163, 164, 166, 168, 169, 170, 171, 172, 173, 174, 178, 179, 182, 184, 185, 199, 202, 206, 207, 211, 212, 213, 215, 216, 217, 218, 220, 221, 222, 223, 224, 226, 229, 232, 233, 235, 237, 242, 243, 247, 249, 250, 260, 261, 262, 265, 266, 267, 269, 271, 272, 273, 275, 276, 278, 279, 280, 283, 284, 288, 289, 290, 293, 295, 299, 301, 302, 304, 305, 307, 308, 309, 310, 312, 313, 320, 321, 323, 324, 325, 326, 328, 329, 330, 343, 346, 347, 348, 349, 350, 352, 353, 356, 357, 358, 359, 361, 363, 365, 366, 367, 368, 369, 370
tolerance, 221, 310
Tooilan, 292
Toomer, Jean, 15, 16, 106
Tracol, Henri, 18, 321
Transfiguration, 250
transform, 88, 114, 127, 154, 208
transformation, 19, 38, 46, 88, 107, 110, 125, 153, 228, 280, 297, 300, 327, 349, 352
transmutation, 62, 88, 127, 128, 131, 138, 209
transmute, 88, 293
Transubstantiate, 285
Transubstantiate, 282
Tree of Life, 120, 180
Triad, 56, 59, 61, 83, 151, 152, 153, 357
Triamazikamno, 121, 122, 147, 148, 149, 150, 151, 163, 234, 255, 286
Triangle Editions, 80
Trimurti, 89
Trinity, 89, 121
Tritocosmos, 238, 240, 255
Trogoautoegocrat, 62, 234, 293
Trogoautoegocratic, 234
two-brained, 57, 58, 305

U

unconscious, 39, 44, 45, 57, 65, 108, 127, 249, 264, 286, 287, 335, 369
unconsciousness, 118
understanding, 20, 24, 33, 35, 36, 37, 38, 62, 65, 70, 80, 88, 111, 113, 114, 136, 141, 143, 147, 149, 164, 168, 173, 174, 204,

207, 212, 213, 218, 219, 233, 243, 246, 268, 270, 272, 274, 279, 282, 291, 299, 301, 327, 329, 341, 359, 360, 369
Union, 128
universe, 22, 50, 68, 69, 70, 81, 82, 89, 96, 98, 126, 131, 143, 146, 147, 149, 150, 151, 153, 154, 158, 164, 171, 172, 180, 197, 212, 230, 234, 236, 241, 287, 295, 302, 330, 331, 333, 338, 340
USA, 13, 18, 24, 165, 167, 168, 169, 172, 182, 183, 194, 196, 198, 200, 201, 202, 203, 206, 373, 374

V

Vedanta, 321
vein, 193, 333
Venus, 43, 45, 135
vibration, 46, 71, 89, 95, 118, 145, 150, 151, 152, 153, 230, 274, 277, 289, 292, 293, 310, 312, 330
Views from the Real World, 267, 268
Vishnu, 121
vivifyingness, 230

W

Walker, Kenneth, 15, 18, 71, 91, 92, 94
Washington, 16, 18, 139, 280
Water, 44, 45, 47, 128, 134, 135, 136, 164, 172, 184, 197, 202, 220, 239, 241, 260, 325, 359, 370
Weak Force, 237
Webb, James, 222
Wellbeloved, Sophia, 19, 24, 28, 41, 63, 102, 373
Will, 52, 61, 114, 168, 171, 173, 182, 183, 184, 186, 194, 196, 198, 200, 201, 202, 203, 204, 205, 218, 235, 237, 238, 241, 249, 250, 252, 364
Wisdom, 67, 70, 72, 73, 74, 77, 83, 90, 94, 102, 103, 121, 168, 170, 173, 175, 183, 193, 195
womb, 128

Word, 169, 234
Word-God, 234
Work, 14, 15, 16, 17, 18, 19, 24, 25, 26, 64, 85, 106, 110, 111, 112, 113, 116, 139, 146, 157, 211, 213, 214, 215, 216, 217, 218, 219, 220, 224, 225, 228, 243, 248, 252, 263, 278, 280, 304, 306, 314, 316, 317, 318, 320, 321, 322, 323, 325, 326, 327, 328, 340, 347, 349, 354, 355, 358, 362
world, 16, 19, 21, 33, 35, 39, 41, 45, 46, 48, 50, 53, 54, 57, 58, 59, 61, 62, 63, 64, 67, 72, 73, 74, 75, 76, 78, 80, 81, 85, 86, 87, 88, 94, 106, 117, 119, 122, 127, 128, 133, 134, 136, 140, 141, 142, 143, 145, 146, 147, 150, 151, 152, 155, 163, 164, 173, 174, 175, 176, 180, 183, 186, 203, 207, 211, 212, 213, 216, 221, 225, 226, 227, 233, 235, 237, 242, 244, 245, 251, 255, 262, 263, 280, 281, 282, 287, 289, 296, 307, 331, 332, 334, 348, 349, 354, 358, 361, 371, 372

Y

Yetzirah, 233
Yoga, 133, 326
   Karma, 83, 96
   Kundalini, 116, 127, 128, 134, 135
   Mantra, 285
   Tantra, 133, 134

Z

Zen, 214, 326
Zigrosser, Carl, 312, 366
Zirlikner, 289
Zodiac, 43, 171, 181, 183, 184, 185, 199, 201
   Aquarius, 46
   Aries, 43
   Cancer, 44, 184, 202
   Capricorn, 46
   Gemini, 43
   Leo, 44
   Libra, 45, 171

Index

Pisces, 46, 184
Sagittarius, 45
Scorpio, 45, 184, 202
Taurus, 43

Virgo, 44
Zoroastrian, 94
Zuber, Rene, 70, 71, 72, 73, 76, 105

www.ingramcontent.com/pod-product-compliance
Lightning Source LLC
Chambersburg PA
CBHW080725230426
43665CB00020B/2615